Biography PIKE Zebulon

Citizen

Citizen Explorer

CITIZEN EXPLORER

EXPLORER

The Life of Zebulon Pike

JARED ORSI

OXFORD
UNIVERSITY PRESS

OXFORD
UNIVERSITY PRESS

Oxford University Press is a department of the University of Oxford.
It furthers the University's objective of excellence in research,
scholarship, and education by publishing worldwide.

Oxford   New York
Auckland   Cape Town   Dar es Salaam   Hong Kong   Karachi
Kuala Lumpur   Madrid   Melbourne   Mexico City   Nairobi
New Delhi   Shanghai   Taipei   Toronto

With offices in
Argentina   Austria   Brazil   Chile   Czech Republic   France   Greece
Guatemala   Hungary   Italy   Japan   Poland   Portugal   Singapore
South Korea   Switzerland   Thailand   Turkey   Ukraine   Vietnam

Oxford is a registered trade mark of Oxford University Press
in the UK and certain other countries.

Published in the United States of America by
Oxford University Press
198 Madison Avenue, New York, NY 10016

Portions of the following publications have been reprinted in this book, with permission:
"Zebulon Pike and His 'Frozen Lads': Bodies, Nationalism, and the West in the Early Republic,"
Western Historical Quarterly 42 (Spring 2011): 55–75. Copyright by the Western History Association.
Reprinted by permission.
"Reading with Pike: The Mystery of His Affection for James Wilkinson,"
Wagon Tracks: Santa Fe Trail Association Quarterly 21 (May 2007): 17–20.
"An Empire and Ecology of Liberty," in *Zebulon Pike, Thomas Jefferson, and the Opening of the American West*,
eds. Matthew L. Harris and Jay H. Buckley (Norman: University of Oklahoma Press, 2012), 139–160.
"State Making and Unmaking (and Making It Back at All): Following Zebulon Pike Across the Plains in
1806," in *The Grasslands of the United States: An Environmental History*, ed. James E. Sherow (Santa
Barbara: ABC Clio, 2007), 159–175.

Library of Congress Cataloging-in-Publication Data
Orsi, Jared, 1970-
Citizen explorer : the life of Zebulon Pike / Jared Orsi.
pages cm
Includes bibliographical references and index.
ISBN 978-0-19-976872-1 (alk. paper)
1. Pike, Zebulon Montgomery, 1779–1813.   2. Explorers—West (U.S.)—Biography.
3. West (U.S.)—Discovery and exploration.   4. West (U.S.)—History—To 1848.
5. United States—Territorial expansion—History—19th century.   I. Title.
F592.P653O77   2013   973.4'8092—dc23
2012048606

1 3 5 7 9 8 6 4 2

Printed in the United States of America
on acid-free paper

For Rebecca, Renata, and Carlos
and
Richard and Dolores

Contents

Acknowledgments

ZEBULON PIKE ASSEMBLED his 1810 account of his travels from the leaves of a diary written in the field, maps hastily sketched on site, scraps of paper wadded into rifle barrels and stuffed into soldiers' clothing, and his memory of two eventful years of adventuring in the West. The resulting volume contained so many errors of style and detail that his publisher wrote in the preface that perhaps no other "book ever went to press under so many disadvantages." Although my book surely contains some flaws as well, I can hardly blame them on disadvantages. Indeed, I have been blessed with tremendous support in the research, writing, and editing of this work.

Pike was an explorer, but he went nowhere that other human beings had not already been. I am no different. I have benefited from the work of Jack Kyle Cooper, Elliott Coues, W. Eugene Hollon, Donald Jackson, Doug King, Frank Sanders, and other Pike scholars who have gone before me. I wish particularly to acknowledge the Lewis and Clark scholar Clay Jenkinson, who more than anyone else inspired me to undertake this project. Between 2001 and 2003, he led three Colorado Humanities summer teacher workshops, which I attended as a collaborating historian. His enthusiasm, depth of knowledge, humane spirit, and energizing teaching style first got me excited about North American exploration, and his invitation to me to address the 2002 seminar on Zebulon Pike launched this project.

My father, Richard Orsi, the historian I most admire, read every word of the manuscript, most of them more than once. Yet again, I have written a book that I could not have completed without him. My colleague at Colorado State University, Mark Fiege, reviewed multiple drafts of all of the chapters as well and offered keen insights and oft-needed encouragement. He also recruited me to read drafts of his scholarship, from which I learned much that has informed my own. Graham Peck of Saint Xavier

University gave the book possibly the closest scrutiny of anyone. I thank him for challenging me and never letting me off the hook. To these three incredibly generous readers, I am much indebted.

Thank you as well to many others who gave feedback on drafts of chapters, articles, conference papers, grant applications, and other pieces that eventually added up to the book you now hold: Fredrik Albritton-Jonsson, Ruth Alexander, Mark Aloisio, participants in Steve Aron's Autry Museum western history workshop, Karla Brown, Jay Buckley, Nathan Citino, my colleagues in the Colorado State University faculty seminar, Nina Erlich, Nichelle Frank, the members of the Front Range Early American History Colloquium, Matt Harris, Eric Hinderaker, Adrian Howkins, James Hunt, Nadine Hunt, Nancy Scott Jackson, Prakash Kumar, David Lewis, Ann Little, Brian Luskey, Dianne Margolf, Jean Muirhead, Barbara Oberg, Leo Oliva, Dolores Orsi, Peter Orsi, Jim Sherow, Kayla Steele, Elliott West, Alan Taylor, Sam Truett, the history graduate students and faculty I met with at UC Davis, Doug Yarrington, and the anonymous readers at the *Journal of American History*, the *Journal of the Early Republic*, Oxford University Press, University of Oklahoma Press, and the *Western Historical Quarterly*. Finally, Oxford's Susan Feber was an incisive reader at every stage of this project, and her editorial suggestions made it a much better book than it otherwise would have been. Thank you to her, Marc Schneider, and the staff at Oxford for bringing this work to fruition.

One attribute that distinguishes this biography from most other works on Pike is its extensive examination of Pike's family background and youth. This was made possible by my mother-in-law, Nadine Hunt, an accomplished genealogist, who located many of the family history resources for chapter one and gamely followed even the faintest of leads to their conclusion. Another distinctive feature is that this book is informed by my reconnaissance of many of the landscapes of Pike's life and travels. Visiting the forts, paying respects at cemeteries, and hiking in his footsteps gave me a deeper feel for his experiences and mind than I could otherwise have developed. On these expeditions, I benefited from many guides, including Kevin Black, Richard Gould, Trina Houser, Rick Manzanares, and especially John Murphy, who first conducted me up the slopes of Mount Rosa. My daughter Renata provided delightful companionship in scouting the Arkansas River, Fort Massac, Fort Kaskaskia, the Wet Mountain Valley, and the Pike stockade.

Many able and kind archivists, curators, librarians, and others, guided my exploration of research materials: Mary Antoine, Barbara Austen,

Peter Blodgett, Doug Ernest, Doug King, Naomi Lederer, Rick Manzares, Dena Rosenberry, Wendy Rotweiler, and Bridget Striker. Graduate research assistants also aided my inquiry: Kelly Barlow, Ryan Flahive, Stephan Greenway, Tao Hui, and Eric Saulnier. Mayra Cerda helped with Spanish translation and Sophie McKee with French. Thank you to former students Jessica Murski and Brian Lenz, whose photos from my classes' field trips grace the pages of this book. To my great fortune the final stages of this project overlapped with the graduate studies of Clarissa Trapp. Clarissa managed the complicated task of securing illustrations for the book and carried out many hours of other research. Her incredible organizational skills were topped only by the good cheer with which she tackled every assignment. I also want to acknowledge the superb scholarship of another graduate student, Jenika Howe, whose work on the history of energy sharpened my own thinking on the subject and whose master's thesis appears in this book's notes and bibliography, the first time, I believe, I have had the pleasure of citing one of my graduate student's writing.

For research and writing suggestions and help conceptualizing the project, I am grateful to Fred Anderson, Wayne Bodle, William Cronon, Lil Fenn, Sharla Fett, Robert Gudmestad, Susan Guinn-Chipman, Drew Isenberg, Ari Kelman, Paul Mapp, Chris Moore, Leo Oliva, Kip Otteson, Roy Pike, Dave Rogers, Greg Smoak, Bill Swaggerty, Louis Warren, David Weber, and Terry Young.

Thank you to my physician friends Dr. Doug Krohn, Dr. Bruce Paton, and Dr. Li Tai for sharing expertise, recommending medical literature, and reading drafts. I could not have written chapter five without them.

The Colorado State University history department staff, especially Lorraine Dunn, Nancy Rehe, and Robin Troxell, took an interest in this project throughout its evolution and provided timely, professional, and indispensable administrative support. They and office staff at universities everywhere are the unsung heroes of all academic scholarship.

Generous funding came from the Charles Redd Center for Western Studies, Colorado Humanities, Colorado State University's History Department, College of Liberal Arts, and Provost's Office, the Huntington Library, Occidental College, and the Santa Fe Trail Association. Thank you to ABC Clio, the University of Oklahoma Press, *Wagon Tracks*, and the *Western Historical Quarterly* for permission to reprint passages previously published.

The maps were produced by the Geospatial Centroid at Colorado State University by Steve Chignell, with cartographic consultation by Sophia Linn. Maps were created in Esri ArcMap v.10 software, using publicly available datasets from naturalearthdata.com and shadedreliefarchive.com.

For friendship and hospitality on research trips, especially the year my family and I spent in Pasadena, thank you to Felice Alter and Carl Hinds, Mat and Jaxon Alter, Jamie and Tim Ankeny, Michelle, Tommie, Ashley, and Robbie Bianco, Laurie, Randy, Allison, and Erica Bretall, Paul Cheng and Li Tai, Collette and Elise Connor, Andor Czigeledi, Julie, Bob, and Chris Franz, Jim and Nadine Hunt, Leslie and Jim Leibold, Bonnie Lynn Sherow and Jim Sherow, Ken, Christine, and David Marcus, Alison, Kevin, Ashley, and Ryan Oliva, Don and Suzie Orsi, Rae Orsi, Richard and Dolores Orsi, Graham, Rosemary, Nicola, and Sylvia Peck, Mark, Beth, and Jack Pesek, Jenny Price, Allyson, Damaso, Katie, Matt, and Danny Saavedra, Jessica Yant, Sean Zielenbach, and the families and staff at Pasadena's Willard Elementary School, especially Lilia Romero and Andrea Stalder.

Thank you to my daughter Renata, aka "Maria Pike," and my son Carlos, aka "Doctor Robinson," for all the make-believe games with Pike plots we've shared. Thanks also to Carlos for a memorable trip to Oklahoma City. And thanks to both Carlos and Renata, who, at ten and twelve, respectively, were astute and enthusiastic proofreaders. Finally, I owe my deepest debt of gratitude to my wife Becky for enduring the many costs this project has exacted and for helping to make it and its author a little better along the way.

Citizen Explorer

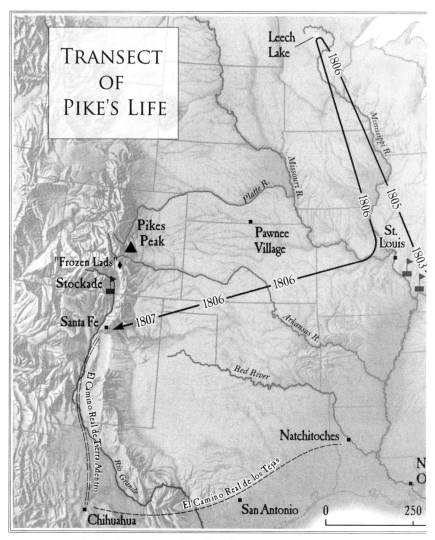

TRANSECT OF PIKE'S LIFE

Leech Lake

1806

Mississippi R.

Missouri R.

Platte R.

1806

1805

Pikes Peak

Pawnee Village

St. Louis

1803

"Frozen Lads"

Stockade

1806

1806

Santa Fe

1807

Arkansas R.

El Camino Real de Tierra Adentro

Rio Grande

Red River

Natchitoches

N
O

El Camino Real de los Tejas

Chihuahua

San Antonio

0

250

FIGURE O.I Map by Steve Chignell and Sophia Linn.

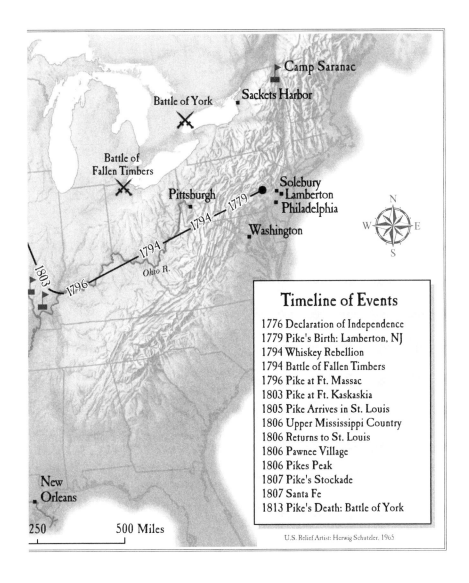

Camp Saranac

Sackets Harbor

Battle of York

Battle of
Fallen Timbers

Pittsburgh

1779

1794

Solebury
Lamberton
Philadelphia

Washington

1794

1803

1796

Ohio R.

N
W   E
S

New
Orleans

Timeline of Events

1776 Declaration of Independence
1779 Pike's Birth: Lamberton, NJ
1794 Whiskey Rebellion
1794 Battle of Fallen Timbers
1796 Pike at Ft. Massac
1803 Pike at Ft. Kaskaskia
1805 Pike Arrives in St. Louis
1806 Upper Mississippi Country
1806 Returns to St. Louis
1806 Pawnee Village
1806 Pikes Peak
1807 Pike's Stockade
1807 Santa Fe
1813 Pike's Death: Battle of York

250   500 Miles

U.S. Relief Artist: Herwig Schutzler. 1965

Introduction

IN THE "BOSOM OF A GRATEFUL COUNTRY"

IN JANUARY 1807, deep in the snows of the Rocky Mountains, Captain Zebulon Montgomery Pike faced a wrenching decision. He was the commander of an American military expedition to explore the southwestern reaches of the Louisiana Purchase, and he had become badly lost. Since early December, the men had trudged through snow drifts and sloshed across streams. When the horses gave out, they hefted seventy-pound packs into the teeth of the Sangre de Cristo Mountains. By January the party was desperate—too weak to go on, too imperiled not to. On the seventeenth, several men got wet crossing Grape Creek, and by evening privates John Sparks and Thomas Daugherty were hobbling on frozen feet. Pike wrote in his journal that the men faced "every probability of losing them." Further travel for the two young men was clearly impossible, and yet to leave crippled men in the wilderness promised them almost certain death. Furnishing them with as much food and ammunition as he could spare, and promising to return when he could, he left them.[1]

Two weeks later, from the safety of a camp on the yonder side of the Sangres, Pike sent five men back to retrieve the "frozen lads." The party found Sparks and Daugherty alive but still unable to travel. In a dark and desperate gesture, the two soldiers removed some bones the frostbite had separated from their feet and sent them back with the rescuers, begging Pike "by all that was sacred, not to leave them to perish far from the civilized world." Pike was mortified. "Ah! little did they know my heart," he wrote in his journal, "if they could suspect me of conduct so ungenerous." Before he would desert them, he vowed, "I would for months have carried the end of a litter, in order to secure them, the happiness of...being received in the bosom of a grateful country."[2] As water and air sucked the heat out of his soldiers' bodies and the nation could do nothing to support them, Pike found solace in a nationalist idea—the republic's promise to reward citizens' virtue.

Pike's ideological response to material hardship raises this book's core question: how did Pike himself and the early republic more generally develop and sustain nationalism when their ideals bumped up against the physical challenges of the North American environment? This is both a personal and a national question. How did a person like Pike, when the chips were down, retain his attachments to the nation, and what enabled the nation during its early years to create enough Pikes to avoid splintering or dividing internally? Pike's life, one man's path to nationalism, opens up a window for understanding nature and nationalism in the early republic—not because he was typical of the nation or causally essential to its development—but because he and the nation grew up together.

Pike was born in January 1779, in Somerset County, New Jersey. At the time, his father and compatriots were fighting a war to win the right to conduct the greatest democratic experiment the world had ever known. They fought, as Thomas Jefferson had put it, for the independence to pursue life, liberty, and happiness. Both Pike and his nation would confront some of the greatest challenges to their independence in encounters with the difficult North American environment. Pike's parents had previously lost a nine-day-old baby and would bury two more youngsters and a teenager. History has not recorded why they died, but the early republic's children succumbed with tragic frequency to cold, hunger, viruses, infections, parasites, disasters, and other assaults to which nature subjected them. Nations, too, faced environmental dangers, not the least of which was sheer physical space. Many who considered the problem, including the widely read French philosopher Montesquieu, believed that large republics would fragment, cracking along the fault lines of the many and diverse interests contained within their borders. In the first *Federalist Paper*, Alexander Hamilton acknowledged that "We already hear it whispered in the private circles of those who oppose the new Constitution, that the thirteen States are of too great extent for any general system, and that we must of necessity resort to separate confederacies." The next six *Federalist Papers* labored to allay this widely held fear. Despite long odds, however, the nation overcame physical distance to succeed as a republic, and Pike survived physical hardships to grow into a man of great fortitude. For both, confronting and overcoming environmental obstacles strengthened their independence and gave it long-term endurance.[3]

Pike grew up during the nation's turbulent early years and joined the army at the age of fifteen. As a young adult, he transported supplies up and down the Ohio River and its tributaries and briefly commanded Fort

Kaskaskia in the Illinois country. He is best known for his exploits between 1805 and 1807, when he led two military expeditions to explore the Louisiana Purchase. The first of these took him north to the headwaters of the Mississippi River. Home barely three days from that ordeal, he received orders to embark on a second. On that one, he crossed the Great Plains to the Rocky Mountains, where Spaniards arrested him as an intruder in their territory and escorted him into northern Mexico. They interrogated him, seized his documents, and marched him across Texas back to American soil. Thereafter, Pike's career took off. He rose to colonel by the time the War of 1812 broke out and then to brigadier general before it ended.

At the end of his life, Pike was more highly regarded than Meriwether Lewis. Although today remembered along with his partner William Clark as America's first and greatest continental explorer, Lewis died tragically in 1809, likely by his own hand. He was in debt, and financial scandal and political impotence haunted him. He had not published the journals from his historic voyage to the Pacific, and he had sunk deep into depression. None of this constituted the makings of a national hero. By contrast, Pike, today the nation's dimly remembered second continental explorer, eventually outranked the elder Lewis militarily and died gloriously in 1813 in the American victory at the Battle of York. His compatriots lamented his great national sacrifice and made him the subject of admiring biographies and epic poetry. For a few years, he was one of the brightest heroes in the pantheon of American military martyrs. More than military prowess and psychological stability, however, distinguished Pike's brief celebrity from Lewis's early ignominy. Pike's story provided the raw material for hagiography because his life reflected America's central promise.

That promise was independence. The independence won by the Revolution was national, to be sure, but also personal. The revolutionaries had sacrificed for a high ideal—the right to be self-governing states, independent of British guardianship. For that sacrifice, they sought the reward of individual independence. Personal independence was like a three-legged stool, on which the members of Pike's generation might elevate themselves. One leg, liberty, freed individuals to pursue happiness without interference from the state. A second, prosperity, usually through property ownership, liberated individual white males from subordination to other men. Finally, gentility and refinement proved to others that one had attained high station in life and admitted an individual to the company of influential people who could further advance one's liberty and prosperity; gentility, one historian has said, was a "resource" for "all who sought worldly advancement."[4] Here, then, was the bargain: white males sacrificed for their country's independence, and their country rewarded them with the fruits of personal independence.

Pike accepted this bargain. From an early age, he aligned his interests with those of the nation. As an ambitious young man, he absorbed the era's cultural advice that happiness lay in self-discipline, civic virtue, and a moderated appetite for personal self-aggrandizement. Republican citizens, the advice held, must always subordinate self-interests to those of the larger community. Refracting these lessons into a code of personal conduct that fit the frontier roughness he experienced as a youth, Pike concluded the best way to achieve the independence he coveted was through physical sacrifice for the nation. He dedicated the rest of his life to persuading the nation to reward him for these efforts. Therein lay his nationalist sensibilities: he believed in the promises of the Revolution, sacrificed for them, and sought to claim their rewards.

Not everyone in Pike's time shared those convictions. Liberty, prosperity, and refinement eluded his father and many other Americans who attempted to claim independence while working the land. By the late 1780s, backcountry Americans rebelled, from Georgia to Massachusetts. As they did, they echoed the rhetoric of the Revolution and insisted its promises were yet to be fulfilled. In Pike's teenage years, his western Pennsylvania neighbors were barricading roads, withholding their taxes, assaulting tax collectors, and acquitting sheriffs charged with refusing to maintain order.[5] It was not always clear whether Jefferson or Montesquieu was right.

Pike's life laid a transect through this landscape of promises, some fulfilled, others not. Ecologists and other scientists use transects—poles or strings or anything else that connects two points—to observe phenomena within a given space. The space might be a patch of prairie grasses, three-feet square, or it might be an acre of forest. Whatever the size, by following the line and appraising and recording whatever it touches, an observer can often gain a reasonable understanding of the entire space, merely from the sample of what the transect crosses. For historians, transects can capture the tension between the mechanistic Enlightenment ideals of Pike's time and the messy organic realities of life in the early republic's West. On one hand, transects are linear, making them anomalous in nature, which itself produces almost nothing straight. Reductively, transects convert the complex relationships of an ecosystem into recordable, quantifiable, and thus (it is often hoped) controllable data points. In this regard, the use of a transect resembles the early republic's project of laying surveyors' chains to grid land into fungible parcels and its attempts to draw and defend precise national boundaries where empires had tolerated more fluid spheres of influence. On the other hand, a well-placed transect can evoke webs of connections. After counting touches and recording coordinates, an observer can also follow the tendrils that snake away from the line through unexplored thickets into hitherto undiscovered clearings. Both aspects of transects, the one that distills a clear trajectory and the one that encourages attentiveness to messier contexts and relationships, are useful for historians.

Citizen Explorer follows Pike as he moved along his life's transect. Whenever he stopped—to trade for horses or hunt for food or read a book or raise a flag—the book takes advantage of his pause to explore away from the transect and follow whatever touches it into the contexts in which he was embedded, treating those contexts ecologically. For example, it understands people's bodies, including Pike's, not just as vessels that contain historical characters but also as organisms, which required food, water, shelter, clothing, warmth, rest, and security. Much of what goes under the categories of politics, economics, and culture at some level rests upon bodies' attempts to obtain these life necessities or the consequences of their failures to do so. Particularly important is energy. Organisms, the scientist Vaclav Smil wrote, "be they cells or civilizations, maintain themselves in highly improbable states of order and organization." This is possible only by concentrating large amounts of energy in defiance of the universe's dissipation of it. Animals do this by eating and then growing fur, muscles, and other body parts that help harness and retain energy from their environment. Humans have the additional ability to make tools such as sailing ships, plows, and mills that capture even larger amounts of power. And they can sell crops or furs to acquire capital with which they can purchase other energy sources, such as labor, at another time or place. They can also burn crops, steal cattle, or regulate trade in order to limit their rivals' capacity to concentrate energy. Thus, while economies require property, capital, labor, and resources, according to Smil, "energy is the only unsubstitutable *and* unrecyclable input into every human activity, and as such it is the ultimate limiting factor of development." At the base of much human activity, then, lies ecology—the knitting of organisms and their environments into relationships tied together by the circulation of energy.[6] By examining the ecological relationships in which Pike was embedded, we can watch him and other Americans as they assembled the material foundations on which to build a republic, and we can observe the challenges they faced along the way.

Energetics, however, cannot by themselves explain an individual's biography, much less the workings of an entire society; consequently, this book integrates its material approach with social, cultural, economic, and political analysis. For example, when Pike offered Pawnees on the eastern Plains protection by the United States if they would give up western raiding and instead trade exclusively with Americans, he was, at one level, offering a diplomatic and economic transaction. When he specifically asked them to sell him horses, he also sought to acquire energy with which to propel his men and their provisions across the Great Plains so that he could explore the West and stake his nation's claim to it. More deeply still, the encounter was a contest over whether the Indians' seasonal migrations or the nation's carefully surveyed land grid and commercial networks would be the primary means for extracting energy from North America's grasslands. Pike's life thus exposes the social, cultural, political, economic, and environmental arrangements by which the young republic extended its sovereignty over distant lands and peoples. Not only did Pike embrace this nation-making project, but his life, which touched the American Revolution, the 1785 Land Ordinance, the Ohio Valley Indian wars, the Whiskey Rebellion, the Louisiana Purchase, the Aaron Burr Conspiracy, and the War of 1812, turns out to be an extraordinarily well-placed transect.

Pike's life trended east to west. It began in New Jersey, where his father joined the Continental Army that fought to give life to the Declaration of Independence. After the Revolution, the Pikes headed west. First they settled in eastern Pennsylvania, where they owned a mill and a bit of land and came as near as they ever would to resembling the American yeomanry that Jefferson romanticized in *Notes on the State of Virginia*. From there, they crossed the state, their circumstances deteriorating from Jefferson's ideal along the way. In Pittsburgh, the Pikes encountered a pair of armies, one composed of rebellious farmers and the other belonging to the Constitution's more perfect union. Pike and his father joined the latter, moving down the Ohio River to fight Indians and establish the nation's power to impose the Land Ordinance's grid of opportunity on the Northwest Territory. At St. Louis, the transect branched and followed Pike's two western adventures. First, it ran north toward the source of the Mississippi River, which the United States claimed after the Louisiana

Purchase but which was in practice ruled by independent Indians and British traders. Later, the line headed southwest to the Spanish borderlands, where Pawnees, Comanches, and Spaniards were masters of the country.

More than just a journey through space, the transect also traced a cultural path through a range of nationalist sensibilities in the early republic. Geographically, it began on the Atlantic seaboard and ended at the far reaches of the American frontier. In terms of sensibilities, it began where nationalism was most cultural and ended where it was most material. In his first inaugural address, for example, Jefferson, who had never traveled more than a few dozen miles west of Monticello, described the United States in cultural terms, as a citizenry knit together by one heart and one mind. The nation rested on citizens who metaphorically sacrificed some of their freedom and bound themselves together around their mutual assent to the nation's founding principles, namely national independence and the guarantee of personal liberties it implied.[7] While things may have appeared this way from the refined spaces of Jefferson's surroundings, from the rebellious western Pennsylvania counties and the violent Ohio Valley of Pike's young adulthood, nationalism looked rather different. There, sacrifice was no abstraction or metaphor but a daily physical experience that registered on people's bodies through infant mortality, back-breaking labor, and confrontations with Indians and the elements. Not long before Jefferson's heart-and-mind address, federal military force had been required to put down whiskey rebels in Pennsylvania, who insisted the nation had not honored or rewarded sacrifices of frontier settlers. Pike did not join the Whiskey Rebellion, but he did share his neighbors' physical trials. By adopting the bargain of independence, he offered his body and life to the nation-state in exchange for the rewards of belonging to this promising republic.

As army duties took him further west down the Ohio River into the Indiana and Illinois territories and beyond, he found nationalist sensibilities growing even more contingent on local and material conditions. Rumors of secession swirled through the backcountry, and some settlers contemplated another move for independence—or even a dash into the arms of Spain—if the United States could not unlock the Spanish stranglehold on New Orleans and open the Mississippi River to the transport of American goods on which frontier settlers' livelihoods depended. At Fort Massac on the Ohio, a man of dubious national allegiance, General James Wilkinson, introduced Pike to Aaron Burr. Burr had recently been expelled from Jefferson's brethren of one heart and mind and was seeking to convert frontier disgruntlement into land speculation, filibustering, or some other scheme that would restore the liberty, prosperity, and gentility he had lost after killing Alexander Hamilton in a duel in 1804. Further west, Pike also crossed paths with Auguste and Pierre Chouteau, the French patriarchs of St. Louis's most powerful fur-trade family. Although hardly republicans, the Chouteaus eagerly ingratiated themselves to their new American rulers in order to continue their commercial success, and they shrewdly moved to make themselves the Jefferson administration's indispensable servants. These and other frontier ties to the nation were less like nationalist sensibilities than mere national attachments—practical decisions to belong to and cooperate with a national community for profit and security. Such attachments, however, endured only so long as the nation met westerners' needs and advanced their ambitions.

In the places Pike visited beyond the United States' control, attachments grew thinner still and more material. Indians of the Mississippi Valley and Great Plains saw Americans and other visitors as potential trade partners and allies, who could enhance the natives' security and prosperity. There, however, attachment ended. They had little interest in joining the independent nation, especially not if the bargain called for the sacrifice of their land, sovereignty, and way of life. At the end of Pike's transect, he met subjects of European empires, who opposed Jefferson's community of one heart and mind. They had no attachment to the nation, just engagement as competitors who were occasionally forced by American power to cooperate. To follow Pike, then, from New Jersey, where his father joined the Continental Army's campaign to make an independent people of one heart and one mind, to the gates of the British North West Company's fur-trade posts on the upper Mississippi or to the streets of Spanish Santa Fe, is to travel a path from places where American nationalist ideas mattered most to where they mattered not at all, and from places where material concerns were merely a part of the nationalist bargain to places where they were paramount.

Pike followed this path both to pursue his own independence and to serve his nation. Through his work and that of others like him, the United States inserted itself into westerners' material lives to induce attachments in people and places where nationalist sensibilities were weakest. In mapping the land and gathering data on the people, Pike carried out some of the first steps to extend Ohio's grid westward. In cajoling fur traders, Indians, and foreign rivals into commercial relationships to be regulated by US laws, he lured them toward dependence that would make attachment to the young nation-state necessary for their continued survival and prosperity. He was not often successful in these endeavors, but in serving as his nation's agent, he lived out his own nationalist sensibilities, sacrificing physically in the hopes of being rewarded with personal independence.

A funny thing happened, though. As he traveled along the transect, he became increasingly dependent on the very people and places he was trying to attach to his nation. Beyond St. Louis, American institutions and values could no longer guarantee Pike and his companions a meal or protect their bodies from danger. To survive, Pike needed help from the people who lived in the places he had come to incorporate into the nation. At the furthest reaches of the transect, the material nearly overwhelmed the cultural entirely, as the geographic knowledge Pike brought to the Rocky Mountains failed him, and hunger and cold so tormented his body that they impaired his ability to think. By luck, he managed to get his party to temporary safety, but his nation had proven unable to support him as he ventured into a faraway and hostile environment. Then the Spaniards arrested him and took him into a very comfortable captivity that presented new challenges to his nationalist sensibilities. First, while still in Mexico, he confronted the embarrassment of being restored to civilized life by a hated and allegedly barbaric national rival. Later, when he arrived home, he faced accusations that his sacrifice was not in service to his country but to traitors within it. In responding to these challenges, his nationalist sensibilities provided him the tools with which both to make sense of the encounter for himself and to defend his allegiance to the nation, something which, to his surprise and disappointment, his brief meeting with Wilkinson and Burr at Fort Massac required him to do.

Today the knowledge that the nation survived its early years obscures the initial uncertainty of that outcome. It is hard to imagine an America whose population's national attachments hung in the balance. It is even harder to imagine an America that had to send a junior army officer on arduous and nearly fatal expeditions to assess the degree and quality of such attachments and to try to strengthen them. Zebulon Pike, however, inhabited precisely such a world. As a young man, he understood nationalism instrumentally. He attached himself to the nation because it offered the rewards he desired. Many others made similar decisions. Pike's story, then, is an American story, of a young nation and a young man both coming of age in the generation after the Revolution.

This biography, therefore, sometimes casts its protagonist in a secondary role in the epic dramas that formed the early republic. It devotes two full chapters to Pike's family background and the national context of his early life, and later it occasionally leaves Pike stranded in the Minnesota cold or gazing upon Pikes Peak in order to track what Aaron Burr was doing at the moment, what Spaniards were wringing their hands about, or how a Pawnee chief navigated tribal politics. Lacking sufficient sources about Pike himself during his early years, all previous biographers have rushed over this terrain to get to the ground covered by his two well-documented expeditions. Since the era when his last chroniclers W. Eugene Hollon (1949), Donald Jackson (1966), and John Upton Terrell (1968) wrote, however, literatures of social, cultural, and environmental histories have enriched the historiographical context in which to understand Pike.[8] Equally importantly, they have provided tools with which to ask new questions of old sources and thus to extract the finer details of Pike's portrait.

Accordingly, while the first two chapters recount what the scant documents tell us about Pike's youth and young adulthood, they spend as much time tracing the multigenerational genealogy by which his family's search for independence entwined with the nation's. They also pay considerable attention to other people in his world—to family friends such as the Browns and Bloomfields, to Thomas Taylor Underwood, who fought alongside the Pikes in Ohio and recorded his memories of them, to Thomas Jefferson and others who theorized the agrarian promises of the Revolution, to struggling Pennsylvania farmers, to George Washington who modeled national sacrifice, to intellectuals around the Atlantic world whose writings inspired Pike, to the fictional heroine for whom he named his daughter, and to a slave named Joe. When Pike's story is triangulated with theirs, his true character emerges more fully than in any previous portrayal. An important limitation of previous Pike scholarship has been to overlook his early years and to try to understand him solely on the basis of his later official military writings. The resulting renderings have depicted a flat, unblemished hero, a buffoon, an enigma, or sometimes even a traitor. By taking the tidbits of what we know about his early years and layering them into his life and times, however, Pike appears unmistakably an ardent nationalist, who consciously cast his lot with his nation. Almost all of his subsequent life flowed from this inclination, starting with his first adult decision—joining the military.

FIGURE 0.2 Pikes' Peak, often called "America's Mountain, with the scenic Garden of the Grounds in the foreground. Photo by author.

FIGURE 1.1 Zebulon Montgomery Pike. 1808. Portrait by Charles Willson Peale.
Independence National Historical Park.

"The Happiness of a Free and Independent People"

A FAMILY AND A NATION SEEK LIBERTY, 1635–1794

IN DECEMBER 1794, Zebulon Montgomery Pike joined the army that had just marched against his neighbors. Fifteen years old, he had been born in New Jersey and grew up in Pennsylvania. He came to Cincinnati in the spring of 1793, following his father, also named Zebulon Pike, who had recently joined General Anthony Wayne's campaign to subdue the Indians of Ohio. It is possible the boy departed the city with his father a few months later, when Wayne's men left to build military posts to secure the nation's hold on the wilderness that stretched from the Ohio River to Lake Erie. As a grown man Zebulon Montgomery later claimed he was present in northern Ohio at the campaign's climactic Battle of Fallen Timbers in August 1794. If so, he saw the savage violence of the Northwest and endured the misery of army life even before enlisting. Even if not, the boy surely had heard the stories. The soldiers who shuttled between Cincinnati and the frontier forts reported that Indians lurked in the undergrowth and ambushed unsuspecting travelers. Rations were in short supply. Muscles ached from hacking through the brush on the daily marches and from felling and hauling trees to build fortifications. Mosquitoes bit. Fevers burned. Disciplinary whips lashed.

Young Pike had undoubtedly also heard the news from western Pennsylvania. Farmers there chafed under the national finance measures that favored eastern commerce. The government taxed their crops and foreclosed their farms when they could not pay. Perhaps such stories recalled for Zebulon Montgomery the day when he was six and a Pennsylvania sheriff catalogued his parents' belongings for sale at public auction to cover their unpaid taxes. While Wayne's legion pursued Indians in the summer of 1794, seven thousand angry farmers marched toward

Pittsburgh, saying it had become impossible to pursue life and liberty. A few weeks after Fallen Timbers, Alexander Hamilton and George Washington led the United States Army to intimidate the Pennsylvanians into submission. Despite the wretched conditions of the frontier army and its attack on people like him, Zebulon Montgomery enlisted because, like generations of his family before him, he found national and personal independence compatible. In Ohio, the military laid the material foundations that promised a path to both.

Seeking Independence: New Jersey

The young soldier came from a long line of independence seekers. Although the record traces their stories only sketchily, it reveals a pattern of Pikes, their friends, and their relatives taking risks to improve their lots in life. John Pike was the first Pike to come to the New world. On April 5, 1635, at the age of sixty-two, he boarded the *James of London* in Southampton, describing himself on the ship's manifest as a laborer from Langford. Two months later, he disembarked in Massachusetts as a prominent man. Court records from Essex County, Massachusetts, list him as an attorney. His transatlantic metamorphosis may obscure a more colorful past. John and his two adult sons, who accompanied him to America, appear to have been considerably more educated than most laboring Englishmen of the day. His adult son Robert, for example, wrote long sophisticated letters in a flowing hand. In the 1630s, religious dissenters like John were fleeing the tyranny of King Charles I. Charles, for his part, feared that "danger might ensue to this State, if Our Subjects might at their pleasure passe and depart out of this Realme," and he sought to make such emigration difficult. In 1634, the Privy Council required New England-bound passengers to swear allegiance to the crown and to attend Anglican worship services aboard the ship. A few months after John left, the king issued a proclamation forbidding emigration without a license. As James Shepherd Pike, John's descendent and an ambassador in Abraham Lincoln's administration more than two hundred years later, observed, men who were "hostile to the governing powers" and "zealous [religious] Dissenters who were hastening out of the country" sometimes "found it expedient" to conceal their origins. Registering at the customs house as a man of modest station may have been a ruse to skirt emigration restrictions.[1]

Regardless of his true origins, John prospered in the New world. He helped found the town of Newbury, Massachusetts, acquired property, and practiced law. According to family tradition, he also held "pronounced opinions." Violating the Puritan municipality's laws governing public decorum in 1638, he stomped out of a town meeting, for which the council fined him two shillings and sixpence. On another occasion, he grabbed the coat of a man, who wriggled away leaving John holding the garment, which he shredded in disgust at his antagonist's cowardice. Again, the town prosecuted him for his impetuousness. Despite the frustrations caused by his strong will, however, the New world appears to have been good to John Pike. When he died in 1654, he left a considerable estate to his five children.[2]

One of them, also named John, continued his father's adventurous and independent-minded ways. A decade after his father's death, he left Massachusetts, likely because of religious objections. Although prominent like his father, he sided with a dissenter pastor, John Woodbridge, whose inclinations toward Presbyterianism rankled his Congregationalist flock. Because religious and civil law overlapped, the matter came to court, and John Pike testified that he "strongly favored [the pastor's] doctrine." Sometime after, he moved to New Jersey, where he acquired 320 acres of land and helped establish a town that he and the other founders named Woodbridge, after their controversial pastor. John Pike quickly became one of its leading citizens, as did his heirs. His son, a third John, served as judge, tax collector, lieutenant in its military company, and deputy in the general assembly. He also officiated in 1708 at the ordination of the town church's new pastor, Nathaniel Wade, whom one historian characterized as a man of "dogmatic temperament, very much bent upon having his own way." Wade urged his flock toward Presbyterianism, and when the congregation joined the Philadelphia Presbytery in 1710, the community splintered. Pike men could perhaps appreciate their pastor's truculent disposition, especially when it coincided with their own religious inclinations, and they stuck with the Presbyterian faction. The third John Pike and his brother Thomas were chosen by the community as ruling elders at a church meeting in 1710. Shortly after the church's embrace of Presbyterianism, John's son Zebulon rose to colonel in the king's army. Town records show him as a land and cattle owner and the head of one of Woodbridge's more prosperous families. Like their Massachusetts forebears, the New Jersey Pikes had been a tad pig headed and had done well.[3]

In Woodbridge, the Pikes met another family of headstrong men, the Browns, and the two families' destinies would intertwine into the 1840s. The first Brown to come to the new world, George, had been a troublemaker in his native Scotland. Like many other Presbyterians of his day, he refused to take an oath of allegiance to the English king, preferring a prison sentence to forsaking his religious conscience. In the late summer of 1685, he sailed for America along with a hundred other religious prisoners whom the English Privy Council had released to the custody of a man named George Scot, himself a recently liberated Presbyterian prisoner of conscience. The council banished the convicts to the colony of East Jersey, "never," according to the council's decree, "to return into this Kingdom without license."[4] Aboard ship, Brown had the good fortune to escape a deadly pestilence that raged among the passengers. Scot, however, succumbed, and his son-in-law successor attempted to indenture the bedraggled survivors into his service upon their arrival. George Brown and the others rebelled. They had not endured the gruesome voyage merely to exchange one form of captivity for another. Joining in protest against the indenture and their banishment, they pled to a New Jersey court that the hardships of their voyage had paid their debts to society. The court agreed and acquitted them of all charges. Transatlantic voyages worked miracles, turning laborers into lawyers and prisoners of conscience into free men.

George Brown came to Woodbridge in the early 1690s and joined the congregation that Pastor Wade, the third John Pike, and others would soon build into the First Presbyterian Church. Church records list George, along with several Pikes, among the first members in 1710, and Brown joined Thomas Pike on committees in 1711 to call a new pastor and in 1716 to survey land for the parsonage. George Brown's grandson, also named George, appears to have been close to James Pike, son of Colonel Zebulon, and the two continued the religious alliance between the families. In January 1756, they served together on a committee of church elders that purchased land abutting their own properties and sold it at cost to the church for a parsonage. When he died in January 1779, grandson George had accumulated a sizeable estate. His will lists several properties in Woodbridge Township, including a salt meadow, a woodlot, and a homestead. He owned a slave, Peter, and left his children a total of 330 pounds.[5]

His friend James Pike enjoyed no such success. Like his prominent forebears, he was a landowner and church elder, but possibly because of poor health or simply because the Pike holdings had by this generation dwindled with each round of inheritance, he accumulated little wealth. It is also possible that the Pikes felt the pinch of the economic stress brought on by the Seven Years' War. Whatever the cause, the family's fortunes took a turn for the worse. James's wife, Mary, died in 1757, and his brother died, intestate, in March 1761, perhaps suggesting the death was sudden. In May of that year, thirty-five-year-old James died of unknown causes. He left a bit of land to his three surviving sons and directed that his personal property be sold and the proceeds divided among them and two daughters. He also expressed a wish that his father, Colonel Zebulon, bequeath his home to James's own son Zebulon, which the grandfather did not do. Two of the witnesses to James's will stated that he was not in possession of his senses when he wrote it, and his parents refused to serve as his executors. In their place, his friend George Brown stepped in to administer the estate's affairs, testifying that James had "dyed without a will." There is no evidence that nine-year-old Zebulon ever inherited any of the land his father intended for him. Zebulon's grandfather Colonel Zebulon died the following year, leaving the boy but fifteen pounds and no land, and his grandmother, who died in 1769, left the bulk of her estate to Zebulon's siblings but nothing to him. The prosperity for which four generations of Pikes had crossed oceans, dissented religiously, founded towns and churches, joined the military, and allied with prosperous neighbors had petered out. Zebulon would have to start over.[6]

Family tradition holds that he went to sea. Zebulon's life story was written down by his grandson Montgomery Pike at the end of the nineteenth century. Some of these tales were reprinted in the newsletters of the Pike Family Association and in local newspapers. There is no way of verifying the stories, but their general validity is not hard to imagine. Orphaned at nine and blocked by the vagaries of his father's estate administration from inheriting much of anything, Zebulon learned at a young age that dependence on family was an unreliable way to make his way in the world. A limping economy after the Seven Years' War would have made difficult personal circumstances worse. British mercantilist reforms of the 1760s and 1770s, aimed at restoring the parent country's economy after the war, constricted paper currency, regulated colonial trade, and levied new taxes that often were payable only in specie. Together such measures aimed to wring capital from the colonies in order to pay off war debts, but the effect on farmers like the Pikes and Browns was to restrict access to credit and to force many landowners and the small merchants and artisans who did business with them into tenancy and dependence. It was a bad time for a landless youth to make a life in the countryside.[7]

Family tradition also holds that he was apprenticed, likely by his maternal grandfather, to a saddler, whose trade young Zebulon intensely disliked. Perhaps the comfortable life of his friend John Brown, son of his father's executor, reminded the teenage Zebulon of the opportunity that family tragedy had robbed him of. Woodbridge was not far from New York harbor, where sailoring might have lured him. If he did go to sea, he might have gotten involved in the smuggling that enriched colonists who skirted the ever more restrictive British trade regulations of the 1770s. In the process, he might have developed a disdain for imperious English authority and its simultaneous crackdowns on smugglers. Successful running of contraband could explain family lore that says he returned from sea with a substantial pile of money.[8]

This is all speculation, though. All that is certain is that he lost almost everything at a young age, disappeared from the historical record for a decade and a half, and reemerged as a man of modest but stable means in the mid-1770s, a metamorphosis that his grandson attributed to seafaring adventure. If he had in fact gone to sea and had not been heard from when his grandmother died in 1769, that could explain his absence from her will. Moreover, the ambition, taste for adventure, and footloose spirit that a sojourn at sea imputes to Zebulon square with what we know of his later character.

One clue that he amassed at least some kind of modest means is that he got married. How and where Zebulon met Isabella Brown is not clear. Family legend holds that her parents, James and Dorothy, owned a considerable amount of land in Somerset County, in central New Jersey, but the couple and their landholdings have not been documented, and they have not been located in that county. The puzzle clearly confused historian W. Eugene Hollon, who accepted family lore and called Isabella the daughter of James Brown of Somerset, New Jersey. Later in the book, however, he identified her as the sister of James Brown and the daughter of John Brown of Somerset County, New Jersey. Still later, Hollon called John the son of James, which would make Isabella John's sister. Two constants running through the tangle of Johns and Jameses is that they were from New Jersey and that one of them later owned an estate in Kentucky called Sugar Grove. Wills and land records establish clearly that a John Brown from Woodbridge, Middlesex County, New Jersey, owned Sugar Grove and that he was the son of George Brown and the boyhood friend of Zebulon Pike. George Brown's will, however, names sons John, James, and Benjamin, and daughters Ann, Jenet, Rebeckah, Mary, and Agnis, but no Isabella. It seems unlikely, then, that she was a member of the Woodbridge Browns. As for her true family origins, family genealogists have found only dead ends. Her ancestry, however, is important because the Pike and Brown family genealogies would entwine in subsequent generations, raising questions about inbreeding, legitimacy, and inheritance.[9]

Zebulon, who might have been a lucky sailor, and Isabella, who might have been the daughter of a New Jersey landowner, married in New York, likely on April 17, 1775, and began life together as an independent married couple.[10] The next day, far to the north in the colony where the first John Pike had settled more than a century earlier, another kind of quest for independence commenced. Paul Revere hung two lanterns in Boston's Old North Church steeple and began his famous midnight ride. The shots fired April 19 at Lexington and Concord incited thousands of New Englanders to take up arms against England. Meanwhile, nervous loyalty to parent Britain reigned in New Jersey and most of the other colonies. Moderates called for negotiation with the crown, but radicals demanded liberty. By August, when the king rejected the Continental Congress' pledge of loyalty and request for concessions, war seemed imminent. Regardless of whether Zebulon brought any treasure back from sea or whether Isabella's family owned any land, events bigger than whatever the young couple had dreamed during their courtship were soon to shape their future together.

News of bloodshed at Lexington reached Woodbridge on April 23, when a rider en route from New York to Philadelphia galloped into town. Although alarming, his cries were not surprising. English abuses had been widely discussed in Woodbridge homes and taverns, and tensions were rising. Joseph Bloomfield, a friend of Zebulon Pike and John Brown, had already chosen sides. Bloomfield was two years their junior, and he hailed from one of Woodbridge's founding families. At twenty-two, he had already established a successful law practice. A wealthy man who potentially had plenty to lose from the upheaval of rebellion, Bloomfield nevertheless joined the radicals who burned sacks of tea in the Greenwich Tea Party, New Jersey's 1774 version of the more famous Boston incident, and distributed militant hand-copied newsletters at New Jersey taverns. Like many in the middle colonies, Bloomfield hated the king's taxes and soldiers, resented the arbitrary closure of the western country to settlement, and chafed at the crackdowns on smuggling seafarers. Scarcity of cash and credit had driven many landowners and others into dependency and were beginning to unite some colonists around the belief that greater equality of political power and wealth were necessary to secure personal independence. From the perspective of middling colonists like the Pikes, Browns, and Bloomfields, Great Britain's taxes, soldiers, and trade restrictions presented the chief obstacle to the independence of colonists. The

New Englanders who fought at Lexington and Concord were saying the colonies must resist such violations of personal liberty, and if the king did not yield, then they should break from England. Bloomfield's father, Moses, agreed, declaring that the citizens of Woodbridge were "determined to stand or fall with the liberties of America."[11]

Still, when the rider hurtled into Woodbridge, the implications were anything but clear. The colonists had few ties to one another; a man from Virginia would more likely have visited London than Boston. They did not think of themselves as a common people. Many dismissed the trouble at Lexington and Concord as solely Massachusetts' problem. Like other colonists, the people of New Jersey felt themselves to be Englishmen more deeply in the 1770s than at any point in their history. Surely they felt that attachment more keenly than had their ancestors who had escaped religious persecution by misrepresenting their origins on ships' manifests or who had come to the new world as convicts banished from England. Mid-eighteenth-century white English subjects were the freest people in the Atlantic world and exercised greater influence over their government and their lives than any other citizenry. The thriving commercial empire to which they belonged stretched from India to North America, brought the world's finest luxuries to their ports, and opened lucrative markets for the fruits of their labor and that of their slaves. In the colonial Atlantic world, the surest path to liberty and prosperity started with being an Englishman. Or did it?

That question divided Woodbridge families. Like Bloomfield, Zebulon Pike's friend John Brown doubted that the path to independence lay through the British Empire, and he joined the New Jersey militia before the year was out. Zebulon's sister Jennet felt similarly, though her husband Philip Gage was a loyalist. After Gage joined the king's army, local authorities seized his land and put it up for public auction. Meanwhile, neighbors considered Jennet a steadfast patriot. According to one Continental Army officer, her neighbors hid their treasure at her home on Strawberry Hill whenever marauding redcoats swept through town. Because of such trust, local historians have suggested, state authorities allowed her to purchase back her husband's confiscated property. Philip died before the war ended, but Jennet's support for the patriot cause was honored with the naming of the local Daughters of the American Revolution chapter for her.[12]

Zebulon, whose friends and family members had already declared in favor of independence, almost certainly was sympathetic to the New Englanders, but he does not appear to have acted on that immediately. Isabella was pregnant, and caring for their family must have occupied at

FIGURE I.2 Cross Keys Tavern, Woodbridge, N.J. After the Revolution, Jennet Pike Gage would raise an American flag in front of this building. From the collection of the Woodbridge Public Library.

least as much of their attention as politics. The couple's whereabouts in 1775 are no more certain than their political leanings. If Isabella was indeed the daughter of the Somerset County landowner James Brown, then it is possible they went to farm in Somerset County. Whatever the couple did, over the course of the first year of their marriage, the events of Lexington and Concord snowballed into a war for independence that became impossible to ignore. American general Richard Montgomery's martyrdom at the battle of Quebec on the last day of the year came to symbolize the heroic sacrifice of the patriot cause throughout the colonies. Thomas Paine told colonists that their lot lay together and that rebellion made common sense. Delegates to the Continental Congress appointed a committee to draft a statement declaring a new, independent nation. And Woodbridge's native son Joseph Bloomfield went to war. "God Grant," he wrote in his diary, "that the United efforts of the Colonies may be crowned with success & that they may be made a free great and happy People." Sometime around then the itch for independence—perhaps from England, perhaps from his father-in-law's farm—began nagging Zebulon Pike.[13]

In 1776, he joined the New Jersey militia as a private. It is likely that he was among the new recruits to whom George Washington read the Declaration of Independence in New York on July 9, 1776, and according to his later testimony, he saw action the following month when fifteen thousand English troops pinned Washington's hapless army against Long

Island Sound. By luck and secrecy, Washington guided the soldiers across the water, thus snatching the cause of American independence from early defeat. In October, Zebulon fought at the Battle of White Plains, and presumably followed Washington as the fighting moved south across New Jersey late in the year. No indication of what Pike thought of all this has survived, but the search for personal independence he had inherited from his forebears was rapidly becoming entwined with the nation's.[14]

His militia term expired in December 1776, and Zebulon presumably returned to Isabella, though probably not to Woodbridge. Located on one of the main routes between New York and Philadelphia, the town had seen the war pass through repeatedly. Five British regiments encamped there, and the soldiers brutalized the townspeople. Fighting in the area was heavy and frequent. Isabella may well have fled the dangerous counties of Middlesex and Somerset. In any case, by early 1777 the Pikes appear to have moved to Pennsylvania. Although initially slow to embrace the patriotic cause in 1775, once the colony fell into the hands of the rebels it radicalized. The Pennsylvania constitution of 1776 echoed the Declaration of Independence, proclaiming that government's purpose was to secure and maintain individuals' "natural rights." It also abolished property requirements for voting, which enabled ninety percent of its white male population and a sizable number of free black men to cast ballots. With such provisions, Pennsylvania was reenvisioning citizenship. In theory, the political power that came with the vote would secure access to the credit, cash, and land that so many had been unable to obtain under recent English reforms. The vote for a government that would protect their rights and liberties was thus also a vote for personal independence.[15]

To advance this cause, Zebulon rejoined the military on March 1, 1777, this time serving in Washington's Continental Army. He enlisted as a cornet in Colonel Stephen Moylan's fourth regiment of the Continental Light Dragoons, in which most officers and all soldiers were Pennsylvanians. Meanwhile, Washington had fatefully crossed the Delaware in December and was pushing the British northward, back across New Jersey. By June, Moylan's fourth regiment was in the vicinity of Woodbridge. Zebulon might have been among the mounted soldiers that British forces sighted on June 24, near Jennet's residence on Strawberry Hill. Fighting erupted in and around Woodbridge over the next few days in what came to be called the Battle of Short Hills.[16]

Four days after the haze of gun smoke settled over the township that his ancestors had carved out of the wilderness in their search for independence, Zebulon formally declared his loyalty to the revolutionary cause. Earlier that month, the Pennsylvania legislature had passed a law requiring white males over the age of eighteen to take an oath of allegiance to the state that had just drafted a constitution and declared its independence from England. The law's preamble explained the oath as a measure to distinguish loyalists of "sordid or mercenary motives" from patriots who "at the risk of their lives and fortunes, or both, rendered great and eminent service" to the cause of "independence." In other words, the legislators aimed to sort out the Philip Gages from the Jennet Pikes, who throughout the land were jumbled up in the same towns, the same churches, and sometimes the same households. The activities of Tories like Gage, the preamble said, were "inconsistent with the happiness of a free and independent people" living in "a free and independent state." The June 28 entry in the "Bucks County Allegiance Book" shows that Zebulon Pike appeared before a justice in Solebury Township, just north of Philadelphia, and swore to "renounce and refuse all allegiance to George the Third, king of Great Britain, his heirs and successors," and to "be faithful and bear true allegiance to the Commonwealth of Pennsylvania as a free and independent state." He also promised to oppose "all treasons or traitorous conspiracies...against this or any of the United States."[17] Once again a Pike had broken from England.

After this, Zebulon and Isabella left almost no trace of their experiences of the Revolution. Zebulon would have been frequently on the move. The Continental Light Dragoons, including Moylan's fourth regiment, have been described by one historian as "Washington's eyes." As a mounted cavalry force, the Light Dragoons were charged principally with scouting and gathering intelligence, usually moving in advance of Washington's infantry. If Zebulon did have any experience as a saddler, that would have equipped him for mounted service. During the summer of 1777, Moylan's fourth regiment moved throughout New Jersey. It was Moylan himself who spied the British fleet as it sailed from New York Harbor in July and relayed that information to Washington, who correctly surmised the English were planning to attack Philadelphia. Accordingly, the general moved his troops, including the fourth regiment, southward, to meet this new threat, and Zebulon saw action in the second half of the year at Brandywine and Germantown in the Philadelphia campaign. After losing Philadelphia to the British, the fourth regiment and the rest of Washington's army settled in for a hard winter at Valley Forge.[18]

Isabella's whereabouts are somewhat murkier. She might have accompanied the Dragoons during some or all of this time. Wherever the Continental Army went, women followed. There were, for example, six laundresses listed as part of Moylan's fourth regiment in May and June 1777. Moreover, it was not uncommon for the wives of officers to join their husbands during long encampments. It is also possible that the couple's apparent move to Pennsylvania in 1777 was to escape to safer territory as the war raged through Middlesex, Somerset, and other New Jersey counties. Despite its small size, New Jersey hosted more Revolutionary War battles than any other state, and the worst of the fighting was during the early years. In the comparative safety of Pennsylvania, Isabella may have lived with friends or relatives, or perhaps in Solebury, where Zebulon had sworn his allegiance to the patriot cause. She and Zebulon likely were together at least some of the time, however, because she conceived again in the spring of 1778.[19]

In addition to adventuring in the cavalry, Zebulon's responsibilities during this time ranged from orderly duty to combat. Much of the junior officers' energy went simply to enabling a cavalry regiment to function at all—recruiting and retaining soldiers and acquiring and maintaining horses. When Zebulon joined in 1777, the regiment had only 180 men—well below its intended capacity but remarkably high considering the worthless paper money he and his comrades received as pay.[20] In July of that year, the soldiers had not been paid for six months, and nineteen men deserted. Thereafter, maintaining the manpower of the regiment was a constant struggle.

So was feeding the horses. Most likely Zebulon spent his first few months in the Continental Army trying to purchase mounts for the regiment. Whether patriot or loyalist, American colonists were smart businessmen. They knew a raw deal when they saw one, and they often refused to sell their horses to officers like Zebulon Pike, who offered only scrip in exchange. When they did sell, they demanded premium prices. Throughout the war, the Continental Light Dragoon regiments were in constant search for more horses. If they had too few horses to ride, however, they had too many to feed.[21] Early in 1778, Washington dispatched the fourth regiment and its starving horses from Valley Forge to seek fresh feed in New Jersey. Whether he remained at Valley Forge or departed for New Jersey, Zebulon was learning that military success depended on keeping the bodies of men and beasts alive and in condition for combat.

In the spring, it is possible that he was among those detailed to monitor British-occupied Philadelphia or that he was among the fourth-regiment officers who took unauthorized furloughs to visit family in the city in April. Perhaps he saw Isabella on such occasions. Soon, though, he was mounted again. As British commander General Henry Clinton abandoned Philadelphia and marched toward New York, Moylan's cavalry pestered the redcoats and relayed their whereabouts to Washington. Pike fought at this drama's climactic battle on June 28 at Monmouth in central New Jersey, and the fourth regiment again harassed Clinton's troops as they continued northward. After the redcoats crossed the water back into New York, fighting in New Jersey subsided for much of the rest of the war. The fourth regiment wintered near the township of Middlebrook, in Somerset County, New Jersey.[22]

Perhaps to join her husband, the pregnant Isabella came to the vicinity of Middlebrook at some point in 1778. There, on January 5, 1779, she gave birth to her first surviving child. The couple named their son Zebulon after his father and great-grandfather, and gave him the middle name of Montgomery, apparently in honor of the martyred general of the Battle of Quebec. In 1817, one of Zebulon Montgomery Pike's first biographers identified the birthplace as a locale then called Lamberton, only a few miles from the Continental Army's Middlebrook quarters. If, as family tradition holds, Zebulon Montgomery was born in Washington's winter camp, it marked the beginning of a martial life for a child whose name honored a military father and great-grandfather and a Revolutionary War hero, and whose entire adult life would be spent in the army.[23]

Little is known of Zebulon Montgomery's early years, except that they passed with his father mostly absent. The fourth regiment's theater of action shifted to the north in 1779 and 1780. It wintered in Connecticut until the American governor asked them to leave, most likely tired of the expense his state shouldered boarding what he called a "southern regiment." Many of the soldiers' terms were about to expire, and they were just as happy to return home anyway. As their numbers dwindled in early 1780, Moylan ordered Zebulon and another officer to spearhead recruitment. Pike met with George Washington in February regarding these efforts, which at first were fruitless. By April the regiment had dwindled to only eighteen soldiers. Perhaps partly due to Zebulon's work, however, the numbers eventually rebounded, and by July the regiment numbered at least ninety-five. That summer, Pike and his comrades fought under General Anthony Wayne at Bull's Ferry, New Jersey, on the Hudson River in a raid on a British supply station. In actuality, "fought" may not be the most apt term for the escapade, which more closely resembled cattle rustling and which inspired the English officer John Andre's satirical poem,

FIGURE 1.3 Battle of Quebec martyr, Richard Montgomery, from whom Zebulon Pike got his middle name. 1784–1786. Portrait by Charles Willson Peale. Independence National Historical Park.

"Cow Chase." In September, Zebulon possibly joined the regiment's overnight dash to West Point, which thwarted Benedict Arnold's treason and enabled Wayne to execute Andre and exact some measure of revenge for conspiring with Arnold as well as for the Englishman's mocking verse. The year 1781 brought the fourth regiment to Yorktown for the battle that led to the British capitulation in October. Zebulon likely participated in some capacity, for Washington's orders place him there on November 4, less than three weeks after the surrender. The following year found them on the Georgia frontier, engaged in heavy fighting, as the combat dragged on while diplomats hammered out the armistice. In July 1783, when the fourth regiment of the Continental Light Dragoons finally went home, it consisted of only two troops, one without horses, and each commanded by a captain, one of whom presumably was Zebulon Pike. In Philadelphia, they were mustered out, "after being received with the ringing of bells by the joyous and gratified populace."[24]

While bells rang in Philadelphia, flags waved in Woodbridge, as Jennet Pike Gage raised the stars and stripes over the town for the first time. One day at the end of the Revolution, she went into the woods near her home with a black man named Joe, most likely her slave, to select the tallest, straightest old hickory tree they could find. Joe felled the tree, trimmed the branches to make a good pole, and dragged it with a yoke of oxen out of the forest to the front of the Cross Keys Tavern, across from the town commons. There, on the main road between New York and Philadelphia, the black man and the white woman planted the pole in the ground and raised an American flag. It was perhaps under this flag that on July 4, 1783, while the fourth regiment was preparing to be mustered out of the Continental Army, Joseph Bloomfield's father Moses mounted a platform with his fourteen slaves and addressed the citizens of Woodbridge. The nation had just won its freedom, he said, and he could not reconcile that with his ownership of human beings. In front of his friends and neighbors, he publicly declared independence for fourteen men and women in the name of an independent nation.[25]

In Woodbridge, and across the newly united states, flags symbolized such independence. For a hundred and sixty years, Pikes like Jennet and Zebulon had left their homes, made new ones, endured hardship, and taken risks to gain control over their own lives and beliefs. They had sacrificed much to pursue the prosperity they hoped would be the fruits of such self-reliance. Twice they had parted ways with England, once with Massachusetts. They had founded towns and churches, owned land, and served in the military. Although not afraid to break with communities and institutions that constrained their liberty, they had flourished largely by collaborating with neighbors like the Browns and serving society. Now, Pikes had helped found a new nation, whose independence they hoped would protect and advance their own. Although the details of the stories varied, similar paths brought John Brown, Joseph Bloomfield, Isabella Brown, Zebulon Pike, and many others to the task of birthing a nation of free people. As the irony of a black man's felling a tree to fly the flag of freedom indicated, the task was far from complete in 1783. But to people like the Pikes, Browns, and Bloomfields, and maybe even to Joe, personal and national independence had become inseparable. The standard that flew from Jennet's makeshift pole symbolized both.

Promises Kept, Promises Broken: Pennsylvania

After the war, farming and independence interlocked as the core of the Revolution's promise to free, white males like Zebulon Pike, Sr. The origin and purpose of government, Paine had written, echoing Locke, lay in people's surrender of part of their property in order to secure the rest of it. Colonial rule, he complained, jeopardized property.[26] During the economic crunch of the 1760s and 1770s, scarcity of cash and credit had left farmers unable to pay their debts and forced them into dependency, their misfortune rippling throughout society to strangle the entire economy. Only national independence could secure the property ownership necessary for personal independence. And only farmers, independent as they allegedly were of the despotic influence that commercial men exercised over wage laborers, consumers, and ultimately the government, could maintain the self-sufficiency necessary to uphold a republican nation in the face of the many selfish pecuniary interests corrupting it. Although Zebulon likely had little experience cultivating the land, most Americans at the time, including demobilized soldiers, sought opportunity in the soil. For now, he would try his hand at the plough.

Initially, though, the army's demobilization was not smooth. In the waning days of the Revolution, the mysterious Newburgh Conspiracy warned Americans that the threats posed by a standing army had not disappeared with the redcoats. By March 1783, Continental Army officers worried they would not collect the pensions Congress had promised, and they also feared losing their social standing upon returning to civilian life. Working with nationalist politicians who hoped to frighten Congress into passing a national impost tax to finance the pensions, a small cadre of officers threatened to defy civilian authority and refuse to surrender their arms until they were paid. George Washington helped thwart the conspiracy by addressing five hundred of his officers and warning that a military coup would jeopardize the national independence that was nearly within their grasp. At one point in his speech, as he mishandled some papers and reached for his glasses, he begged his listeners' pardon, pleading that he had not only gone gray in service to his country but blind as well. The performance swayed many of the officers, who recognized that their leader had suffered and sacrificed along with them. They agreed to wait a little longer for their pay.[27] Soon after, the Continental Army began to be disbanded. Congress never provided for military pensions, and when some officers, including Zebulon Pike, formed a military honor fraternity, the Society of the Cincinnati, they were roundly criticized. America committed itself to remembering the war as a people's cause, in which ordinary men and women had stepped forward to sacrifice and defeat the hated redcoats, thus both revealing American citizens' heroism and discrediting the need for professional soldiers. Washington himself resigned his general's commission and went home to Mt. Vernon to farm, which won him accolades as the epitome of a selfless citizen who had suffered for his country and then declined the glory and power he might have seized as a general, instead preferring the civilian agrarian life on which a republican nation might be founded. In so choosing, he set a model for many others, including Zebulon Pike, who had responded when the nation called in the 1770s and now dutifully left the army when the nation asked.

Zebulon's foray into farming initially met with some success. During or shortly after the Revolution, he acquired a property in Solebury Township in Bucks County, Pennsylvania, the same place he had sworn allegiance to the state in 1777. The Pikes also seem to have dabbled in some kind of frontier land speculation. On August 11, 1784, Zebulon purchased a 298-acre tract from a Philadelphian named John Whitmer. The land was in Bald Eagle Creek Township, in the hills of western Pennsylvania. The deed described Zebulon as "a late Captain of honor in the Pennsylvania line" and the property as "a parcel of land called Good Luck." The Pikes appear never to have settled there, however. Bucks County tax records for 1785 show that Zebulon owned forty-nine acres in Solebury, a pair of horses, a cow, a grist mill, and a saw mill. There were no servants in his household. Together this property was valued at 845 pounds, and he paid 2 pounds and 14 shillings in taxes. Compared to others in the same tax records, such holdings mark the Pikes as far from wealthy but still modestly prosperous. By earning a sufficient livelihood on the land, the couple was living out the promise of the Revolution.[28]

This was just what Thomas Jefferson had in mind. In the late summer or early fall of 1780, around the time Zebulon served with Wayne in the Hudson River theater, the Virginia governor Jefferson received a letter he could not put down. A French diplomat at Philadelphia had sent a questionnaire to members of the Continental Congress inquiring about various details of the states' populations, resources, and other matters. Knowing of the governor's interest in natural and human history, a member of Virginia's delegation had passed the questionnaire on to Jefferson. All through 1781, Jefferson worked on his lengthy reply, before sending the French diplomat in December a response that would eventually become *Notes on the State of Virginia*. In it, he outlined his vision for America. Farmers like the Pikes were near and dear to Jefferson's heart. In what was destined to become the most famous line of *Notes*, Jefferson wrote that "those who labor in the earth are the chosen people of God, if ever He had a chosen people, whose breast He has made His peculiar deposit for substantial and genuine virtue."[29]

Jefferson believed land ownership enabled farmers to exercise both economic and political independence. For this reason, they formed the

FIGURE 1.4 Thomas Jefferson. 1791–1792. Portrait by Charles Willson Peale. Independence National Historical Park.

foundation on which to build a nation. Laborers in manufacturing and other pursuits required customers and employers for support, and were therefore dependent. "Dependence," Jefferson added, "begets subservience." The mobs of Europe's cities were to pure government what sores were to the human body. Although in practice most agriculturalists in the early republic also relied on markets for their produce and rarely resembled the purely self-sufficient yeomen of Jefferson's imagination, he nevertheless believed that husbandmen such as Zebulon and Isabella depended on nothing but the soil and their own industry and thus formed a bulwark against corruption and national degeneracy. Since "the manners and spirit of a people" were what "preserve a republic in vigor," Jefferson wrote, farmers were the antidote to the "canker which soon eats to the heart of its laws and constitution." As long as "we have land to labor," he said, "let our workshops remain in Europe." Jefferson's protégé James Madison and many others agreed. Farmers, Madison wrote, were "the most truly independent" of all classes, the "best basis of public liberty" and the "bulwark of public safety." In theory, the more Pikes the better.[30]

For Zebulon and Isabella, however, farming did not make good on the Revolution's promise. Over the course of the 1780s, they fade in and out of the historical record, but even these scant documents indicate that the fortunes of the recent "Captain of honor" and owner of property called "Good Luck" took a turn toward dependence. Zebulon was unable to pay his taxes in January 1785, and the Bucks County sheriff seized his assets to pay the bill. Given a farmer's seasonal cycle of spring debt and fall harvest, it seems possible that the timing of the sheriff's visit reflected crop failure the previous year. According to the property seizure warrant, the couple's personal items amounted to four horses, a mare, a wagon, a feather bed and bedding, a dozen chairs, two tables, two iron pots, one brass kettle, two guns, a case of pistols, and two swords, all of which were appraised and confiscated. The following year, Zebulon and Isabella sold the "Good Luck" parcel, perhaps due to continued fallout from their tax troubles.[31] The buyer was John Kinsey of Solebury, one of the witnesses who had signed the sheriff's warrant the year before. The couple also apparently lost the saw and grist mills that year because their tax records for 1786 and 1787 list only the forty-nine-acre parcel in Solebury. Over the period, their tax burden decreased accordingly, indicating a gradual decline in the property they owned. No Bucks County tax records for the Pikes survive thereafter, indicating either that Zebulon was no longer a landowner or that he had left the county. His absence from the tax rolls perhaps confirms local lore, dating to the late nineteenth century, that in the late 1780s, the Pikes were renters. By the end of the decade, they must have been on the move because between 1789 and 1791, they vanish from the historical record entirely, including the 1790 census. In struggling, however, they were hardly alone.[32]

Pennsylvania in the 1780s produced woeful tales like the Pikes' far more often than success stories. Pennsylvanians suffered under the consequences of a second vision of the promises of the Revolution. Unlike Jefferson's, this one was not agrarian. Rather, it was associated with men like Alexander Hamilton, who believed the path to independence lay not on the land but through the nation's factories and commercial centers. Pennsylvania's Robert Morris, one of the richest men in America, embodied this vision. He believed that national independence rested on faith in the nation's credit. This, he averred, could most effectively be established through land, liquor, and poll taxes to obtain funds with which the government could redeem the public debt it had created to finance the Revolution. Such taxation would channel wealth from "men...who are idle...and extravagant" to "monied men" and "the mercantile Part of Society," who "could render it most productive." Under the influence of Morris and his allies, Pennsylvania and the national government began to restrict paper currency toward the end of the Revolution. After the war, Pennsylvania and other states also levied taxes, collectible in specie. At the same time, speculators bought up the depreciating paper currency, war bonds, and other obligations the Continental Congress had issued to finance the war. Given the uncertainty of when and if the government would make good on its obligations, unpaid former soldiers and other holders of the government debt could rarely afford to hang onto the notes in the cash- and credit-starved economy. They sold the obligations to investors at significant discounts. After buying the paper at bargain prices, speculators held it until they were able to influence the state legislatures to redeem the debts. They then sold it to the state at face value plus interest, often for gold and silver. The state, in turn, taxed its citizens— the very people who had been forced by economic circumstances to sell their paper—in order to fill the public treasury to purchase the paper. These and other measures resembled the steps Great Britain had taken after the Seven Years' War, and they yielded similar results—economic crunch and rebellion.[33]

As in the 1760s, restricted cash and credit set off a wave of foreclosures. Credit networks collapsed, as eastern creditors called in the debts of western merchants, who in turn demanded payment from their farmer customers. Families like the Pikes often had only their land to cover their debts, and foreclosures became rampant. In one county, there were 3,400 writs of foreclosure issued between 1782 and 1792 among a population of only 5,000 families. In another, the foreclosures amounted to two-thirds of the population. Between 1785 and 1789 in Northumberland County, where Zebulon and Isabella had purchased the "Good Luck" parcel, the sheriff delivered more writs of foreclosure than there were taxpayers. By the end of the decade, most Pennsylvanians—in fact the bottom ninety percent of them, according to the historian Terry Bouton—were worse off economically than they had been at the start of the American Revolution. The sheriff who visited the Solebury farm of Zebulon and Isabella in 1785 was only one of many to seize the assets of middling Pennsylvanians whose dreams of independence were dashed by postwar hard times.[34]

Hardship set Pennsylvania families on the move. Many foreclosed property owners abandoned their homesteads. Others fled even before the sheriff arrived. In the western county of Westmoreland, most of the families foreclosed in the 1780s could not be found anywhere in western Pennsylvania in the 1790 census. Neither could the Pikes, perhaps because they did not want to be found. After a four-year absence from the historical record, however, during which time Zebulon, Isabella, and little Zebulon Montgomery presumably shared the economic misfortune of so many of their neighbors, Zebulon reappeared in the spring of 1791 in western

Pennsylvania, where a pair of armies would soon converge in a dispute over the meaning of the promises of the Revolution.[35]

Securing the Land, Securing Independence: Ohio

Both Pike and the armies came to western Pennsylvania because of a pair of laws Congress passed in March of 1791 to establish order and maintain national independence in the backcountry. The first act was the so-called whiskey tax, which taxed distilled alcohol to finance the national and state debts the federal government had consolidated under the federal Funding Act of 1790. Most of the $60 million debt was owed to speculators who had purchased the government notes at discounted rates after the Revolution but to whom the Funding Act promised full repayment. The whiskey tax outraged western grain farmers and many other struggling Americans. They already had taken a loss on the notes they had sold at a discount; now they would bear the burden of taxes as the government redeemed those same notes to the benefit of the speculators.[36]

The other act raised an army. Since the Revolution, Indians and American settlers had clashed in the Ohio Valley, and in 1789 the federal government built Fort Washington near Cincinnati to enforce American power in the area. The following year, General Josiah Harmar led US troops to retaliate for Indian depredations and met an ignominious defeat that President Washington and others blamed on the ill-disciplined militiamen Harmar commanded. Washington and Secretary of War Henry Knox preferred regular soldiers but knew Congress would never approve a standing army. The March 1791 act struck a compromise by creating a class of soldiers known as levies. These were volunteers who enlisted for short terms, which satisfied the opponents of standing armies. At the same time, the soldiers served under the command of the national government, not the states, which Washington and Knox hoped would ensure the uniformity and discipline of regulars. Congress authorized the recruiting of up to two thousand levies, the beginnings of the first federal army.[37]

Taxes and armies obliged Zebulon Pike to make a choice. Even before the whiskey excise, western Pennsylvania was hardly the place for someone like him to seek agricultural prosperity. It suffered from credit and cash scarcities even more acutely than Bucks and other eastern counties. By the time Zebulon arrived, western Pennsylvanians had for some years resorted to unusual measures for resisting the rampant foreclosures. Tax collectors refused to collect taxes. Sheriffs refused to foreclose. Judges and juries refused to convict. Neighbors refused to bid at auctions. And militiamen were useless for punishing resistance; they often were leading the protests. Starting in the fall of 1787, angry farmers barricaded roads to make it impossible for law enforcement officers to cart away debtors' pots and pans and beds and livestock or for speculators to get to auctions to buy them. The rebels justified their disobedience with the rhetoric of the Revolution, which they believed had empowered them to defy any government that deprived them of liberty. Zebulon had joined such a rebellion once before. He had also joined an army. This time, he would have to pick one or the other.[38]

By offering a specific outrageous act, the excise tax focused the disparate but long-standing grievances that had accumulated among farmers in western Pennsylvania. Whiskey was a staple of the western economy, sometimes circulating as currency. With Spanish officials closing the Mississippi River port of New Orleans to American trade from upstream, many western farmers converted their grain into alcohol, less bulky and more dear, and profitably shipped it over the rugged Allegheny passes to eastern markets. For a government that could not protect them from Indians or Spaniards to tax one of the few methods they had for overcoming distance, mountains, and specie shortages was, to many westerners, the last straw. Western Pennsylvania erupted. Settlers closed more roads and attacked more tax collectors. Some disgruntled folks even began talking about forming an independent government or rebelling in concert with disgruntled westerners in other states. In the context of the ongoing French Revolution, such words sounded an alarm that echoed through the eastern financial houses and halls of government. By August 1794, a militia of seven thousand angry farmers was marching toward Pittsburgh in the infamous Whiskey Rebellion.[39] Eventually, the federal army that Congress authorized in March 1791 would be required to suppress the revolt the excise tax of that same month later triggered.

Failure made Zebulon Pike a good candidate for rebellion. In 1791, he turned forty years old. His family now numbered four children, including twelve-year-old Zebulon Montgomery, seven-year-old James, one-year-old Maria, and infant William. Zebulon had accumulated little of value to pass on to them. For eight years, he had pursued the Jeffersonian agrarian independence the Revolution promised, but he had not attained it, and he must have wondered how he would support his growing family. Many like him—Pennsylvanians who had tried to live out the Revolution's promise of personal independence—were rebelling. Zebulon, however, would not be among the army of farmers who marched to Pittsburgh in the summer of 1794. His only taste of success had come in uniform. As a Revolutionary War soldier, starting out as a private, he had won promotion into officer ranks and had been entrusted with important assignments. He had rubbed elbows with Anthony Wayne, the Marquis de Lafayette, and George Washington, and after the war he had helped to found the Society of the Cincinnati. As late as 1786, he still called himself "Captain."[40] The honor and status that his forefathers had enjoyed came to Zebulon only through the army, and his dignity as an officer contrasted sharply with the ignominy he had experienced as a farmer when the sheriff rummaged through his belongings and sold them for delinquent taxes. Because of his military background, when order and liberty clashed, Zebulon would side with the nation-state that in his experience made liberty possible.

By June of 1791, Zebulon was on a boat headed down the Ohio River, away from Pennsylvania's chaos. Almost no record remains of his whereabouts or activities for the next four years and nothing is known of Isabella and the children during this time. But it is likely they remained in Pittsburgh, for he was headed for war. Recently a down-and-out farmer, Zebulon was now a captain in the levies. His destination was Fort Washington, where he and the other recruits authorized by Congress that March joined General Arthur St. Clair for a campaign against the confederation of Northwest tribes that had defeated Harmar. When he disembarked in August, Zebulon began a new phase of his life. He was about to join the effort to help the new nation seize the Ohio country—land where Americans had found that the promises of the Revolution could be kept. While Pennsylvania's economic problems and brewing fight over whiskey taxes made it a landscape of discontent and a microcosm of a nationwide wave of frustration with the central government's inability to keep the promises of the Revolution, neighboring Ohio became a beacon of the benefits of federal power.

The Ohio country that Zebulon came to defend was born out of the states' land cessions to the national government in the 1780s. With the Land Ordinance of 1785, the Confederation Congress undertook to impose administrative order on the tangle of rivers and forests and prairies north and west of the Ohio River, beginning where the river intersected the Pennsylvania border. Largely the brainchild of Jefferson's supremely rational mind, the act gridded the Northwest Territory into six-mile-square townships composed of thirty-six 640-acre, one-mile-square rectangular sections. The sections would be numbered, surveyed, and sold at auction for a minimum of one dollar per acre. The proceeds from disposal of the public domain would fill the national treasury and at the same time provide opportunity for personal independence to farmers who had failed in Pennsylvania and elsewhere. Most significantly, the grid standardized the land, reducing complex, faraway ecologies to fungible units with fixed boundaries that could be measured, recorded, bought, sold, subdivided, taxed, and adjudicated by easterners like Jefferson who had never seen the places they were managing. Along with subsequent laws—such as the 1787 Northwest Ordinance's standardization of government in the territory and the Constitution's provisions empowering the nation to establish uniform currency, bankruptcy rules, weights and measures, and foreign exchange rates—the Land Ordinance aimed to convert the messy variability of local commercial customs into a regularized national system that could administer a far-flung and regionally variegated republic. A lynchpin of that centralized government power, the land grid enabled property to circulate in a national market and brought everyone who wanted to participate in that market into dependence on the nation-state that administered it.[41] Ohio, then, encapsulated the promise of the Revolution: interlocking personal and national independence through property ownership to fulfill the private dreams of people like Zebulon and Isabella Pike and support the public ambitions of the nation-state against corruption, national degeneracy, and internal and external hostilities. To carry it out, a benevolent centralized government would broker the bargain.

All this exacted a terrible price from the people who already lived in Ohio. The Indians of the Northwest had never accepted the sovereignty that the United States claimed over the region. They maintained that the proper boundary between themselves and the young nation was the Ohio River, the demarcation established with the British Empire in the 1768 Treaty of Fort Stanwix. The stream of farmers surging over the Appalachians and Alleghenies in the 1780s not only alarmed Spaniards at New Orleans but also outraged the Miamis, Shawnees, Wyandots, and Delawares, who formed a loose confederation to stanch the flow. Since the Revolution, the British had armed and egged on the natives in hopes of preventing American trans-Appalachian expansion. Ohio became a bloody battleground between natives and newcomers. Indians understood that without reliable supply lines, the settlements would soon wither and the invaders would straggle back across the mountains. Consequently, they often focused their attacks on surveyors and on people transporting goods and supplies in the territory. As one early Ohio Valley pioneer put it, the "indispensable business" of transporting supplies also became the "most dangerous." Meanwhile, settlers retaliated, launching vicious offensives of their own, all the while demanding protection from the national government. Like most other native peoples in North America, the confederation tribes did not consider land a commodity to be gridded, bought and sold, and converted into capital to circulate in a national economy. They understood that such land use would endanger their ways of life, and they pitted themselves implacably against it.[42]

Zebulon Pike arrived at Fort Washington in late August 1791 to contest this very question with the Indians. Although Zebulon had responded to the nation's call for the levies, recruiting had mostly gone badly, resulting in a force of men whom one observer said "were purchased from prisons, wheel-barrows and brothels at two dollars a month." When Pike arrived, St. Clair's forces numbered fewer than six hundred men, a motley crew of militia, levies, and regulars. Morale was low. Rations ran short. Autumn frosts would soon be killing the forage necessary for the horses to transport supplies and soldiers. On September 17, the ill-disciplined troops, including the company Pike commanded under General Richard Butler, began their northward march. Miserable weather slowed their progress over the next seven weeks, until the exhausted party halted one night without building any defensive works. The men woke at dawn the next morning, November 4, 1791, to the sound of gunfire. Confederation Indians quickly surrounded the camp as the militiamen panicked. Officers shouted orders but could not control the troops. Almost immediately, the battle turned into hand-to-hand combat, and the soldiers stampeded for safety. By 9:30, St. Clair was fleeing with them. General Butler had been killed, and Pike took charge of the entire regiment. Gathering his men, he told them they must retreat in orderly fashion or die. Under his guidance, they loaded on the run, stopping to fire, and then resumed the retreat while reloading. Pike's cool leadership had saved his charges, but the rest of the army was not so lucky. In less than four hours of fighting, more than 600 of St. Clair's 1,400 troops had perished, including 69 of the 124 officers, and 258 men were wounded. St. Clair had also lost 400 horses and $33,000 in supplies and equipment.[43]

St. Clair's debacle and continuing pressure from disgruntled westerners finally overcame congressional opposition to standing armies. In March 1792 Congress authorized the formation of a large army, the United States Legion. Washington tapped Zebulon's former commander, the popular Revolution hero, Anthony Wayne, to head the legion, which was composed

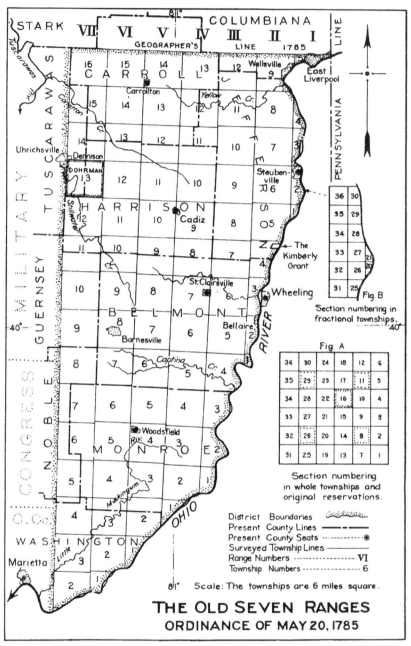

FIGURE 1.5 The Land Ordinance of 1785 began by carving the so-called Seven Ranges into a set of squares. From there the grid would fill Ohio and the Northwest and eventually most of the territory all the way to the Rocky Mountains. Ohio Department of Natural Resources, Division of Geological Survey.

of 5,414 soldiers and divided into four sub-legions. Pike immediately enlisted and received a captaincy in the third sub-legion as one of Wayne's 193 officers. Meanwhile, recruits from around the nation began streaming toward Wayne's headquarters near Pittsburgh. Lieutenant Thomas Taylor Underwood, who served with Pike in the legion and wrote about Pike and life in the frontier army, said that as the enlistees marched to the frontier, their fellow Americans thought it a pity that so many fine young men were going off to be slaughtered as St. Clair's men had been.[44]

Wayne, however, was determined to surprise his doubters. In contrast to the impetuous marches into the wilderness by Harmar and St. Clair, Wayne intended to form a disciplined and efficient force that would advance no faster than supply lines could support, gradually extending American control of the environment. In November, he moved the troops twenty-two miles down the Ohio, beyond the lure of liquor and other temptations that beckoned from Pittsburgh. There, Pike and his fellow officers drilled the men in the skills they would need to succeed in Ohio. They marched and practiced their weapons. In the woods they learned to build fortifications and fought mock battles with comrades dressed as Indians. The following April, the men boarded flatboats and sailed for Cincinnati, where again they camped just out of reach of the town's distractions. As the drills continued, punishments were harsh, with court martial proceedings that often sentenced culprits to fifty or a hundred lashes. "They improved daily in discipline," Underwood wrote in his journal, and Wayne later called them the best-trained soldiers he had ever seen. Meanwhile, restless Ohio settlers wondered when Wayne's legion would quit drilling and get down to the business of rousting Indians.[45]

Wayne, however, moved methodically. He knew that in the contest for Ohio, whoever could best keep themselves fed, rested, clothed, healthy, and supplied in the region's difficult environment would prevail. Indians depended on the Britons for food and weapons. From Fort Miamis on American soil on the south shore of Lake Erie, the British provided arms, supplies, and tactical advice to Indians resisting the American advance. British support also maintained natives' confidence in the face of Wayne's more numerous force. But Americans faced their own obstacles. Ohio was only sparsely settled and a long way from the manufacturing and staple-producing centers of the United States. In between, the Alleghenies and Appalachians formed a significant barrier. Moving whatever provisions Wayne could acquire through the brush and bogs of Ohio would be slow, difficult, and dangerous. "More than...all the Hostile Indians of the

FIGURE 1.6 Anthony Wayne. ca. 1850–1880. Engraving by Samuel Sartain from the original painting by Charles Willson Peale. Ohio Historical Society.

Wilderness," Wayne wrote to Secretary of War Henry Knox in March 1793, he dreaded the "very gloomy pro[s]pect, & scarce a hope of seeing or receiving any other reinforcement of troops or supplies." He would proceed cautiously.[46]

Accordingly, in the fall of 1793, when the troops were beginning to look well-seasoned, the legion marched northward along a chain of forts in the Great Miami Valley, following St. Clair's ill-fated path of two seasons earlier. After passing the last stronghold, Wayne ordered the construction of Fort Greenville, where Pike and the other officers settled in and played handball for the winter while soldiers escorted the army's supply contractors' caravans between Cincinnati and the forts. The legion advanced once again the following summer, building more forts, each a day's march apart. As they proceeded, the surveyors, escorted by riflemen, went first, examining the landscape and charting the course. Next came the scouts, fanning out over the countryside. They were followed by the road cutters, also with a rifle guard, hacking their way through the thick summer underbrush and wending around the ubiquitous swamps. Behind them came the advanced guard and then the main body of the army, divided into two columns of soldiers, approximately 250 yards apart, with one piece of artillery at the front of each column and one at the back. The cavalry flanked the two lines, a hundred yards away on either side. In between the columns and behind them ranged the army's livestock—its energy-saving pack horses and ambulatory meat supply of cattle and hogs. Two more cannons also rolled along. Finally, the rear guard came up behind. Frequently, the troops stopped to build bridges over the creeks and swamps that the wagons could not cross, and every night, the men halted early to cut trees to build breastworks to protect the supplies and guard against surprise attacks. Reveille awakened Zebulon and his comrades each morning an hour before dawn, and the columns formed once again and marched until it was light enough for roll call. In this manner, they made but fifty miles in twenty-four days, advancing no faster than the secure transport of their vital supplies would allow.[47]

As the legion inched northward, Indians fled their villages, seeking protection from the British at Fort Miamis. Meanwhile, Wayne's troops burned lodges and destroyed crops along the way, slowly extending American mastery of the environment into northern Ohio. On August 8, 1793, when the Americans reached a Miami village at the confluence of the Auglaize and Maumee rivers, they found cooking fires still smoking but the town deserted. Up and down the Maumee, on both sides as far as the eye could see, and up the Auglaize, too, grew fields of corn, potatoes, pumpkins, beans, cucumbers, and other produce, all, Underwood wrote, "in great perfection." Without a fight, Wayne had seized what he called "the grand emporium of the hostile Indians of the West." A chain of forts and a scorched earth had shifted the balance of independence in the Ohio country, enabling Americans to feed and clothe themselves and field an army indefinitely while forcing the Indians to rely increasingly on a British lifeline. The natives' patrons, Wayne calculated, would soon tire of supporting dependents, and the confederation would have to come to the bargaining table.[48]

Now in possession of his adversary's food supply, Wayne sent messages of peace. The British are no longer able to protect you, he warned the natives. Come join the American side. He had a large army, he said, but would rather talk than fight. While he awaited an answer, his soldiers feasted on the Indians' crops and destroyed the leftovers. Receiving no reply to his overtures, Wayne resumed marching down the Maumee. Meanwhile, on August 18, the Indians began fasting in preparation for battle. Wayne, however, also anticipated an imminent clash and halted to build yet another post, Fort Deposit, to hold supplies. By the time his men sallied forth on the twentieth, leaving Captain Pike in command of this last stronghold, many of the hungry Indians had retreated to other villages downstream in search of food, while the ones who remained were weak from fasting for longer than they had planned.[49]

The American columns marched at daylight and proceeded for two hours. Near an area of thick undergrowth and fallen trees, likely downed by a past tornado, the advance guard drew fire and beat a hasty retreat, losing some men in the process. Quickly, the main columns formed for battle, and heavy fighting commenced almost immediately. Indians fired from the cover of the downed logs, loading, shooting, and dropping down to load again. The Americans' horses faltered in a ravine that crisscrossed the dense woods and separated the legion from the Indians. Nevertheless, Wayne's charge was successful. The Battle of Fallen Timbers, as the skirmish came to be called, lasted only seventy-five minutes, with the three thousand Americans and fourteen-hundred natives both suffering thirty-some deaths. When the outnumbered Indians finally fled toward Fort Miamis, they found the gates locked. Wayne had been right: the British were not a reliable ally.[50]

Upon learning that the Indians were fleeing, William Campbell, the British commander of Fort Miamis, had ordered the gates closed. Inciting Indian opposition to American expansion was one thing; engaging Americans directly was quite another. His orders did not include triggering a war between the United States and Great Britain. For the next few days, while the legion buried its dead, Wayne taunted the British, whose fort stood on American soil. He sent flag bearers and trumpeters and even led several hundred soldiers up to the gates and around the garrison. By letter, Wayne demanded Campbell's retreat. But Wayne did not want to start shooting first either, and he lacked the supplies to carry out a prolonged siege. In the end, he marched his troops four rainy days back to the confluence of the Maumee and the Auglaize, destroying miles of Indian crops on the riverbanks along the way.[51]

As the grand emporium smoldered and the natives' ersatz British allies locked the gates, the confederation's morale evaporated and many turned to the Americans for support. When the main part of Wayne's legion retreated to its winter quarters at Fort Greenville in November, a party of Indians waving white flags overtook the columns and accompanied the soldiers to the post. All winter, they crowded around Fort Greenville to receive food and supplies to endure until spring when, Wayne announced, peace talks would commence, a schedule he undoubtedly timed to coincide with the season when the natives were least able to feed themselves. The talks opened in June, but proceeded slowly. On the twenty-ninth, five hundred Indians camped around the fort, but the chiefs had still not had an audience with Wayne, who was waiting for all the tribes to arrive before beginning negotiations. They demanded to meet with the general and to eat as the Americans ate. Wayne responded by giving each leader a sheep.

FIGURE 1.7 Woods where the Battle of Fallen Timbers took place. American horses stumbled and threw their riders as they crossed trenches like this one. Photo by author.

On July 3, he raised the American flag and addressed them: "Brothers—I am extremely happy upon this occasion to...inform you, that tomorrow, will be the great day, famous, for the independence of the United States." The cannons will roar in celebration, he said, to "declare Liberty and independence" and the flags will fly as "emblems of peace." By mid-July, as the talks dragged on, the army was feeding more than 1,700 Indian men, women, and children. In August, when Wayne and his guests concluded the Treaty of Greenville, in which the confederation surrendered most of Ohio to the United States, the contrast between independent Americans and dependent Indians had never been starker.[52]

Wayne's victory had changed Indians' and settlers' relationships with the Ohio environment. Americans conquered Ohio partly by conceiving a particular brand of liberty and partly by concentrating the energy necessary to implement it. This was nothing new in North America. The Pike family had been doing it since 1635, when the first John Pike and his sons boarded a ship whose sails harnessed the energy equivalent to four thousand men at oars. Such energy-tapping devices were essential to creating the conditions that enabled Zebulon and his comrades to invade Ohio a century and a half later. As the historian David Nye has put it, "although it is possible to row

FIGURE 1.8 Battle of Fallen Timbers. ca. 1895. Painting by R. T. Zogbaum. Ohio
Historical Society.

across the Atlantic, Europeans could not have settled in the New world or
dominated without the sailing ship. The new colonies would have made no
economic sense." Transporting North America's bulky commodities such
as lumber and cotton would have been unimaginable. Wind-powered ships
also brought droves of colonists to North America along with the ancestors
of the slave Joe—human muscle power to rearrange the landscape—and
earned the seafaring orphan Zebulon enough capital to marry. Warfare
required an even greater mobilization of energy than colonization, and the
Revolution was powered in part by the horses Zebulon Pike tended, the
bodies of the soldiers he recruited, and the meat of the cattle he rustled with
Wayne at Cow Chase. After the war, the water wheel at his Bucks County
saw mill was one of thousands that captured the hydropower to provide
energy for the clearing of forests to benefit people who sought liberty in
private property ownership and the houses, fences, barns, and pastures that
came with it. The resulting ecological change made it harder for Indians to
gather the energy that powered their way of life.[53] Like so much else about
the conquest of North America, Wayne's victory at Fallen Timbers was not
so much militarily decisive as it was ecologically transformative. By burning
natives' crops and severing their ties to the British (who had imported guns
and other energy sources for the Indians), the legion changed the balance
of literal power in Ohio. The ecosystem that had once supported Indians by
the end of the eighteenth century favored Americans. The people who

sailed the Atlantic, sawed forests into fences, and waged and won a war for liberty had successfully concentrated the energy necessary to extend an American vision and practice of independence over much of the eastern portion of the continent, a juggernaut their offspring would continue.

The Alignment of Region and Nation

Meanwhile, Wayne had begun recruiting to replace soldiers whose enlistment terms were nearing an end.[54] One of the recruits who replenished the ranks after the Battle of Fallen Timbers was Zebulon and Isabella's fifteen-year-old son Zebulon Montgomery. By the time he enlisted, he must have known the outlines of his family's story: how his fourth great-grandfather left England to seek prosperity and follow his conscience, how the prosperity built by the Pikes' first few American generations had dissipated through family tragedy and the economic downturn of the 1760s, how this misfortune had robbed his father of opportunity even before he passed from childhood, how Zebulon, Sr., had gone perhaps to sea and certainly to war to seek independence, and how farming had failed him before the new army gave him a second chance. For generations, Pikes had struggled and sacrificed to gain and then regain independence. After the Revolution they lost that independence on the land and then recovered it in the military.

The nation, too, had gained independence through the military. It had won a great war for liberty against the mightiest empire in Europe. It had put down the Pikes' disruptive Pennsylvania neighbors, who themselves rebelled in the name of independence. And it had wrested control of environments far from Philadelphia and forced the peoples who lived there into cooperation, if not complete allegiance. Through the army, the nation had exerted its power in order to maintain and expand its sovereignty in the face of challenges from Europeans, Indians, and its own citizens. After opening the land of the Ohio country for American settlement, the army, with its demand for food, clothing, tools, weapons, alcohol, and other goods stimulated regional economic development. For many, including Zebulon Pike, Sr., the army also charted an avenue for social advancement. For these reasons, he and other Ohioans equated the nation's interests with their own.[55]

Joining the army, then, must have made sense to the teenage son of a hard-luck Revolutionary War veteran. Zebulon Montgomery's own family's experience had taught him to associate independence with personal prosperity and liberty as well as with the sovereignty of the nation that enabled those things. Throughout his life he displayed an affinity for the order and hierarchy that underwrote national independence, while also cherishing the individual autonomy necessary for personal independence. At the age of fifteen, he surely did not yet understand all of this; however, these ideas and impulses had already begun to shape his character. Over the course of his life they stirred in him an intense commitment to the nation-state and set him on a life path of sacrificing for his country in hopes of attaining the independence that generations of Pikes had pursued.

2

"Be Always Ready to Die for Your Country"

THE BARGAIN OF INDEPENDENCE, 1794–1805

THAWING ICE CRACKLED through the western Pennsylvania forests in mid-February. For the next several weeks, the streams awakened as snows melted and spring rains filled the channels. In shady spots, lingering chunks of ice that clung to the shore broke off and bobbed in the chilly waters cascading from the mountains of western Pennsylvania. French Creek, Buffalo Creek, Sandy Lick, the Kiskiminetas—together they filled the Allegheny River, frothing southward to join its more placid southerly partner, the Monongahela. The two rivers' contrasting moods intermingled at their meeting. Having flowed for some distance through gentler terrain and warmer climes already free of frost, the sluggish Monongahela meandered toward the confluence. The mountains' Allegheny still carried ice in its clear waters and pushed excitedly across the Monongahela's channel.[1] Their forks birthed a third river, the Ohio.

In the early years of the republic, the Ohio River was the artery connecting the nation to its western provinces. Mighty and unrelenting as the Allegheny, lazy and inexorable as the Monongahela, the Ohio coursed a thousand miles southwest to the Mississippi River. Below the forks, the Ohio sometimes cut a deep, narrow channel, canopied with trees leafing out in the warming spring sunshine. At other times, blooming shrubs dipped their limbs into the rolling waters. Halfway between its headwaters and its mouth, the Ohio dropped over stair steps of horizontal limestone strata. Although it dropped almost perpendicularly in some places, for most of the way through the falls, the river ran through a channel of fairly even slope, which it had worn down for millennia. In wet seasons, the rapids were hardly noticeable. But as the midsummer sun blazed and the flow dwindled, rocks protruded through the ripples. Fall

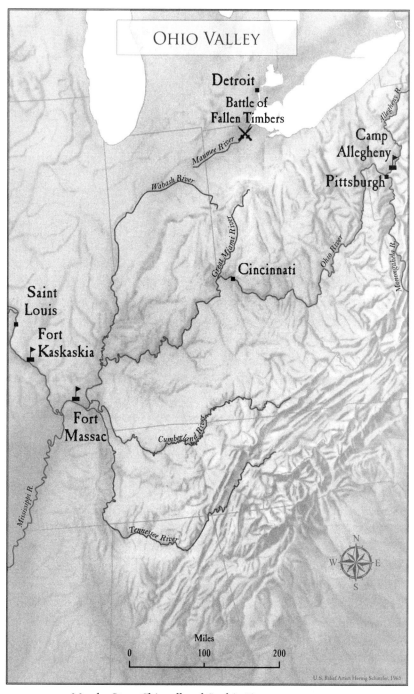

FIGURE 2.1 Map by Steve Chignell and Sophia Linn.

rains filled the channel, but by December, it frosted up again, and the new year found the surface of the beautiful river frozen stiff at its confluence with the Mississippi. All winter, blocks of ice ground against each other, rumbling and awaiting the early spring thaw, when the waters would roll down to the Gulf of Mexico.[2]

The Ohio brought young Zebulon Montgomery to the West and introduced him to the physical sacrifices that over the course of his army career would bind him to the nation. For several years after he joined the army, he frequently waded into the Ohio's waters to load, steer, and command boats carrying the bountiful produce of the Ohio Valley countryside—energy gathered and concentrated by the army and redistributed to those who wished to make use of it. His job as transporter of the army's supplies was among the most important on the frontier because it both connected the West internally and linked it to the East and ensured circulation of goods and capital, and thus energy. Even with the Indian menace quelled, Wayne's chief concern remained provisioning. In the weeks after Fallen Timbers, there had been no salt to season the food, and the contractors had run out of beef. "Very pore beef & musty flour poor living," grumbled the Pikes' comrade, Lieutenant Thomas Taylor Underwood. Another officer worried, "Our Armey [is] Almost Exaustead by their Dailey fatigue and the Weak Nurishment of Only ½ a Ration of Bread." With deprivation, morale and behavior deteriorated. Some men stole rations or plundered civilians. Others deserted. To independent men in harvest season, starving in the wilderness made little sense when laboring on their farms would support their families and fill their stomachs. To shore up the men's sinking spirits and his thinly stretched supply lines, Wayne invoked the help of the Almighty. On September 2, 1794, he gathered the soldiers for religious services for the first time. The legion's chaplain David Jones struck a rallying note, drawing his sermon from Romans 8: "if God be for us, who can be against us?" Four more men ran away later that day, taking good horses with them. As grumbling and desertion continued, Jones appealed to St. Paul's sterner writings, in which order trumped liberty. "Let every soul be subject unto the higher powers," he preached on October 19 from Romans 13, "for there is no power but of God: the powers that be are ordained by God. Whosoever therefore resisteth the power, resisteth the ordinance of God.... Wilt thou then not be afraid of the power? Do that which is good."[3]

Although in the aftermath of Fallen Timbers, the younger Pike numbered among the recruits, not the deserters, the willful fugitives and

Reverend Jones's grave call to obedience together manifested one of the army's greatest challenges: without adequate supplies, soldiers suffered. In the face of such hardship, the army could not retain the loyalty or compliance of independent men. These difficulties were national, too. Most people distant from America's centers of power and wealth faced considerable adversity, and the national government often proved unable or unwilling to support them. The constitution had promised an antidote to the misbehavior of rebels who had followed embittered Revolutionary War veteran Daniel Shays, but even after its ratification, the Pikes' Pennsylvania neighbors and many others had revolted. Rumors of secession and alliance with rival Spain flashed across the frontier territories and states, as the nation conceived in rebellion against authority struggled to enforce virtuous behavior on people who felt the government was deaf to their struggles and who believed they had a right to block roads, conspire with Spaniards, and desert armies in the name of liberty. How could a nation compel such a population to "do that which is good"?

Pike began life in the army amid this tug of war between liberty and order. Like the Whiskey rebels, the Mississippi Valley secessionists, and Wayne's hungry deserters, Pike suffered in the backcountry. Instead of rebelling, however, he charted for himself a very different path to independence, one that reconciled nationalist virtue and frontier hardship.

Provisioning and Personal Growth

The day the council at Greenville closed, Wayne ordered Zebulon Pike, Sr., further west to assume command of Fort Massac. Pike departed Fort Greenville with a hundred men, including his son, Zebulon Montgomery, and arrived at Fort Massac on September 5.[4] Overlooking the north bank of the Ohio River thirty-eight miles above its confluence with the Mississippi, the fort occupied the site of an abandoned French post, built in 1757. To extend American presence into the interior of the continent, President Washington ordered the fort's reconstruction in 1794. Its first commanding officer had overseen the construction of a few buildings to provide temporary security, but when the Pikes and the other soldiers clambered out of their boats, the place hardly resembled a fortress.

On September 8, fifty men felled trees and dragged them out of the forest, fashioning them into pickets. Over the next few days, they dug a moat and posted the pickets vertically into the ground with sharp tips pointing to the sky and forming a stockade enclosing the buildings. As the new inhabitants entered the fort through its main gates on the river side to the south, the officers' quarters stood straight before them across the courtyard, along the north side of the fort. Captain Pike—and Isabella and the children if they were with him—would have taken up residence there. As an enlisted man, Zebulon Montgomery would have occupied a wooden bunk in either of two eight-room two-story barracks to the west and east.[5] Bastions at the corners enabled surveillance of the well-traveled Ohio River.

After the fortifications were finished, Captain Pike sent his son in search of two deserters who had left camp, perhaps when they realized the grim living conditions or while sweating through the heavy construction. Indeed, Fort Massac's dark and musty quarters were hardly comfortable. Made of hewn logs, the walls had a few paned windows facing the courtyard, and the men could peep outward through a handful of smaller squares, ranging from six to eighteen inches. Only some of the rooms had fireplaces, and the wind that whistled through the cracks chilled the men in the winter, while mosquitoes and other pests entered through the same chinks to torment the inhabitants in the summer. The soldiers sustained themselves with hunting and fishing and, by the next spring, a little gardening. Although the younger Pike did capture the two runaways, the austere conditions that underlay the men's misbehavior made provisioning

FIGURE 2.2 Reconstructed soldiers' barracks as they might have looked ca. 1802. Fort Massac State Park, Illinois. Photo by author.

Captain Pike's most immediate concern, just as it had preoccupied Anthony Wayne in Ohio. This essential duty became his son's first significant army assignment.[6]

As Captain Pike's party rowed the last few miles down the Ohio River to rebuild Fort Massac, Wayne was at Detroit, his new western headquarters, writing orders for Zebulon Montgomery Pike. "You are to proceed with all possible dispatch for Fort Washington," the general wrote, where the commander "will order you the necessary supplies of Provision." From there, Zebulon Montgomery was to descend the Ohio with the same barges and crew that accompanied him upstream and "deliver the dispatches and stores committed to your charge" to Fort Massac. The following month, Lieutenant Underwood, who had been assigned to Fort Massac with the Pikes, undertook a similar journey. Departing with twelve soldiers, perhaps including the younger Pike, Underwood proceeded up the Ohio to the Cumberland, which he followed into the interior of Kentucky and Tennessee. He visited Colonel Andrew Jackson and other local dignitaries along the way before turning north to deliver letters and pick up the payrolls at Fort Greenville. On his way home, the quartermaster at Fort Washington gave him a flatboat loaded with provisions for Fort Massac. After the two-month sojourn, Underwood returned to Fort Massac on December 30, carrying the news of Captain Pike's promotion to major. Whether or not Zebulon Montgomery accompanied Underwood, the journey, like the orders from Wayne, exemplified the kind of duty Pike performed for the next decade as he traveled the Ohio and its tributaries, visiting planters, merchants, and officers, and moving the supplies that were so essential to survival and morale in the West.[7]

But the network involved more than just supplying the army. Like the water itself, the region's traffic emanated from the western slopes of the Alleghenies. The Alleghenies consisted of a series of parallel north-south ridges that alternated steep grades with deep valleys. No sooner would travelers hump over one rise than they would behold another, with the promise of monotonous repetition of their labor looming on the horizon. Tree-strewn and cluttered with boulders, the roads were often impassable in heavy rains and completely inaccessible in winter. Summer heat was unbearable. What traffic did cross the passes came on foot or on beast and transported only low-volume refined goods, for there were no water routes connecting east and west. Horses could ease the journey somewhat but they frequently gave out along the way. All this and plenty of rattlesnakes, too.[8]

Because of the difficult and expensive mountain crossing—and because water flowed downhill with little investment of energy by humans or animals—farmers and artisans on the western side of the Alleghenies found it more profitable to float their bulky produce two thousand miles down the Ohio and Mississippi to New Orleans rather than haul it three hundred overland miles to Philadelphia and Baltimore. Fanning out along the Ohio Valley's many navigable waterways, they shipped the fruits of their labor downstream to port cities like Cincinnati, where trading vessels docked at the wharves. There, traders sold their wares and picked up more before continuing on to Louisville, St. Louis, and New Orleans. The boats that Zebulon Montgomery guided were but a few of the many laden with flour, whiskey, peach brandy, cider, bacon, iron, potters' ware, and cabinet work. The wooden bowls from which Captain Pike's men ate and the ceramic mugs from which they drank came to Fort Massac via this thriving trade. So did the glass panes in the barracks windows that Zebulon Montgomery and his comrades peered through. A receipt in the younger Pike's name indicates that in 1798 he brought to the post a shipment of nails, flannel, thread, crosscut saws, handsaws, whipsaws, cables, padlocks, wire, and materials for "mending the Garrison Flag."[9]

Little went upstream, however. In addition to the falls and the mountains, the current itself made upstream transport a slow, expensive, and therefore rare undertaking. From Cincinnati, a vessel took about a month to arrive at New Orleans, and the difficult and dangerous return voyage by land or boat required about three or four. In 1807, 1,800 vessels docked at New Orleans but only eleven went upstream. Instead, commodities often traveled down the rivers in seaworthy craft built at Pittsburgh or elsewhere and then sold in New Orleans for continuing on to Gulf and Atlantic ports. Boats unfit for an ocean voyage were scrapped for lumber, while their crews caught ships to Philadelphia or Baltimore and then crossed back over the Alleghenies by land.[10]

Despite the one-way flow, the system circulated energy, labor, commodities, and capital over great distances. Alluvial overflows enriched soil that nurtured crops. Spring rains watered them. Summer sun warmed them. Human industry harvested them in the autumn, and the current carried them downstream. Sunlight, soil, water, and labor produced goods to be sold in New York, London, and Paris. Energy became capital, which people used to hire or enslave more labor, cultivate more land, and continue the process. This system tied the interior of North America to the Atlantic world economy and enabled people like Zebulon Montgomery

Pike to make a living. In addition to transporting army supplies, he dabbled in private goods on the side, and at one point he even appears to have contemplated leaving the army for the more lucrative domain of commercial supply contracting.[11] The system also enabled the nation-state to extend its power to the west. With Fort Massac as a western base, the Pikes and their comrades extended the Ohio Valley's spider web of supply networks and replicated the process of landscape control through concentration of energy with which Wayne had conquered Ohio.

While Zebulon Montgomery was carrying the produce of the Ohio Valley, his father was enforcing the nation's western boundaries. In March 1796, when a Spanish barge with eighteen oars on each side rowed up the Ohio, Major Pike ordered a cannon ball fired over its bow. The Spanish captain huffed ashore, insisting that the mission was peaceful, but given the tense relations between the two nations, Pike's bellicose greeting made sense. The previous October, the American and Spanish governments had established the United States' southern boundary through the Treaty of San Lorenzo, but Andrew Ellicott, who dined with Pike at Fort Massac later that fall on his way to survey the boundary, did not believe that Spanish officials intended to adhere to it. He also feared that Spain and France would conspire against American westward expansion. Indeed, late in 1795, news had reached the Mississippi Valley of a peace between Spain and France.[12]

Fort Massac lay just upstream from the Ohio's confluence with the Mississippi, where the North American empires of Britain, Spain, and the United States collided. Because commerce did not travel up the Mississippi and Ohio nearly as easily as it went down, the Ohio-Mississippi circulatory system was vulnerable to being choked, and Spain understood this. After the Revolution, Spain's North American frontier neighbored a republic with a burgeoning population and an ideology that all of those new bodies had an inalienable right to land. As Americans flooded west, Spanish officials grew nervous that the Mississippi River, which divided the two nations' holdings, would prove a porous border. To hem in the westward moving settlers, Spain closed the port of New Orleans to American shipping in 1784. Simultaneously, the Spaniards tried to lure disgruntled westerners into secession from the union, overtures that sometimes found willing ears. Part of Major Pike's job was to see that the rumors of disloyalty did not come to fruition, and doubtless the need to exert American strength at the confluence of the Ohio and Mississippi influenced his decision to fire his cannon.

Not everyone, however, perceived the vital national interests in the rivers that westerners did. In the aftermath of the Revolution, Federalists were ready to cede the river's navigation rights to Spain in exchange for favorable trade relations that would head off the threatened secession of New England from the Articles of Confederation. As a result, many westerners began to doubt whether a federal government dominated by Atlantic states could be trusted to promote frontier interests. Kentucky and Tennessee became fertile ground for secessionist movements in the 1780s and early 1790s. A former Continental Army officer, James Wilkinson, one of the ringleaders of the abortive plots, secretly took an oath of loyalty to the Spanish government, as did Andrew Jackson and many others. In 1787, Wilkinson sailed down the Mississippi with a boatload of goods and quietly negotiated with the Spanish governor Esteban Miró for a dispensation opening New Orleans to Wilkinson and his friends in exchange for kickbacks to Spanish officials and the promise to agitate for secession in the interior.[13]

In the context of questionable western loyalties, Pike's shot across the bow reflected the main purpose of Fort Massac, enforcing US sovereignty in the West. Among other duties, Pike and his men inspected cargo and passengers on the Ohio to establish a federal bulwark against the smuggling, filibustering, secessionism, and foreign intrigue with which frontier residents frequently flirted. The same year that he fired on the Spanish visitors, Major Pike also arrested two French military officers suspected of trying to foment rebellion. US citizens also posed a threat to national authority, and Pike's successors at Fort Massac burned the cabins and fences of American squatters who illegally violated treaties and occupied Indian lands. Despite the 1795 Treaty of San Lorenzo, which temporarily reopened New Orleans to American shipping, geopolitical tensions put frontier posts like Fort Massac on a hair trigger. After the Spanish captain came ashore, he presented Pike with a Spanish flag, and then Thomas Taylor Underwood and another officer took him hunting. Later, as the Spaniard departed, he thanked the Americans for their hospitality, but Major Pike suspected the visit had been intended to test the fort's strength.[14]

Pike's previous guest, the surveyor Andrew Ellicott, had groused in his journal and in correspondence to Major Pike about the miserable circumstances of his western travels, especially getting stuck in the ice at the confluence of the Ohio and the Mississippi. Pike, who had suffered similar difficulties, sent a letter commiserating with the surveyor: "[I] am only sorry I have it not in my power to render you more comfortable." He assured Ellicott, however, that in the end, the hardship would be "Gratefully acknowledged by your Countrymen."[15] Pike's equanimity in the face of struggle, whether felling trees, enduring the elements, or weathering challenges from imperial rivals, reflected a faith that his country would reward sacrifice. While that faith did not always bear out in his own life, his son internalized the same conviction.

Meanwhile, the son was growing into a man. A symbolic turning point in his maturation came on the Fourth of July in 1796. That evening, he and Major Pike set out to sail across the Ohio. About 150 yards from shore, a squall blew up, capsized the boat, and dumped both men into the current. "Save yourself & let me goe," the major reportedly cried as the boat sank, but the seventeen-year-old shouted, "I will take you safe to shore." Zebulon Montgomery must have been a powerful swimmer, because he paddled to shore in rough waters, dragging his father along by the hair. Underwood recorded the episode, perhaps sensing that it marked a transition in both men's lives. The younger Pike was making a name for himself with his physical prowess and strength of character, and he received his first officer's commission as second lieutenant in March 1799. By November he earned promotion to first lieutenant. In 1801, he supervised construction of a new post just downstream from Fort Massac, Cantonment Wilkinsonville, of which he was named the first adjutant. Meanwhile, his duties continued to take him all over the Ohio Valley. He spent parts of 1799 and 1800 at Camp Allegheny in Pennsylvania, before moving on to assignments at Fort Washington, near Cincinnati, Fort Knox, near Vincennes, Indiana, and finally in 1803 at Fort Kaskaskia on the Mississippi, where he served as adjutant and briefly as commander. Throughout some or all of this period, he continued to shuttle provisions, but he was no longer sent on small errands and instead of traveling under command of a superior officer, he supervised the transport crews himself.[16]

While the son's career ascended, the father's fortunes once again declined. In May 1797, the army reassigned Major Pike to Fort Pickering, near modern Memphis, Tennessee. Like Fort Massac, Pickering was a key western post, suggesting his superiors' continued esteem for his abilities, but while posted there, he suffered some kind of injury or illness, which he later maintained caused a long physical decline that eventually rendered him unable to walk. Nevertheless, after Fort Pickering, he continued to win prestigious appointments over the next few years, including two stints at the Inspector General's office in Washington, and commands of Fort Wayne and Detroit, even as his health continued to deteriorate. In March 1804, the adjutant general wrote to Major Pike, relieving him from his last command and placing him on a furlough that became nearly permanent. In 1805, he met with Secretary of War Henry Dearborn, who informed him that his mind and body were no longer capable of performing military service. Dearborn promised Pike lifetime pay and emoluments of a major, but told him not to expect any more promotions. Sometime after this, the old soldier retired to a farm near Cincinnati in Lawrenceburg, Indiana. Like many frontier officers, he had previously purchased the parcel in hopes of speculating in western lands. But like his first foray into agriculture, this one yielded chronic debt, and he would spend much of the rest of his life petitioning the government to keep Dearborn's promise. By the time he reached his seventies, he was unable to walk across his room without assistance, and he signed his pension applications in unsteady handwriting. Frontier hardship had taken its toll on Major Pike, who had earned in turn the plaudits of his superiors and a pension in old age. It was not the personal independence he had once hoped for, but it did reflect a life of nationalist virtue. It would be a model for his son.[17]

Declaring Independence: The Education of a Young Soldier

By the time he arrived at Fort Massac, Zebulon Montgomery's education had been sporadic, comprising little more than what he had learned as a child from a tutor in Bucks County and whatever piecemeal education was available at the army posts his father bounced between in the boy's teen years. By adolescence he had not distinguished himself with any particular talent, learning, or trade.[18] Young men without prospects—especially when they invoked the language of liberty as whiskey rebels, or for that matter when they mounted the barricades in France or raised arms against masters in Haiti—alarmed intellectuals of the eighteenth-century Atlantic world and inspired much pedagogical writing, from essays to advice literature to fiction, which examined the problem of making liberty and order compatible.

Pike never commented directly on this conundrum of independence or the new pedagogy that formed the backdrop of his life, but he was undoubtedly aware of one of its key texts. Among the century's most widely read novels was Samuel Richardson's 1748 *Clarissa*, and because

Pike's wife and daughter were both named for its heroine, it seems unlikely that he was not at least familiar with its outlines. Clarissa Harlowe, Richardson's protagonist, was the daughter of an overbearing patriarch who sought to marry her to a wealthy suitor. Family social rank, not Clarissa's prospects for life as an independent adult, motivated the father, and the headstrong Clarissa fled with another man, Mr. Lovelace, who eventually abandoned her.

The plot epitomized a century-long Atlantic-world conversation about proper pedagogy that had begun with the English philosopher John Locke's *Essay Concerning Human Understanding* (1690) and *Some Thoughts Concerning Education* (1693). Although better known today for his writings on political theory, Locke was also a foundational thinker on the development of the human mind and character and the pedagogy necessary to promote that. Each person, according to Locke, was born a *tabula rasa*, onto which life's experience would write the individual's character. Properly educating such children, then, did not lie primarily in the era's common practice of stifling youngsters' innate sinful tendencies and exacting obedience. Rather, Locke and others advocated readying children to function as independent adults by cultivating their reason and thus forming their minds and morals before the world corrupted them. Locke's treatises and Richardson's novel suggested that tyrannical parents who demanded complete submission and neglected to nurture the moral independence of their children would render them, like Clarissa, morally incompetent and thus vulnerable to damaging themselves and society. From Richardson and the authors of similar works of the era, Pike's generation learned to pursue their own happiness independently.[19]

They learned from other sources, however, to temper that pursuit. If many postrevolutionary Americans were excited by the national prosperity that unchained individualism promised, they were also troubled by the avarice, deceit, selfishness, and rebellion it threatened. As a result, an inchoate group of moralizing nationalist editors, preachers, politicians, playwrights, novelists, poets, educators, almanac writers, and other intellectuals sought to teach not just personal independence but also public virtue to Pike and other ill-educated Americans with meager prospects. Among the nationalists' many strategies was to exalt the sacrifice and discipline of gentleman warriors like Richard Montgomery, who had died at the Battle of Quebec. The paragon of such public virtue was George Washington. Mason Locke Weems's widely read *Life of Washington* (1800) extolled the recently deceased president as an independent and successful man and a pillar of the nation who epitomized industry, self-control, and sacrifice. Such figures, the nationalists hoped, would both bind Americans as a nation in common gratitude and provide models that Americans could be induced to imitate. Essentially, the nationalists' solution to the order-liberty conundrum was that of Genevan-born French philosopher Jean-Jacques Rousseau, who advised masters in *Emile: or, On Education* that a child "ought only to do what he wants, but he ought to want to do only what you want him to."[20]

Although Zebulon and Isabella bequeathed to their son no land, they advanced his moral education by providing him an entrée into the army. Whether or not Pike read Weems or similar works, his family's military background ensured an early exposure to the appreciation of Washington and the national service he embodied. Continental Army officers like Pike's father were among the nation's earliest and most ardent advocates of nationalist sacrifice, inspired partly by their loyalty to and admiration of Washington. As a new soldier, Pike fashioned himself into the kind of ambitious young man to whom such literature was addressed. Henry Whiting, an army officer and early Pike biographer, reported that people who knew him admired his "resolute spirit" and "ardent longings after distinction." John Williams, Pike's messmate and fellow junior officer,

FIGURE 2.3 George Washington. 1848. Portrait by Rembrandt Peale. Independence National Historical Park.

described him as "zealous, ardent and persevering." Had Pike lived longer, Williams predicted, it would have carried him "to the highest honors ... in the military profession under the Republic." Such aspirations seemed attainable to many young men of Pike's day, for no longer was it universally agreed that good birth was the only path to high social rank. Locke and others had argued that individual self-improvement was possible through cultivation of mind and habit, and Weems promised that young men who imitated Washington's discipline could win acclaim and fortune. The British poet William Shenstone, whose *Essays on Men and Manners* Pike read, advised readers "to enjoy the amusement of reading," which "paves the way to general esteem."[21]

In particular, Pike sought to train his reason. The army duties that kept him busy from dawn to dusk were never enough to exhaust his energies, and to make up for his deficiencies in formal training, he set about self-education by evening candlelight. Late into the nights he studied, reading widely, in the kind of "studious and rational retirement" Shenstone advised. Occasionally Pike paused to pontificate on what he had learned. "Let me intreat your attention," he wrote to his thirteen-year-old sister Maria in 1803, "to the cultivation of your mind—for ... a long life, is all to little; to acquire the art of living virtuous and happy." Regarding his brother George he observed, "unless he makes rapid advances in learning ... I am afraid he will not make that figure in Society nature has calculated him for." Constantly, he chided his siblings for their spelling, grammar, and handwriting, often himself butchering the very language he was admonishing them to treat with care. "Your letter is wrote well with respect to language," he informed Maria on one occasion, "but is two much crowded." In another letter, he reproached George: "you have made several mistakes in your letters to me, than which, there is nothing which so certainly shews a want of Education. You likewise use Capitals to frequently." However annoying the youngsters must have found such nagging, it was advice that Pike followed assiduously.[22]

By the time he received his first officer's commission in 1799, Pike had taught himself French and basic mathematics and had become, according to Williams, "a tolerable good english scholar." He also pursued "scientific improvement" and "wrote a good hand." Later he would undertake to learn Spanish. This and other learning, according to an 1820 biographer, befitted a "gentleman" and "elevated and adorned" Pike's character as a soldier. Eschewing his western Pennsylvania neighbors' rebellion, Pike instead endeavored to fashion himself into a gentleman officer, in the mold of his namesake Richard Montgomery or Weems's Washington. Like Rousseau's Emile, Pike had learned to seek independently what the nationalists wanted him to desire.[23]

He did not, however, get all this from the source the nationalist elite would have preferred. Not trusting weighty matters such as child raising to tyrannical parents like *Clarissa*'s Mr. Harlowe, or even well-intentioned but struggling folks like Zebulon and Isabella Pike, advocates of the new pedagogy on both sides of the Atlantic sought to compensate for parental deficiencies by publishing advice literature. To the American nationalists, however, the ever-popular English advice dispensers like Lord Chesterfield and the sentimental fiction like *Clarissa* merely deceived aspiring young Americans like Pike into looking abroad for inspiration on virtue.[24] But try as they might, the nationalists could not prevent people from reading according to their own tastes and forming their own opinions on virtue. Members of Pike's generation read the works of Weems and other nationalists, but they also devoured English advice literature and sentimental fiction.

Pike did, too. Among the most influential of his nocturnal readings was Dodsley's *Economy of Human Life*. Robert Dodsley was one of the most significant English publishers of the eighteenth century and a promoter of the careers of Alexander Pope and Samuel Johnson. In 1750 he published a curious little book called the *Economy of Human Life*, which purported to be a translation of an ancient Tibetan book of wisdom. Its almost certainly fallacious introduction narrated a fantastic tale of a Chinese emperor who sent a scholar to recover documents archived in Tibetan monasteries. One of these texts so enthralled a British traveler in China that he translated it into English and sent it to an unnamed nobleman, who passed it on to Dodsley. Under cover of oriental antiquity, the text offered more than a hundred pages of western Enlightenment advice on education, self-discipline, sacrifice, family, happiness, and other subjects. It was reprinted dozens of times in five languages over the next seventy-five years in both Europe and North America. Although usually referred to in Pike's lifetime as Dodsley's *Economy of Human Life*, the anonymous authorship is today generally attributed to the century's most famous English mannerist, Lord Chesterfield.[25]

Pike's own copy has not survived, but contemporary references to it indicate that it had considerable effect on him. He carried it with him frequently, and shortly after marrying gave a copy to his wife, who later

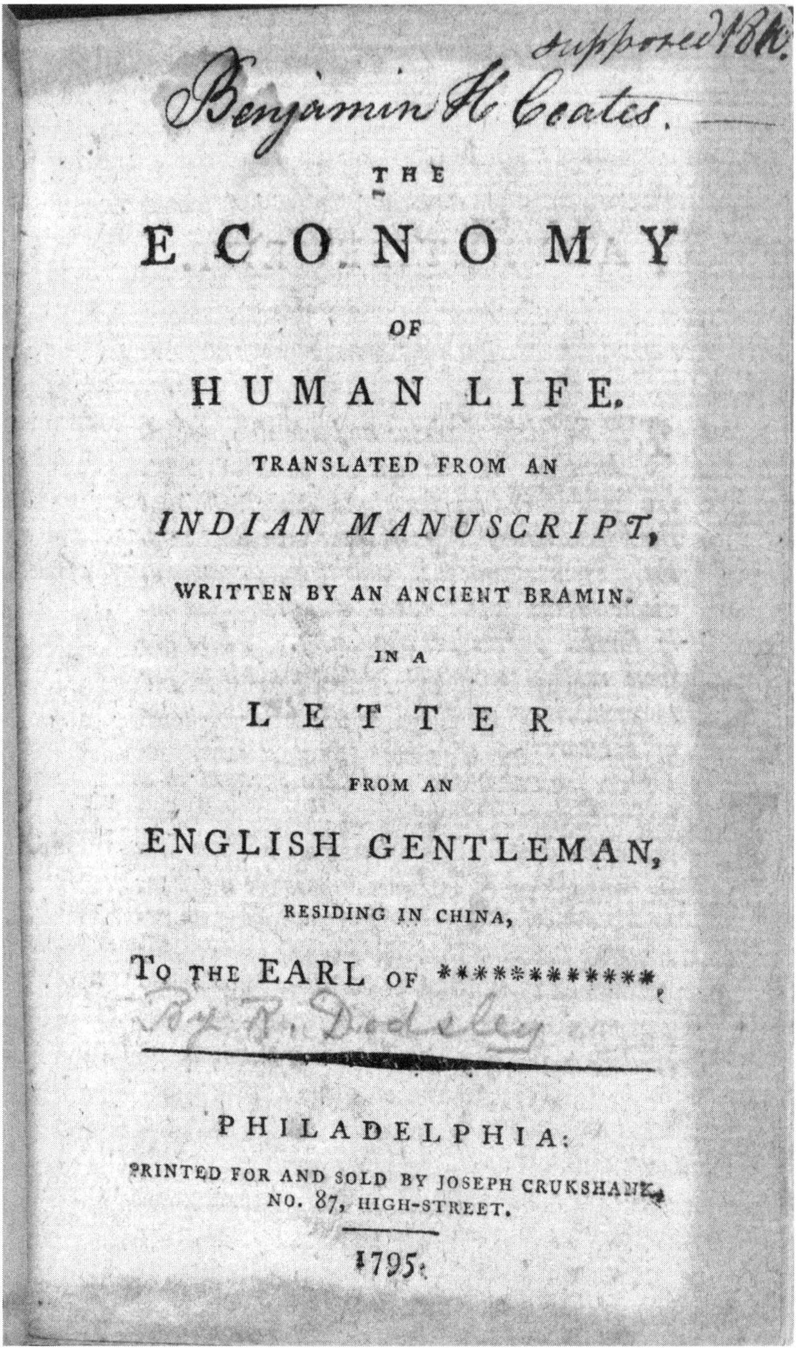

Benjamin H Coates. *supposed BK.*

THE

ECONOMY

OF

HUMAN LIFE.

TRANSLATED FROM AN

INDIAN MANUSCRIPT,

WRITTEN BY AN ANCIENT BRAMIN.

IN A

LETTER

FROM AN

ENGLISH GENTLEMAN,

RESIDING IN CHINA,

To THE EARL OF ************.

By R. Dodsley

PHILADELPHIA:

PRINTED FOR AND SOLD BY JOSEPH CRUKSHANK,
NO. 87, HIGH-STREET.

1795.

FIGURE 2.4 Cover of 1795 edition of Robert Dodsley's *Economy of Human Life.*
Courtesy, American Antiquarian Society.

called it a "cherished memorial of her husband's virtues." He scrawled notes and bits of wisdom in the margins and blank pages of his own copy, employing the volume as something of a commonplace book. Pike's letters frequently reflected the ideas, advice, and even the writing style of the book. In 1809, for example, Pike prescribed to his despairing brother George one of Dodsley's favorite remedies, fortitude, advising the younger sibling to persevere in his hardship, for "fortitude is the first gift of the soul—without which we sink into the depth of littleness & vice." And he asked that it be passed upon his death to his son, "as the gift of a father who had nothing to bequeath but his honour, and let these maxims be ever present to his mind as he rises from youth to manhood." Quite possibly, in more than one weary moment of nocturnal study, Pike pondered Dodsley's inquiry into the traits of "he that hath acquired wealth...power...and honor." Such a person, Dodsley said, "hath shut out idleness from his house; and hath said unto sloth, Thou art mine enemy. He riseth up early, and lieth down late; he exerciseth his mind with contemplation, and his body with action, and preserveth the health of both." This was an era of self-conscious imitation among young men. Like Washington copying *Rules of Civility* or Jefferson transcribing Milton and Shakespeare into his commonplace book, Pike adopted a behavioral muse to script his actions in pursuit of the improvement he coveted.[26]

Among its many insights into Pike's character, Dodsley's volume may provide some clues to his curious unflagging defense of the scoundrel James Wilkinson. As the commander of the United States Army starting in 1797, Wilkinson continued the kind of duplicity he had engaged in Kentucky in the 1780s, and by 1805, had entangled himself in the grandest of conspiracies, Aaron Burr's mysterious designs on northern New Spain and possibly Louisiana. Despite this, Pike remained a lifelong admirer and ardent defender of the general, a stance that one of Pike's biographers considered a "paradox in the otherwise unblemished life of Zebulon Montgomery Pike."[27]

Dodsley, however, helps unravel the paradox. In the decade after Pike joined the army, Wilkinson tapped him for important military posts and errands to Washington, where he began to meet powerful military and civic leaders. In 1805, the general assigned him the first of two high-profile expeditions to explore Louisiana. Over these years, Pike came to think of his mentor as something of a father figure, writing to Wilkinson on one occasion "not only as my general, but as a paternal friend." Dodsley was clear about how to think about such a man: look upon your "benefactor with love and esteem," and "the hand of a generous man is like the clouds of heaven, which drop upon the earth, fruits, herbage, and flowers." Ingratitude in the face of a mentor's largesse, according to Dodsley, would have been "like a desert of sand, which swalloweth with greediness the showers that fall." Once Pike's mind was made up about Wilkinson, Dodsley's advice might also have helped him close it: "When thou hast proved a man to be honest, lock him up in thine heart as a treasure; regard him as a jewel of inestimable price." There is, then, perhaps less mystery than might appear in Pike's scandalous loyalty to Wilkinson. Pike simply believed his benefactor to be a good man and treated him as Dodsley said a patron should be.[28]

Pike's defense of Wilkinson illustrates the paradox of didactic literature in the context of the American tension between liberty and order. In reading advice tracts to surmount his educational deficiencies, Pike demonstrated that he had bought into the nationalists' faith that human reason could be trained to be selfless and virtuous. In selecting foreign reading matter, however, and interpreting it through his own experience, he had come to the abominable conclusion that the nation's enemy was a friend. In cases like Pike's lay the limits of didactic literature as a tool to impose authoritative order on a nation of independent men and women who freely chose what to read and how to interpret it. The nationalists had only

FIGURE 2.5 General James Wilkinson. 1796–1797. Portrait by Charles Willson Peale. Independence National Historical Park.

partly replicated Rousseau's experiment with Emile. Pike would read, which the masters wanted him to do, but he would respond according to his own lights.

Sometimes he even defied authority. As a young soldier, he often visited his father's boyhood friend Captain John Brown, who now owned a sizable Kentucky plantation called Sugar Grove just downriver from Cincinnati. During his visits, Pike became smitten with Clarissa Harlowe Brown, the captain's eighteen-year-old daughter. Clara, as Pike called her, was a striking woman. Some years later, a grand-niece remembered her as "tall, dignified, and rather austere," projecting an "awe-inspiring appearance." She was also well-educated and well-mannered—as Lockean pedagogy demanded republican daughters to be, the better to prepare their own children for virtuous citizenry. She kept a diary in French, and she would later take pride in the library of great works in English, French, and Spanish she would collect over the course of her life. Not only did she embody the "virtue and modesty" that Dodsley took as the feminine ideal, but Pike believed she both shared his ambitions for distinction and was willing to make any sacrifice for their fulfillment. It seemed a perfect match.[29]

Captain Brown, however, disapproved. He was the beneficiary of an independence story far more successful than the Pike family's, having remained in Woodbridge as a prominent landowner and town official after the Revolution, before moving west in the late 1780s and accumulating an estate that eventually totaled more than twenty thousand acres and dozens of slaves. A man of such substance must have been alarmed by his daughter's interest in the middling Pike. Brown's gravestone, which can still be picked out among the thickets on the southern bank of the Ohio, calls him "A Patriot and Soldier of the Revolution...a true Republican...[who] Braved an Emigration to the Western Wilds at an early Period." Perhaps, like another republican slave-owning father of the era, Thomas Jefferson, Brown believed that upon his own daughter's shoulders rested the future education of his family. Jefferson once remarked that he educated his own daughter out of fear "that in marriage she will draw a blockhead." To Captain Brown, the twenty-two-year-old Pike, who ranked near the bottom of the army promotion ladder, must have looked like his well-educated daughter's blockhead. Like Richardson's fictional Mr. Harlowe, Brown preferred preserving family social rank to promoting his daughter's independence, and feared that Pike was playing Mr. Lovelace to the captain's real-life Clarissa.[30]

In the summer of 1801, Zebulon Pike and Clara Brown married anyway. This was a daring move. Captain Brown was a wealthy man, who could easily cut off Clara's inheritance. The ideology and rhetoric of independence, however, justified their leap. Although Locke, Richardson, and other writers had insisted on filial obedience, their critiques of tyrannical parents also handed a sword to rebellious children. Moreover, the metaphors of maturing children breaking away from overbearing parents infused not only the era's fiction but its political theory as well. Thomas Jefferson, Thomas Paine, and many others had drawn upon family and life-cycle metaphors to justify the colonies' break from their imperial parent Great Britain, and Pike saw his own rebellion against the tyrant of Sugar Grove similarly. Honoring the new bride and reflecting the sentimental fiction the couple had absorbed, they named their first-born child, conceived in filial rebellion, Clarissa Harlowe Pike.[31]

In a letter to his father shortly after the marriage, Pike marshaled the rhetoric of independence to defend his impertinence. Acknowledging the force of patriarchy near the beginning of the letter, Pike conceded that "my conduct as connected with Capt—Brown…may possibly be a little too independent." But he justified his behavior by adopting the language of Jefferson and Paine. "Nothing," he insisted "can justify an unconditional submission to the will of any man…should I be confined to the walls of a prison still shall my soul be free." In the last few lines of the letter Pike implied that Captain Brown held some financial power over the young couple and perhaps over Pike's parents, too. It is not unimaginable that the planter had offered one or more of the parties some financial carrot or stick in an attempt to stop the marriage. Whatever it was, something provoked Pike to write that he scorned the "assistance of any man who should grant it under the Idea that I thereby forfeited either my right to speak or act, agreeable to my own will & and Laws of my country." While he insisted that he would "willingly receive the advice of those either my Superior in Rank or Age or connected with me by consanguinity"—presumably such as his own father—he rejected authority "derived from pecuniary motives," that is, the sort of power that Captain Brown may have wielded. Pike believed, with the American nationalists and the advocates of the new pedagogy, that dependent men could not also be virtuous. He concluded decisively and unmistakably in the idiom of the Revolution: "Whilst I have breath I will never be the slave of any man." Like many others, Pike found in the Revolution a justification for assertiveness and even defiance in the pursuit of personal autonomy and self-interest.[32]

By the time he was an adult, Pike had absorbed both the eighteenth century's challenge to parental authority and its revolutionary political ideology. With the help of Dodsley, he bent them to fit his own circumstances and in the process seized for himself some of the independence that Captain Brown had attained but that had eluded Pike's own family and so many others. Pike's modest success in this regard, and his association with a nationalist military, deepened his commitment to the independent nation that espoused those principles. "Be always ready to die for your country," he scrawled one day on a blank page in Dodsley's *Economy of Human Life.* Thus the pedagogy of independence both enabled Pike's misconduct as a son and ensured his compliance as a citizen. Pike's compliance, however, did not take place in the comforts of the eastern states. He did not learn virtue and citizenship in parlors by fireside as Dodsely, Weems, Richardson, and others presumably expected. Rather, Pike abided by those lessons in the West, where frontier hardship would lead him to refine them further.[33]

Embodying Virtue

Even for officers like Pike, military life on the frontier was far from comfortable. He and his family and army comrades suffered bodily all the time, as pain, fatigue, hunger, boredom, illness, despair, extreme temperatures, insecurity, and other miseries afflicted them relentlessly. By the time Pike's father reached his early fifties, he was a broken man, no longer fit for command, a shadow of the gallant revolutionary officer of his youth. He "had grown grey" in his patriotic army service, the younger Pike lamented in 1802, as rumors swirled that the old soldier was now to be discharged with but three month's pay. "That's the end of...[a man] who has bled & spent his youth in the service of an ungrateful country," Pike wrote; "fine encouragement for the sons to tread in the footsteps of their fathers." That he, too, might bruise and bleed and prematurely age only to be discarded when his body reached the end of its utility haunted Pike for the rest of his life. In 1810, still in his early thirties, he despaired that army life would soon "render me unfit for any duty or profession."[34]

Acquaintances remembered Pike's body and physical behavior. He stood "about five feet eight inches," his messmate John Williams recalled, "tolerably square and robust.... His Complexion was then Ruddy, eyes blue, light hair, and good features." In deportment he was "gentlemanly," his manners "agreeable and polished," though he was generally "reserved" and "somewhat taciturn" except "when incited." Boyhood schoolmates recalled him similarly: "slender form, very fair complexion, gentle and retiring." They, too, noticed his "combative energies" when he was "put to a test." To Williams, Pike's "appearance was military yet somewhat peculiar[.] He generally leaned or inclined his head on one side so that the tip of his Chapeau touched his right shoulder when on parade." In the food and drink he put into his body, he was "uniformly abstemious and temperate." It is not surprising that acquaintances would recall details of Pike's posture, behavior, and physique, for bodily discipline was of great importance to his generation.[35]

Pike and his comrades grew into adulthood during a revolution in manners that designated the human body as an important site for the exercise and display of virtue. Americans increasingly accepted the idea that one could gain access to the higher levels of society through behavior, especially bodily self-discipline, which Locke had suggested was a stepping stone to moral behavior. Advice literature emerged to counsel aspiring youths on how to comport themselves physically. A young George Washington, for example, copied the 110 precepts of *Rules of Civility*, an advice tract first set down in 1595, from which he learned helpful tidbits such as "When in company, put not your Hands to any Part of the Body, not usually Discovered." In 1774 the likely author of Pike's cherished *Economy of Human Life*, Lord Chesterfield, posthumously published what became his most famous work, *Letters to His Son on the Art of Becoming a Man of the World and a Gentleman*, which quickly became a bestseller in the colonies. Walking quickly in the streets, Chesterfield warned, was "a mark of vulgarity, ill-befitting of the character of a gentleman." "Lolling supinely" or sitting with the "stiff immobility of a bashful booby" were even worse. But that was not all. According to the historian C. Dallett Hemphill, Chesterfield and other widely read mannerists also cautioned against excessive shivering, scratching, snapping fingers, rubbing hands, drumming tables, biting nails, tapping toes, and tossing the head—this last piece of advice apparently escaping Pike's attention. He undoubtedly did, however, absorb numerous doses of bodily advice from Dodsley, who condemned the "vain" and "arrogant" man who "clotheth himself in rich attire…walketh in the public street, casteth round his eyes, and courteth observation." Even Shenstone, whose *Essays on Men an Manners* did not discuss bodies extensively, reminded Pike to clothe himself simply, for "men of quality…do not need the assistance of dress." No bodily position or action was too minute to escape the scrutiny of those who would read into it evidence of a person's virtue.[36]

Pike, however, lived not in refined eastern enclaves, but in the West. There, bodily discipline involved considerably more suffering and endurance than simply walking at a measured pace or remembering not to scratch. He spent most of the middle and late 1790s moving men and supplies along the Ohio River and its tributaries, work Williams recalled as "arduous and unremitting." Pike and his crews picked up provisions at Pittsburgh and other towns and distributed them throughout the Ohio Valley, loading and depositing additional goods all along the way. In wet seasons, the river current tested their strength. In dry seasons, they labored against the constant danger of snags and shoals, portaging their boats and goods when the water ran too low. All cargo descending below the falls at Louisville, including the boats themselves, had to be dragged or hauled on the backs of men and animals. Hours and days were frequently passed in boredom, waiting for floods to subside or drying rain-drenched baggage in the sun. The men who guarded the goods at night from the thievery that plagued early American transportation spent many sleepless hours with their heads nodding and eyelids drooping. Chesterfield's admonition against shivering must have had little meaning to men who waded into the early spring Ohio waters with chunks of ice floating by. For Pike and the men he commanded, most of the time on the river was spent wet, cold, hot, hungry, burdened, bored, sunburned, mosquito-bitten, or tired. To be sure, farming and other endeavors by which a frontier man might earn his bread hardly offered a life of ease. Still, Pike seemed to believe the afflictions that battered the bodies of western soldiers were extraordinary, and by 1802 he was considering "quitting the service."[37]

Dodsley offers some clues about why he stayed. The quality that Dodsley most extolled was the same one that Pike recommended to his younger brother George, fortitude. Dodsley devoted an entire section of the book to it and laced many other parts with the principle as well, repeatedly advocating endurance of misfortune and physical pain. "As the camel beareth labour, and heat, and hunger, and thirst, through deserts of sand, and fainteth not, so the fortitude of man shall sustain him through all perils," Dodsley said. "Think not of thy pain," he later advised. "The body was created to be subservient to the soul." As the body was the soul's physical covering, damage to it need not be mourned any more than a tear to a garment. Even the body's death—if it be noble—was not to be avoided or feared. Pike saw in his father a model of such fortitude, admiring him as "an Old Patriot and soldier," whose pain paid the price of making a nation. His father's example, in conjunction with Dodsley's counsel, may have helped Pike accept the physical hardship of a soldier's life, considering it a great virtue.[38]

Pike may have found additional models in men like George Washington. After the Revolution, the gentleman warrior foiled would-be conspirators among his officers by reminding them of the physical toll the war had taken on him. In retiring when his military prowess was no longer needed, returning to civic life when called to serve his country as president, and setting a lasting democratic precedent when he declined to run for a third presidential term, Washington epitomized for Pike's generation the virtuous men who surrendered self-interest for the good of the nation. In twice relinquishing personal glory to facilitate peaceful exchange of power in the young republic, he both served his country well and won even greater acclaim for himself. Not every citizen, however, could match Washington's sacrifice. As Dodsley said, "all are not called to guiding the helm of state; neither are their armies to be commanded by every one." Pike had not inherited the promises of the Revolution the way Captain Brown and George Washington had; he had no property, wealth, education, office, or glory to sacrifice. He did, however, have his body. One day, in the margins of Dodsley, next to the entry on "Sincerity," Pike scribbled, "Should my country call for the sacrifice of that life which has been devoted to her service from early youth, most willingly shall she receive it." He would stay in the army.[39]

In remaining in the military, Pike found a pathway to virtue through bodily self-discipline. He denied his body sleep in order to study. He denied it alcohol as an exercise in restraint. He let the Ohio River pummel him with its current and chill him with its icy water. He even changed his mind about his father's deterioration, taking heart when the nation did not discharge the old soldier and instead kept him on the payroll at full salary. In 1808, he reassured his father of "the great obligations which your country was under to you" and declared the nation's generosity to be "a more liberal allowance than is made for Invalided officers by any other power in the world." If the public gratitude and social standing accorded his father was the reward for mental and physical discipline, the alternative to such moral self-improvement, Pike believed, was "poverty—Ignorance, insignificance—and . . . contempt." The advice-givers and nationalists had taught Pike that sacrifice was virtuous, and the hardship of western life led him to interpret sacrifice in terms of his body.[40]

Pike was hardly the only one to arrive at such a conclusion. When soldiers failed to exercise such discipline themselves, officers imposed it on them. During the War of 1812, for example, Andrew Jackson grumbled that it required only "a few privations" to reduce his soldiers from "the highest elevation of patriots—to mere w[h]ining, complaining, sed[it]ioners." To prevent them from deserting entirely at one point, Jackson felt "compelled to point my cannon against [them]," a step he found "grating" but necessary, just as "an affectionate parent" would be obligated "to chastise his children." Only through such discipline, he wrote to his wife, could his men avoid "disgrace" and "return [home] cloathed with a good reputation, praised by all." He thanked God for giving him the "fortitude to do my duty under every circumstance...like a true patriot."[41]

Once Pike became an officer in 1799, he, too, felt the duty to discipline the bodies of his troops. One cold December morning in 1800, he was in command of seventy men and a ten-craft fleet that consisted of light-duty company boats and heavy, provision-laden commissariat boats, which required constant labor to manage on the river. Shortly after the sound of the reveille, the soldiers began scrambling for the company boats to avoid the toil of poling and rowing the heavy commissariat vessels. Pike snatched a flaming log from one of the campfires and flung it at the slackers. Then he hurled another, and another, commanding John Williams to join him. According to Williams, the tirade had a "salutary and instantaneous effect" and quickly brought the soldiers "to a sense of duty and order." Like Jackson, who pointed a cannon at men who shrank from duty, Pike considered shirking physical discomfort the worst kind of dishonor. It was a violation of the virtue of self-sacrifice, a crime that warranted pelting with firewood.[42]

He continued such discipline after hours. His own candle-light studying contrasted with the carousing of the soldiers and male and female civilians who congregated about the forts. "Avoid the allurements of voluptuousness," Dodsley cautioned, "and fly from her temptations....When her wine sparkleth in the cup...then is the hour of danger." Following Dodsley's admonition, Pike cut a rare figure of moderation in the army camps, where wine—or, rather, corn whiskey—sparkled in many a cup. As Williams recollected, the "extensive use of Ardent Spirits" posed "the most vexatious evil and obstacle" to army discipline. One night, Pike and Williams prowled the bushes outside the camp, halting occasionally to listen, hoping to interdict the traffic of liquor into the barracks. Around ten o'clock, several fellows sauntered down the path carrying jugs of their favorite spirits. Jumping from the undergrowth, Pike and Williams gave them a chase and captured both men and contraband. In disciplining his own body, Pike sought to attain virtue; in disciplining other men's bodies, he demonstrated his independence and endeavored to inculcate virtue in his charges.[43]

Success in doing so earned him a promotion. In 1803, he was assigned to Fort Kaskaskia, where he served as adjutant for the Illinois country and eventually assumed command of the post. The fort stood on a high bluff across the Kaskaskia River from the town of the same name, a couple of miles upstream from its confluence with the Mississippi. The settlement dated to a 1703 French Jesuit mission and developed over the next century into a military stronghold and an important fur trade center. When the French botanist Andre Michaux visited the town in 1795, it had forty-five families, mostly French traders, whom he described as living under mean circumstances. With the arrival of Pike and other American soldiers in 1803, the town began to grow, and within a year it had nearly doubled in size and boasted a land office, a post office, and a school.[44]

The first year in Kaskaskia, however, was hard. Clara was a new mother living among men at the fort. The river and steep hill isolated her from the town, whose women Pike considered "by no means sociable" anyway. As for the men, the fur trade and military post attracted the rough assortment of soldiers, trappers, and other itinerants who populated frontier towns and whose company Pike disdained. His letters that year record that Clara was chronically "nervous," "low spirited," "miserable," and "lonesome," symptoms perhaps of postpartum depression or other afflictions. To make matters worse, Pike caught the measles, which rendered him "scarcely able to hold a pen." A few months later, Clara came down with a summer fever that incapacitated her for a month, an affliction that Pike gratefully acknowledged remarkably did not pass to the still suckling infant. By September, he hoped the turning seasons would soon "restore us to our pristine vigour," but soon young Clarissa developed what appears to have been a severe throat malady. Throughout that troubling year, Pike also wrote tender letters on a variety of family troubles—disputes between Isabella Pike and Captain Brown, the continued uncertainty of his father's career, the difficulty his parents had finding a place to live, and the trials of his nearly invalid tubercular brother James, who lacked money even to pay his postage and who was considering moving back home with his struggling parents. After a year of trials, Pike wrote with relief to his mother in November that "Our little Girl . . . is now considerably better." The man who had forced soldiers to wade into icy waters and hurled fiery timber at them when they balked bore the illness and other troubles of his family with a heavy heart.[45]

This reflected the era's masculinity norms, which extolled male capacity for perceiving and responding to the suffering of others and called for men, even military men, to show the kind of sensitivity that Pike's family letters expressed. Dodsley, for example, contended that compassion was just as much the responsibility of independent, virtuous men as discipline. "Extend thy hand," the publisher said, "to those who have none to help them." A man who enjoys both riches and reason will "protecteth the poor that are injured." Pike fretted about Clara and the baby, wrung his hands over James's intractable problems, and mourned his father's decline because those bodies merited not discipline, but compassion. On occasion, Pike even applied such advice to soldiers he commanded. "Vain" and "arrogant," Dodsley said, was the man who "treateth his inferiors with insolence." Upon that man, Dodsley assured Pike, would "his superiors in return look down." Bodily virtue for an independent man entailed more than discipline of those in his charge: "Thou who are a master, be just to thy servant.... Severity and rigour may create fear, but never command his love." Instead, "mix kindness with reproof, and reason with authority; so...his duty shall become his pleasure." Not unlike Emile.[46]

For the rest of his career, then, Pike would mix sympathy with discipline. His inconsistent but timely flourishes of compassion and his steady resolve to require of himself whatever he demanded of others would win him a reputation for human decency among his men. Even more unflagging was his own self-conception of being a leader of both compassion and fortitude.

An Intriguing Proposition

Toward the end of that hard year of 1803, Meriwether Lewis and William Clark came to Fort Kaskaskia. President Jefferson had recently purchased Louisiana from the French, and the exact extent of the acquisition was uncertain. British subjects encroached on the territory's northern reaches and Spaniards contested its southwestern boundaries. Just like Ohio in the 1790s, Louisiana needed to be secured. To that end, Lewis and Clark were recruiting men for their expedition to the Pacific and left Kaskaskia with twelve. They also acquired a pirogue, a French boatman, and an interpreter. Although, they were not looking to add officers such as Pike, Lewis did have an intriguing proposition. After departing Kaskaskia, he wrote to Pike that Jefferson planned to dispatch subsequent expeditions to

FIGURE 2.6 Meriwether Lewis recruiting soldiers at Fort Kaskaskia. *Gass' Request.*
Courtesy of Michael Haynes—mhaynesart.com.

explore the rest of Louisiana, which were going to be led by the army's "most capable officers." Did Pike, Lewis asked, want to lead one?[47]

He did. Pike itched for adventure and the chance to escape the sickly backwater that was Kaskaskia, where he and his family had suffered so much, where his wife felt isolated and lonely, and where he chafed against the pervasive drunkenness that so insulted his stern bodily discipline. In Louisiana, Pike imagined his own kind of intoxication, the chance to distinguish himself in service to the nation. Thus Lewis's offer appealed to his deepest sensibilities. Coming of age in the generation after the American Revolution, Pike was a child of the new pedagogy of independence. The long transatlantic revolution that lasted from Locke's tabula rasa to the French guillotine had unleashed a tension between liberty and order. In suggesting that personal experience formed character, in opening the upper levels of society to broader segments of the populace, and in justifying rebellion against authority, the pedagogy of independence both enhanced personal freedom and portended social chaos. These tensions played themselves out in Pike's life. To reconcile them, he drew from his lifetime of disciplined responses to the cultural environment of the English-speaking Atlantic world and the physical environment of the North American frontier. If his family background, military upbringing, and nocturnal studying of Enlightenment literature gave Pike the conceptual categories to imagine independence and virtue, the hardships of life on the frontier taught him practical lessons about bodily fortitude that convinced him of its connection to civic virtue in a republican nation. If Dodsley and other literature captured for Pike the eighteenth century's revolutionary but abstract ideas about nature, nation, and bodies, the difficult Ohio country translated them into the concrete practices of daily life and persuaded him that the best way to achieve the fruits of independence and to earn his compatriots' gratitude and a measure of distinction was to sacrifice his body for his nation.

Lewis did not have the authority to make Pike an explorer, much less a distinguished one, but James Wilkinson did. In the spring of 1805, the general ordered Pike to lead twenty men to explore the upper Mississippi River and confront Indians, Britons, and the elements. Here was Pike's chance to put his sensibilities to the test and claim his place in the nation.

3

"A Barrier to Their Trade"

ESTABLISHING AMERICANS IN THE UPPER MISSISSIPPI COUNTRY, 1805–1806

RIFLE BLASTS CRACKED the cold Minnesota air as Pike ordered his men to shoot down the British flag. Fifty feet in the air it hung from a staff at the entrance to the British North West Company's fur trading post at Leech Lake near the headwaters of the Mississippi River. After several shots, the Union Jack broke from the pin that held it and fluttered to the ground. An American flag was hoisted in its place. The commander of the fort that day in February 1806 was Hugh McGillis, a Scottish agent for the company and the superintendent of its Fond du Lac department. He must have found the ceremony an ungrateful gesture. Ten days earlier, Pike had hobbled up to the fort on ankles swollen and sore after several days of wandering in the snow. He had journeyed six hard months from St. Louis up the Mississippi in search of its headwaters, but the last days had been among the hardest. By day he and a companion had trudged through two-foot snow drifts and "dismal...swamps," picking their way along the chain of lakes that constituted the Mississippi in those parts. By night they had shivered by smoldering campfires while snow fell and their liquor froze in its keg. Many times they lost their way when snow obscured the lakes' inlets. Cold and hungry one evening, they knocked at the gates of McGillis's post at nearly ten o'clock. The hospitable Scotsman opened the doors and fed them hot coffee, biscuits, butter, and cheese. Over the next ten days, Pike partook of the trader's food and companionship. McGillis, for his trouble, was treated to the desecration of his country's standard. But to Pike this was no mere display of ingratitude. Rather, he believed he was enforcing the sovereignty of the United States, for McGillis was in violation of American law.[1]

The furs that the North West Company acquired at the Leech Lake establishment and other trading houses in the Fond du Lac department

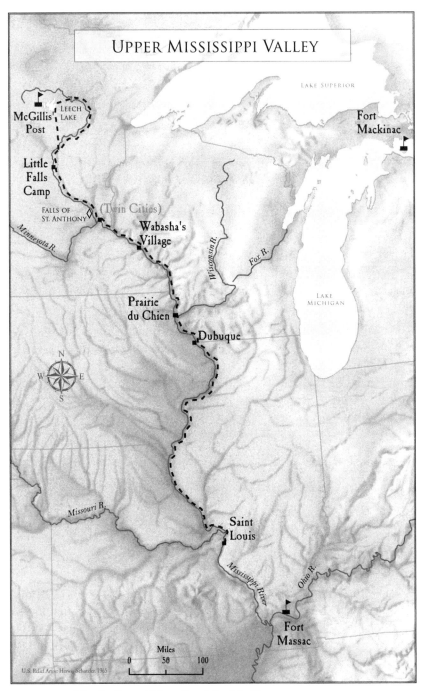

UPPER MISSISSIPPI VALLEY

LAKE SUPERIOR

McGillis'
Post

LEECH
LAKE

Fort
Mackinac

Little
Falls
Camp

FALLS OF
ST. ANTHONY

(Twin Cities)

Minnesota R.

Wabasha's
Village

Wisconsin R.

Fox R.

LAKE
MICHIGAN

Prairie
du Chien

Dubuque

N
W E
S

Missouri R.

Saint
Louis

Mississippi River

Ohio R.

Miles
0   50   100

U.S. Relief Artist: Herwig Schutzler, 1965

Fort
Massac

FIGURE 3.1 Map by Steve Chignell and Sophia Linn.

found their way in traders' canoes across northern Minnesota to Lake Superior and from there to Lake Huron's Georgian Bay and Lake Nipissing, then down the Ottawa River to Montreal. There, they were loaded onto ships bound for London and points beyond. Considerable time, distance, and hardship may have separated Pike's point of departure at St. Louis from the Mississippi headwaters, but in the logic of the fur trade they were practically neighbors. Pelts collected by St. Louis traders and sent downstream often rotted quickly in the warm, damp climate of New Orleans. As a result many merchants opted for a lengthier but cooler northern route to market. They sent their hides by boat up the Mississippi to Prairie du Chien and then on the Wisconsin River to Lake Michigan and eventually on to Montreal. Some of them might have ended up as a hat or coat on a rack in a London boutique, right next to ones that had passed through McGillis's hands. McGillis's crime was that his did not stop at the United States customs house at Fort Mackinac on their way to London; nor did the wares he imported to trade to the Indians in order to acquire the furs.

Whether through Fort Mackinac or not, many paths brought the wealth of the North American interior into Atlantic world commerce. At the base of that commerce lay an ecological relationship among individuals, the state, and nature. Commerce in the Atlantic world dealt largely in commodities: molasses, tea, coffee, cocoa, sugar, tallow, spices, cotton, indigo, tobacco, lead, coal, salt, furs, and, of course, human beings. Each of these captured energy from the sun and stored it in plant, animal, or mineral matter. The market converted this stored energy into capital—as when a fashion-conscious Londoner paid cash for a hat made from a beaver pelt. Capital could then be invested in machinery, animals, and labor, and thus

FIGURE 3.2 Fort Mackinac. Built by the British on an island in the strait between Lake Michigan and Lake Huron, the fort switched to American control after Jay's treaty. Under both empires it served as a post for controlling the flow of goods, especially furs, on the Great Lakes. Photo by author.

reconverted into energy to manufacture things or provide services. When Pike shot down the flag, he was not only asserting the state's sovereignty over the Mississippi Valley but also over the lucrative conversion of energy into capital that began there.[2]

But many other competitors vied to control those networks, men who inhabited the nation's territory but who felt little or no attachment to the United States. To end the abomination of Americans having to beg for shelter on their own soil from men enriched by profiting at their expense, the United States had to establish itself—literally, in sense of the word's Latin root, to make itself stable—in the upper Mississippi country. This required feeding and clothing its agents and keeping them safe. By gaining control over land, energy, and capital, the nation could transform its loyalists from hobbling supplicants into self-sufficient agents, who not only enjoyed biscuits and butter themselves but also controlled the distribution of such amenities in order to render rivals dependent and force them to abide by American rules. The West was a place of elaborate connections but dubious attachments. Pike went up the Mississippi to strengthen the attachments by asserting the state's control of the connections.

Bound for St. Louis

News of the Louisiana Purchase reached the Mississippi Valley in the summer of 1803 and stirred Pike to pen a short treatise on the territory in August. He had long been interested in the mysterious contents of the province, having seen bushels of salt belonging to a St. Louis man and alleged to have come from a giant saline mountain somewhere out West. In 1804 he published the piece in *Medical Repository*, a widely respected journal of medicine and natural history founded in 1797 to promote American independence of European science. The article reiterated many of the era's misconceptions about North American geography, including the mountain of salt and volcanoes he had heard lay up the Missouri River. He also averred that there was a short, easy route between the Missouri and the streams that ran to the Pacific, maybe even via a lake from which the western rivers flowed. Santa Fe could be reached in just fifteen or twenty days on foot from St. Louis.[3] One day, some of these fallacies would cost him dearly; for now, they fired his imagination.

The opportunity for independent, virtuous men to profit from this blank spot on the map tantalized Pike. It abounded in minerals: lead in the Mississippi Valley, silver near Santa Fe. And the furs! "If a company of sufficient capital was to establish itself at St Louis," Pike predicted, "it might rival the famous N. W. Company of Canada." Moreover, he foresaw few competitors. The European population was small, and the most powerful Indians were also the "furthest removed from our frontiers" and wielded only bows, arrows, spears, and clubs. In Louisiana, Pike saw an empire for the taking, a place so dimly known that it could be filled in with any fantasy or scheme. "It is highly desirable," he wrote, "that it should be explored." Within a year, Pike headed for St. Louis to do just that.[4]

With a growing population of approximately a thousand people, St. Louis was the commercial hub of the middle part of North America, The salt, lead, and furs that Pike touted poured in via waterways, as did merchandise from Philadelphia and Baltimore. Refined and educated, its business leaders were known not only in New Orleans and Montreal but also in the trading houses of London, Paris, and Geneva.[5] Commercial success seemingly set them and their town on an orderly path to full incorporation into the liberty-loving United States of America, which had bestowed on its newest territory the very political institutions that had spread the promises of the Revolution into Ohio. What Thomas Jefferson called the "empire for liberty" was rolling westward, taking its course through St. Louis.

For Jefferson the words implied no contradiction. The American empire he imagined coalesced not around a coercive metropolis but around an idea: republicanism. The Revolution, he believed, had awakened Americans' republican love of liberty and opposition to monarchy and aristocracy. In visionary statements, such as his first inaugural address, he called Americans to "unite with one heart and one mind" and become a "brethren of the same principle," a virtuous citizenry joined against the foes of republicanism. As Jefferson told James Madison, no nation was ever so well fit as the United States to advance both "empire and self government." An expanding empire would guarantee liberty's spread, while a common commitment to liberty would knit the empire together and prevent it from becoming despotic. Each bolstering the other, empire and liberty would check the centrifugal forces that vast geographies and heterogeneous cultures had always imposed on nations that dared to span great distances—the very energies that Montesquieu had warned of and that had frightened the founders into writing a constitution.[6]

Pike absorbed Jefferson's hopes for the nation, but the interior of North America teemed with people indifferent or even resistant to the empire's liberty. The Indians who paddled to St. Louis with canoes full of furs had barely heard of it. Louisiana's French and Spanish inhabitants had done quite well for years without it. Even Americans who flocked to the frontiers often came more for opportunism than as apostles of principle, and a few of them came to escape it or undermine it entirely. During its less than half-a-century of existence, St. Louis had adapted to many regimes and given its loyalty to none. Its population jumbled people of European, African, and Indian origins and from all four of the empires that contested North America. It also was home to unclassifiable people of mixed heritage and uncertain freedom statuses who defied the taxonomic order that arranged people according to their race and citizenship. Such an assortment would not easily consent with one heart and mind to the principles of a national community. A common pursuit of self-interest, however, drew many people to the city in the spring and summer of 1805, along with Pike. One came as Jefferson's emissary. Another came to plot against the president. The three would meet briefly on their way to St. Louis and their futures would entwine.

When Pike's benefactor James Wilkinson left Washington for St. Louis on April 25, 1805, he was at the apex of his power. In his late forties, he was the ranking general in the United States Army, and the Senate had recently confirmed his appointment as governor of the territory of Upper Louisiana. Jefferson had instructed Wilkinson to reduce Louisiana's trade with British Canada and to oversee the transfer of southern Indians from Orleans Territory to Upper Louisiana Territory.[7] But Wilkinson had bigger plans than that.

What they were is not clear, but they had percolated for some time. Looking for ways to profit from the American acquisition of Louisiana, Wilkinson had recently renewed his relationship with the Spaniards. In 1804, he wrote a lengthy report for the Spanish crown, drawing upon his extensive geographic knowledge of the West and his intimate understanding of its social and political affairs. In the report, he advised Spanish officials of how best to resist American expansion, including a recommendation that they capture Lewis and Clark. He also counseled them to use their possession of the Floridas to make upstream Americans dependent on Spanish goodwill for access to coastal ports on the Gulf of Mexico, to fortify Spanish holdings on Texas's border with Louisiana, and to organize Indians to resist American expansion. In return, he asked for an annual pension of $4,000 and back-pay for previous services of $20,000. Concurrently, he also wrote to Jefferson with data from the same font of geographic knowledge, warning the president about Spanish designs— some of which Wilkinson himself had instigated.[8] As the United States and Spain faced off over the uncertain borders of the Louisiana Purchase, teetering on the brink of war, Wilkinson was maneuvering to the middle. Stationing himself as the most powerful man at the border, he could make both sides dependent on his knowledge and goodwill.

From St. Louis, he also planned to tap the lucrative flow of western resources to Atlantic world economies, while using his powers as governor and general to hamstring his competitors. Perhaps he intended to set himself up as head of a St. Louis fur trade empire of the sort Pike had envisioned. A few obstacles, however, blocked that path. The St. Louis fur trade was a crowded playing field. Dealers had already exploited the Osage and Missouri Rivers to the west, and British traders like McGillis pressed down from the north. Wilkinson eyed Louisiana's untapped rivers, including the Arkansas and Platte, as alternative entry points to the fur trade for a latecomer like himself. When he arrived at Fort Massac in June 1805, he sought out Zebulon Montgomery Pike, who was there on garrison duty, and ordered him to lead an expedition to the northern reaches of the Louisiana Purchase. The young lieutenant assumed the project was the fulfillment of the invitation Lewis had made the previous year. And so it may have been, for Wilkinson was a master at crafting his own plans to coincide with national interests. Pike's journey up the Mississippi, then, was not so much a matter of exploring unknown, empty wilderness as it was a response to just how crowded the West was getting.[9]

As Wilkinson descended the Ohio River, another traveler a few weeks ahead of him was growing impatient to meet with him. Aaron Burr's term as vice president had recently ended and now he, too, headed West. His stormy tenure in the nation's second-highest office began when he and his running mate Thomas Jefferson tied in the election of 1800, forcing the contest into a bitter clash in the House of Representatives, which eventually selected Jefferson as president. Sometime after Jefferson took office, Burr, who had once been useful to the Republican ticket for his ability to attract voters from his populous home state of New York, became a potential threat to Jefferson's desire to pass the presidency on to his protégé and fellow Virginian, the secretary of state James Madison.[10] Pushed off the ticket for the 1804 election, Burr instead ran for governor of New York, a divisive election that he not only lost but that also embroiled him in a verbal

FIGURE 3.3 Aaron Burr. 1802. Portrait by John Vanderlyn. Negative #6227. Collection of The New York Historical Society.

joust with the New York Federalist Alexander Hamilton. The feud turned violent in July, and when the two dueled at Weehawken, New Jersey, Burr shot and killed Hamilton. By the following April, Burr was a fugitive, descending the Ohio River and hoping for a meeting with Wilkinson.

Burr's plan was only somewhat clearer than Wilkinson's, but it had to do with restoring his standing in the national community. Dueling was illegal, and Burr soon found himself under indictment in New York and New Jersey. A fugitive from the law in two states, deeply in debt, his law practice ruined, and hated equally by the followers of Jefferson and Hamilton, Burr had made himself an enemy of Jefferson's "brethren of one principle." "How honorable, how glorious the situation of our Nation!" mocked the *New York Evening Post*, when Burr gave his vice presidential farewell to the Senate; "Her second magistrate presiding in the first branch of the Legislature, while he stands indicted for murder."[11] His future prospects in the East were dim.

In the West, however, Burr might rekindle his career. Many westerners were only too eager to see Federalists like Hamilton poked in the eye—or worse—and among them dueling was no black mark on one's political résumé. The West, especially the part south of the Ohio River, which had not benefited from federal efforts to clear Indians, stimulate the economy, or grid the land nearly so much as the Old Northwest had, was a place filled with people with grievances against the national government. At the heart of their complaints was the Mississippi River. Through the river's mouth at New Orleans, Jefferson wrote, "the produce of three-eighths of our territory must pass to market, and from its fertility it will ere long yield more than half of our whole produce and contain more than half our inhabitants." Those inhabitants, Madison wrote in March 1803, were "bound to the union not only by the ties of kindred and affection," but also by other considerations that "flow from clear and essential interests." France, which had recently acquired Louisiana from Spain, he acknowledged, believed that holding the mouth of the river would enable it to "command the interests and attachments of the Western portion of the United States." In heading west, Aaron Burr thought he might be able to take advantage of some of this.[12]

As he traveled down the Ohio in 1805 a few weeks ahead of Wilkinson, he sought out wealthy, connected, and adventurous men disgruntled with the federal government. If Burr presented himself as a kindred spirit who resented the eastern establishment that had rejected both him and them, such men might form the political base for his return to national office. In its most benign incarnation, Burr's plan was simply to cultivate a new constituency from which to resuscitate his political career.[13]

With Burr, though, there was always more. The previous August, he had approached British diplomat Anthony Merry in Philadelphia. According to Merry, Burr told him that westerners were eager to secede from the union. They awaited only assurance of aid from a foreign power. Burr proposed that Great Britain employ him to "effect the Separation of the Western Part of the United States from that which lies between the Atlantick and the Mountains." If the British were not interested, Burr baited, perhaps the French would be. Later, he proposed something similar to a Spanish official.[14]

Many of his contemporaries and some subsequent historians believed Burr was plotting to splinter the nation. Certainly, the ambitious westerners he conversed with could well have helped him raise a private army to make good on the plans he outlined to Merry. They might have been just as helpful, though, in raising a corps for a raid on New Spain or to colonize lands in Louisiana that Burr was looking to speculate in. Any of these plans, or a combination of them, would have mitigated his exile from the national community. And all of them appear to have been on his mind. All of them would also have benefited from association with Wilkinson, with whom he finally rendezvoused at Fort Massac in June.

What they discussed is unknown. They had been corresponding in code, and if Burr was planning to revive his political career or speculate in land, Wilkinson's extensive knowledge of the West would come in handy. If he was aiming to capture New Orleans, either to sever the West from the union or to launch a filibustering campaign, he needed the support of the man who commanded the United States Army, or at least assurance that Wilkinson would look the other way. Burr was equally useful to Wilkinson. He could charge Burr for information, like he did the Spaniards. He also may have hoped Burr's plans would maintain the US-Spanish tensions that had long profited Wilkinson. Or, Burr may just have contributed another iron to Wilkinson's fire. As he described himself to Major James Bruff a few days later, the general was a man "fertile in schemes," advancing many plans at once. According to Bruff, Wilkinson also told him, "I have now a grand scheme in contemplation that will not only make my fortune, but the fortunes of all concerned." He may have seen in Burr's projects the chance to advance his own. Pike, who also came to Fort Massac at the time, later said he did not participate in the conversations between the general and the former vice president and that Wilkinson said nothing of Burr except to laud him as a man of talents and to praise his farewell address to the Senate. Perhaps not coincidentally, though, Wilkinson first informed Pike at this time that he would lead the expedition up the Mississippi.[15]

Thus, three men with entangled lives but different dreams crossed paths at Fort Massac for four days in early June 1805. One of them schemed to exploit the fuzzy imperial boundaries in order to build himself a commercial and possibly a political fiefdom. Another sought to regain his standing in a national community that had once esteemed him but had now exiled him, possibly ready to carve out a new nation for himself if he could not gain readmission to his own. The third, a young man itching for adventure, unwittingly joined them. As they parted, Burr went south to New Orleans, in a boat provided by Wilkinson and armed with introductions to the city's elite. There, he tested the waters for his plans before heading to St. Louis for another conference with Wilkinson in the late summer. Wilkinson, meanwhile, went directly to St. Louis to assume the governorship. And Pike began preparations to move his family to St. Louis and ready himself for a long journey.

As Pike was headed for St. Louis, another man desperately wanted to get out of the city. Pierre Chouteau, along with his older half-brother Auguste, was co-patriarch of the city's leading fur trade family, and he yearned to go to Washington in order to establish his membership in the national community that had just engulfed his world. By 1805, the Chouteau family and their many associates were used to having to attach themselves to new masters. Founded in 1764 to service a fur trade monopoly the French government granted to Pierre's father, St. Louis had barely gotten off the ground before its inhabitants learned that France had ceded its North American territory to Spain as a result of the Seven Years' War. The Chouteaus spent the next few decades ingratiating themselves to Spanish rulers, insinuating themselves into the bureaucratic elite's social networks, and inviting them into business ventures. By the turn of the century, their efforts had produced a formidable family business that drew furs and other western resources from the tributaries of the Mississippi and sent them through New Orleans and Montreal to European and American ports around the northern rim of the Atlantic. With the October 1802 news of Louisiana's retrocession to France, the Chouteaus prepared to learn to play their game with yet another set of officials. But the sudden purchase of the territory by the Americans set them off balance.

Pierre Chouteau was no republican. He was used to operating in governments of men, not laws, and with officials who could issue edicts to further the business ventures of their friends. Accordingly, he went to Washington in the spring of 1804, escorting a delegation of Osage Indians and hoping to curry favor with American leaders. Once in the capital, Pierre turned on his charm for the president, presenting himself as the great friend of both the Osages and the Americans, the indispensable bridge between them. To Chouteau's delight, Secretary of War, Henry Dearborn, appointed the French-speaking merchant as Indian agent for Upper Louisiana. At the same time, however, Chouteau's habit of sparing no expense in courting strategic friendships alarmed the cost-conscious Jefferson administration, and rumors arrived from the West that Auguste and other St. Louis residents were protesting the governing structure that had made Upper Louisiana a district of Indiana Territory. Pierre Chouteau "seems well disposed, but what he wants is power and money," Secretary of the Treasury Albert Gallatin wrote to Jefferson. "He may be either useful or dangerous." Chouteau had provoked Gallatin's doubts by making the kind of request that Spaniards had often granted: to control trade licensing and to direct all government commerce with the Indians, a monopoly that did not sit as well with a republican government. Returning to St. Louis with half his loaf, Chouteau still trusted face-to-face relationships among gentlemen, which had served him well under the Spanish

FIGURE 3.4 Pierre Chouteau. 1897. Portrait attributed to Clarence Hoblitzelle. Missouri History Museum, St. Louis.

regime, and the following year in 1805, he volunteered to lead a delegation of Sauk and Fox leaders to Washington, another opportunity for him to woo American officials.[16]

Although Chouteau hardly exhibited the heart and mind Jefferson expected would attach lovers of liberty to the empire, he was ready to play by republican rules if it would serve his interests. Like McGillis and the people Burr courted, Chouteau was in between. He and the rest of

St. Louis' French elite held the instrumental, shifting, western loyalties that the United States needed to acquire if it was to become a continental empire of liberty and attach St. Louis and its hinterland to the United States. For Jefferson, citizenship entailed assent to principles. To Chouteau, a nation's principles meant little more than a set of rules to facilitate the fur trade. Citizenship meant the right to do business.

But Chouteau never got to Washington in 1805. Instead, James Wilkinson arrived in St. Louis and quickly incorporated the Frenchman into his own plans. On July 10, he issued a proclamation that seized for himself as governor the very power for which Chouteau had lobbied the Jefferson administration. The order prohibited anyone from ascending either the Mississippi or Missouri Rivers or entering Indian territories for the purpose of trading, except "by permission under my hand."[17] Later that month, Wilkinson sent Chouteau west to the Osage villages, to solidify their affection for the new American regime and to gather intelligence about the tribes' relations with Spaniards. While Chouteau was gone on Wilkinson's errand, the powers in Washington instead tapped Captain Amos Stoddard to lead the second Indian delegation to the capital. If Wilkinson did not engineer this outcome himself, it likely delighted him. Chouteau was both an asset and a rival. The general needed Chouteau as a bridge to even less attached people like the Osages, but allowing Chouteau to be the primary broker between Washington and the Indians would foil Wilkinson's desire to play that role himself. While Chouteau was courting the Osages to the west and Stoddard was preparing to travel east, in between Washington and the Indians was James Wilkinson, in the middle, in St. Louis. Even without Aaron Burr stirring things up, the city was a place of dubious loyalties.

Indian attachments beyond St. Louis were even more tenuous. In 1805, Iowas, Osages, Sauks, and Foxes streamed toward the city in anticipation of the second delegation to Washington. That summer, more Indian travelers arrived, sent by Meriwether Lewis from further up the Missouri. The Jefferson administration invited them all to the capital in hopes of solidifying their attachments to the American government. Indians, however, were hardly among the brethren of one principle. They were curious and desirous of the prestige the trip might bring them as individuals within their tribes. More than anything, though, like Chouteau, they hoped the United States might serve their existing interests by providing better, cheaper trade goods and placing them in better standing vis-a-vis their rivals. They also understood that cultivating relationships with multiple empires enhanced their leverage to play each off against the other. When Washington had something useful to offer, Indians embraced it; when it did not, they resisted. Even in accepting trade, they often modified the items, turning them to uses other than those intended and imagined by whites.[18] Beyond the homelands of the Indians lay the subjects of other European empires, McGillis and his cohort of British traders eyeing the upper Mississippi and Missouri rivers as trapping grounds to extend the reach of their fur trade empires, and Spaniards in Santa Fe futilely looking for Lewis and Clark and determined to hold back American expansion.

Thus, as Pike and so many other people converged on St. Louis in 1805, citizenship in the western United States was thin and shifting. The people most likely to assent to republican principles with their hearts and minds lived in the East. South of the Ohio and the further west Pike traveled, allegiances grew weaker and more contingent and instrumental. Wilkinson and Burr and the people they courted manipulated republican principles and institutions to advance their own ambitions. Chouteau, who lacked any attachment to republicanism, was willing to play by its rules to acquire its privileges. Indians seeking to pit the United States against other tribes as well as against Spaniards and Britons strove to incorporate the Americans by taking what was useful and rejecting what was not. At the far margins of the nation-state's reach, British and Spanish rivals were connected to the nation only as competitors who sought to undermine US sovereignty. But with all these kinds of peoples converging on St. Louis in the year after the Americans took control, each thin attachment was also a potential connection.

Paths of commerce and communication radiated outward from St. Louis, forming a giant spider web ensnaring much of the interior of North America. As Jefferson wrote, the city was "the center of our Western operations, whether respecting the Spaniards, Indians or English."[19] The Ohio River, which brought Wilkinson west, connected the city to the republic, and Pike was about to follow another strand northward up the Mississippi River, which connected St. Louis to the Great Lakes, the St. Lawrence River, Hudson Bay, and the Atlantic world markets. Aaron Burr, meanwhile, was headed down the Mississippi, following that thread of the web to New Orleans, from which St. Louis spun connections not only to the Atlantic world but also to the Caribbean, Veracuz, and Mexico City. Other gossamers fanned westward up the Missouri, Platte, Osage, and Arkansas rivers. The spider at the center was James Wilkinson, tying himself to all the threads nature had woven so that he could sense and respond to movement anywhere the web reached, whether political shifts in Washington or Madrid, or environmental ones on the Great Plains. As Pike prepared to ascend the Mississippi, he was charged with securing the attachment of one of these connections.

From St. Louis to the Falls of St. Anthony

On July 30, the same day that Wilkinson wrote Chouteau's Osage journey orders, the general also penned Pike's instructions. The timing of the two letters was no accident, for Wilkinson was contemplating many expeditions. As he had written to Secretary of War Henry Dearborn a few days earlier, "Our relations to Spain & Britain on our Southern, Western & Northern *unexplored* frontiers Suggest the expediency of attaching to us, all the Nations who drink of the waters which fall into the Gulph of Mexico." Foremost in his mind were the Comanches, one of the most formidable military powers on the southern plains and uneasy allies of the Spaniards since the 1780s. Wilkinson told Dearborn that he would try to arrange a meeting with the Comanches, who lived "between the Osages and St. Afee" and who "have it in their power to facilitate or impede our march to New Mexico." He also informed Dearborn that he was sending Pike up the Mississippi and Chouteau to the Osage towns. As it turned out, the ambitious attempt to contact the Comanches would have to wait until the following spring, but before the year was out, Wilkinson dispatched the two expeditions he mentioned in this letter as well as a third under the command of his son, Lieutenant James B. Wilkinson, who followed the Missouri to the Platte. There is also some evidence that Wilkinson launched or planned to launch a trio of privately financed trips, one up the Yellowstone, one up the Platte, and one to Santa Fe, though the outcomes of these mysterious treks have been lost to history.[20]

Pike's voyage thus constituted one part of the general's multipronged efforts to gather the rivers and peoples of Louisiana into the American fold, which he was simultaneously endeavoring to make *his* fold. "You are to proceed up the Mississippi with all possible diligence," Wilkinson's instructions to Pike began, taking the course of the river, measuring distances, and noting tributaries and other landmarks. Keep a diary, Wilkinson also directed, and make note of weather and natural resources. "The government" is especially interested (and so was Wilkinson) in obtaining information about Indian populations and the quantity and species of fur-bearing animals in which they trade, prices and trading partners, too. Find suitable sites for forts and get the Indians' permission to build them. Tell them it will "increase their trade & ameliorate their condition." Go as far up as you can—to the headwaters if possible—but come back before the water freezes. Take the latitude of all significant points (Wilkinson had no instruments to lend him to help with longitude, and may have decided anyway that the river itself would furnish sufficient longitudinal information for any site as long as it could just be ascertained how far upstream the point was). Wilkinson also ordered Pike to "procure Specimins of whatever you may find curious in the mineral, vegetable Kingdoms." Echoing his statement to Dearborn, he told Pike to "spare no pains to conciliate the Indians and to attach them to the United States." Give them flags and other trifles and invite them to St. Louis. Notably absent from this litany of tasks is any instruction to harass McGillis or any other traders. But Pike, who appears to have carried a copy of Wilkinson's licensing proclamation of July 10, would spend a considerable amount of time doing just that. He would also fail to get back before the rivers froze. For these and other transgressions, Wilkinson would later write to Dearborn that Pike had "stretched his orders." More than mere disobedience, however, the young soldier's delay in returning and his treatment of McGillis reflected his zeal to make a mark for himself by carrying out what he took to be his government's very clearly conveyed, if unstated, instructions to do everything in his power to learn as much as possible about the upper Mississippi and to attach its lands and people to the nation. After all, Wilkinson also told him the official instructions should "yeild to your discretion in all cases of exigency."[21]

Much of the exigency that Pike would face on the journey resulted from Wilkinson's own delay departing Washington and getting down the Ohio River that spring. Pike did not set out from St. Louis until August 9. He was getting a very late start.

Launching the empire for liberty turned out to be a tedious task. Pike and his crew departed up the Mississippi about four o'clock in the afternoon in a seventy-foot keelboat. His party consisted of one sergeant, two corporals, and seventeen privates. They carried provisions for four months. As they advanced, Pike generally walked on shore, surveying the land and making notes, while the men labored to move the boat against the current. Private John Sparks and other hunters supplied the crew with game, and the men caught fish in the river. They made good progress the second day out but had to halt when a severe storm blew up late in the afternoon, and they spent their third morning drying their baggage. The squall notwithstanding, the late-summer water ran low in the river, and they were "much detained" by having to wade into shallow spots and haul the vessel upstream. On August 13 they ran aground on sandbars. The fourteenth and fifteenth brought more rains. On the sixteenth one boat caught "fast on a log" and they could not extricate themselves until eleven a.m. Frequently, the islands, bars, and other obstructions confounded their attempt to follow the main channel of the river. They enjoyed smooth sailing on the nineteenth before ramming a snag while maneuvering around a sandbar at nine in the morning. By the time they plugged the leak and bailed enough water to haul the boat to shore for repairs, the supplies and clothing were soaked, and the party spent the afternoon airing out again. To make up the lost time, they continued well into the evening, only to mire in sand unseen in the darkness. By the end of the first week of snags and shoals and too much water in the boat but not enough in the river, the men were "quite galled and sore."[22]

But they were not alone. Far from being unpeopled, the Mississippi was a freeway of travelers, many of them St. Louis-bound, and late summer 1805 was rush hour. Pike found signs of Indian camps and met a Frenchman and his Indian wife scrabbling by on an unimpressive homestead. The party passed Indian canoes frequently and three other vessels, which Pike did not identify. Twice Pike and his men camped with parties of Michilimackinac traders, each with several boats apiece, headed downstream to St. Louis. On August 21, Pike got to try out his Indian speech. He informed a band of Sauks that "their Father at St. Louis" had sent Pike and other "young Warriors" in all directions to meet Indians and discover how best to help them. Pike also reminded them that they had agreed by treaty "to apprehend all Traders who came amongst them without license" and that Pike would inspect for licenses on his way back to St. Louis. He also asked them about establishing an American trading house among them, but the cagey Sauks informed him they would have to check with the rest of their nation first, and they invited him to wait a day while they sent an emissary to another village. Pike's words missed the boat, so to speak. As he learned a few days later from a St. Louis-bound trader, he had been talking to the wrong people. His audience was a marginalized village within the Sauk and Fox nations, out of favor among the people at the time because of their leader's role in an unpopular 1804 treaty. In Pike's haste to get upstream, however, such subtleties escaped him. He declined their suggestion of sending an emissary a few miles to the main village. Instead, he dashed off letters to Wilkinson and Clara and resumed his course. He was in a hurry at his next stop, too, where he left two men and a pair of dogs who did not return to the boats on time. Pike grew anxious for them over the next few days, but continued on, considering their absence "not extraordinary; as they well know that my Boat never halts for any persons on shore they will endeavour to strike the Mississippi ahead of us."[23]

The men were still missing when Pike dined on September 1 at the establishment of the Frenchman Julien Dubuque, near the present site of the city bearing that name. With the consent of the Spanish government, Dubuque had operated a lead mine on lands ceded to him by Indians. Learning with dismay from Dubuque that the mines were six miles distant and that no horses were available, Pike determined he would be unable to inspect the operation as Wilkinson had requested. Dubuque, however, appears to have been misleading the American, for the mines were in fact much closer than Pike reported. "What is the date of your grant of the mines from the savages?" Pike asked him. "The copy of the grant is in Mr. Soulard's office at St. Louis," Dubuque replied. "What is the date of the confirmation by the Spaniards?" Same answer. And the extent of the grant? Same answer. Pike did manage to learn that the mines produced between 20,000 and 40,000 pounds of lead annually, but on the whole, he found Dubuque's responses to "carry with them the semblance of equivocation."[24]

And why shouldn't they have? The United States had not yet confirmed title to his grant but already the devious Wilkinson had sent a young subordinate to ask pesky questions about the legitimacy and value of Dubuque's establishment. The tight-lipped Frenchman's situation resembled Chouteau's. Both had done well under the Spanish administration of Louisiana and were still maneuvering to continue that success under republican rules. Like Chouteau, Dubuque positioned himself as a middleman, upon whom both local Indians and the United States would depend. When Pike arrived, Dubuque was outfitting a band of chiefs to visit St. Louis, calculating that facilitating their travel to American cities would enhance his own standing among the tribes.[25] Also like Chouteau, Dubuque gave no assent to the republican principles Pike esteemed. Years of shifting imperial rule had taught both Frenchmen and Indians to maintain flexible loyalties and to adapt in practice rather than heart and mind. Dubuque's attachments, then, ran only as deeply as the Americans' willingness to let him keep taking lead out of the ground and sending it down to St. Louis in exchange for goods and cash. If the United States could facilitate *that*, then he would cooperate.

Pike's four hours with Dubuque, however, did yield reunion with his lost men. They had wandered along the well-timbered banks of the river for six days with almost no food until they met some traders and Indians, who gave them corn and shoes, restored their "strength, and Spirits," and brought them to Dubuque.[26] Separated from their comrades, they could barely find their way or feed themselves in this country without help from the locals. Their plight showed that Americans had yet to establish themselves on the Mississippi. Meanwhile, Pike's first two attempts to attach Louisiana's inhabitants to the national community ended inconclusively. Both the Sauks and Dubuque were hospitable but noncommittal. Making little headway on that front, Pike turned his attention to seeking fort sites.

With a chain of forts, the United States could do all the things that Pike had thus far failed to accomplish. It could station permanent agents to inspect Dubuque's mines, take note of the subtleties of Sauk and Fox politics to ensure the United States was not parleying with the wrong villagers, and remain around if necessary to talk to the right ones. Forts could import and store the food and other necessities to support Americans in an unfamiliar environment, and provide the kind of security that had eluded Pike's lost men. Perhaps most importantly, forts could direct through a handful of controllable places the massive and chaotic flow of traders' barges and Indian canoes that Pike had seen traversing the Mississippi watershed. At these places the United States civil and military authorities and their agents could more easily ensure that licenses were being obtained, that Indians were not being plied with alcohol, and that foreign traders were not attempting to lure the lucrative commerce into orbits of rival empires. All this would establish—make stable—the American hold on Louisiana.

On September 4, Pike arrived at one such potential site, Prairie du Chien. Founded under English rule in 1783 but taking its name from an older French settlement nearby, Prairie du Chien lay just above the mouth of the Wisconsin River, which flowed from the northeast, broadening to nearly half a mile wide as it met the Mississippi. The bluffs on the west side of the Mississippi angled steeply into the river, but on the east bank, a crescent-shaped plain, a mile wide and eight miles long, skirted the front of a range of "high bald hills," separating them from the two rivers. On this low-lying, fever-infested spit of land stood twenty-six frame houses that made up the town. Another eleven homes dotted the vicinity, including some across the Mississippi, for a total of thirty-seven dwellings, which

Pike estimated to be home to some 370 permanent white residents. Inside, the homes had whitewashed walls, and some boasted furniture of "elegance and taste." The permanent population and the civilized decor made Prairie du Chien the largest and most substantial white settlement on the upper Mississippi, and it marked the confluence of more than just a pair of rivers. A hundred and twenty miles up the wide, sandy-bottomed Wisconsin, boatmen portaged easily into the Fox River watershed, which drained into Lake Michigan and ultimately the Atlantic Ocean. Although Prairie du Chien obtained its corn from a nearby Fox village, its manufactured goods came from Europe and the United States, via Fort Mackinac. The shacks on the swampy spit where the Wisconsin joined the Mississippi marked the gateway between two great watersheds of commerce by which animal furs drained from North America's interior into Atlantic world markets. It was just the sort of place from which a nation might command a vast hinterland.[27]

Establishing Americans there, however, first required unscrambling the human attachments, which were even more mixed up than in St. Louis. The population nearly doubled every fall, when traders stopped at this staging ground before making their way into the wilderness to winter. The population swelled again in the spring, as the traders, along with a few hundred Indians, met again to swap pelts, goods, and stories. During his stay, Pike heard a babel of languages, which taxed even basic communication. At one point, Pike found himself speaking French to a trader, who translated to a Sioux, who in turn translated to some Winnebagos. In the vicinity of Prairie du Chien, he met people of Sioux, Winnebago, Sauk, Fox, Menominee, British, French, and American origin and every conceivable mixture thereof, the traders having made "transient connexion with the Indian women." Among this eclectic collection of permanent and temporary villagers there were as many national and tribal allegiances as there were racial combinations.[28]

One man exemplifying the fluid attachments within the village was James Fraser, who Pike said welcomed him warmly and "procured me every thing in his power that I stood in need of." Pike, who often mistook hospitality for attachment to the United States, described Fraser as an American showing "Spontaneous effusions of good will" toward his "countremen." Fraser was more complicated, however. Born in Vermont in 1775, he later moved to Canada. At Montreal, he clerked for Josiah Bleakley, who sold furs and acquired goods on behalf of the Chouteaus. His better-known brother, Simon Fraser, explored far western Canada for the British North West Company and superintended its fur trade operations there. James Fraser would later support the British in the War of 1812. To Pike, Fraser contrasted with Prairie du Chien's French Canadians, whom he disparaged as ignorant hypocrites whose "natural good manners" were motivated more by "fear" than by genuine "good will." Transient and mongrel, the place was as unruly as it was strategic, and Pike marveled that the "heterogeneous mass" of people and liberal use of "spirituous liquors" did not spark more "murders and affrays."[29]

Pike and his men spent four days at Prairie du Chien resting, reprovisioning, and trying to strengthen that American presence. On the first day, some of the leading traders at the settlement accompanied him to examine promising fort sites. Pike's first choice lay atop one of the high bluffs across the Mississippi. The hill he selected had a flat summit, access to plenty of timber, and a spring nearby. It held a commanding view of the rivers' confluence. The next day, he also selected another location, three miles up the Wisconsin, but considered this one more vulnerable—timber would have to come from across the river, and the site had poorer access to drinking water. It also had blind spots, which made it susceptible to attack along a small channel in front and a hill three-quarters of a mile behind. Pike blazed trees to mark both places, but he clearly preferred the former. By securing access to water, fuel, building materials, and views on the west-bank site, the United States could command the entire confluence, and thereby hold a vast hinterland against "any European power who might be induced to attack."[30] Although the government never built a fort there, the unassuming Iowa prominence he recommended bears his name today, making it the original Pikes Peak.

While his men bested the locals in jumping and hopping contests, Pike prepared to leave. Fraser, who was taking several canoes to winter among Indians upstream, accompanied him for a few weeks. Pike also swapped his keelboat for a pair of round bottomed "Schenectady barges," twenty or thirty feet shorter than his unwieldy vessel, which locals told him would have difficulty ascending St. Anthony Falls, the most formidable geologic barrier on the upper Mississippi. In the evenings, he composed a letter to Wilkinson reporting his judgment of the locale, but at the end of the letter, he turned to some subject that he later chose to delete when he published his correspondence. The excised portion no longer exists, but references to it in the closing paragraph indicate that he contemplated the possibility of war with Spain. "The field of action," he wrote, "is the sphere for young men, where they hope and at least aspire, to

FIGURE 3.5 Confluence of the Wisconsin and Mississippi Rivers, looking east from Pikes Peak across the Mississippi at the Wisconsin River. Photo by author.

gather laurels of renown, to smooth the decline of age; or a glorious death." Whatever caused him to pause at the confluence of the Mississippi and Wisconsin rivers and ponder war in the Southwest and the opportunity for bodily sacrifice and national gratitude it might offer for men like himself remains a mystery. Wilkinson, however, surely read the lines with great interest, for Aaron Burr was due in St. Louis any day.[31]

As Pike left Prairie du Chien, two powerful men far away were thinking about rivers. Upon their concerns hung the fates of nations. One was Nemesio Salcedo, the *comandante general* of Spain's *provincias internas*. Established in 1776 as part of the Bourbon king Carlos III's reforms to streamline administration of Spanish America, the Internal Provinces were a huge bureaucratic jurisdiction, independent of the viceroy, who governed the rest of the colonies, and stretching from the deserts of Chihuahua north to the Columbia River watershed and from the Great Plains to the Pacific Coast. They included a large portion of land that the United States claimed it had acquired in the Louisiana Purchase. On September 9, 1805, from the city of Chihuahua, Salcedo wrote to Joaquin del Real Alencaster, the governor of New Mexico, alarmed at "the frequency with which the Subjects of the United States of America Navigate the

Misuri River." Lewis and Clark had made it up the Missouri, and where they had gone, other Americans would surely follow. The Missouri, Salcedo reminded Alencaster, was "the Key point to the Internal Country of New Spain," and guarding New Spain required guarding that river. He ordered the governor to send a party to the Pawnees, who lived near the Platte River, lavishing them with Spanish gifts and asking them to capture Americans and bring them to Santa Fe. Like Pike and his superiors, the Spanish government courted the attachment of Indians.[32]

Salcedo had good cause to worry, for unbeknownst to him, 1,200 miles away in St. Louis, Wilkinson was thinking about rivers, too. He had written Dearborn the day before with new intelligence about the Arkansas River and the best route to New Mexico. "Should We be involved in a War," he advised, "it...becomes extremely desireable it should be reconnoitred, and this cannot be done, with any prospect of safety, or Success, before we have brought the...Commanchees to a conference, because they reign the uncontrouled Masters of that Country. This I understand may be best accomplished through the Panis."[33]

A few days later Aaron Burr paid him a visit. Back from New Orleans, he arrived in St. Louis on September 11 and stayed for more than a week. One day, he and Wilkinson rode out to inspect the army post at St. Charles, and they conferred several other times as well. Two accounts of the visit survive, and, as is generally the case with stories about Wilkinson and Burr, they conflict. According to Burr's later statement, they "settled the plan for attacking Mexico," a story that Burr biographer Milton Lomask says gains credence from reports from leading Americans in St. Louis that Burr and Wilkinson had approached them with such a plan in mind. This was the filibuster plan—Burr would raise an army of disgruntled westerners financed, possibly, by Britain and lead this private army to invade Spain's northern territory. It also may have been the "grand scheme" Wilkinson had mentioned to Major Bruff. Either way, it was illegal under American neutrality laws, and to accomplish it, Burr needed to control New Orleans, or at least know that US officials there would not interfere—something that only James Wilkinson could guarantee.[34]

Wilkinson, however, recalled the encounter differently. As he testified when later accused of conspiring with Burr, he first grew suspicious of Burr during that visit. Burr, the general alleged, made wild statements about the "imbecility of Government" and the readiness of the "people of the Western Country" to "revolt." Wilkinson claimed he wrote to the secretary of the navy to warn that "Burr is about something, but whether internal or external, I cannot discover." The letter, however, has never been found.[35]

Meanwhile, to the north, Pike waited impatiently in a downpour to confer with Wabasha, a prominent Sioux chief he had met at Pairie du Chien. Wabasha, at the moment, was embarrassed. He had expected Pike three days earlier and planned a feast. When Pike did not arrive, the villagers started the party without him. Now they were hung over. Wabasha sent word by messenger that he would prefer to host Pike the following day. After waiting for the weather to clear and the Indians to sober up, Pike went to Wabasha's village to do the sort of plying of Indians that Salcedo and Wilkinson were contemplating far to the south. With pistol in his belt and sword in hand, Pike met Wabasha on the bank of the Mississippi and accepted an invitation to the chief's lodge. At the lodge, he sat upon a pillow, with Wabasha on his right and Fraser and an interpreter on his left, a pipe leaning on a pair of crutches before him. Wabasha expressed his desire for friendship with the United States and reminded Pike that he "had never been at War with their new father, and hoped always to preserve the same good understanding that now existed." He gave Pike the pipe to take to other bands of Sioux upstream as a "token of our good understanding; and that they might see his [Wabasha's] Mark, and imitate his conduct." Pike accepted the pipe as the "Gift of a Great Man, and a Brother" and replied that Wabasha and other natives now fell under the "protection" of the United States. The government, he said, would establish posts to supply Indians with their "necessaries" and send agents to attend to their business. The United States also sought peace between the Chippewas and Sioux. Finally, they ate—"wild rye and venison." Before parting, he gave presents to Wabasha: "two Carrots of Tobacco, four Knives—a half pound of Vermillion and one Quart of Salt," and an eight-gallon keg of rum.[36] Instead of warning about trade regulations, as he had the Sauks—who lived closer to St. Louis and fell more firmly under American control—Pike invited Wabasha's band into family-like relations of dependence that promised them material benefit. With this two-and-a-half hour ceremony in which Pike ate Wabasha's food and accepted the pipe and then offered gifts from his own realm, a Sioux chief and an American lieutenant symbolically agreed to exchange the wealth of nature and nations and pledged friendship to interlock their worlds even more tightly in the future. Pike then departed. An even grander exchange lay ahead.

A few days later, while hunting in the hills above what is now Winona, Minnesota, Pike gazed over the Mississippi. As far as he could see, the river wound in channels between bluffs that rose right out of the river, forming countless "beautiful Islands." His boats cruised below him, "under full Sail, with their flags displayed before the Wind," carrying his nation's interests onward against the Mississippi's current. Such "sublime and beautiful prospects," he wrote, "a man may scarcely expect to enjoy" more than "twice or thrice in his life." His spirits soaring, Pike did not want to come down from the mountaintop. He tried to persuade his companions Fraser, Sparks, and Corporal Samuel Bradley to camp on the bluffs and enjoy the moment, but Fraser, his mind on his boatload of goods, insisted on rejoining the vessels as soon as possible.[37]

On September 21, the party camped on what has come to be known as Pike's Island, in the middle of what is now Minnesota's Twin Cities, and prepared to make a large real estate purchase. Out of the sails from the boats, his men fashioned a billowy chamber into which filed six of the leading men of the Mdewakantons band of the Santee Sioux, whose French names Pike butchered: Le Fils de Penichon, the leader of the nearby Mdewakantons village and the grandson of a French trader, Le Petit Corbeau, at whose village Pike had breakfasted two days before, Le Grand Partisan, Le Orignal levé, Le Demi Douzen, Le Beccasse, and Le Boeuf qui Marche. Pike also found several traders in the area and roped them into leaving their boats for the afternoon to witness the deal: Duncan Graham, a Scottish trader who would later serve in the British Army during the War of 1812, Murdoch Cameron, whom Pike called "a Scotchman by Birth and Englishman by prejudice," and Cameron's unidentified employee. The Vermonter-turned-Canadian Fraser also joined the talks. Pike began by announcing the American acquisition of Louisiana and his intent to purchase part of it a second time, this time from the Mdewakantons. Specifically, he wanted parcels around the confluence of the Mississippi and St. Peter (today the Minnesota) rivers on which to build a fort and establish Americans.[38]

At the time Pike arrived, Santee prosperity had reached both a peak and a crossroads. Four bands comprised the Santee, and of these only the easternmost, the Mdewakantons, met with Pike. Although the bands intermarried and cooperated, they were growing apart. During the late eighteenth century, the other three bands had begun moving out of the deciduous forests of the Mississippi Valley onto the prairies to the West, following the bison herds and transitioning from woodland lifeways to a horse-borne economy of spring and fall horticulture and summer and winter hunting. The Mdewakantons, who numbered about two thousand, however, remained a woodland people. According to Pike and other early visitors, they grew a little corn and some beans, and a staple of wild rice. They extended this subsistence niche by exploiting their position as the easternmost Sioux band to become the best supplied with European manufactured goods. Piled in the canoes of traders like Fraser, Graham, and Cameron were guns, powder, lead, traps, and axes, with which the Santee enhanced their abilities to take furs from beaver, otter, fox, mink, bear, raccoon, fishers, muskrats, deer, and occasionally bison, and barter them to Europeans and Americans. The traders' boats also bore kettles, cloth, blankets, and even foodstuffs. Competition among Euro-American traders enabled the Mdewakantons to drive the terms of the bargains and to incorporate what they found useful and reject the rest. In the spring, the canoes went home with furs stripped from animal carcasses, and the Mdewakantons went west with the kettles and other items to the James River and other rendezvous sites, where they exchanged the manufactured goods with the western Sioux bands for horses, meat, clothing, teepee covers, and other products of the western prairies and plains. As middlemen between the horse-borne western Sioux and the water-borne traders, the Mdewakantons bridged the new plains culture and older woodlands worlds of the Sioux nation.[39]

In some respects, Pike's arrival enhanced their position. On the land he was proposing to purchase, Pike announced, the father would establish trading posts, which were "intended as a benefit to you." The traders who currently visit you, he said, "are single men who come far in small boats." Perhaps Fraser or Graham or Cameron flinched; Pike was talking about them. The Americans, Pike promised, would do better. They were "many and strong." They would come "with a strong arm, in large boats." From them, you will be able to "procure all their things at a cheaper and better rate." In addition, the Americans would station agents, who would serve the Mdewakantons and make sure the traders who came among them were "good men." So far so good, Le Petit Corbeau and the others must have thought. More traders meant more bargaining power for the Mdewakantons.[40]

"Another object your father has at heart," Pike continued, "is to…make peace between you and the Chipeway's." Because the woodland lifeways and seasonal rhythms of the Chippewas, who also inhabited the upper Mississippi, resembled those of the Mdewakantons, they competed for the same natural resources and access to the same traders. The two peoples had been in episodic conflict since the late seventeenth century. Four decades earlier, the fur trader Jonathan Carver, who wintered among the Santees in 1766 and 1767 and whose narrative Pike had read, had been among the first to describe this conflict. When his Mdewakanton friends asked him to lead them into battle against the Chippewas, Carver did some quick calculations. If he refused, he would anger people upon whom he depended for food, shelter, and safety. But in his future travels, he might need the Chippewas. He could not afford to cross them, either. Plus, he was not very keen to pick a dangerous fight with which he had no truck. Instead, he negotiated a truce. Word of his skillful diplomacy spread among both groups, and they asked him to be their king, an invitation that smacks more of European vanity than the reality of Indian politics. Still, making peace saved his hide (and hides) and enabled him to continue to survive and profit from the forests. He understood that conflict among Indians was hazardous to his person and bad for business. The British Empire recognized this on a larger scale in 1786, when officials invited the Santees and Chippewas to a peace conference at Fort Mackinac. What was true for individuals like Carver was also true for nation-states and fur companies. The more Indians fought, the fewer furs came off of mammals and onto canoes bound for market.[41]

Pike, then, was only the latest visitor to seek peace among the locals. At the council under the sails, he promised that on his way home he would escort Chippewas and Mdewakantons together to St. Louis to forge a lasting friendship "under the auspices of your mutual father." Acknowledging that in order to meet him the Mdewakantons had interrupted a retaliatory war party against the Chippewas, Pike said, "I know it is hard for a warrior to be struck and not strike again." If the chiefs were wondering how the Chippewas might interpret such an apparent show of weakness, Pike had an answer. "I will send (by the first Chipeway I meet) word to their chiefs:—That, if they have not yet felt your tomahawk, it is not because you have no legs or the hearts of men, but because you have listened to the voice of your father." Woe to the Chippewas "if the chiefs do not listen to the voice of their father, and continue to commit murders on you," for "they will call down the vengeance of the Americans."[42] Pike sought to replicate in the upper Mississippi country the material prosperity that came with the federal pacification of local violence in his boyhood Ohio. And, like Carver, he assumed the Mdewakantons wanted a ruler anyway.

However sensible it may have seemed to Pike, this was a bigger demand than the parcels of land he had inquired about. In asking them to accept an American father, Pike requested that the Mdewakantons cede to a faraway power control over the competitive local relationship that secured them the basic necessities of life. In contrast to the fort, dependence would not enhance their middleman's niche. Unsurprisingly, they rejected this demand.

But they did sell the land. Under the treaty, the Mdewakantons could "pass, repass, Hunt, or make other Uses of the said Districts as they have formerly done," but they ceded "full Sovereignty and power" over it to the United States. On the surface, middleman ecology remained mostly intact. Then Pike trotted out the paperwork. "We are a people," he explained, "who are accustomed to have all our acts wrote down, in order to have them handed to our children." He asked the chiefs to "sign in the presence of the traders now present." But Le Petit Corbeau and company balked. They told Pike that they "conceived the word of honor should be taken for the Grant, without any Mark." Although Pike managed to convince them to sign, their hesitance rightly puzzled him. In fact, it indicated big differences in their perception of the agreement. The Indians understood peace in terms of relationships—for example, the honor that came from keeping word mutually agreed upon. For Pike, however, peace meant gridding the lands into sections and owners. Antagonisms among competitors must be institutionalized by a central power in signed treaties and contracts that drew lines on the land and governed who could use which piece of land for what purposes and under what conditions. Whereas European empires had tolerated fuzzy social and geographic boundaries on their peripheries, in republics and empires of liberty, which required their citizens to unite behind the state with one heart and mind, each parcel of land must be designated according to its acceptable uses—pass, repass, or hunt—and there must be one ultimate sovereign. Trade must be conducted only with licensed partners. And only certain goods might be exchanged. Mdewakanton lands must be separated from Chippewa. For Pike and his superiors the treaty was not about relationships established by smoking pipes or keeping promises, so much as it was about categories—categories of land or nations or trade partners. The nation-state would administer these categories—policing their boundaries and guaranteeing those inside the categories a share of the benefits of this ordered world in exchange for compliance with the rules that distinguished Sioux hunters from Chippewa ones, American traders from British ones, licensed merchants from unlicensed ones, traffic in legal goods from traffic in contraband.[43]

Thus, in a tent of sails on the beach of an island in the Mississippi, an American soldier concluded a large real estate transaction with seven Mdewakantons with French names, as four pro-British traders looked on to legitimate the whole thing. That night, Pike wrote to Wilkinson, "We have obtained about 100,000 Acres for a song." He overestimated his triumph, however. The Indians' desire to enhance their middlemen position and the Americans' desire to establish posts by which to control the transformation of nature's bounty into the market's capital provided just enough common ground to exchange a little property. It was not enough to smooth relations between the Mdewakanton and their Chippewa neighbors. In fact, gridding the land intensified conflict in the long run. By eliminating the flexible fuzzy-edged territories and buffer zones that Indians and empires had constructed to accommodate their rivalries, American attempts to broker peace provided new grounds for hostilities over the sharply distinguished borders. The Indians also misjudged the agreement, underestimating the degree to which they would be sucked into Pike's world. It would take until 1819, but the United States would eventually build Fort Snelling on the site Pike bought. With the establishment of the fort and the elimination of competition from British and other traders, the United States could make all the rules. This meant fewer options for the Mdewakantons and ecological dependence on the United States. In 1827, a chief lamented that without the traders, the people would starve. In contrast, he said, the western Sioux could still jump on their horses and feed themselves without help from the Americans. "We my Father cannot do this." But the day when Americans had established themselves enough to command the environment and when Indians would depend on them still lay in the future. More immediately, it was Pike who would struggle.[44]

From the Falls of the St. Anthony to a British Trading Post

To this point, Pike had traveled through well-known territory, with plenty of help. Dubuque had fed him. Traders and Indians had rescued his lost men. A merchant at Prairie du Chien traded him two boats he needed to navigate the river. Fraser guided him through the complicated physical and social landscapes upstream. Wabasha gave him the pipe. Cameron and the other traders broke out their liquor to lubricate the deal with the

Mdewakantons. After the council, Graham swapped him another still nimbler craft with which to ascend the Falls of St. Anthony, and then Pike and the traders parted ways. Before departing, Pike closed and sealed a pair of letters, one to Wilkinson detailing the terms of the real estate purchase, and the other to Clara, and gave them to Fraser. Those would be the last letters he would send downstream until April, and with them, he bid "a last adieu to the civilized World."[45]

As the weather chilled and the level of the water in the river dropped, the cost of his late start became daily more apparent. "This Voyage could have been performed with great convenience," he wrote in his journal, "if we had taken our departure in June." By October 16, Pike and his men had reached the pine forests of central Minnesota, near the point where the Mississippi bends northeast at the beginning of a big arc that forms a backward letter C and returns the river northwest to its headwaters. The night before, they had camped at the foot of Little Falls, and two inches of fresh snow fell overnight. Additional morning flurries offered "poor encouragement for attacking the rapids, in which we were sure we must wade to our necks." Determined to ascend the river to the "highest point ever made by the Trader's in Bark Canoes," Pike ordered his men into the river to shepherd the vessels upstream. For four hours they labored until their limbs numbed. Resting on shore about two-thirds of the way up the cascade, they discovered their boats were leaking. Four of the men had been "rendered useless" by the travails, and Sergeant Henry Kennerman began vomiting blood. Corporal Bradley urinated some as well. With six men incapacitated, Pike's discipline finally yielded to compassion. "If I had no regard for my own health and constitution," he acknowledged, "I should have some for those poor fellows, who, to obey my orders were killing themselves." He halted the operations and allowed the men to eat their breakfast. After the repast, they dragged the boats ashore. Pike resolved to make a winter camp at which to leave some of the men, while the rest of the party advanced upstream.[46]

He stayed at Little Falls for seven weeks, laying in stores, repairing boats, and building new ones. He gathered venison hams to bring as presents to Wilkinson and other friends in St. Louis the following spring, and he built a small fortress to shelter his men while he continued ahead. All of this violated Wilkinson's orders to return to St. Louis by winter. Had Pike pressed on, he might have completed the rest of his journey in that time.[47]

Sheer folly partly explains the delay, for Pike and his men, now completely on their own for the first time, did some of their best blundering during those days. In the first week, the men felled pines for lighter canoes, but as they took shape, Pike judged them too small. Anxious to move on, however, he allowed the work to continue. On the twenty-eighth of October, the men loaded the slightly-too-small dugouts and brought them to the head of the rapids, where the vessels quickly sank, drenching the baggage and cartridges. Then, while trying to dry the powder over a fire the next day, Pike blew up a pot and "nearly...a Tent and two or three men up with it."[48]

Feeding themselves went no better. One day, while some of the men were working on a second batch of canoes, Pike took half a dozen comrades hunting. Before leaving, Pike bragged he would bag an elk, a boast he later called a "very foolish resolution." At one point, he saw in the distance a herd of a hundred and fifty, with "a large Buck with horns of at least four feet leading...and one of equal magnitude bringing up the rear." The hunters followed them all day, getting merely a single shot off, which served only to scatter the target. They did shoot a doe, but "yet not knowing how to track we lost her." They then hit an elk and before they could pursue it, saw a buck deer. Pike shot it between the eyes, and it keeled over. He stepped up to claim his quarry, his foot on the horns, when it leapt up and bounded off. Distracted from the wounded elk, they pursued the deer, certain it would fall at any moment from exhaustion. But it was they who wearied, and the buck escaped. They wounded many more animals before giving up, "Hungry, cold and fatigued," and without a single carcass to carry home. The American hunters terrorized the forest animals around Little Falls all the next day as well but captured nothing. Finally at sundown, Pike got his elk. "This was the cause of much exultation...we having been two days and nights without Victuals."[49]

And so the next few weeks went. Snow fell and melted and fell some more. The temperatures dropped. "Extraordinary cold," Pike wrote one night.[50] "Freezing," he scrawled on others. Hunting parties went out. Sometimes they got something; sometimes they got nothing. Sometimes they just got lost. At one point, food got so low that Pike had to break out the hams he had packed for Wilkinson. Several men fell through the ice into the river. The canoes were going badly, too—his men wrecked yet another one in early December while dragging it across jagged ice. "So many disappointment's almost wearied out my patience," an exasperated Pike wrote.[51]

The setbacks drove him to the edge. On the night of October 31, two days after the accident with the powder, he found himself "powerfully attacked with the fantastic's of the Brain." Cooped up, beset by ineptitude, hungry, cold, and bored—"my Books being packed up"—he felt "entranced." In that moment he better understood the carousers he had so disparaged back in the Ohio Valley, and it was suddenly clear to him "why so many persons who have been confined to remote places, acquired the habit of drinking to excess; and many other vicious practices."[52] Deep in the woods on All Hallows' Eve, this self-disciplined teetotaler was spooked at how his physical exhaustion had given way to mental incapacity. Far from the world in which they understood how to take care of themselves reliably, even basic tasks like eating and traversing the icy terrain posed challenges, and only barely did they avoid blowing themselves up. Under such conditions and despite their frontier experience in and around the forts of the Ohio Valley, Pike and his party made mistake after mistake, which delayed their advance for weeks.

In addition to ineptitude in an unfamiliar environment, there is perhaps another, more calculated, reason why Pike delayed. As the season advanced and the temperatures plummeted, the landscape changed in small but significant ways, and he appears to have waited for it to complete its metamorphosis. "River thickening," he wrote on November 7, as snow blanketed the Mississippi and the flow congealed to ice. He did not record exactly when he made his decision, but sometime around then Pike must have changed his mind about how he was going to get upriver. Three days after first making camp at Little Falls, Pike was preparing for an imminent resumption of his journey, and his actions in those early days were not those of a man planning on settling in for a seven-week hibernation. But when the first round of canoe-building failed and the second set was yet incomplete in mid-November, the thickening river apparently gave Pike an idea. Thereafter, he frequently recorded the freezing and thawing of the river, as if observing carefully, waiting for the time when its transformation from liquid to solid would enable his departure. When he finally set off from Little Falls on December 10, it was not by boat but by sled.

Pike split the party in two. He left Sergeant Kennerman in charge of the rump of the party, which would stay behind at the fortress. He gave Kennerman explicit instructions for coping with the variety of misfortunes that Pike anticipated might befall the group, and he detailed how to ration provisions if supplies dwindled. He then asked Kennermen to care for the expedition's journals and Pike's personal baggage and ordered him to "observe the strictest discipline and justice in your command." For misbehavior, offenders would have to "account to a higher tribunal," an injunction that Pike was later dismayed to have to enforce. He instructed that "one month after the ice has broke...if I am not arrived, it is reasonable to suppose that some disastrous events detain us." In that case, go back to St. Louis, bringing "US property" to the "assistant military agent" there and "my baggage" to "Mrs. Pike." To the men going upstream with him, he gave a morbid pep talk about "the real danger we had to encounter." Whether due to blundering or river thickening or both, the delay had cost the expedition precious time, the difference between safety and suffering. Now, the Minnesota winter was bearing down on them.[53]

James Wilkinson was undoubtedly much warmer in St. Louis. By late November, Pike's communication from the edge of civilization at the Falls of St. Anthony had found its way downstream and into the general's hands. On the twenty-sixth, a day on which Pike recorded that the ice was "getting very rotten" and fretted that "the men fell through several times," Wilkinson wrote a lengthy letter to Henry Dearborn. He groused about the self-interested loyalties of Pierre Chouteau and reported that Potawatomis had killed some Osages and taken sixty-three more as captives. Now the Osage were in St. Louis demanding the United States make good on the oft-made promises to enforce peace among Indians. Trouble threatened from the West as well. "Our situation at New Orleans," he informed Dearborn, "is a defenceless one." Reports indicated that the Spaniards had the American army out-manned and out-mounted and that there was evidence of their "intention to bring forward a respectable force to that frontier." Wilkinson promised the secretary he could defeat them, but he needed more men, horses, and money. He also needed manufactured goods, and lots of them, to give as presents to the Indians. Alliances with the tribes—one of his plans for seizing the strategic initiative he had outlined in his letter to Dearborn on September 8—now took on defensive urgency. He had received intelligence that the Spaniards had given a "Commission" to a Pawnee chief, irrefutable evidence, Wilkinson said, "that the Mexicans have an Eye to the Indian Nations of the [Mis]souri." "No time should be lost," he continued, in convening a conference on the Arkansas River with the Comanches, Pawnees, and Osages "to attach & bind the whole to our Interests."[54]

Wilkinson was probably not expressing a sense of real danger. Rather, his alarmist letter was yet another of his efforts to stir the western cauldron in whose bubbling he always found opportunity. Still, the letter set out the reasoning for a grand western expedition: returning Osage captives to their villages, wooing Plains Indians, and checking Spain's ambitions.

Wilkinson appears to have been contemplating Chouteau for this delicate mission, but when the following spring came, it would not be Chouteau leading the expedition but rather a certain lieutenant, who, at the moment Wilkinson was sounding the alarm to Dearborn, was trying to keep his men out of the thickening Mississippi River.[55]

The river had not yet frozen quite enough. After leaving the camp at Little Falls on December 10, some of the men pushed and pulled a pair of sleds over the prairie and through wooded bottomlands from which snow was melting, exposing bare patches between the trees. Three others towed a canoe through the shallow Mississippi, occasionally dragging it over the rocks. One sled fell through the ice into the river on the fourteenth and ruined some cartridges. The men broke a sled runner on the seventeenth and fell through the ice again on the twenty-eighth. With the river too slushy to sled on and too thick to boat on, they clawed their way upstream, making but a few bends of the river each day. Some days were better. "The River being froze over," Pike wrote one day, they were able "to make three times the Distance." They zipped along over well-packed snow on December 19, making 10 miles, and they "proceeded with some degree of ease and speed" when the "River was compleatly shut with ice" on December 27. Even good days, however, could turn bad. On January 4, they made twenty-eight bends in the river, but shouts awakened Pike that night. Flames were engulfing his tent, and before he and his companions could douse the blaze, he lost his leggings, moccasins, and socks, "no trifling misfortune in that country." "Thank God," though, "that the powder (three small Kegs) which was in the Tent, did not take fire, when I should infallibly have lost all my Baggage, if not my life also." It all pushed even the relentless Pike to the edge. "Never did I undergo more fatigue," he wrote.[56]

Along the way, the party encountered ever more frequent signs of human beings. They heard gunfire and passed vacant Indian encampments. They had learned from a Menominee man that British trading houses dotted the lakeshores on the other side of the pine-covered ridges, only a day's march away. Pike, however, would not reach them for a month-and-a-half, while he kept his course to the arcing Mississippi, which first traveled away from the posts before bending back toward them. On January 2, the party met four Chippewas, an Englishman, and a Frenchman in the employ of the North West Company. The Englishman, likely James Grant, announced that he had a lodge six miles distant, to which he took Pike and one corporal the following day and gave them a good breakfast.

Grant also invited Pike to meet him at a post on Lake De Sable, just off stream, near the easternmost point on the river's great bend. Several days later, Pike met a pair of Frenchmen on snowshoes, each carrying packs that Pike estimated at 180 pounds. They informed him that Grant had passed the party and gone to the fort. The countryside was crawling with human beings who ate well and moved with facility. They did not seem to be suffering as Pike's men did.[57]

January 7 dawned frigid. "The cold was so intense," Pike wrote in his journal, "that some [men] froze their noses—some their fingers and some their toes." To continue on at all, they took to building fires and waiting while someone tramped ahead to build another. Then the rest of the explorers would straggle up and warm themselves while someone else went to build another blaze further along. It was a "very hard days march." The next day, certain he was nearing Grant's Lake De Sable establishment, Pike, together with corporal Bradley, scouted ahead of the party. Directions from a Chippewa man and a dangerous but successful night-time crossing of a trackless frozen lake brought them to a light and a large stockade. Grant opened the gate and welcomed them, with "the greatest hospitality."[58]

Even as he stood in the snow outside the post, Pike was sufficiently distracted from his hunger, fear, and fatigue to be "surprized" at how substantial it was. The trading house was twelve years old, and Pike reveled in the civilization it offered. He was tickled to eat roasted beaver and boiled moose head and taste in neither the least flavor of gamey "Des Bois." The residents grew potatoes and purchased wild oats from the Indians. They trolled the lakes for several species of fish and hunted deer. The storerooms held flour, pork, salt, coffee, tea, and sugar for sale (though Pike considered the prices exorbitant), and there were horses obtained from the Indians. Together, it added up to "such a degree of regularity, as to enable the Superintendent to live tolerably comfortable." What a contrast its residents posed to the cold, hungry men dragging sleds upstream and taking turns lumbering ahead to set fires to keep the others warm.[59]

It was a troubling contrast indeed. The British had grown comfortable in the very landscape in which Americans struggled. Through trade and industry, mapping and markets, and a lengthy but efficient supply line that brought necessities from their homelands to this remote place, the British had rendered the local ecosystem both familiar and profitable. They had established themselves. Men who counted it a success when they spent a day without falling through the ice and had something in their bellies when they lay their heads on the frosty ground at night had a long way to go before they could call this place home. Even before witnessing the splendor of Grant's establishment, Pike was awed at the "searching spirit of trade" and the "enterprize" of the North-Westers. He was also dejected at what their mastery of the land implied for his own country's prospects of displacing them. These were "people who had penetrated from *Lake Superior*, to Lakes little more than Marshes." They were everywhere, and they seemed to have the people and the land doing their bidding. There would be much "difficulty of putting a Barrier to their trade."[60]

On January 20, the party left the trading house, heading for the even more substantial North West Company posts at Leech Lake, near the headwaters of the Mississippi, the residence of Hugh McGillis. As he often did, Pike went on ahead of the rest of the party. On January 27, he spent the day "putting my Gun in order, mending Mockinsons &c." As he did, he was conscious of every one of the more than 1,200 river miles that separated him from St. Louis. The day's mindless chores gave Pike ample time to brood, and he "felt the curse of solitude." How did the North-Westers do it, he wondered, "contenting themselves in this Wilderness for 10, 15, and some 20 years?" It must be Indian women, he decided. That would not do for him, though. No, not even the "wealth of Nations" would induce him to "remain secluded from the Society of Mankind, surrounded by a savage, and unproductive Wilderness, without Books, or other sources of Intellectual enjoyment, or even being blest with society of the cultivated and feeling mind of a civilized fair." Until they secured the material foundations that underlay independence, republican men and women could not thrive here. He had plenty of wood that night, but only one blanket. He "found it very cold."[61]

Encounters with the British

The steam that wafted from McGillis's coffee pot five nights later rendered the upper Mississippi country less remote. The fort was 150 feet on each side, with three gates, picket walls thirteen-feet high, corner bastions, a parade ground, and a flagpole fronting the lake. There were 109 employees on the payroll and seventy-nine more women and children whom Pike classified as "belonging to the Establishment." The complex, which was as substantial as Fort Massac, consisted of a stockade enclosing several buildings, each more than fifty feet in length, some underlain by cellars, others covered by lofts. A cooper and a blacksmith plied their trades. As director of the Fond du Lac department, McGillis enjoyed a residence eighteen-feet square, with a private bedroom, kitchen, and office. Next to McGillis's quarters was a trading shop and adjacent to that was a large storeroom and a well-filled ice house. The stores included "packs of peltries; also chests with 500 bushels of wild rice" and produce from the five acres of gardens northwest of the post. Pike dipped into these supplies to equip Private Theodore Miller, who went out to bring in the other men. They arrived with frozen noses, ears, and chins, undoubtedly grateful to partake of McGillis's bounty. Pike also obtained clothing from McGillis, for "my legs and ancles were so much swelled, as not to be able to wear my cloth's." Obviously, there was much to learn for his nation about how to survive and profit in the upper Mississippi country from these comfortable and hospitable North-Westers. So, Pike stayed awhile—and took careful notes.[62]

First, he rested. "Remained all day within Doors," he wrote on the first day. "Spent the Day in Reading" led off his entry for the second. During these and other down times at the fort, Pike sated his cravings for books. Predictably, he selected from McGillis's library works on uncharted lands and moral self-improvement. First he read the Compte de Volney's account

FIGURE 3.6 Hugh McGillis. "Hugh McGillis (1767–1848): a partner in the North West Company" [n.d.] (Archives of Ontario. Acc. 3634 S. 358).

of his travels in Egypt and then William Shenstone's *Essays on Men and Manners*.[63]

Pike did not just wait around for his limbs and joints to stop swelling, however. He conferred with a trader named Anderson, who ran a trading house nearby, and quizzed him over breakfast about the company's operations. Pike also conversed with McGillis, and the two later went to visit Anderson's and other outposts around Leech Lake. On these excursions, Pike traveled comfortably by horse-drawn sleigh, in which he sat with his legs flat on the bottom and his feet in front lodged in the boot of the craft, while his back reclined against a cushion. He wrapped himself in a buffalo robe and donned a fur cap—both of which were also undoubtedly borrowed from McGillis's supplies—and he coursed over the frozen winterland, "bid[ding] defiance to the Wind and Weather."[64]

From these excursions—and from wearing the clothing and eating the food from McGillis's stores—Pike learned the outlines and extent of the Fond du Lac operations. The company was draining the watersheds of the Mississippi River and the Red River of the North of fur-bearing mammals—bears, beavers, badgers, wolverine, deer, foxes, fishers, lynxes, martens, minks, otters, raccoons, and muskrats. Pike even got wind of plans to push down the Mississippi and tap into the lands exploited by the Michilimackinac traders Pike had met between Prairie du Chien and the Falls of St. Anthony. All this was but part of the North West Company's fur trade empire, which stretched from Hudson Bay down to the St. Lawrence River, upstream through the Great Lakes and across the watersheds of the upper Mississippi and Missouri to the Rocky Mountains and back north and across the Canadian plains to lakes Winnipeg and Saskatchewan. Pike learned during his stay that the company had sent an expedition that year across the Rocky Mountains to the Pacific. He must also have managed to get a look at the post's bookkeeping, because he compiled a table of the packs of peltry that had come through the Fond du Lac posts in 1804–1805, with details of the weight and kinds of furs in each one. In total, 233 packs, each weighing in the neighborhood of a hundred pounds, left the district annually.[65]

Pike sampled the company's imports: blankets, cloth, bindings, gunpowder, balls, shots, tobacco, traps, axes, guns, knives, and more, all of which could be used or traded in order to concentrate energy. The company brought such items from Atlantic workshops to the storage house at the west end of the post on Leech Lake, and persuaded the Indians to rearrange their relationship to the land and the creatures in it in order to acquire the goods. Thus the North West Company gained what Pike termed "great and almost unlimited influence" over the Indians. From the moment the heat radiating from the coffee cup warmed his hands the night he knocked at McGillis's gates, Pike learned both intellectually and bodily that the traders of the Fond du Lac department had already figured out how to survive in the upper Mississippi country. As they moved beyond survival to profit, they connected the savage wilderness Pike had cursed and rendered it productive for the British. Pike and his men with frozen noses had been sent to do this for the United States but had yet to accomplish it. For now, they struggled to stay warm, and the hospitable, comfortable North-Westers poured them coffee. They hungered, and the North-Westers opened their storehouses. When they couldn't tug clothing over their swollen limbs, the North-Westers wrapped them in the skins of bison. In keeping the Indians under thumb and channeling some of the region's stored energy through the hands of the company, McGillis and his comrades had established themselves. Sovereignty on the upper Mississippi was based more on environmental mastery than on discovery or treaties. As Pike put it, aptly using the same words as he had to describe the sleigh cutting through the snow, the North-Westers "bid defiance to every opposition," including Pike and his party, who were both guests and rivals.[66]

That would not do. After a few days of eating from McGillis's larder and wearing the Scotsman's clothing, Pike wrote him an official letter, accusing him of dodging US customs and operating without trade licenses. By not fully paying for what profited him, McGillis lowered his costs and thus undercut competitors who did follow the rules. To Pike's mind, McGillis cheated both the nation and those who sacrificed for it of their legitimate chance for prosperity and independence, not to mention $26,000 in customs revenue.

That was only the half of it, though. Pike also worried that in the event of war between England and the United States the British government would employ the North West Company's establishments to gain a military foothold in the area.[67] Moreover, the company was selling liquor to Indians and working devious diplomacy to lure native attachments away from the US government and American-licensed traders. By distributing medals and British flags to Indians and flying the British flag themselves over their posts, the North-Westers were accustoming Indians to treating British power "as that which alone has authority in the country," which might lead them to give Britain their allegiance. Pike considered such acts "injurious to the *honor* and *dignity* of our government." No less than the competitive market advantages gained by avoiding customs duties, the North West Company's symbolic diplomacy threatened American ability to direct the flow of furs through hands friendly to the United States.

"The law," Pike admonished McGillis, "directs...a total confiscation of your property, personal imprisonment and fines." Pike, however, preferred magnanimity. "Having discretionary instructions," he continued, maybe wondering where his next meal would come from and what he would wear if he tried to arrest McGillis, "I am willing to sacrifice my prospect of private advantage" and forego this "first opportunity of executing those laws." Instead, he merely ordered McGillis to begin complying with American law. A few days later Pike's men shot down the British flag.

Pike also courted the Chippewa chiefs who came to the fort. Make peace with the Sioux, he asked them, give up your British flags and medals for American ones, and send some chiefs with me to St. Louis. They willingly smoked Wabasha's pipe, and they gave up their British tokens, "generally, with a good grace." But some resisted even that, and none were too keen to go down the Mississippi. One offered his calumet instead, asking "Will not my pipe answer the same purpose?" Another said he preferred to visit his American brothers at Fort Mackinac in the spring. A third begged off on the grounds that he was needed up north to keep the peace. Others did not even feel compelled to offer any reasons at all. To goad them into the trip, Pike said he regretted their "hearts...[were] so weak." Other "Nations would say, what, is there no soldiers at Leach, Red and Rainy Lakes, who had the Hearts to carry the Calumet of their Chief to their father?" This taunting persuaded a pair of warriors to undertake the journey, but as Pike distributed gifts, the Chippewas "attempted to get more liquor." Pike, with "a firm and manly denial, convinced them I was not to be played with." This was not the last time that Pike would use masculine posturing to cajole Indians, nor the last time he would discover how thin a victory it actually won him.[68]

For all his bluster, Pike obtained satisfaction from neither McGillis nor the Chippewas. The two warriors changed their minds and went home on the tenth day of Pike's homeward journey, and McGillis consented without complying. His letter to Pike was as cooperative as it was disingenuous. "Your address...has attracted my most serious consideration," McGillis began. "I shall at as early a period as possible, present the agents of the N. W. Company with your representations regarding the paying of duties." He also promised never to fly the British flag or to engage in diplomacy with Indians. Nor would he distribute liquor, medals, or flags to them.

And he acknowledged the company "indebted" for Pike's forbearance in not enforcing a penalty for violations. Indeed, he appreciated "the inestimable advantages arising from the endeavors of your government, to establish a more peaceful course of trade in this part of the territory." He and the other North-Westers, he said, "know not how to express our gratitude to that people whose only view seems to be to promote the happiness of all, the savages that rove over the wild confines of their domain not excepted."[69]

Then McGillis really poured on the flattery: "It is to you, sir, we feel ourselves most greatly indebted, whose claim to honor, esteem and respect, will ever be held in high estimation by myself and associates. The danger and hardships by your fortitude vanquished, and by your perseverance overcome, are signal, and will ever be preserved in the annals of the N. W. Company." Pike and his men, McGillis said, had "exposed their lives in a long and perilous march through a country, where they had every distress to suffer, and many dangers to expect," all "with a view to establish peace in a savage country."[70] No description could have attuned more closely to Pike's vanities if he had written it himself. The man in McGillis's letter suffered distress and by fortitude vanquished danger, not to advance personal interests but rather to bring order to his nation's chaotic frontier and to promote the happiness of its subjects. So closely does the portrait resemble Pike's own self-image that McGillis probably deserves some credit for astute observation of the American during their two weeks together in close quarters and discerning, as a result, precisely how to manipulate his American visitor.

Whether shrewd or lucky, McGillis could afford to be so agreeable because Pike was dependent and the cagey North-Wester was not. He could indulge Pike in shooting down the flag and see it as no more than empty symbolism. Pike had overstepped his orders by a long shot. He was supposed to be home before winter, and his orders said nothing about harassing British traders. Not even James Wilkinson's active imagination contemplated bullying North-Westers at their own headquarters. American influence over land and people simply did not reach that far. In passing beyond his orders, Pike had also surpassed his nation's ability to do anything for him. He had no maps, scant pull with the Indians, and little ability even to meet the biological needs of his party in this unfamiliar ecosystem. Grand promises and vague threats of American power were all he had to sustain the expedition. Without the North West Company's post, Pike would have been reduced to lighting fires to warm his men on their march and fishing his sleds out of the icy rivers every so often—that is if he could hunt enough game to keep the soldiers alive. McGillis, in contrast, was established. Just as he was able to impose his rules on Indians and landscapes, so, too, was he able to ignore the rules that Pike wanted to impose on him. When you eat a man's bread and wear his clothes, it is hard to make him do things your way.

After the two-week charade, in which the lieutenant pretended to enforce American sovereignty and the trader pretended to comply, Pike left with a new sled and some dogs courtesy of McGillis, who subsequently carried out none of his agreements. North West Company papers contain only a single documentary record of Pike's visit, a journal entry from a faraway post that mentioned that a party of American soldiers had visited McGillis on an errand "to oblige us to pay the usual duties."[71] Although he apparently accomplished nothing to force North West Company cooperation, the drama gave Pike some useful practice navigating the contradictions of enforcing American sovereignty over hosts upon whom he was utterly dependent, a situation that would become increasingly familiar to Pike during his adventures the following year.

Homeward Bound

The homeward journey was mostly uneventful. Well-outfitted by McGillis and taking a shortcut across the reverse C of the northern Mississippi, the party made good time. Upon returning to Little Falls, Pike discovered that Sergeant Kennerman had broken out the liquor and sold it liberally to the men at the camp. He had also used up much of the stores, including Pike's cache of gift hams. Most outrageously, he had opened Pike's trunk and sold some of his commander's personal belongings as well. Pike spent another month at the camp, court-martialing Kennerman, restocking the supplies, and entertaining Indians and traders (and struggling mightily to hunt enough food to feed his many hungry guests). He also watched the ice on the Mississippi daily, waiting once again for the river to change its state. It thawed by April 6, and the men cleaned out their rooms and sang and danced late into the night. The next morning they were on their way by boat for the much faster downstream trip to St. Louis. "Every heart appeared rejoiced at the Idea of leaving this savage Wilderness."[72]

Overall, the expedition can be termed a limited success. Pike did not find the exact headwaters of the Mississippi, but he reached the general vicinity. The peace between the Chippewas and Sioux did not last, but it did endure during the time he spent among them. He brought no chiefs to St. Louis, but a few straggled downstream on their own behind him. He did not establish an American presence, but he stayed alive, and so did his men. His greatest achievement was to begin mapping the web of connections that knitted people and land together in the upper Mississippi country and beyond. He learned the paths by which goods found their way from Atlantic world factories through the Great Lakes and into canoes like Fraser's, bound for Indian villages. He discerned the vast extent of the North West Company's operations. He also came to understand the connections among Indians, their rivalries, their economies, and their politics. Little of this was completely new knowledge when he brought it back to St. Louis, but Pike was one of the few people who had assembled all of it in one place.

Together with his journal and a brief narrative report on the rivers and Indians, Pike compiled a chart.[73] Along the left side, he listed fifteen different ent Indians groups. Each had its own row, divided into twenty-one columns providing data on population, geography, trade relationships, species of peltry, optimal trading post locations, diplomacy, and other topics. He also produced a table giving French, Indian, and English names for rivers and other natural features. Yet another chart listed the 115 packs of furs that had passed through the Fond du Lac Department in 1804 and 1805, detailing weight, species, and other information for each one. Finally, there were maps, flawed to be sure, but some of the most detailed yet drawn for that part of the world. Together these documents began to reveal the upper Mississippi to Americans in the systematic categorizations by which the Enlightenment era's intellectuals liked to organize knowledge. He had spent nearly eight months there gathering a dazzling amount of information and undergoing a variety of experiences. Upon returning home, he put it all into narrative and tabular form, gridding the upper Mississippi and rendering it intelligible and manipulable for the state.

The young lieutenant, who a year before had been dying for an assignment that would test his endurance and patriotism, took pride in his accomplishments. It had been cold. Men had bled and so had he. They had been hungry. They had been lost. As he wrote to Wilkinson, "without vanity," they had suffered "as many hardships as almost any party of Americans ever experienced, by cold and hunger."[74] Pike's offer of bodily suffering in service to his nation was hardly over when he returned to St. Louis on April 30, however. Troubles with Spaniards and Indians had been brewing while he was gone. Burr had continued hatching plan after

Names of the different nations of Indians, as pronounced in the English Language	Primitive names as given by the savages themselves	Names given them by the French or Spaniards	No. of Warriors	No. of Women	No. of Children	No. of Villages	Probable No. of Souls	No. of Lodges of the Roving Bands	No. of Fire Arms	Primitive Language	Traders or Bands with whom they traffic	Amount of merchandise necessary for their annual consumption	Annual return of Peltry in packs	Species of Peltry
Osage Grand Village	Wasbasha	Grand Osage	502	852	341 Male	1	1695	214	500	Osage	Of St. Louis	Dollars. 10000	1000	Deer-skins, black Bear-skins, Otter, Beaver, and some few Buffalo robes.
Ditto	Ditto	Petit Osage	250	241	{574 O. {159 B. {353 T.	1	824	101	250	Ditto	Ditto	8000	300	Ditto.
Ditto	Ditto	Total..Osage	500 1252	700 1793	300 B. 974	1 5	1500 4019	200 516	450 1300	Ditto	Of Arkansaw			Ditto.
Kans	Kanas	Kan	465	500	600	1	1565	204	450	Ditto	St. Louis	8000	{250 deer, {15 beaver, {100 otter. {——— {365 total.	Deer, Beaver Otter, Bear and Buffalo skins.
Pawnee Village of the Republic.	Pawnee	Panis	308	530	560	1	1618		200	Pawnee	St. Louis and Kans	8000		Deer, Buffalo, and a few Beaver and Otter.
Pawnee Grand Village	Ditto	Ditto	1000	1120	1000	1	3120	90	300	Ditto	St. Louis, and possibly once in three years a few Spaniards	15000		Deer, Buffalo, and a few Beaver and Otter.
Pawnee Village of Pawnee Loups	Ditto	Ditto	485	500	500	2	1485	40	200	Ditto	Ditto.	8000		Ditto.
		Total..Pawnees	1993	2170	2060	3	6223	174	700					
Tetau	Camanches		2700	3000	2500		8200	1020	270	Camanche	Spaniards of North Mexico.	30000		Buffalo robes and Horses

FIGURE 3.7 Like the surveys of the Land Ordinance of 1785 (see Figure 1.5, chapter 1), Pike's chart of his Mississippi voyage organized remote data in a grid format, easily intelligible to and administrable by officials who had never seen the place the document described. Chart published in Pike's *An Account of Expeditions to the Sources of the Mississippi...*, 1810. Courtesy of Special Collections, Colorado State University Libraries.

The positions most proper for trading establishments.	Nations with whom at war.	Nations with whom at peace or in alliance.	Names of the Chiefs or Principal Men.			Remarks.
			Indian.	French.	English.	
On the middle branch of the Osage river, between the Grand and Little village.	Tetaus.	Little Osage.	Cahagatonga.	Cheveux Blanche.	White Hair.	Grand and little medal, colors, &c. 1st chf.
	Potowatomics.	All the Pawnees.	Watchawaha.	Jean La Fou.	Second chief, son-in-law to White Hair.	
	Arkansaws.	Sacs.	Tawangaha.	Fils de Canard.	He who drives villages.	Literally from the Indian.
	Cherokees.	Reynards.	Ichesohungar.		Wise Family.	Son Cheveux Blanche.
	Chickasaws.	Delawares.	Hapause.		Pointed Horn.	First Soldier.
	Chactaws.	Shawanese.	Chaperanga.	Bonnet du Bœuf.		
	Creeks.	Kickapous.	Gihagatche.		The Chief himself.	
	Padoucas.	Otos.	Shenga Wassa	Belle Oiseau.	Beautiful Bird.	Accompanied me to the Pawnees.
	Caddoes.	Missouries.	Wasaba Tunga.	Sans Nerve.	Without Nerve.	
		Mahaws, &c.	Ogahawasa.		The Son-in-Law.	
		Kans uncertain.	Tourmanzara.		Heart of the Town.	
Ditto and above the Gr. Osage, on the Arkansaw and on the side of the Missouri.	Ditto.	Ditto.	Tuttasuggy	Le Vent.	The Wind.	First chief Little Osage.
			Watchkesingar.	Soldat de Chien.	Soldier's Dog.	Second do.
			Nezuma		The Rain which Walks	Brother first chief.
			Tetobasi.	Sans Oreille.	Without Ears.	First Soldier.
			Tarehem.		The Yellow Skin Deer.	N. B. 49 of the Little Osage have been killed since under our government.
			Maugraine.		The Big Rogue.	
	Ditto.	Ditto.				The enumeration of the Grand and Little Osage village was taken by myself. The calculation of the Arkansaw village is by the estimates of the chiefs of the Grand Osage. For farther explanation relative to that village, see lieutenant Wilkinson's report, Appendix, Part II. [No. 2.] p. 20.
The entrance of the Kans river, or at the village.	None, if at peace with the Osage.	With all their neighbors.				The men are from actual enumeration; the women and children by estimation.
Ditto.	Tetaus and the Indians of Kans, Osages, and all the New Mexico, also Panis Indians of the east. Loups.	With all the Pawnee and Panis Indians of the east.	Characterish.	Loup Blanche.	The White Wolf.	
			Iskatappe.	L'Homme Riche.	The Rich Man.	
			——	——	Republican Chief.	N. B. The population of the Pawnee republic is from actual enumeration; but the others from information.
					Two sons of Characterish.	
Entrance of the La Platte	Ditto, except the Panis	Ditto.				
Ditto.	Ditto, and Pawnee republic.	Ditto.				
High up the Red river and near the mountains on the Arkansaw.	Pawnees and Utahs, Osage and Kans.	With all the Spanish Indians.				

plan, and so had Wilkinson. Their schemes were no clearer in April than they had been in August, but the sense of urgency about them had not diminished. Within three days of rejoining Clara and Clarissa, he learned of his next assignment. He and seventeen of his twenty-two men, with battered bodies but plucky spirits, would soon be headed for another, bigger adventure. They had no way of knowing that their next journey would be even harder.

4

"Young Warriors" of the "Great American Father"

CROSSING THE PLAINS, JULY–NOVEMBER 1806

IN OCTOBER 1806, on a high promontory above the Republican River, Pike stopped and looked back at the Pawnee village where he had spent the last two weeks. En route to the settlement, his party had struggled through heat and cold and chilling rains, and their guide had led them astray while both men and horses hungered. When they arrived at the village, the Pawnees fed them, and Pike's men rested their weary bodies and purchased fresh horses. But the Americans quickly wore out their welcome, and violence nearly erupted when Pike tried to continue his expedition in defiance of the Pawnees' efforts to turn it back. Through good luck or shrewd diplomacy that morning, Pike had marched his men without incident to the summit from which he now beheld from a safe distance the source of his aggravation. With the tense days now behind him, he felt "relieved from a heavy burthen."[1]

That burden was both diplomatic and physical. Pike had come among the Pawnees—and the Osages, whom he had visited a few weeks before—to announce to them the United States' purchase of Louisiana, to request their allegiance to their new American fathers, and to invite them into commercial and diplomatic relationships. In short, he had come to incorporate both groups into his nation. At every step, however, friction among westerners hindered his task. The Osage cooperated with him only minimally, and the Pawnees verged on hostile. Rivalries among the white merchants who competed for Indian trade threatened to undo his efforts more than once. Mastery of the prickly terrain of native diplomatic customs eluded him, and divisions between and within the tribes further complicated his efforts. With good cause he welcomed the end of the Indian diplomacy stage of his voyage.

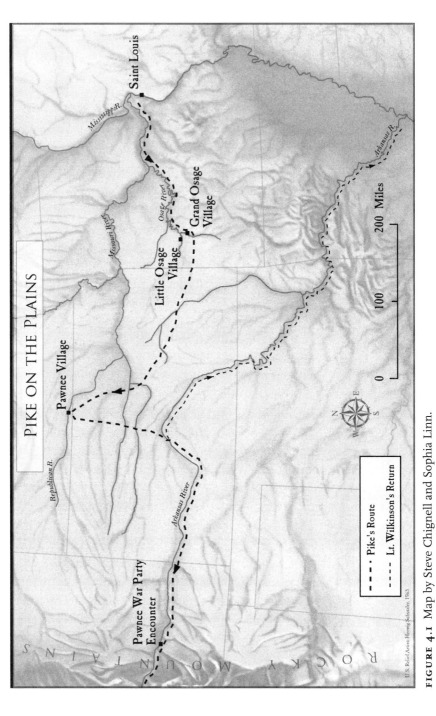

FIGURE 4.1 Map by Steve Chignell and Sophia Linn.

FIGURE 4.2 View of Pike's promontory from the Pawnee Village site, now a privately owned field of corn, near modern Guide Rock, Nebraska. Photo by author.

Pike also bore his burdens physically. At the simplest level, the problem involved moving bodies and baggage through space. Wherever boot and hoof touched earth or wherever paddle slapped water, Pike and his comrades expended energy to overcome physical friction. Acquiring such energy demanded eating, drinking, sleeping, and staying warm, each of which deducted additional energy costs. Sustaining his party and moving it forward occupied Pike on an hourly basis, but it was also a microcosm of a national problem. The second law of thermodynamics asserts that energy in the universe is unevenly dispersed but constantly moving toward a state of uniform distribution. That is, energy moves from where there is lots of it to where there is less. This is called entropy, and all societies labor against it constantly. In doing so, they neither create nor destroy energy, but, rather, harness its flow by temporarily concentrating it in human bodies, animals, ship sails, water wheels, or other useful channels. Indian tribes and the early republic both accomplished this by farming sunshine. Whether harvesting crops, eating animal flesh, or burning wood, all peoples in preindustrial North America consumed energies that plants had absorbed from the sun and photosynthesized into usable fuel for humans.

But natives and republicans differed radically in the social, political, and economic arrangements they set up to enable this. Pike went among the Osages and Pawnees to ensure that the nation's energy system would subsume the natives'. This task demanded not only overcoming the many diplomatic frictions already present in relations within and among the tribes, traders, and American government, but also getting people on the plains and prairies of mid–North America to change the way they drew energy from their environment, something that implied changes to their entire way of life. All the while he had to acquire or import the energy necessary for himself and his party to stay alive while moving through unfamiliar, difficult environments. A heavy burden indeed.[2]

Reasons for Pike's Western Expedition

The buzz in St. Louis held that this second expedition involved more than the Pawnees. Some alleged that Pike was going to spy on the Spaniards, though for whom—Jefferson? Wilkinson? Burr?—was not clear. Aaron Burr had talked too much during his 1805 western sojourn, and before he returned east, rumors were swirling up and down the Mississippi and Ohio rivers. On August 2, 1805, the *United States Gazette*, a Federalist newspaper in Philadelphia, published a startling exposé. Burr was recruiting "adventurous and enterprising young men from the Atlantic states" (a description that fit Pike reasonably well) for a project that would carve a new nation out of western states. After rewarding his followers with public lands seized from the United States, he would sweep south to capture Mexico. News of the conspiracy spread westward and likely reached Wilkinson before he met Burr in September. Or he learned it around the same time from Daniel Clark, with whom Burr had conferred in New Orleans and who wrote to Wilkinson of a "horrid" tale circulating on the lower Mississippi. "Kentucky, Tennessee, the state of Ohio, with part of Georgia and Carolina," Clark warned, "are to be bribed, with the plunder of the Spanish countries west of us, to separate from the Union." Wilkinson, one of Clark's associates said, was rumored to be Burr's "right hand man." If so, Pike's western expedition could have gathered geographical and political information for Burr's maneuvers or possibly provoked an incident that would bring Spain and the United States to war and provide cover for filibustering.[3]

Like Wilkinson and Burr, the US government, too, had reason to explore Louisiana. In the spring of 1806, Spain began massing troops in

Texas to contest the boundaries of the Louisiana Purchase. As Salcedo's and Wilkinson's letters the previous September had attested, both nations considered alliance with Pawnees and other Plains tribes, who controlled the territory between the two empires, crucial to gaining the upper hand in this dispute. Moreover, since the late seventeenth century the Pawnees had been acquiring horses and slaves from New Mexico and the southern Plains and exchanging them for guns, ammunition, and metal goods from European traders from the Mississippi Valley and Great Lakes. Competition for trade with the Pawnees, and fear that the tribe was falling into an imperial rival's political orbit, had spurred French and Spanish expeditions to the region in the eighteenth century, as both sides vied to incorporate the tribe into their transatlantic empires. By the time the United States entered the fray, the West was filled with traders of various ethnicities and nationalities competing to buy and sell the commodities bound for Atlantic world markets. The Chouteaus and other dealers had been doing business in Louisiana under several flags long before the Americans showed up. They and their rivals were more interested in ensuring continued financial success than in following the laws of the United States.

With Spain pressing from without and Burr and the traders from within, the American state's political and economic survival in the West required ecological success—that is, control over the processes by which westerners concentrated energy. In the months leading up to Pike's western expedition, the newspapers carried stories about the US government exploring and surveying western territories, settling land claims in Louisiana and the Northwest, hearing Tombigbee River settlers' grievances against Spain, establishing western roads and postal routes, hassling Spain over navigation rights on western rivers, regulating Indian trade, and trying to fix the borders of the Louisiana Purchase.[4] All this centralized power over the landscape, over trade in the land's wealth, over movement through space, over property rights, and over boundaries that excluded foreign rivals from tapping American resources. It also facilitated westerners' capture of energy and transfer of it to markets that converted it into capital. If the United States established itself as the arbiter of commerce in the West, Indians, Europeans, and restless Americans who wanted to prosper there would have to cooperate with the government. To own land, trade, travel, communicate, and enjoy security from aggressors, they would depend on the state. By directing energy flows and shaping the lives of organisms from beavers to cotton plants to human beings, the American state was creating a national ecosystem, one that was designed both to invigorate the western economy and to consolidate national power in the West. With a national ecosystem, Americans, their ideas, their institutions, and their ways of doing things would be as comfortable on the grasslands of Louisiana as on the streets of Philadelphia.

That was why Pike was traipsing around the Plains in the fall of 1806. "You are to proceed withoute delay," Wilkinson instructed Pike in June, "to the Cantonment of the Missouri," to embark on a multifaceted mission that would help establish Americans in the West. The first task was to escort Indians to their villages. Part of the group consisted of a delegation of two Pawnees, five Osages, and an Otoe, who had been to Washington, DC, to meet with Jefferson. The usually cost-conscious president had spared no expense entertaining Indians at the capital, and the federal government shelled out more than seven thousand dollars to convey them to Washington and back. Pike's escort would be the final leg in a grand journey intended to impress them with the larger world of which they were now a part, particularly the nation-state's power to shape that world. The second and larger portion of Pike's retinue consisted of fifty-one Osage men, women, and children whom Potawatomis had captured and whom the US had ransomed. In response, an angry Thomas Jefferson had written that the Potawatomis must be "strongly reprimanded, and no exertion spared to recover and restore the prisoners....The Indians on this side of the Mississippi must understand that that river is now ours, & is not to be a river of blood."[5] American power must prevail in the West. Without it, aspiring men like Pike, whether American or Indian (and Jefferson did hope that one day Indians would aspire as Pike did), could not achieve the civilized independence that Jefferson considered necessary for a republic's prosperity. Whether with trips to Washington as carrots or presidential reprimands as sticks, Jefferson was determined to bring the Indians under Washington's influence. In this, Zebulon Pike, first lieutenant in the US Army, upon whom fifty-nine Indians now depended for their safe transport through their own territory, was one of his agents.

In addition to Indian diplomacy, Wilkinson asked Pike to firm up American understanding of western resources, in particular to explore the rivers of the Great Plains. With the United States and Spain on the brink of war over the disputed boundaries of Louisiana, Wilkinson had justified the expedition to Secretary of War Henry Dearborn as a mission to find military routes to Santa Fe. Wilkinson therefore ordered Pike to ascend the Arkansas River to its headwaters and then to return by the Red River. Along the way, Pike was to note "the Geographical structure; the Natural

History; and population; of the country." He was also "to collect & pre-serve, specimens of every thing curious in the mineral or botanical Worlds" and to record distances, direction, latitude, and the astronomic data necessary to calculate longitude upon return. In possession of such envi-ronmental data, a centralized state could tighten its sovereignty in the West. It could tax, maintain security, organize land ownership, enforce borders, and regulate trade. In a subsequent set of instructions on July 12, the general added, "Should you discover any unlicensed traders...you are to arrest such person or persons and dispose of their property as the law directs."[6] Pike would be the state's eyes and hands in its new territory.

Make alliances with Indians. Explore strategic transportation routes. Gather environmental data. Lean on unauthorized traders. To Jefferson and Dearborn, it would have appeared another piece of their stratagem to extend US mastery over westerners' relationships with the land and to preclude its exploitation by rivals. To Burr it would have looked like exactly the intelligence his machinations required. And to Wilkinson, who never did anything without something in it for him, it would point out avenues for directing some of the stored energy and potential capital of the Great Plains and Louisiana into his own hands.[7] Once again, the general pack-aged many people's interests—some to advance state power, some to challenge it—under cover of diplomatic and scientific exploration. Pike, who probably understood little of this many-layered plan, got underway from St. Louis on July 15, 1806. Americans did not know how wide the Plains were or how big the mountains that loomed beyond. As he had the previous year, he was leaving too late, poorly informed about the distance and difficulty of the project. It would not be long before he had to set aside much of both the state making and unmaking projects in favor of simply making it at all.

Among the Osages

This season's party numbered twenty-three, including two lieutenants, a doctor, a sergeant, two corporals, sixteen privates, and an interpreter. Seventeen of the men had accompanied Pike up the Mississippi. Having as yet no command of his own, he had borrowed his men once again from their commander, Captain Daniel Bissell. "They are a Dam'd set of Rascels," Pike wrote Bissell, "yet in the Woods they are staunch fellows and very proper for such expeditions as I am engaged in." The men left no record of their opinion of this arrangement, except for private Henry Kennerman, demoted from sergeant after breaking into Pike's stores at Little Falls. Complaining of illness four days out from St. Louis, he secured permission to depart temporarily from the boats and never returned. Several new men joined these veterans: Sergeant Joseph Ballenger, Private John Wilson, Lieutenant James B. Wilkinson (the general's son and Pike's second-in-command), and an interpreter, Antoine F. Baronet Vasquez, a mixed-race trader who spoke French, Spanish, and faulty English. Pike considered Vasquez "one of the finest young men I ever knew in his situation...as firm an American as if born one." Three days before departure, and without clear explanation, General Wilkinson directed Pike to take along a civilian physician, John Hamilton Robinson, "as a volunteer...to attend your sick." One simple explanation for Robinson's attachment to the party is that Wilkinson, himself trained in medicine, thought the expedition ought to have a doctor. Robinson's subsequent actions, however, have invited speculation that his assignment entailed more than just doctoring. A Virginian three years younger than the twenty-seven-year-old Pike, Robinson had arrived in St. Louis the year before and endeared himself to the general. After serving Wilkinson, apparently unofficially, at Fort Bellefontaine, Robinson left that employment two weeks before Pike's party embarked. Wilkinson may have chosen Robinson as a personal agent to carry out tasks too shady to be entrusted to the upright, nationalistic Pike. Whatever the reasons for his assignment, Robinson would be both friend and nemesis to Pike.[8]

Heading west from St. Louis and the last frontier outposts across the modern state of Missouri, Pike and his rascals followed the Missouri River to the Osage River. They traveled in a pair of flat-bottomed boats that Pike referred to as barges or bateaux. As he had done on the Mississippi voyage, Pike walked on shore, hunting or scouting the countryside. Hunters, including the crackshot John Sparks, again fanned out into the woods to chase game to feed the party's seventy-four mouths. Pike generally followed the boats along the bends in the rivers, while Lieutenant Wilkinson escorted the Indians on foot along a more direct overland route, the rivers bearing the considerable weight of their belongings as well as the expedition's gear. The party embarked at five a.m. when they could, though to Pike's great annoyance, they frequently had to wait for the Indians to get going. They also waited out low water that slowed the craft and periodic violent thunderstorms that filled the rivers and drenched the baggage. As soon as the gear dried, Pike would hurry the crew onward, taking advantage of the high water that followed the cloudbursts. On a good day, the party could travel as much as thirty river miles, though turns in the river made the actual advance more modest. One day, the boats made thirteen river miles, but the bends in the river carried them in "almost a perfect circle," so that the party camped just three miles as the crow flies from where they had stayed the previous night. Finally, on August 18, not far from the Osage villages, fallen timber and debris blocked the river entirely. The Indians having departed overland for their homes a few days earlier with Lieutenant Wilkinson, Pike sent word to the village asking for horses to carry the goods the rest of the way.[9]

Sometime before the debris blocked Pike's water passage, Wilkinson and his charges arrived at the village of the Little Osages. Along with the Big Osage village five or six miles away, the Little Osages had for many decades constituted the tribe's primary settlement in the area. Each numbered between 1,500 and 2,000 residents, though many inhabitants were siphoning off to a third village to the southwest on the Arkansas River, the result, according to Pike, of Pierre Chouteau's efforts a few years before to splinter the Osages and establish a rival center over which he could maintain his influence. A hundred and eighty fully painted horsemen came out to greet Wilkinson's party a half-mile from the town and escorted the captives to the village, where a thousand people poured out to welcome them. While wives embraced husbands and children embraced parents, Tetobasi (Sans Oreille, or No Ears) made a speech. "Osage," he cried, "you now see your wives, your brothers, your daughters, your sons, redeemed from captivity. Who did this? [W]as it the Spaniards? No. The French? No. Had either of those people been governors of the country, your relatives might have rotted in captivity... but the Americans stretched forth their hands, and they are returned to you!! What can you do in return for all this goodness? Nothing: all your lives would not suffice to repay their goodness." Pike apparently had completed this first leg of his mission with great success.[10]

Pike himself arrived a few days later to a "flattering" reception. Camping halfway between the two villages at a place he named "Camp Independence," he began preparing for a council with the villages' leaders. "My brothers," he addressed them on August 22, "You see... by the release of your women and children from captivity, how sincere is the friendship of your American father." He also delivered a message of friendship from General Wilkinson and asked the Osages to accompany the expedition to the Pawnee villages, to make peace with the Kaws and Comanches, and to provide him some horses to carry the baggage. "I address myself to both villages," he

FIGURE 4.3 Osage Chief Pahuska, or Ca-ha-ga-tonga, called White Hairs and Cheveux Blanche by Pike. *Payouska* (Pawhuska, ca. 1752–1832)—Chief of the Great Osages. ca. 1806. Drawing by Charles-Balthazar-Julien Fevret de Saint-Memin. Negative #1111. Collection of the New York Historical Society.

concluded, "as if they were one, for it is the wish of your Great Father that they should be as one nation, take counsel together and be strong."[11]

But they were hardly one. The Big Osage chief, Ca-ha-ga-tonga (Cheveux Blanc, or White Hairs), replied briefly to Pike acknowledging the request and promising a full reply the next day. Then he turned to Tuttasuggy (The Wind), the head man of the Little Osage village and the leader among the captives, and upbraided him. "I am shocked at your conduct," Ca-ha-ga-tonga said, before rebuking Tuttasuggy for taking the visitors first to his own village without stopping at the Big Osage village on his way. Tuttasuggy held his tongue and left the council soon after. Pike pleaded that American ignorance of geography had led to this diplomatic slight and later confided to his journal that Ca-ha-ga-tonga's display of wounded pride stemmed from a desire to show the Americans his own superiority over the chief of the Little Osage.[12]

Rivalries divided the white men as well. A few days earlier, a French St. Louis resident known as Lamie had arrived among the Osages after paddling with two armed men up the Osage River. Lamie claimed to be collecting debts for Chouteau's rival, Manuel Lisa, but Pike suspected he was up to something more. Lisa had established himself as a competitor of the Chouteaus, and it was the Osage River trade monopoly that Lisa had teased from Spanish officials in 1802 that had inspired Pierre Chouteau to persuade some Osages to defect to the Arkansas. Now, Lisa was planning to woo Comanches and Spaniards to tap an as yet undeveloped trade with Santa Fe, the same commercial treasure for which Wilkinson was prospecting. On July 17, two days after the expedition departed Fort Bellefontaine, a sheriff from St. Louis had shown up at Lisa's behest and arrested the interpreter Vazquez for unpaid debts. Pike stopped to write a letter to General Wilkinson about the affair. When Vasquez returned to the city, Wilkinson personally assumed responsibility for the debt and wrote to Pike condemning the "despicable Intrigues" of Lisa and the Chouteaus. Lisa "dined here yesterday," Wilkinson huffed, "& left me this morning before the arrival of your letter—this was well for him." In a subsequent letter, Wilkinson explained to Pike that Lisa's maneuvers stemmed from a grander design to tap the Santa Fe trade, something "without the sanction of Law" and "injurious to the United States" (not to mention Wilkinson's own commercial schemes). "You must take all prudent & lawful means to blow it up." The day after receiving Wilkinson's letter, Pike learned about Lamie.[13]

FIGURE 4.4 Manuel Lisa. Early nineteenth century. Artist unknown. Missouri History Museum, St. Louis.

Pike interrogated the trader at Camp Independence, but could find no solid evidence of wrongdoing other than traveling in Louisiana without a license. When he asked Ca-ha-ga-tonga, the chief offered only that Lamie had come in advance of Lisa's upcoming commercial visit. Pike could spare no men to arrest Lamie and return him to St. Louis, so he took the man's deposition, detained him in camp for "sufficient time to alarm him," ordered him and his companions back to St. Louis, and sent word to the acting governor to prosecute the troublesome interloper. Vazquez, who may have taken a measure of vindication in officially witnessing Lamie's deposition, attributed the affair to the shenanigans of Lisa and/or Chouteau. Whatever their origins, the intrigues complicated Pike's mission of incorporating the Osages.[14]

After Pike interrogated Lamie, the Osages' hospitality cooled. Pike conjectured that Lamie was influencing the conduct of Ca-ha-ga-tonga and Noel Mongrain, the chief's mixed-race son-in-law, whom General Wilkinson had instructed Pike to employ as interpreter. Mongrain was refusing Pike's request to accompany him to the Pawnees as an interpreter, though he had performed a similar service the previous year for Chouteau. A frustrated Pike contemplated invoking military law to compel Mongrain's cooperation, for to let such a "scoundrel" best him would lessen "the dignity of our government." But he appears not to have done so, noting in a letter to General Wilkinson only that he had "brought...Mongrain to reason," without saying how. At the same time, Pike was struggling to purchase horses from the Osages, but Ca-ha-ga-tonga secured only ten from a herd that Pike estimated to number seven or eight hundred. Pike griped to Lieutenant Wilkinson that rumors in the village held that Lamie's employer (whoever that was) "could have obtained horses plenty." Even in western Missouri, not far from American towns and lying on the ruins of old trading posts, the reach of the American state faltered. Fractures among the white men who competed for Indian trade enabled the Osages to remain independent of all of them. They did not subject themselves to Wilkinson, Chouteau, Lisa, or Spaniards, nor would they to this latest American and his handful of soldiers. Pike's boasts of American power amounted to little more than bluster, and he was therefore impotent to discipline Lamie or to compel the villagers to sell their horses.[15]

Ecology made things worse. The energy costs of travel in the North American interior had long posed significant obstacles to the expansion of the United States.[16] From the Ohio country to the Mississippi River, the republic had expanded by traveling mostly downstream. West of St. Louis, Pike and others went upstream, which was harder, but still by water and through lush environments. Although rainstorms and river bends occasionally delayed his progress, fertile riparian lands supplied game, water, and fuel. The rivers' waters supported the loads of boats, reducing the human and animal energy necessary to move through space. Beyond the Osage villages, Pike navigated a different environment, one that changed the energetics of travel. Crossing the prairies from the Osage villages to the Pawnee town on the Republican River required him to travel north, perpendicularly to the west-to-east flowing rivers. Consequently, he sold one of his boats for a hundred dollars, entrusted the other to Tuttasuggy, and switched from waterborne travel to an overland march. Away from the rivers, in the largely treeless grasslands, however, the necessities of life were harder to come by. Travel was hard, and often dangerous. Hence Pike's need for horses—he needed a new energy source to replace the buoyant waters—and hence his dependence on the Osages, who sold him horses only slowly and at high prices. Pike's impotent dealings with Lamie, Ca-ha-ga-tonga, and Mongrain underscore the tangled relationship between diplomacy and state authority on the frontier. Pike's mission aimed to incorporate traders and Indians into the nation, but doing so first required their cooperation. Trapped in this predicament, Pike released Lamie and delayed the expedition's departure while he haggled with the Osages over horses and paid whatever price they asked. Without Osage support and unable to spare the horses or men necessary to escort the unlicensed traders back to St. Louis, Pike was able only to intimidate them and try to boast of the extent of American power. At this first opportunity to extend American sovereignty, energy demands compromised that objective. It would not be the last time.

Among the Pawnees

The late-summer sun of September still blazed as Pike and his men labored on blistered feet in search of the Pawnee village. The mounted Osage guides who had accompanied them—even the patriotic speechmaker Sans Oreille—had deserted them, taking some of the energy-saving horses with them. The few Osages who remained so feared the Kaws, whose hunting grounds the expedition was skirting, that they dragged the party far out of its way to avoid a clash—another energy debit. On this detour, game, water, and firewood were sometimes scarce. On September 14,

Pike dispatched Vasquez, Robinson, and one of the Pawnees from the Washington delegation to scout ahead for the village. In the meantime, the party inched forward. A rainstorm drenched their baggage and delayed them two days, and they halted early another day for fear of not finding water. Some of the men suffered severe headaches, and everyone was thirsty. As Lieutenant Wilkinson remembered it, the march was painful, the sun oppressive, and the terrain irregular and broken. Both men and horses were spent. Lost among the hills and salty river valleys, where vegetation was sparse and sand was plentiful, Pike anguished over his scouts' delay. To the exhausted travelers, ill-prepared for extracting the energy and water necessary for survival on the tall-grass prairies, the Pawnee village, which they finally reached on September 25, was an oasis.

Among the rolling hills a few miles northwest of where the Republican River crosses the modern Kansas-Nebraska line, smoke rose from the bowl of a pipe. Taking a whiff or two, the Republican Pawnee chief Sharitarish extended his hand, and greeted Pike with a hearty "Bon jour!" He and Pike and Lieutenant Wilkinson then proceeded up a hill, followed by Pike's sergeant and color bearer and a caravan of laden horses led by American soldiers and the remaining Osage Indians, while some three hundred Pawnee men, nearly naked and mounted on horses, galloped along the procession's flanks. On a hill above the Pawnee village, Sharitarish passed the pipe among the Pawnees, who, one by one, presented it along with a horse to the eight Osages. After the horse-smoke, the soldiers and Osages made camp across the river from the village. Meanwhile, Sharitarish invited Pike to his lodge for dinner, possibly of pumpkin soup with corn and bison meat or perhaps cornmeal mixed with bison marrow. That evening, after the meal and conversation ended, an undoubtedly weary Pike made his way up to his companions' camp with a Pawnee youth burdened with corn for the rest of the party to eat.[17]

Pipes, horses, corn—these were the props of welcome at the Pawnee village. At one level, the Pawnees were receiving traditional rivals, the Osages. That required the peace pipe. Most likely the pipe bowl was made of catlinite, a reddish mineral quarried in southwestern Minnesota. For centuries, different tribes had come from hundreds of miles to obtain the treasured stone, which was easily molded when recently quarried, and even enemy groups suspended hostilities while sharing the excavation site. Even after the stone left the quarries and circulated throughout the Plains, it continued to cement peaceful relationships among the Indians who exchanged it, and once fashioned into pipes, those pipes became the

FIGURE 4.5 *Uncertain Welcome.* Pike and his comrades arrive at the Pawnee village. Courtesy of Darrell Combs. Painting displayed at the Pawnee Indian Village Museum, Kansas State Historical Society.

prop for ceremonial acknowledgment of bonds, even among foes like the Pawnees and Osages. Smoking together transcended the traditional hostilities. At another level, the Pawnees were welcoming business partners. In contrast to the Osages, Euro-Americans like Pike were a pleasing sight, for commerce with the Europeans and Americans on the periphery of the grasslands had for half a century formed a pillar of the Pawnee economy. Welcoming this diverse assemblage of friend and foe required a complex ceremony of gift and ritual that took up most of the day.[18]

But Pike was no trader. He came to seek alliance with Indians and to gain knowledge of their land to stake his nation's claim to the West. From the Pawnees, he needed food, a safe place to rest, and horses to continue his journey. The horses and corn exchanged that day would help replenish the explorers' dwindling energy reserves and enable Pike to venture beyond the village. Even the pipestone would eventually draw the Indians into the North American commercial world, as British and American companies would annually sell thousands of manufactured catlinite pipes to Plains Indians by the 1860s.[19] Thus, as it had historically, the movement of commodities around the grasslands connected peoples and their environments and knitted their fates into common destinies. At a deeper level, whether they realized it or not, in welcoming Pike and his Osage companions with pipes, and horses, and corn, the Pawnees were also sustaining Pike in his larger objectives, and thus they were also tightening their attachment to an American world.

The Americans were not the only ones interested in incorporating the grasslands. Over dinner, Sharitarish informed Pike that Spaniards had visited the village a few weeks before in pursuit of American explorers. Pike assumed the Spaniards were after him, though they almost certainly sought not him but Lewis and Clark. Nor were arrests their only objective. The Spaniards, too, recognized the importance of controlling faraway rivers and people, and their mission to the Pawnees involved some six hundred men and more than a thousand head of livestock. Their goal resembled Pike's: swaying the Pawnees into their orbit. Just as Pike's expedition had flowed from the pen of Wilkinson's September letter to Dearborn, this Spanish voyage, under the command of Lieutenant Facundo Melgares, came in response to Salcedo's letter the next day. Melgares warned the Pawnees that the Americans were a little people, but enterprising, and that they would soon threaten the Pawnees' lands. Indignantly, Pike wrote to Dearborn that the Spanish expedition aimed to impress the Pawnees with Spanish power and persuade the them to ally with it. To counter such efforts, Pike held a dinner for the chiefs two days later and presented them with gifts, which he "conceived would have a good effect, both as to attaching them to our government, and in our immediate intercourse." In that act, Pike sought to further both the national goals of his expedition and his immediate chances for survival. The Pawnees' world was growing larger. For more than a century, they and their ecosystem had been the object of competitive diplomacy driven by interests that made more sense from the vantage point of Madrid, London, and Paris than from the North American prairies. Now Washington was joining the contest. When Pike learned of Melgares's visit the night of the Pawnee welcome ceremony, he had traveled only twelve miles that day but had gathered news of continental significance. Rested and well-fed after spending a few days at the village, Pike began to inform his generous hosts of American power.[20]

A Spanish flag flew from a staff outside Sharitarish's lodge on the day that Pike chose to convene his "grand council." During the four days Pike had been with the Pawnees, he had orchestrated what he took to be a peace agreement between his Osage companions and a party of Kaws who had come to the village after Pike. Now, he would parley with his hosts. On the twenty-eighth of September, some four hundred Pawnee warriors gathered with the Osages, Kaws, and Americans under the Spanish flag. "My Brothers," Pike addressed the Pawnees, "here is an American Flag which I will present you—but it must never be hoisted by the side of that Spanish one which I desire in return." In addition to the flag, Pike presented other gifts and also declared his intention to travel west to meet with the Comanches. He asked the Pawnees to supply him with some horses for that trip, as well as an interpreter. He also invited some chiefs to accompany him first to the Comanches and then to Washington. The Pawnees agreed to discuss these requests, but were initially silent about the flag. Perhaps they understood that more was at stake than a piece of cloth, that Pike was implying a new set of lifeways as well.[21]

Pike arrived at the Pawnee village during the fall harvest, the most bountiful time of an annual cycle of subsistence that was organized both temporally and spatially and that enabled the villagers to extract energy from a diverse collection of sources that would see them through all but the leanest of Great Plains years. The heart of the Pawnee ecosystem was the village. It was there in the spring that the women cleared fields and planted their gardens with corn, beans, squash, melons, sunflowers, and pumpkins. During the weeks that the women tended the crops, the Pawnees performed the religious ceremonies to ensure a bountiful harvest. Despite tribal ceremonies and women's labor, the local ecosystem supported the Pawnees only partially. By the time of Pike's visit, their horse herds had outgrown the available forage, and by itself, horticulture on the Plains had always been a risky subsistence base on which to depend. So in June or July, once the crops were sufficiently established against weeds, the villagers extended their caloric and nutritional base by moving to the west and southwest, to the hunting grounds between the Platte and the Arkansas rivers. There they hunted bison, whose flesh supplied food and whose body provisioned much of Pawnee material culture. This space was a borderland, with many groups—Comanches, Kiowas, Arapahos, Cheyennes, Wichitas, Kaws—hunting in the area, sometimes harmoniously, sometimes not.[22]

When the prairie goldenrod bloomed in late August, it was time to leave the hunting commons. Sometimes, bands of warriors would detach from the tribe to raid other Plains peoples or the Spanish pueblos of the Rio Grande Valley. These forays further extended the Pawnees' subsistence base by importing horses, captives, and manufactured goods from other ecosystems. Meanwhile, the rest of the tribe went back to the villages for the harvest. There, bison meat was burned in the fields, and offerings of corn were made. Religious ceremonies again accompanied the close of the agricultural cycle. Some of the produce was consumed; the rest was dried and cached for the winter. As the days shortened and temperatures dropped, the Pawnees returned to the western hunting grounds, this time to chase bison, deer, elk, bear, and other creatures for their thick and commercially valuable winter hides, with which the Indians purchased sundries from traders from St. Louis, Santa Fe, and British posts on the upper Mississippi. If their harvest had been bountiful, the tribe would have a little left in the caches to tide them over when they returned to their villages to plant again the next spring.[23]

Like other North American Indians, the Pawnees managed their ecosystem throughout the year. They burned grass in the fall to promote growth of forage the following year. They scattered the seeds of fruits to create orchards on the outskirts of villages. They fallowed their fields to maintain soil fertility. They regulated their collection of wild potatoes, onions, berries, and other plants both to supplement their diet annually and to assure a long-term supply.[24] Thus, Pawnee ecology entailed moving over vast distances, managing the local environment, and tapping the energy and resources of faraway places—from the pipestone quarries of southwestern Minnesota to the plains of western Kansas to the Valley of Mexico to the factories of early industrial Philadelphia and London—to supply what the village environs could not. From their perspective, which flag unfurled at the chief's door mattered little. What mattered was maintaining all the relationships that allowed them to flourish.

To Pike, however, the flag was everything. His aunt had raised one to celebrate the triumph of the Revolution. He had shot down McGillis's near the headwaters of the Mississippi. To him, flags symbolized the republic, and republics used very different strategies for concentrating energy than did Indians. Like the Pawnees, Americans in the early republic sought to tap faraway ecosystems, but they did so primarily by sending emissaries on commercial errands, not by seasonally relocating the people of an entire village. The European and American factories on which the Pawnees increasingly relied in turn depended on an even larger system—the Atlantic world and the flow of commodities between places. But the circulation of energy in the Atlantic worked quite differently. Europeans and Americans, with their land surveys, armies, sailing ships, water wheels, and other ingenious devices for harnessing energy from sun, wind, and water, consumed land voraciously. These technologies also demanded that other peoples give up their traditional methods for concentrating energy. Private property rules assigned plots of land to individuals and restricted everyone else from using them. The hunting commons of the Plains Indians was an alien concept to the new nation-states of the Atlantic world, which were scrambling to mark off boundaries to gain exclusive sovereignty over resources and to ensure that whatever crossed those boundaries profited the state's citizens. As settlers cut down forests to build fences and homes and marked off parcels of private property, Indian seasonal mobility and sharing of territorial sovereignty grew increasingly untenable, first in John Pike's New England, then in Zebulon Pike's Pennsylvania and Anthony Wayne's Ohio, and soon, Zebulon Montgomery Pike intended, on the Great Plains.[25]

The flag Pike offered, then, was an exclusive one, one that reflected republican methods for extracting energy and goals for establishing sovereignty. "After next year," he proclaimed to the Pawnee, "we will not permit Spanish officers, or soldiers, to come into this country to present medals or Flags." To do otherwise would have violated the very core of the Enlightenment concept of the nation: sovereignty. Nations, the era's thinkers posited, were sovereign, internally self-sufficient and externally independent of all other entities. Like Isaac Newton's solar system or Adam Smith's market, nations were to be self-regulating systems that would function in perpetuity as long as there was no external interference. Contested spaces like the Great Plains hunting grounds that were shared by rival powers and where access to resources was not regulated by a single authority presented an uncomfortable anomaly. The United States was willing to take up arms to define its boundary with Spanish Texas; it would not tolerate multiple sovereignties on the Plains any longer than it had to. "The river is ours now," Jefferson had indignantly written in marshaling the power of the federal government to discipline the Potawatomi outrages against the Osages in the Mississippi Valley, and now Pike had come to show that the rivers of the grasslands, too, fell under the sovereignty of the United States.[26] It would not do to have a portion of the nation's land tied to both Madrid and Washington.

What he found, however, was a landscape in which American sovereignty was in fact quite feeble. Although he rejoiced in his diary that the Kaws and Osage "avow themselves to be under the American protection," he complained in a letter to Dearborn of the Melgares expedition's "infringement of our territory." As for the Pawnees, they were "at present decidedly under Spanish influence." He recommended that the United

States remedy that by withholding arms, ammunition, and clothing for a few years and encouraging the Osages and Kaws to harass the Pawnees until they were sufficiently distressed to "feel the necessity of a good understanding with the United States." Restricting the commercial strategies by which the Pawnees extended their own ecosystem would, he believed, persuade them to join the national ecosystem.[27]

Even then, however, US sovereignty would face an additional obstacle in its dependence on waterborne transportation. The Platte and the Kansas rivers were not reliably navigable all the way to the Pawnee villages, he reported. The United States could establish trading posts at the points where the Platte and Kansas rivers joined the Missouri, but to do so would first require "influence sufficient to guarantee to them [the Pawnees] peace and a safe passage through the nations of the Kans, Otoes, and Missouries," who lived between the Pawnees and the Missouri.[28] This, in turn, required making peace among traditional enemies, hence his efforts to reconcile the tribes.

Offering the flag to the Pawnees, then, not only demanded that they sever Spanish ties, but also required that they abandon raiding other Indians, a request to which the Pawnees could not readily assent. Raiding not only tapped distant energy sources and imported meat, slaves, horses, and hides into the Pawnee world, but also shaped power relations within the tribe. It enabled males to display bravery and other masculine traits with which they enhanced their status, and it maintained hierarchies of authority over time. To suggest, as Pike did, that Indians should abandon raiding in favor of participation in an American commercial network was to disrupt both the Pawnees' ecology and their social structure. To Pike, however, raiding, and the intertribal tensions it aggravated, complicated the establishment of American sovereignty, and so he did his best to stamp it out. Expelling Spaniards who sought Louisiana's resources, controlling travel along the rivers, eliminating raiding—these were the steps by which the grasslands would become American. In terms of diplomacy, Pike was entering a contested space for the purpose of bringing it under exclusive American control and removing it from the influence of an imperial rival. Ecologically, the encounter was a clash of two incompatible methods for concentrating energy.

The chiefs' silence about the flag indicated their hostility to such prospects. So Pike reiterated his demand: "My Brothers; You cannot have two Fathers—your former Fathers the Spaniards have now no further Authority over you." This was language the Pawnees could understand. Pike had labored over his speech by the evening campfires, selecting his words carefully, and tediously translating them all into French. He drew upon a wealth of American knowledge about how to talk to Indians. Chasms may have divided native and Euro-American culture in some regards, but in others, their outlooks overlapped considerably. Gender was among these areas of congruence, and here it served Pike well in bridging the Pawnee and postrevolutionary American worlds and their distinct understanding of equality and hierarchy. Pike called the Pawnees brothers, language they and he both would have interpreted to establish bonds among equals. Furthermore, Jefferson usually addressed Indians as children, rhetorically subordinating even chiefs to his authority and thus to the sovereignty of the American state. Consequently, Pike, too, invoked the unequal language of parenthood, demanding that the Pawnees choose between Spanish and American fathers (and implicitly denying the possibility of continued autonomy). In the social contract theory of Pike's era and in the ideology of the American Revolution, Pike was Jefferson's son as well— equal among his citizen brothers, subordinate to Jefferson, the representative of the law of a sovereign state to which they had willingly ceded some of their natural freedom. Fatherhood metaphors would have appealed to the chiefs as well, for in Pawnee society, fathers gave gifts and ensured fairness and social stability. Thus, in invoking both brotherhood and fatherhood, Pike, who had accepted subordination to the state because of the opportunity it gave him to pursue individual life, liberty, and happiness, invited the Pawnee to join him as a brother in relationship with a wise, gift-giving father. Pike had chosen his words well. After a silence of some time, an old man rose. He went to the door of the chief's lodge, took down the Spanish flag, and laid it at Pike's feet. "This," Pike wrote, "gave great satisfaction to the Osage and Kans."[29]

The Pawnees' faces, however, "clouded with sorrow, as if some great national calamity was about to befal them." The bounded, sovereign, regulated, hierarchical national ecosystem that Pike's flag symbolized heralded an ecological revolution. In a nation, the state drew boundary lines on the ecosystem, and it brokered the energy transfer by sanctioning licensed trade and punishing that which was illicit. The flag that Pike offered to the Pawnee on the Republican River at the end of the harvest season heralded property lines to identify who could farm where. It heralded fixed boundaries among peoples to determine who could hunt where. It heralded taxes and courts. It meant few trading partners instead of many. It meant no more raids. It heralded an ecosystem regulated not

by seasons, but by the state. The downfaced Pawnees could not have anticipated all this in detail, but their somber visages indicated they understood enough of Pike's offer to resist it. Sharitarish took the Spanish flag
in his right hand and the American one in his left, declaring that he
esteemed two fathers. He reminded Pike that while the Americans gave
only fragile symbolic gifts, Spaniards gave the Pawnees horses, with which
they hunted and kept themselves alive. He also reiterated Melgares's
warning that the Americans would take Pawnee lands and drive off their
game. Exclusive alliance with the Americans, he understood, would disrupt the Pawnees' balance of farming, hunting, raiding, and commerce.
Even Pike realized, as he wrote in his journal, that his demand that the
Pawnees reject the Spanish flag in favor of the American carried "the pride
of nations a little too far."[30]

More importantly, his demands jeopardized his immediate well-being.
How, Pike wondered, could he with twenty troops hope to compel the
Pawnee cooperation that eluded the Spanish commander with hundreds?
Although he was inaugurating the Pawnees' future attachment to a
national ecosystem, for now he had to survive in the grasslands and was
still subject to its constraints, including the fact that traveling north-south,
perpendicularly to the rivers, required tremendous amounts of energy.
For this, he needed the Pawnees' horses. Perhaps with horses on his mind,
Pike took up the Spanish flag himself and congratulated the Pawnees for
showing themselves to be "dutiful children in acknowledging their great
American father." Assuring them that he did not wish them to "embroil
themselves in any disputes between the white people," he returned the
Spanish colors, warning the Pawnees never to fly them in the presence of
American soldiers. At this the Pawnees burst into cheers and applause.
But the tense negotiations over the flag hint at deeper Pawnee resistance
to submission and the new ecology that would come with it. Pike attributed this resistance to Spanish influence, but it sprang from something
more than affection for Spaniards or even fear of reprisals from Santa Fe.
Rather, it was rooted in a different vision of the ecology of human life and
a desire to retain environmental independence. That resistance, along
with Pike's dependence on the Pawnees, would complicate the part of his
mission that lay beyond their village.[31]

After the parley came the quarrel. On the day following the grand
council, Sharitarish was in a foul mood. Frank, Pike's Pawnee guide who
had been to Washington to meet Jefferson, had come back conceited. He
had flaunted his American medal before the elders, and then he had run

off with the wife of an Osage man who was staying in the chief's lodge. Sharitarish threatened to kill the young man, the insult done to a guest being the same as an insult done to the host. These Americans and their companions were becoming a troublesome lot. The next day, Sharitarish informed Pike that he would not allow the Americans to continue their journey. The Spaniards, too, he said, had wished to venture further into Pawnee territory, and Sharitarish had turned them back. He intended to do the same to Pike. Pike retorted that the "young warriors of his *great American father were not women* to be turned back by *words.*" He intended to proceed, and if Sharitarish tried to stop him, Pike's troops "were *men,* well armed, and would *sell our lives* at a dear rate to his nation." Moreover, Pike threatened, "our *great father* would send our young warriors there to gather our bones and revenge our *deaths* on his people." Sharitarish continued to argue the point, but, finding his words had no effect, concluded that "it was a pity," and was silent. Pike left the chief's lodge and returned to camp, "in considerable perturbation of mind."[32]

The encounter perturbed Sharitarish as well. Like Pike, he had to pursue immediate and long-term goals simultaneously, and the arrival in quick succession of the Spaniards and Americans complicated his predicament. The Pawnee world was rapidly outgrowing his ability to understand or control it. The grasslands had long been an ecologically and culturally dynamic place, but the Pawnees had always held their societies together in the face of centrifugal forces by developing broad and flexible subsistence strategies and social institutions that organized power in the villages. These, however, were disturbed by the challenges represented by interlopers like Pike and Melgares. In recent decades, smallpox had swept through their villages, and Euro-American commerce had led the tribe to live in larger villages and depend more on bison hunting and less on agriculture. Now, in the fall of 1806, Spain and the United States teetered on the brink of war. Troops were massing along the Sabine River in the disputed territory between Texas and Louisiana, and it appeared that the conflict might soon engulf the Pawnee villages in Nebraska. Writing to Wilkinson, Pike observed that it would be easy for soldiers to follow his path with "baggage waggons, field artillery, and all the usual appendages of a small army" en route to Santa Fe. The prospect that the villages and hunting grounds might become way stations for warring empires shuttling between St. Louis and Santa Fe threatened to undermine the strategies with which the Pawnees had coped with their expanding world. Securing a place for his people in this suddenly larger and less stable world

must have weighed heavily on Sharitarish's mind that fall as he responded
to the nearly simultaneous local disruptions caused by Pike and Melgares
as well as the global implications of those visits.[33]

Nor were the local disruptions necessarily trivial to Sharitarish's exercise
of power. In his official report, Pike mistakenly described the Pawnee
chieftainship in concrete and certain terms. It was the same as the Osages',
he said, a hereditary aristocracy, with fathers handing down the position
of chief to sons. Such neat categories satisfied the Enlightenment impulse
toward Linnaean style classification, but they only begin to capture the
complexity of authority in Pawnee society. There were indeed hereditary
chiefs—many of them. Every village had a hereditary chief, who was considered to be a descendent of the founder of the village. There were also
elected chiefs, whom the tribe elevated as a reward for merit or excellent
character. These positions were not heritable. Whatever their path to leadership, however, chiefs of all ranks had limited power, something that Pike
did recognize. "They merely recommend," he observed, "and give counsel
in the great assemblage of the nation." Above all, chiefs like Sharitarish
were responsible for the welfare of their people. Pawnee villages were
voluntary assemblages of families, and they could split at any time that
factions grew incapable of maintaining harmony. New villages (and thus
new chieftainships) could be created by dissenters and old ones could be
dissolved. To hold these loosely knit communities together, generosity,
humility, wisdom, and diplomacy were among the character traits prized
in chiefs.[34]

Sharitarish had emerged as the principal chief of the Republican village
only shortly before the Spanish and American visits. The four bands that
comprised the Pawnee nation—the Skiri (Loup), Chaui (Grand), Kitkahahki
(Republican), and Pitahawirata (Tappage)—had been living on the Platte
River and its tributaries since at least 1600 and perhaps earlier. Prior to
their first mention in European documents, Pawnee history is sketchy, but
it is certain that the Grand Pawnees, who occupied the Loup Fork to the
north, intermittently sought to require the other bands to live under their
protection and rule. Only the Skiris successfully maintained their
independence. In the late eighteenth century, the Republicans lived sometimes among the Grand and sometimes independently. When Pike arrived,
they were independent, a disgruntled warrior having apparently broken
with the Grand Pawnees some years past to establish the village on the
Republican River. This warrior and his followers were joined by Sharitarish,
a Grand Pawnee, who for unknown reasons moved his family to the

Republican village and managed to usurp the chieftainship from the village's founder. Whether Sharitarish was a hereditary chief among the Grand Pawnees and his move was yet another one of that tribe's frequent efforts to incorporate the Republicans or whether he was an elected chief or some other person of ambition who calculated that a move to the Republican village would serve his purposes is unclear. Whatever the chief's motives, Pike identified him as the main leader of the Republican village in 1806, though factions following Sharitarish and the village's founder still coexisted.[35]

Authority in the village was precariously balanced, and Pike's arrival disrupted it. Nothing better exemplified this trouble than his two young Pawnee guides. Both appear to have been men of little consequence until they decided, without tribal consent, to venture east into the expanding world. Somehow, they made it to Washington posing as chiefs and snookered Jefferson into awarding them medals and a letter addressed to the village. Their return threatened traditional authority lines within the village. Offended at their unauthorized sojourn, the villagers scorned the young men and prohibited them from wearing the medals. Frank eloped with the wife of Sharitarish's Osage guest, and the other young man left at some different time. Neither was heard from again. When Pike presented a medal to the second-ranking Pawnee chief, the man refused it, remarking that if similar awards hung from the necks of men as unimportant as the two Pawnee youths, then of what value could such things be? The well-ordered lines of authority among the Pawnees were jeopardized by contact with the larger world. Sharitarish could ill afford to appear overly friendly to the Americans who had brought such chaos to the village.[36]

That meant resisting Pike's immediate needs as well as his nation's larger objectives. The day after his run-in with Sharitarish, Pike and his men attempted to trade for the horses they so badly needed.[37] Several of the mounts they had bought from the Osages had sore backs and needed to be left behind.[38] The men had no luck, however, as Sharitarish had apparently prohibited it. That night, a mounted party of Pawnees raced toward the Americans' camp at full speed as if intent on attack, retreating only at the last possible moment. Such feints became so frequent and menacing that Pike put the camp on guard day and night. The Americans acquired two horses on October 3, but none on the fourth. Finally on the fifth and sixth they managed to purchase enough horses to depart— though Lieutenant Wilkinson called them "miserable horses at the most exorbitant prices."[39]

On the morning of October 7, 1806, the Americans took down their tents and loaded their horses, not knowing whether Sharitarish intended to block their departure by force. Just in case, Pike had taken steps to ensure the Pawnees would pay dearly. His men filed out of camp, mounted and well-armed, their swords drawn. It is not clear what happened next. Lieutenant Wilkinson's account of the parting is too short to be definitive, and Pike's and Sharitarish's versions differ considerably—even the time of day is in dispute. According to Pike, his men rode around the Pawnee village and halted while he went to talk to Sharitarish. The men of the Pawnee village were stirring about with their arms, but there was no sign of a serious attempt to stop the Americans. After taking leave of the chief, Pike joined his party, pausing on a summit above the village for the view that relieved his "burthen."[40]

Sharitarish's version, which he related to American Indian agent George C. Sibley in 1811, was more dramatic. With five hundred warriors, he met Pike's armed party on the Plains. Unarmed, Sharitarish approached Pike and once more tried to dissuade him from proceeding, but Pike remained firm, saying that only death could stop his advance. Sharitarish stood in silence. Pike's men braced themselves in their saddles, while the Indians strung their bows and fixed their arrows. A single word from Sharitarish could have shed much blood. "Brave young chief," he addressed Pike, "you are free to pursue your journey—were I now to stop you by destroying you...I should feel myself a coward." If the "Spanish chief...wishes you stopped let him do it himself if he is able."[41] Pike and his men then rode out of sight, though not out of mind. Sibley reported that five years later, villagers still talked of the brave young American's visit.

Sharitarish's account may well be true. Sibley claimed that Pike himself later confirmed it. If so, it reveals a sagacious chief who diffused a charged moment. By marshaling his warriors and demonstrating beyond doubt that he held Pike's fate in his hands, Sharitarish cast himself as brave, wise, and merciful—brave for standing up to the Americans, wise for not feeling compelled to counter Pike's youthful brashness with violence, merciful for letting the Americans pass unmolested when he could have destroyed them. He also absolved himself of any responsibility to the Spaniards by casting Pike as their problem to solve on their own. In playing peacemaker, Sharitarish preserved his authority among his followers and maintained the village's independence of both Spaniards and Americans. In effect, he restored the lines of authority that Pike's visit had disrupted, and he refused to choose a flag. Even if the account is embellished or untrue, it seems to have been the accepted story in the village at the time of Sibley's visit in 1811, meaning that Sharitarish with this stand, or with some clever revision of community memory, had used Pike's visit to bolster his position in local politics. At the time, the Republican Pawnees were living at the Grand Village, and Sharitarish was the principal of both groups.[42]

As he departed the village, Pike wished the Pawnees no evil, only that "I might be the instrument in the hands of our government, to open their ears and eyes with a strong hand, to convince them of our power."[43] The irony escaped Pike. This first leg of his journey aimed to alter Pawnee reliance on seasons and space and to depend instead on the benevolent dictates of the state. But it was the Pawnees who had fed and restored the hapless Americans and then declined to stop their advance by force. As he worked to incorporate the Pawnees into a national ecosystem, Pike had found himself dependent on theirs.

His encounter with the Pawnees was a clash between two irreconcilable systems for concentrating energy from the environment. In economies that depended entirely on organic fuel sources, as both the Indians and Americans did, everyone had to live within the limits of the energy they could harness from the sun, which ultimately required trade-offs among different land uses. The Pawnees, for example, could not grow pumpkins and chase bison on the same piece of land. They solved this through mobility, migrating seasonally hundreds of miles to tap energy sources in a variety of different ecosystems. Pike's people, in contrast, divided sections of land among individuals who stayed put and extracted whatever they could from those plots, sending their surpluses to market to acquire whatever their own parcels did not supply. In native society, work—the labor that concentrated energy—implied no rights beyond the usage of the resulting energy; in Pike's world, work conferred nearly absolute ownership of the property and the right to prevent other people from using it or passing through. Because seasonal mobility required that many people be able to use land at different times while private property required single owners who used it at all times, Pawnee mobility was inimical to the promise of yeoman farming after the Revolution that had fired the dreams of Jefferson and Pike's parents. These two methods for concentrating energy could not long coexist.[44]

The long run favored the republic. Ships, mills, property lines, land surveys, armies, slave labor, and markets were building an American engine that could harness much of the continent's energy—and eventually the world's—and convert it into wealth. Even Pike's sojourn among the Pawnees foreshadowed his nation's future triumph in this contest. The inflated prices the Pawnees had managed to extract from Pike in exchange for supplying him the horsepower necessary to travel overland on the Plains tied the tribe just a little more tightly to the United States. To pay for the horses, Pike gave the Pawnees notes that were redeemable only by taking them to American officials in St. Louis. Thus, even in getting the better end of a horse swap, the Pawnees inched closer into dependence on the American government, on which they now relied to recoup Pike's debts. By the 1830s, only a generation after Pike's visit, the accumulation of many such small defeats, plus the combination of smallpox and other diseases, warfare with the Dakotas and Oglalas, and Euro-American market penetration had reduced the Pawnees to a dependent people. By treaty in 1833, the Pawnees ceded much of their territory, gave up their weapons, and agreed to live as a sedentary farming people in exchange for annual annuities, supplies, agricultural training, and military protection from the US government.[45]

But on the Republican River in 1806, Pike could tap none of this American power. The Pawnees were still masters of their country and made Pike return the flag, pay high prices for horses, and clench his white knuckles around the reigns as he rode out of town. The young republic could muster the wherewithal to launch him from St. Louis, but he did not travel far before passing beyond the United States' ability to support the journey, and after leaving the Osage villages, his energy needs began to outstrip his capacity to meet them on his own. Pike's struggles to incorporate the Osages and Pawnees into a national ecosystem, a failure borne of his material dependence on them, reveals the physical limits of the nation's ability in 1806 to impose nationalist order on remote, independent people. When there were no Pawnees around to help him, he would be in trouble.

Across the Plains

From the Pawnee village, Pike crossed the Plains looking for the Comanches and the Arkansas River. As he made his way south and then west, he chose to follow the Spaniards, despite their intent to arrest foreigners like him. After departing the Pawnee village, Melgares's party had returned to Santa Fe along a route probably well-known to their guides as well as to generations of native peoples, but to which Pike was oblivious. As the Americans followed the Spaniards' several-week-old path across the Plains, Pike's men counted the remains of the Spanish campfires and piles of livestock manure. By this crude calculation, Pike guessed he was following a contingent in which both livestock and men numbered at least in the hundreds. Bringing their own food and energy supply on their journey not only secured the Spaniards' temporary place in the Great Plains environment, but the enormous herds of men and beasts left an unmistakable scar of ashes, beaten-down grass, and animal droppings, which, even weeks later, were frequently visible to Pike. In the grasslands, which were so stingy in meeting visitors' needs, everyone required food, fuel, and water. Since these could be found easily in only a few spots, there were actually few places that human strangers were likely to go. To find them, Pike decided to follow the Spaniards, calculating "that they had good guides, and were on the best route for wood and water." Pike now depended on the very people who were after him.[46]

When the Americans reached the Arkansas River in mid-October, they paused for ten days while the men fashioned two canoes, one from a small cottonwood and another from the hides of bison and elk, and the party prepared to divide. During the respite, Pike recorded one of his journal's few scientific observations—a lengthy description of a prairie dog—and also wrote to General Wilkinson, reporting himself to be in a "positive mood" and his men as being in "good spirits." He compared the feats of his voyages to those of Lewis and Clark and asked whether he had been promoted to captain, a wish that would be granted within a few weeks, without his knowledge. If so, he hoped the expedition's soldiers would be attached to his company when he returned, and he asked the general to use "his influence" to obtain for them "the same, or similar rewards, to those who accompanied Capt. Lewis." On October 28, Lieutenant Wilkinson, five soldiers, and the two Osages who remained with the party launched the boats to head downstream and back to the United States. They carried letters and copies of maps and other records documenting the expedition's route and findings. Lieutenant Wilkinson, however, was hardly in the "good spirits" Pike attributed to him. Bitter that Pike had not divided the provisions to his liking, he complained that in "Stores, Ammunition, Boats & Men" he was "perhaps more illy equipd than any other Officer, who ever was on Command." Indeed, his detachment suffered numerous hardships before making it home.[47]

Later that day, Pike and the fifteen men who remained in his party began to make their way up the Arkansas River, aiming to find its headwaters.

Traveling by foot and horseback, they rose most days before the sun and camped an hour or so before it set.[48] The horses were heavily laden with tools, supplies, and the dried meat from game the men killed. As the men plodded upstream, the banks of the river swarmed with bison. On November 4, Pike estimated a herd to number three thousand animals, and on the sixth, the party "feasted sumptuously" on the meat of a cow that he declared was the "equal to any meat I ever saw." As the November days grew shorter, the leaves of cottonwoods that grew along the water courses glistened gold in the afternoons. The first snow fell, and forage grew scarce. A few of the horses gave out. The party also saw signs of Indian war parties and thereafter advanced, "with rather more caution than usual."[49]

"*Voila un savage*," Vasquez's cry rang out on the twenty-second, breaking the morning silence. Suddenly Indians were everywhere. Some ran from the cottonwoods and willows that lined the riverbank. Others circled up onto a promontory above. Pike no sooner got off his horse to greet them than someone mounted it and galloped away. Similar misfortunes immediately befell his comrades. As the chaos settled and the marauders returned the horses, Pike learned that the Indians were a Pawnee war party, returning from an unsuccessful search for Comanches. There were sixty of them, half with guns, the rest with bows and arrows, and they seemed undecided as to whether Pike was friend, foe, or prey. Pike feared they would vent their frustration upon any easy target.

To placate them, he offered tobacco, knives, fire steels, and flints. They called for ammunition, corn, blankets, and kettles. Pike refused. He needed such items to acquire and conserve energy in this difficult land. Everyone smoked, drank, and ate, and then Pike got up to leave. As the Americans packed the horses, the Pawnees tossed the presents away in disgust, and several pairs of grasping hands surrounded each soldier. They snatched pistols and tomahawks. Axes, canteens, and a sword all melted into the fray. Pike managed to mount his horse and shout a threat into the air, loud enough to be heard. He would kill the next man who touched the baggage. The Pawnees withdrew. The Americans rode on and by nightfall put twelve miles between themselves and the site of their humiliation.

That evening, Pike reflected on the day. He felt "mortified, that the smallness of my number obliged me thus to submit to the insults of a lawless banditti, it being the first time ever a savage took any thing from me, with the least appearance of force."[50] To Pike, the attack represented lawlessness, but it looked different from the Pawnees' perspective. Raiding was another stage in their annual ecological cycle. After this party's attempt

FIGURE 4.6 Pike encountered the Pawnee War party in the vicinity of this spot, not far from modern Nepesta, Colorado. Photo by author.

to acquire resources by raiding the Comanches had failed, Pike's party presented an opportunity for the dispirited warriors to compensate for the breakdown of their regular ecological strategies, and maybe to save some face among the villagers at home. Pike, with his small force and his dependence on the vital energy contained in his dwindling stores of powder and corn could neither appease them with gifts nor stop them by force. Indeed, he was fortunate not to lose even more than he did. Thus, he endured the theft of one of the postrevolutionary world's dearest things: property. And that truly rankled his sensibilities. The trouble was, the gridded lines that divided Pike's property from the Pawnees', that divided American commerce from Spanish commerce, that divided allegiances to the United States from allegiances to Spain, and that divided the lands over which the flags of nation-states flew held no sway in the grasslands. Pike and his men had once again passed beyond their nation's influence and ability to protect them. For the next three months they would see no one—American, Indian, or Spaniard—and there would be times when they would have welcomed almost any sort of company. To support themselves from here on, they could rely only on each other and whatever their minds and bodies could wrest from the land.

5

"Frozen Lads"

INTO THE ROCKIES,
NOVEMBER 1806–FEBRUARY 1807

PIKE HAD NO more success finding the Comanches than the Pawnee raiders did, but on November 15, he saw something else. Riding ahead of the caravan, at around two o'clock he spotted a "small blue cloud" on the horizon. Lifting his spy glass to his eye, he supposed it to be a mountain. At first, he mentioned his suspicions only to Doctor Robinson, but within half an hour there was no concealing the discovery. Everyone could see it. The party paused on the prairie and raised "three *cheers* to the *Mexican mountains.*" Their destination was in sight. Two days later the party broke camp and "pushed with an idea of arriving at the mountains." At nightfall, however, Pike could detect "no visible difference in their appearance." Although he found the mountains "easily . . . imagined" and familiar to all "who have crossed the Alleghany," he did not really understand what he was seeing. He had not yet acclimated himself to the long sightlines, clear air, and soaring heights of the West. The possibility that he could see a mountain and still be more than a hundred miles away from it was not something he could wrap his Ohio Valley mind around.[1]

Underestimating the aerial distance to the crest he called the Grand Peak was only the first mistake Pike made about the Rockies. The pinnacle was not a day's march away, or even a week's. The mountains were nothing like the Alleghenies. And the men were not going home any time soon. More than two months would elapse before they escaped the mountains. In the interim, Pike attempted to climb the summit without food, blankets, or socks. He led men wearing cotton summer uniforms into the mountains on the morning of winter's first blizzard. Three times, he crossed chains of mountains without needing to do so. He left frostbitten men in the snow, contemplated suicide in the wilderness, threatened to

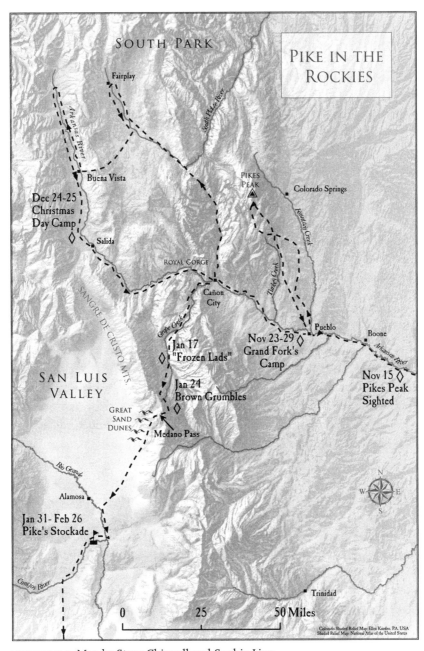

FIGURE 5.1 Map by Steve Chignell and Sophia Linn.

execute a malingerer, and raised an American flag on Spanish soil. Although such behavior was sufficiently strange to have provoked charges of secret orders and even treason, in fact, Pike's terrible ordeal in the mountains underscored his commitment to sacrificing for the nation.

The Grand Peak

Since leaving the Pawnee village, national service had weighed heavily on Pike's mind. As dawn broke on October 17, a steady rain fell and a cold northwest wind blew. He and Robinson were alone, having lost the party two days before. They did not reunite with their comrades that day, and by nightfall Pike's "sensations now became excruciating." First he calculated his dwindling ammunition. Then his mind fixed on the "400 miles" that separated them "from the first civilized inhabitant." Finally he contemplated the possibility of being "cut off by the savages." The predicament jeopardized not only the men's "personal safety" but also "the national objects intended to be accomplished by the expedition." Two weeks later on November 4, after the party had regained its bearings, Pike and his men observed the anniversary of Arthur St. Clair's disastrous defeat in Ohio in 1791. As they paused on the prairie to recall the "fate of our countrymen," Pike and his men were momentarily connected to their distant nation by an anniversary—the kind of event that might have been commemorated in eastern streets or taverns with toasts, processions, speeches, or other tributes by which Americans celebrated heroic national sacrifice and tightened the bonds that made them a nation. Out on the Plains, however, Pike might have recalled his father's stories of the tragedy—how poorly trained men, with thin bonds to each other, and their commanders had panicked and how their lack of fortitude and cohesion turned into a rout when they broke ranks and fled. Now the nation was asking Pike to lead men to stick together and sacrifice with fortitude. On November 11, as the horses weakened and the nights grew chillier, he acknowledged the "impossibility of performing the voyage in the time proposed." But even if he had to spend another winter in the wilderness, he "determined to spare no pains to accomplish every object."[2]

But what *were* the national objects? On the day he resolved to spare no pains, he could already check off many of the tasks Wilkinson had given him. He had transported the Osage captives and the delegation of chiefs to their homes. He had detained unlicensed traders. He had mediated peace between the Kaws and Osages. He had visited the Pawnees. And he had mapped the land and taken latitude and longitude measurements along the way. Although he had not yet located the Comanches, he was headed into their territory. A final set of elliptical instructions remained. "As your Interview with the Cammanchees will probably lead you to the Head Branches of the Arkansaw, and Red Rivers," Wilkinson had directed, as if adding the rivers as an after-thought, "you may find yourself approximate to the settlements of New Mexico." In that case, "You should move with great circumspection" and "keep clear of any...parties from that province." Spanish-American rela-tions, he reminded Pike, were for the moment amicable. To keep them so, Pike was to "prevent alarm or offence." In spite of this injunction, the general added in a subsequent paragraph, "It is an object of much Interest with the Executive, to ascertain the Direction, extent, & naviga-tion of the Arkansaw, & Red Rivers; as far therefore as may be compat-ible with these Instructions and practicable to the means you may Command, I wish you to carry your views to those subjects, and should circumstances conspire to favour the enterprize...you, yourself may descend the Red River...to the post of Natchitoches."[3] Wilkinson never told Pike explicitly to follow the rivers into the mountains. The instruc-tions to explore the two rivers at all were buried as side comments in passages about avoiding the Spanish and furthering the president's interests in exploration. If he reread Wilkinson's letter on November 11, as he decided to advance upstream despite the lateness of the season, Pike would have found only oblique official instructions that left him considerable discretion regarding if and how to carry them out.

Pike could not have known that day that Thomas Jefferson was about to receive a firecracker of a letter. The author was James Wilkinson and the subject was Aaron Burr. In August 1806, Burr headed west from Philadelphia likely intending to raise a private army and attack Mexico. Should that fail, his backup plan was to settle a property he was about to acquire on the Ouachita River, known as the Bastrop parcel. Burr had not yet raised adequate funding for the expedition. Nor had he secured mili-tary support from Britain or any European power. And he had been rebuffed by Commodore Thomas Truxton and Captain William Eaton, disgruntled former military heroes whom Burr had tried to interest in the schemes. Still, the timing seemed auspicious. Relations with Spain had worsened in July, when Spanish soldiers crossed the Sabine River into territory claimed by the United States. Conflict with Spain transformed Burr's plan from illegal conspiracy into patriotic adventuring, and gave it legitimacy among prominent westerners.[4]

Consequently, as Burr crossed the Pennsylvania mountains and descended the Ohio River, he was confident he could enlist financial support and military participation from discontented westerners, who were not hard to come by. He talked to aspiring politicians and courted the sons of military officers. From western Pennsylvania, according to one report, he recruited a "considerable number of single men of conspicuous parentage," men not unlike Pike. Among his first stops was a visit to Harman Blennerhassett, a wealthy Irish attorney who had immigrated to the United States to escape sanction for his illegal marriage to his niece. Near Marietta, the couple took refuge at an estate on an Ohio River island, which Blennerhassett named for himself, an ideal location at which to conceal not only consanguinity but filibustering preparations as well. In a December 1805 letter, the ambitious Blennerhassett had assured Burr that he would "be honored in being associated with you, in any contemplated enterprise you would permit me to participate in" and promised to contribute a small amount of funding toward the project. Burr spent two busy days at Blennerhassett's Island in late August. He hired boat makers to construct vessels and stockpiled foodstuffs and other provisions, enough for the five hundred men Burr said would rendezvous at the island in early December. All was paid for by the credulous attorney, who bought Burr's stories, too. Next, Burr courted prominent westerners in Cincinnati and Frankfurt and then went to Nashville, where he solicited additional vessels and supplies from Andrew Jackson, then commander of the Tennessee militia. Initially, Jackson complied, but he later grew suspicious. He had heard the rumors that Burr's plans included separating the western states from the union. He assented to Burr's request, however, once the former vice president assured him that the expedition targeted Mexico, not the United States, a claim that must have seemed plausible as tensions on the Sabine thickened and the number of Spanish troops on the American side continued to rise. War seemed imminent.[5]

In the confusion, Wilkinson either lost his nerve for going down the line with Burr or saw a better opportunity. Gossip about Burr's secessionist intentions often implicated the general, and it was a bad time for Wilkinson to be associated with unpatriotic activities. He was unpopular in St. Louis and whispered to be a Spanish agent. Word from the East held that Jefferson planned to phase the scoundrel out as territorial governor. With the June arrival of Dearborn's orders for Wilkinson to quit the seat of government in St. Louis and move down the Mississippi in order to repel the anticipated Spanish aggression on the Sabine,

Wilkinson believed he was being eased out as governor. He had two choices. Burr's plans required a war, and Wilkinson had the power to make one. He could provoke hostilities with Spain and join Burr's filibustering in Mexico, knowing that European support had not materialized. Or he could jump Burr's sinking ship and devise some way to stay in the good graces of his two patrons, the United States government and the King of Spain. If Wilkinson was being honest when he rhetorically asked Samuel Smith in June, "Do I expect a war? Surely not," then the general had already made up his mind to choose his patrons over Burr. Dramatically descending the Mississippi to Natchitoches, where he arrived in September, Wilkinson prepared to confront the Spanish forces led by Simón Herrera.[6]

In early October, he received a letter written in code, purportedly from Burr, that claimed the former vice president had obtained military backing from England and that he would deliver five hundred to a thousand westerners to Natchez by early December, ready to embark on whatever Wilkinson deemed "expedient." The plan appeared to be to capture Louisiana and Mexico and to set up a new kingdom in which "Wilkinson shall be second to Burr only and Wilkinson shall dictate the rank and promotion of his officers." This was the infamous cipher letter, which—if Burr was the author—apparently implicated the former vice president in treason. The letter was not from Burr, at least not most of it, and Wilkinson likely guessed as much, but he immediately recognized in it a golden opportunity. Doctoring the letter to condemn Burr and absolve himself, Wilkinson prepared to publicize it. Tilting at imaginary enemies would be easier than challenging real ones.[7]

On October 21, he wrapped himself in the flag and wrote to Jefferson, warning that an army was headed toward New Orleans with the intent of capturing the city en route to an invasion of Spanish provinces. The general promised to resolve the Sabine conflict quickly in order to divert his troops to defend the city. Over the next two weeks, Wilkinson concluded an ingenious peace with the Spaniards. Under the agreement, which was reached on November 5, he pulled his troops back to Natchitoches, and Herrera retreated to the west bank of the Sabine. Until the nations' politicians could settle the matter, neither army would occupy the so-called neutral ground in between. Although Wilkinson did not know it at the time, Jefferson had already sent him instructions to make exactly such arrangements. Yet again, the wily general had managed to cloak a personal scheme in the garb of national interests.[8]

Wilkinson's letter reached Jefferson on November 25, a week before the president's scheduled annual message to Congress. He had been aware of rumors about Burr since January 1806 and had lifted not a finger, perhaps waiting for Burr to commit some act that would sour public sentiment. He came to the brink of action in late October, but suddenly tabled his plans to stop Burr. The letter from Wilkinson, the commander of the United States army, however, converted rumor into official report, and Jefferson could delay no longer. Still, however, he moved cautiously. On the twenty-seventh, he issued a public statement acknowledging the existence of a filibustering expedition and called on officials and citizens to oppose it, but devoted only one paragraph of his December 2 congressional address to the matter. He further downplayed the issue when he refrained from naming either Burr as the instigator or Wilkinson as the informant, thus concealing, if only thinly and momentarily, the high profile of the cast of characters.[9]

On the day Jefferson addressed Congress, Aaron Burr found himself in a courtroom in Kentucky. The rumors of treason had prompted Joseph Hamilton Daveiss, a federal district attorney, to charge Burr with violating a 1794 federal law prohibiting private parties from attacking nations with which the United States was at peace. After a month of summonses, hearings, dismissals, and more summonses, the grand jury rejected indictment on December 5. Over the next week, the homes of prominent Kentuckians filled with revelers, who toasted Burr's victory. Meanwhile, a flotilla of armed supporters slipped away from Blennerhassett's Island shortly after midnight on December 10 and began rendezvousing with other backers until the expedition numbered twelve boats and about a hundred people—far fewer than the number purported in the cipher letter. That same day, Burr left Kentucky for a second conference with Jackson and then headed for New Orleans. But before he reached the city, he learned that Wilkinson was one step ahead of him.[10]

Despite the acquittal, the parties, and the boats, Burr's window of opportunity had already closed. The crisis on the Sabine had abated. The cover for a filibuster was gone. With the neutral ground settlement, Wilkinson had renewed his patriotic credentials and now moved to burnish them by fabricating and then dismantling a Burr plot to splinter the union. On November 12, he wrote a second letter to Jefferson reiterating that the enterprise aimed to capture New Orleans. On the thirteenth, he dispatched his aide Walter Burling to Mexico City to inform the Spanish viceroy that Wilkinson had foiled a diabolical plot against the crown.

For good measure, the general also demanded a reward of 121,000 pesos. Cheeky. Meanwhile, Wilkinson moved his troops to New Orleans. He announced the news of Burr's advancing hordes, declared martial law, and detained Burr's supporters, preparing for the arrest of Burr himself. Thus, in the fall of 1806, Jefferson was dithering in Washington. Wilkinson was writing urgent letters from the Southwest. Boatloads of Burr's friends were floating down the Mississippi, while the former vice president himself was proceeding to New Orleans in hopes of salvaging his plans or at least eluding jail. And on the Great Plains, Zebulon Pike was ascending the Arkansas River, the Grand Peak in his sights, and gathering data about western geography—for someone.[11]

Exactly for whom, perhaps he did not know. Shortly after leaving St. Louis, and four months before sighting the Grand Peak rising from the Plains, Pike himself had given some murky evidence that his expedition might have involved more than following rivers to their headwaters and coming back. Six days into his journey, he received a letter from Wilkinson once again admonishing Pike to avoid alarming the Spaniards. The next day, July 22, Pike penned a response in which he expressed confusion about how to follow those directions. The instructions to meet with the Comanches, he wrote, would lead him toward territory "which is no Doubt claimed by Spain." To cope with this, he proposed deception. If he were to meet any Spaniards in the vicinity of Santa Fe, he would "give them to understand that we were bound to join our Troops near Natchitoches but had been uncertain about the Head Waters of the Rivers over which we passd." If pressed, Pike suggested, he would pay a "visit of politeness" to Spanish authorities, for a trip into Spanish provinces would also "gratify our most sanguine expectations." In other words, Pike planned to tell them he was lost and looking for the Red River to return home.[12]

Getting a look at Louisiana's critical river geography, especially if it occasioned a peek at Santa Fe, would have been of immense value to Burr and Wilkinson. It would have allowed Pike to scout the way to the heart of Spain's northern holdings and assess the military defenses of the region and the loyalties of its people. Or an arrest by Spaniards might trigger an international incident to provide legitimacy for Burr's would-be filibusterers. These might have been the "sanguine expectations" to which Pike referred. Indeed, in his letter to Pike, Wilkinson seemed eager for geographical reports from Pike as soon as possible. But Wilkinson had likely already decided to betray Burr before Pike departed from St. Louis, possibly quite some time earlier. If so, he did not send Pike up the Arkansas for Burr but for Wilkinson. The information Pike could gather in New Mexico and near the headwaters of Louisiana's southwestern rivers could open lucrative Santa Fe commerce to Wilkinson or give him a leg up on competitors to control the fur trade on the as-yet untrapped Arkansas and Red. It might also give him leverage in manipulating the Spaniards and make him indispensable to Jefferson. Or maybe all of these. Pike's reconnaissance could have many benefits for an opportunist like James Wilkinson, useful enough for the general to give his eager lieutenant secret orders to find Santa Fe.[13]

Or not. Pike's instructions and the expedition itself also fit squarely within the larger context of Jeffersonian exploration. After visiting Kaskaskia in 1803, Meriwether Lewis had told Pike that Jefferson planned many expeditions and intimated that Pike might get to lead one. In the meantime, Lewis and Clark had gone and returned. Pike had been up the Mississippi River. Jefferson had sent George Hunter and William Dunbar to explore the Ouachita River in the fall of 1805. And the president had reported enthusiastically to Congress on the results of these western voyages of discovery in January 1806. Later that spring, a party led by Thomas Freeman, Peter Custis, and Richard Sparks set out to explore the Red River, and Jefferson would contemplate an Arkansas expedition in 1807. When Pike returned from Minnesota, Jefferson took great interest in his journal and pushed to have it published and distributed to members of Congress.[14] In the context of presidential enthusiasm for western discovery, a patriot like Pike could easily associate his own travels with the national objects that he mulled over on the prairie in October and that Jefferson had described to Congress back in January.

Perhaps, then, on November 11, as he pondered the lateness of the season and the unknown distance to his destination, Pike had nothing to guide him but what Wilkinson's instructions precisely said: the rivers are of interest to the president; explore them if you can; and stay away from the Spaniards. Even without secret orders to get to Santa Fe, Pike had a history of overstepping commands. Marching upriver toward the Grand Peak without an explicit mandate to do so would not be the first or last time he tested his mettle, and his men's, by disregarding cautious directives and going the extra mile (and many more besides) in service to his nation. Perhaps chagrined by this reputation, Pike had concluded his July 22 letter with an apology for the "enthusiasm of a youthful mind" and a promise to exercise "prudence."[15] If Wilkinson wanted to send someone to

Santa Fe without the explorer knowing the purpose of the expedition, Zebulon Montgomery Pike was his man.

Whatever Pike's objectives, they could be advanced by climbing the Grand Peak. Four days after resolving to spare no pains, he sighted the mountain, later to be named Pikes Peak, and he must have decided immediately to climb it, for it preoccupied him for the next week. He marched intently for it on November 17 and was disheartened to gain no apparent ground. On the eighteenth he halted the party to rest the horses, lay in a supply of meat, and chart the mountains. After putting the hunters to the chase, Pike ascended a small hill not far from the south bank of the Arkansas River, near the place that would come to be known as Rocky Ford, a choice crossing among future travelers. From that promontory, he sketched the peaks—several of them were by now visible—and took compass readings for each. Meanwhile, the hunters killed seventeen bison that day, yielding nine hundred pounds of meat for the trail—enough, Pike estimated, to last a month. He evidently intended continuing the journey for some time. The next day, the party preserved the meat and rested the weary horses, the dwindling number of whom would now have the extra weight of bison flesh distributed among them.[16]

FIGURE 5.2 From Pike's camp at the "Grand Forks" in what is now Pueblo, Colorado, Pikes Peak looms to the north, looking rather like the "height of land." The triangular peak to the right, Mount Rosa, would play a role in Pike's adventures in the upcoming days. Photo by Brian Lenz.

Reprovisioned, Pike once again looked toward the Grand Peak. On the twenty-third, he halted the party in the Y of what he called the Grand Forks, the confluence of the Arkansas and Fountain Creek. Fountain Creek rises northwest of Colorado Springs and flows southeast over a fault between Pikes Peak and the Rampart Range. Then it bends south along the face of the mountains and joins the Arkansas near the heart of what is today Pueblo, Colorado. From the area around the camp, the summit of the Grand Peak was in easy view. With no one around to ask about it, Pike drew on the store of Enlightenment geographical knowledge he carried in his mind from St. Louis. The size, shape, and contents of the little-known but vividly imagined western half of North America had long fascinated geographers, and a considerable body of fact and fantasy about it had accumulated since the late seventeenth century. One of the leading devotees of Enlightenment geography was Thomas Jefferson. Another was James Wilkinson. The two of them collected maps, interrogated travelers, and read widely in the many works that speculated on the locations of rivers, mountains, and a wide variety of incredible phenomena believed to fill the West. Pike, who also read widely and carried maps on his journey, had been exposed to much of this knowledge, as his 1804 *Medical Repository* article had indicated.

At the core of this knowledge was the concept of continental symmetry. This theory, which took hold among British geographers and cartographers in the first half of the eighteenth century, was still prominent in the early nineteenth among men like Aaron Arrowsmith, a leading cartographer of North America, whose work formed part of the map that Jefferson commissioned for Meriwether Lewis and William Clark to take with them to the Pacific. Lewis also carried Arrowsmith's 1802 map of the interior parts of North America. Jefferson and other adherents of continental symmetry held that a great western river, likely the Missouri, must drain the western interior portion of the continent, in the same way the Ohio drained the eastern interior. Like the Ohio's tributaries, the western river's sources must originate near those of the streams that coursed to the Pacific, providing easy connections between the waters of the interior and those of the western coast. A chain of western mountains—about the size of the Alleghenies and Appalachians and a similar distance from the coast— supposedly gave rise to the rivers. Arrowsmith's 1795 map of North America estimated the range to rise 3,520 feet from its base.[17]

Another idea fashionable among Enlightenment geographers was the imagined height-of-land, a steep, high-altitude area from which the great western rivers flowed. First to posit it were French geographers and explorers. Robert Rogers, a Briton who planned to search for a water route across North America in the 1760s, was also an early proponent of this idea, but Pike was probably most familiar with the concept through the work of one of Roger's companions, Jonathan Carver, whose much embellished book *Three Years Travels Through the Interior Parts of North America* Pike had read during his Minnesota journey. Carver claimed to have learned from several Indian tribes, "as far as it was possible to arrive at a certainty without a personal investigation," that the continent's "four great rivers," the Nelson, the St. Lawrence, the Mississippi, and the Columbia, all "take their rise within a few leagues of each other, nearly about the center of this great continent," and flow from the "highest lands in North-America" for two thousand miles along "separate courses" to the seas. Pike himself had speculated in his *Medical Repository* article that the Missouri River and the waters of the Pacific might flow from a single alpine lake.[18]

From Pike's camp at the forks, the Grand Peak must have looked like the height of land. It rose precipitously from the plain and dwarfed surrounding summits. Large rivers, including tributaries of the Arkansas, issued from its slopes, and snow crowned its top. Though still forty-five miles to the northwest, so magnificent a massif looked much closer to a man who expected it to be smaller and had already compared it to the Alleghenies. He decided to park his men in a "defensible situation" and climb "to the high point of the blue mountains." Early on November 24, the men cut down fourteen trees to build a small defensive structure. It was five feet high on three sides, the fourth facing the point of the river. The breastwork completed, he gave instructions to govern the men in his absence and in case of his failure to return.[19]

Climbing the peak was no mere sport. Rather, it was essential to the national objects. Summiting it would enable Pike to "lay down the various branches and positions of the country." From a crest that high, he hoped to see the headwaters of the Arkansas, the Platte, and the Red, and maybe the Missouri, Yellowstone, Rio Grande, and Colorado as well, the river geography that defined the geopolitical borders within North America. Calling the high country around the peak "that grand reservoir of snows and fountains," his subsequent report to Congress asserted he could "take a position in the mountains from whence I can visit the source of any of those rivers in one day." Assuming with Arrowsmith and others that the mountains rose but three thousand feet above him, he took Robinson,

Private John Brown, and Private Theodore Miller, and marched at one o'clock in the afternoon, expecting to reach the mountain by evening and to climb it and return the next day.[20]

The would-be climbers camped that night on the prairie, under a lone cedar tree, far from water and still a long distance from the mountain's base. It was very cold. The next day, Pike grew impatient with Fountain Creek, which paralleled the front of the range and led the party north but gained them no ground toward the west. So the men struck out overland to diagonal over to the foothills. Yet again they marched expecting to summit the peak but only reached the mouth of a small drainage, Little Fountain Creek, by nightfall. They camped at the point where the Great Plains meets the Rocky Mountains, and Pike took a meridian observation and the altitude of the Grand Peak. He did not record the results, but if he calculated with even rough accuracy, he must have been surprised to find it surpassed 14,000 feet. On the morning of the twenty-sixth, underestimating the size and distance of the peak one last time, they cached their food and blankets and began climbing, expecting to return to their provisions at night.[21]

It was a hard climb. For all of the ten hours of daylight the sun gave them, they labored. Starting from a base elevation of about 6,600 feet, they hiked up drainages and contoured hillsides. Sometimes, Pike wrote, the rocks were "almost perpendicular." By the late afternoon, as the last rays of sun melted behind the mountains, the party came to a steep slope. The Grand Peak had remained hidden from view all day, blocked by intervening lesser peaks. Perhaps to get a look at the terrain that separated them from their objective, they started up the slope, toward a pinnacle that appeared to be the highest promontory in the vicinity. The ascent was fierce, requiring the foursome to hoist themselves up a sheer face and grasp with their wearying limbs the jagged edges of boulders and the branches of fallen trees. Sometimes, perhaps, they contoured to ease the steepness and then switched back to maintain upward progress. For perhaps thirty or forty minutes they battled the slope before coming to a cave, a crevice really, just big enough for four tired, hungry men without blankets. With daylight waning and the temperature falling, they crowded into this rocky hostel to share body heat while they tossed and wriggled all night, seeking a comfortable surface on which to sleep, somewhat sheltered from the late-fall chill.[22]

They awoke the next morning, Thanksgiving Day, to a sublime view. Clouds overhung the endless prairies stretching out to the east, while the

FIGURE 5.3 The only cave on the eastern side of Mount Rosa, this is probably the one Pike, Robinson, Miller, and Brown slept in on the night of November 26. Coming from the direction Pike did and picking the easiest route up the steep, wooded, boulder-strewn slope, climbers commonly happen on this spot. Photo by Jessica Murski.

sky above them was clear and blue. The panorama resembled "the ocean in a storm; wave piled on wave." Hungry and sore but dry, the climbers resumed their ascent. It was easier at first, as they reached the shoulder of the mountain in a few minutes and then commenced a half-hour walk along the ridgeline toward the cone of the peak. Then it was back to boulder scrambling and hoisting themselves by crags and branches, soon in snow waist deep. Another half hour of this brought them to the top of Mount Rosa, at 11,500 feet the highest in the chain of peaks southeast of Pikes Peak and affording a 360-degree view that revealed a sight as awesome as it was dispiriting. "The Grand Peak," Pike recorded, "now appeared at the distance of 15 or 16 miles from us, and as high again as what we had ascended, and would have taken a whole day's march to have arrived at its base, when I believe no human being could have ascended to its pinical."[23]

Today, self-congratulatory Coloradans delight in claiming that Pike thought the peak would never be climbed. Well-fed modern hikers enjoying

FIGURE 5.4 Pikes Peak, from Mt. Rosa summit. Photo by author.

the benefits of plastic, nylon, Thinsulate, and Gortex have had little difficulty accomplishing what Pike could not. Deeper understanding of the context of Pike's description of the summit, however, reveals that he intended to say only that the summit could not be reached *under the circumstances* that beleaguered his party. That is, men who had not eaten in thirty-some hours, who had no blankets or socks, and who lacked the provisions to bear another day in the wilderness could not climb it. He made this context clear when he added, "This with the condition of my soldiers who had only light overalls on, and no stockings, and every way ill provided to endure the inclemency of the region; the bad prospect of killing any thing to subsist on, with the further detention of two or three days, which it must occasion, determined us to return." Descending Mt. Rosa's steep slopes by an easier route, they made it back to their base camp on the plain that night and ate for the first time in forty-eight hours. Exhausted, they slept until nine o'clock the next morning and then hiked two days back to the breastwork at the point of the Grand Forks and "found all well."[24]

In addition to the cotton overalls that comprised the US Army's summer garb, Pike brought much to the front of the mountains.[25] In his trunk of papers, he carried Wilkinson's elliptical instructions, which encouraged him toward the mountains, despite Spain's claim of sovereignty over them. He also carried a copy of his reply proposing a daring alibi should he stumble upon Spaniards. By the coincidental timing of his voyage, he carried an association with a mysterious conspiracy involving land and war and maybe treason. In his head, he carried a map of North American geography—a western chain of hills that resembled the Alleghenies and rivers that flowed from a common source, with short portages to streams running to the Pacific. In his heart he carried Dodsley's exhortations to fortitude and a patriot's commitment to national objects. Together these steeled him to spare no pains to accomplish or even surpass every purpose of his expedition. He also carried with him a sense of military fraternity that reminded him of his ties to brother soldiers who had perished at St. Clair's defeat and that filled him with sympathy for the hardships of his own men, whether lost on the Plains or shivering atop Mt. Rosa. In one way or another, each of these things had led him to the Grand Peak, but they had failed to help him climb it. Now it was snowing. In the upcoming months, none of them would serve him any better than the cotton uniforms.

Lost in the Rocky Mountains

On November 30, the party resumed marching up the Arkansas. It was "snowing very fast," and they made only fifteen miles. The next day, with "the storm still continuing with violence," they gave up the folly of continuing, and remained encamped. The horses pawed away the foot of snow that had fallen overnight and gnawed the stubble underneath. They kicked and shook to shoo away the brazen magpies that pecked at the poor beasts' raw backs. December 2 brought the coldest morning yet, but the party gamely took to the trail. Soon they were delayed when a ridge forced them to ford the icy river. The party hastened to build fires but could not manage the task before two men had frozen feet. As the party hobbled on, the terrain became more rugged—the river ran between the mountains—and one horse decided enough was enough. Taking a "freak in his head," it charged back toward the Plains. Pike dispatched some men to find it, and when they did not return that night he grew "apprehensive they might perish on the open prairie." All this for only thirteen miles of progress. The next day was wasted, too. The absent men returned without the lost horse. Pike sent some more men after it, but they returned with the beast too late for the party to march. Pike and Sparks tried to hunt a bison cow but killed only some males. Back at camp the men fashioned the pieces of the bulls' hides into crude moccasins to replace worn-out boots. "The hardships of last voyage," Pike wrote that night, "had now began."[26]

On December 4, the expedition reached a point of decision. In the vicinity of modern Cañon City, several small streams join the Arkansas River. Pike was not certain which was the main branch. In addition, the Spanish trail they were still following had gone cold. For the next five days scouting parties fanned out over the countryside, attempting to determine which branch to follow and where the Spaniards had gone. One party reported ascending what they took to be the main branch of the Arkansas until it dwindled to a brook, babbling between the sheer walls of a canyon too narrow to be passable for the horses. On the ninth, Pike located what he took to be a Spanish camp. Believing that he had reached the headwaters of the Arkansas and regained the Spanish trail, he led the party into the mountains, to the north.

The men might have wondered about this decision. Most of them were illiterate, so they probably knew little of the geography that Pike carried in his head. But they had heard enough talk in St. Louis to know what everyone said—the Red was to the south or southwest of the Arkansas, not to the north. Pike knew this, too. Some of the knowledge he brought to the mountains probably came from the greatest of Enlightenment geographers, Prussia's Alexander von Humboldt. Humboldt traveled extensively in the Spanish new world, visiting Mexico in 1803 and 1804. In Mexico, wary Spanish authorities uncharacteristically opened up their map collections to him, and he compiled their information into two comprehensive maps. Whatever he could not find in the archives, he filled in through interviews with knowledgeable Spaniards. This research yielded what was at the time the most complete map of Spain's North American empire. Before heading home to publish it, his last stop in the new world was a visit to Jefferson in Washington, where the two dined and discussed geography. Little is known of their meeting, but apparently, the Prussian agreed to let Jefferson borrow the map in order to have a copy made, on the promise that no others would be made. Sometime during the winter of 1804–1805, the copy fell into the hands of James Wilkinson, then in Washington lobbying for a leading role in the soon-to-be-organized Louisiana territory. Wilkinson arranged to have his draftsman Antoine Nau make yet another replica.

The map conjectured the relationships between the rivers of northern New Spain, that is (from the US perspective), southwestern Louisiana. The map showed a pair of creeks coming together to form the Arkansas River just about where Pike was camped in indecision at the entrance to the mountains. The next river south of the Arkansas was labeled the Red River of Natchitoches, with headwaters on the eastern side of the mountains, a little north of Santa Fe. Humboldt had not traveled this far north, so his location of the Red's headwaters was speculation, drawn from the work of Bernardo Miera y Pacheco, the cartographer who mapped the 1776 Spanish expedition led by Fray Francisco Atanasio Domínguez and Fray Silvestre Vélez de Escalante. Wilkinson, who got his appointment as governor of Louisiana a few months after Jefferson and Humboldt dined, descended the Ohio River in 1805 to take up the post, the surreptitiously obtained map tucked securely somewhere in his baggage. Pike never mentioned whether he carried a copy of the map on his western expedition, though it seems inconceivable that Wilkinson would have sent his lieutenant west without at least the opportunity to study it thoroughly.

Even if he did not have Humboldt's map, Pike did carry another that also made his northward tack questionable. This map was sketched in Pike's hand and depicted the rivers of the central Plains. It showed areas he never visited and charted a path he never followed, so it clearly was not a depiction of his own explorations. More likely, he conjured it from various sources before he left St. Louis, sort of a compilation of the best information he could assemble to guide him into what was to Americans unknown territory. The map has come to be known as the "Santa Fe Trail map" because it contains the earliest known American depiction of a course from the eastern Plains to Santa Fe, which roughly follows what in subsequent decades came to be the famed commercial route between the United States and New Mexico. Pike also carried a statement of a trader who claimed to have been to Santa Fe in 1797 and provided him some flimsy directions, which probably were the main source of the sketch. What this means is that Pike, who had explicit orders to avoid Spaniards, carried with him a map and directions to Santa Fe. Like Humboldt's rendition, the Santa Fe Trail sketch also placed the Red River's headwaters northeast of Santa Fe, between that city and the Arkansas. Given what Pike likely knew of the Humboldt map and what he drew on his own, turning northward from the tangle of streams that apparently joined to form the Arkansas was not the path to the Red. Rather, to anyone suffering the wintry conditions they were encountering, an easier route to the Red would seem to have been to descend the Arkansas back to the Plains and then to travel south along the front of the mountains until striking the Red.

Men who had cheered a month earlier at the sight of the mountains they understood to be their turnaround point cannot have been happy that Pike decided to turn north. But if any of them grumbled, they did

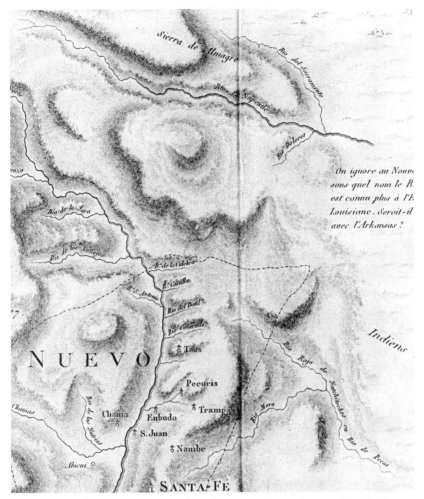

On ignore au Nouv*
sous quel nom le R.
est connu plus à l'E.
Louisiane . Seroit-il
avec l'Arkansas ?'

FIGURE 5.5 This map conjectured by the Baron Alexander von Humboldt map was the source of much grief for Pike. This excerpt shows the Red River, labeled "Rio Rojo de Nachitoches," with headwaters north of Santa Fe near Taos and south of the headwaters of the Arkansas, labeled Rio de Napestle. Note also that the headwaters of the Arkansas are marked with a pair of streams coming together near the place Pike camped December 5–9, when he decided he had found the river's source. David Rumsey Map Collection, www.davidrumsey.com.

not do so in front of Pike, or he did not record it. Perhaps Pike spun a persuasive explanation for them or perhaps they merely bit their tongues. Even if they were inclined to doubt him, questioning the decision of a superior officer was a serious step, one that could bring severe consequences, and obedience must have offered a tolerable path of least resistance. Moreover, anyone wanting to chart a different course had few alternatives. Surviving in the wilderness required cooperation and sticking together. A bickering or splintered party was a doomed party. Men who had already traveled together in Minnesota and across the Plains likely were by now a tightly knit bunch. Commitment to comrades and leaders often holds military men together under the worst of circumstances, so for the time being, the unit's cohesion endured.[27] But the men had been led into the mountains during a blizzard for which they were badly underdressed and had watched a spooked but sensible horse bolt for the Plains; if they had not already begun to wonder about their commander's judgment, the turn to the north might at least have given them pause.

In his journal, Pike explained his northward tack in terms of his desire to follow the Spaniards. The mountains looming to the southwest rose even more sharply than the Grand Peak and others to the north, and perhaps he believed the Spaniards knew a circuitous but ultimately easier path through them. In any case, his entries for the four days he spent where the Arkansas tumbled out of the narrow canyon reveal him to be as concerned with relocating the Spanish trail as with determining which tributary was the main branch. On December 9 he finally "found the Spanish camp" and was itching to move "immediately," except that four scouts were still in the field. With the party reassembled the next day, the men marched northward over the mountains that divide the Arkansas from South Park, one of Colorado's high-altitude prairies. As he advanced, Pike's mind fixated on the Spaniards. The party lost the trail several times again on the eleventh and passed what Pike took to be a Spanish camp on the thirteenth. On the fourteenth, he found it "impossible to say which course the Spaniards pursued." Meanwhile, the adjective "supposed" had begun to creep into his entries as a modifier of the Spanish trail. By the fourteenth, he believed it might actually be Indians, not Spaniards, he was following. Whoever it was, he was "determined to persue them," for "we were some what at a loss which course to pursue," and he wanted to ask directions because "the geography of the country, had turned out to be so different from our expectation."[28]

Meanwhile, Pike had made an important discovery. Scouting ahead on the thirteenth while his men were making camp, he "fell upon a river 40 yards wide, frozen over" and running northeast. "Must it not be the head waters of the river Platte?" It was. Finding and correctly identifying the South Platte was one of the few things he got right during his sojourn in the mountains. For a few days, the party attempted to follow both it and the increasingly stale path of the humans he longed to talk with. Having lost the trail on the sixteenth, they "halted and dispatched parties" to reconnoiter. Pike and Robinson mounted a "high ridge" to take the lay of the land. From the viewpoint above the South Platte, they surveyed the country. They looked for evidence of Spaniards or Indians. They looked for clues about the river geography that so confused them. They looked for a trail to follow. But they saw nothing useful. The party had reached its northernmost point in the Rockies, the vicinity of modern Fairplay, Colorado, where the sources of the South Platte River fall from the mountains into South Park, and they still had found no one to give them directions. With his stalwart soldiers suffering "extremely with cold" and "being almost naked," Pike once again stood on a promontory and decided he had reached the limit of what men could endure. He concluded that the best course of action was "putting the Spanish trace out of the question." He turned the party around "to bear our course south west, for the head of the Red river."[29]

Doubt soon gave way to jubilation. On December 18, they crossed the Mosquito Range on the western side of South Park and peered southwest into a valley. The river they spied "was about 25 yards wide, ran with great rapidity and was full of rocks." The Red? Everything matched: a broad valley, a river too big to be a tributary, west of the headwaters of the Arkansas. They were somewhat further north than Humboldt's map or Pike's Santa Fe Trail sketch suggested, but the river was coursing south. It must bend east after passing a divide between it and the Arkansas. Satisfied that he was nearing his destination, Pike decided "to remain a day or two in order to examine the source." This was the third time in three weeks that he had halted the expedition to tease out a river's origins, not the behavior of a man whose primary objective was Santa Fe. His men must have found the identification of headwaters a more plausible explanation for delay than the one Pike had offered for the northerly foray into South Park. In any case, the men must have assumed, soon they would be turning home, and the sight of the river "gave general pleasure."[30]

But this was December 18, thirty days since the party had packed the nine hundred pounds of bison meat at Rocky Ford, which Pike had estimated would last a month. The next day, it was "snowing and stormy." Pike "sent out parties hunting," but they "had no success." The hunters failed again on the twentieth. "As there was no prospect of killing any game," and the group's provisions would last only three days more, Pike decided to split the party. He ordered Robinson and Vasquez downriver in search of food. If they found some, they were to carry it back to the main stem of the party, which also was to head downstream, with all the horses and gear. Meanwhile, Pike took Mountjoy and Miller upstream to the headwaters, consistent with the behavior of a man who believed he had just found the river whose headwaters he was seeking. The threesome made it to a point not far from modern Leadville, where the river was "not more than ten or fifteen feet wide, and properly speaking, only a *brook*." But the provisions were running out. Pike's detachment killed a turkey and a hare—enough to fill them, but nothing to carry back to the hungry men straggling downstream. So Pike hastened back. It was cold, and they marched into the night, until their "cloathing was frozen stiff, and we ourselves were considerably benumbed." Finally, on December 24, they overtook Robinson and Vazquez. The doctor and the interpreter had not eaten for two days but had just shot four bison. Together, the five men caught up with the others, who also had not eaten. Pike sent some men back with horses to retrieve Robinson and Vazquez's kill, and meanwhile John Sparks, the party's champion hunter, brought in four more cows. "Thus from being in a starving condition," Pike wrote, "we had 8 beeves in our camp," a Christmas Eve feast.[31]

Christmas Day was stormy, and the men passed it "as agreeably as could be expected from men in our situation." They rested and patched raw bison hide into something that passed for clothing and shoes, all the while doing their best to stay warm without blankets, which they had cut up for socks. As for the quality of the victuals, Pike would not stoop to complain, considering such a breach of fortitude "beneath the serious consideration of a man on a voyage of such nature." It was enough not to be hungry. At night, they lay down by fireside, "on the snow or wet ground; one side burning whilst the other was pierced with the cold." If the men were able to sleep at all that night, perhaps they dreamed of the meat they had dried that day for the homeward journey that would commence tomorrow.[32]

By evening the next day, however, Pike's personal attendant Private Thomas Daugherty and another unnamed man had taken so ill that Pike, who was the only one with a tent, sacrificed it to them and awoke the next morning covered with snow. On the twenty-seventh the valley narrowed into a series of canyons, which sometimes left little room to pass on one side or the other. This forced the men back and forth across the river and sometimes, when the nearly perpendicular canyon walls rendered neither side passable, drove the party into the streambed itself. Slipping on the ice and faltering over the rocks protruding from the partially frozen river, the horses fell frequently, and sometimes had to be unloaded so the baggage could be carried around particularly treacherous spots. Despite marching all day, the party made only twelve-and-a-half miles. They saw no sign of bison or horses, and Pike began to suspect that neither wild animals nor Indians "ever take this route, to go from the source of the river out of the mountains." Instead, he speculated, they "must cross one of the chains to the right or left, and find a smoother tract to the lower country." Interlopers such as Pike and his men, however, did not have the luxury of knowing alternative routes, and, anyway, although the canyon occasionally widened, it offered no opportunity for exit during the next few days. Nothing on his maps prepared him for anything like this, and the newcomers were compelled to keep stumbling down the rocky streambed.[33]

Travel was getting impossible for the horses. To relieve their burdens, the men piled the baggage on makeshift sleds, which they dragged over the ice and around the rocks, but still the beasts fell. On the thirtieth some sleds broke, forcing a delay. Then the baggage had to be carried because water ran over the ice. More delay. Whenever the canyon narrowed, the party had to cross. Sometimes the men even had to drag the horses. A few days later the party tried carving tracks for the sleds in the ice and filling them with dirt to get around the cascades. Pike had no idea how much farther the canyon would stretch, and between carrying baggage, repairing sleds, cajoling horses, and carving a path, the party was making only a few miles a day, and getting hungry.[34]

On the first day of 1807, Pike sent Robinson and Private John Brown ahead to hunt and cache what they did not consume so that the rear part of the party would have something to eat when it caught up. On January 2, the party "labored all day, but made only one mile." Pike concluded the horses could continue no farther along the treacherous riverbed. He left Freegift Stout and Theodore Miller behind to advance with a sled, while the rest of the group attempted to escape the canyon. Hauling themselves and the horses upward, they reached the rim and discovered immediately there was nowhere to go. They began descending "an almost perpendicular" precipice, and one of the horses tumbled down. Pike shot it at the bottom. After reaching the streambed again, Pike left two more men to make sleds. Miller and Stout, meanwhile, had passed on ahead. The main party, now numbering only ten, staggered on, and the horses kept falling. Two lost their senses from the bruises and falls and had to be left behind.[35]

The horses were not the only animals in danger of losing their senses. After two days without nourishment, hunger would soon begin to cloud the men's judgment as well. They had not seen Robinson and Brown since January 1, nor Miller and Stout since the 2nd. Neither vanguard had cached any meat for the men in rear. Pike never explained why his party did not eat the fallen horses. Surely the men considered horsemeat poor food, but under dire circumstances they might easily have put aside such culinary preferences. Whatever their reasoning, without food, the men's blood would not carry enough glucose to their brains. To maintain their blood-glucose levels, the men's bodies were breaking down fat and muscle tissue, leaving them weaker, less agile, more prone to cold, and less able to maintain their body temperature. If such conditions persisted, their metabolism would slow to the point of affecting their brain function. Men who could not think straight could not rescue themselves from peril. They had not yet reached that critical point yet, but after two days without food, the men were probably irritable and prone to taking risks in their desperation. Pike could not have understood the chemistry of hypoglycemia, but he knew he was hungry. They had to get out of the chasm, soon.

He decided to split the party again. From a wide spot in the canyon, he sent Vazquez and two soldiers and the horses upward, to find a route to safety. Then he divided the rest into groups of two, with orders to make sleds and drag the gear downstream as they were able. Pike, meanwhile, went down the river alone. Unbeknownst to him, the worst was still ahead: the Royal Gorge, where the canyon sometimes narrows to as little as thirty feet wide and where granite walls soar perpendicularly more than a thousand feet above the river. As they approached the chasm, the men had broken into eight groups, strung out over several miles in and atop the Royal Gorge, entirely out of communication with one another. No one had any food, and each man "had then to depend on his own exertion for safety and subsistence."[36] The party had disintegrated.

That afternoon, Pike caught up with Stout and Miller. The two men were climbing a sheer rock face at a point where the river flowed bank to bank and made the canyon impassable. They had not eaten in two days and were determined to escape the gorge and boil some deer skin for supper. Together the three found a steep ravine covered with a solid sheet of ice and clawed their way up "with the utmost difficulty and danger." At the top, Pike shot a deer but could not locate the kill in the darkness. He went out to hunt again in the morning but could not shoot straight. Upon examining his gun he found the barrel bent—damaged, he supposed, when it banged on the rocks in one of the many falls in the canyon. His spirits sank, for he considered the gun his "grandest resource." Indeed at the moment it was—the difference between eating and not, between madness and maintaining his wits at a time when he had nothing else to save him. Somehow, he managed to pull himself up to a lookout and beheld, at last, the Great Plains. Relief, however, quickly turned to "mortification." A river splashed out of the mountains below, but it was not the Red. Before him lay the very place the party had camped for four days in December and determined to be the headwaters of the Arkansas. The brutal month in the mountains had yielded only the redis-covery of the river they had been following since October. At the end of all his exploring, to paraphrase T. S. Eliot, Pike had arrived where he started and knew the place for the first time. He gathered Stout and Miller and then hap-pened upon Vazquez and the horses. Together, they straggled to the camp they had left on December 10. It was January 5, Pike's twenty-eighth birthday, and he hoped "most fervently...never to pass another so miserably." At night he fired a gun as a signal for the still missing Robinson. No one answered.[37]

They finally killed a good supply of game on January 6, and Pike devoted the next few days to rescuing the remaining men from the canyon and scratching his head as to his whereabouts. If this was the Arkansas, where was the Red? Surely Texas was not one of the places that crossed his mind. But that was indeed where it lay. Contrary to the conjectures of the best Enlightenment geographers, the Red rises in the Llano Estacado of northern Texas, a region so rugged that the river's headwaters eluded pre-cise location until the 1850s. Humboldt had guessed wrong. Pike, who actually went to look for it, missed it as well. So did Major Stephen Long, who later thought he had found it on his 1820 expedition, only to discover that the river he took as the Red was in fact the Canadian, a long tributary that led him back to the Arkansas. Geography doomed explorers looking for the Red to keep finding the Arkansas. Even the Spaniards, who, apart from the region's native peoples, knew the area best, placed the Red's headwaters northwest of Santa Fe on an 1802 map.[38]

By January 9, Robinson and the rest of the party had regrouped, but Pike was still perplexed. "I now felt at considerable loss how to proceed," he wrote. The men were exhausted. The horses were broken and useless. The Red, he believed, still lay somewhere to the southwest. Formulating plan after plan, he rejected them all. Presumably his deliberations included simply to stop and wait out the winter and resume again in the spring when the mountains would be more hospitable. He must also have considered proceeding downriver and turning south along the mountain front, at lower, warmer, less rugged elevations. Eventually, his thoughts returned to something he had already contemplated and rejected, crossing the Sangre de Cristo Mountains, the jagged range to his southwest that sawed up 14,000 feet in elevation. These were the "snow cap'd mountains" whose crossing he had dismissed on December 14 as "almost impossible." Now he would try it.[39]

Over the next few days, the men constructed a small fortress, where Vazquez and Private Patrick Smith would remain to tend the horses and guard the baggage. The rest of the party would advance, locate the best route over the Sangres, and return a few days later, by which time the horses would be rested. During the days the men were building the blockhouse, as Pike called the small structure, is probably when Pike scribbled out "Red" in all his journals, maps, and traverse tables and replaced it with "Arkansas." As he did, he was literally erasing the Enlightenment geography that he had carried into the mountains but that had so consistently steered him wrong. Finding rivers in Louisiana was supposed to be a simple matter: ascend a watercourse to its headwaters, climb a height of land, find all the other rivers. Rivers were not supposed to dwindle to brooks a hundred miles downstream from their headwaters. But as T. S. Eliot later wrote, "We shall not cease from exploration"; neither would Pike.[40]

To some, Pike's actions from the supposed headwaters of the Arkansas and back appear the behavior of a man trying to get to Santa Fe, not one trying to avoid the Spaniards. On December 10, he had turned his back on the direction in which his maps said the Red lay and instead followed the apparent trail of the Spaniards into the mountains to the north. From the same place in January, he rejected the easier options of waiting out the winter or seeking the Red on the Plains but rather turned his face to the southwest, the direction of Santa Fe. This behavior, however, is also that of a man who is trying to get to the Red River and who carries a map showing that the Red lies between himself and the New Mexican capital. The best Enlightenment geography said the Red was south or southwest of the Arkansas, and twice he decided to cross mountains to the southwest. His

FIGURE 5.6 Poncha Pass. Above: looking south from near Pike's Christmas Day camp. If Pike had known he was on the Arkansas and wanted to turn southwest to Santa Fe, this was an easy place to cross.

FIGURE 5.7 Below: his view of the Sangres to the east would have confirmed that the crossing would get no better than Poncha Pass and that if he was going to scale the Sangres, this was the place to do it. The fact that he did not cross Poncha Pass is strong evidence that he did believe he was on the Red River and that in the days after Christmas he was intending to descend it and head home. Photos by author.

official instructions from Wilkinson suggested looking for headwaters, and three times in the past month, he had looked for headwaters. His instructions said to find and descend the Red, and when, on the upper Arkansas, he believed he had found it, he had descended. A man with a mission to Santa Fe would have kept crossing mountains to the southwest after finding the Red. In fact, Poncha Pass, visible from the Christmas Day camp and for at least the day after, beckoned with a much easier crossing than the Sangre route he ultimately attempted. If he were determined to get to Santa Fe, the morning after Christmas was the day to try it. Crossing the Sangres two weeks later from the camp on the Arkansas was a poor decision, one that was to have dire consequences, but it was nevertheless one consistent with the behavior of someone who wanted to find the Red River. The horses, clothing, and guns were failing them. Everything Pike carried in his head had been wrong. Next the men would pit what they had left—their bodies and their commitment to each other—against the mountains.

It must have been a grim scene on January 13, 1807, as Pike carefully divided the gear and weighed each man's pack to even the burden. They took only the essentials—their guns, some basic tools, and probably whatever wraps the men had fashioned from animal hide. Curiously—and fatefully—Pike deemed his trunk of official papers to be among these necessities and brought them along. They carried little food, planning to subsist on what they could hunt. On the morning of the fourteenth, each man hefted his seventy-pound pack and faced into the teeth of the Sangres.[41]

Across the Sangres

The plan might have worked if not for the events of January 17. From the blockhouse, the adventurers trekked southwest for three days through some low mountains, more or less following Grape Creek into the Wet Mountain Valley, a basin that runs north and south between the towering Wet Mountains on the east and the even steeper Sangres to the west. About four in the afternoon, they came around some round hills and caught sight of the prairie. Only an hour or so of daylight remained, but there was no wood or flowing water nearby, and it was bitterly cold. They had not eaten in two days. Retreating to the last good spot for a camp would have been unthinkable to men desperate to press on and now within sight for the first time of the foot of the lofty mountains they aimed to cross. Across the valley, Pike spied some trees and a small stream issuing from the Sangres. The place "appeared to be at no great distance," and he "thought proper to march for it."[42] But Pike had again underestimated the expanse that separated him from a western mountain. Bad luck or bad judgment, the decision to cross the Wet Mountain Valley set in motion events that would unravel the bonds of military fraternity and severely impair the men's ability to think and act rationally.

As the sun set over the mountains and the shadows lengthened, it became apparent that the woods were indeed a great distance away. For four hours their exhausted bodies struggled through the darkness. In the middle of the valley, they crossed Grape Creek. The falling temperatures likely reflected a

FIGURE 5.8 Sangre de Cristo Mountains from the Wet Mountain Valley, on nearly the same date and at about the same time of day Pike saw them. This is the view Pike had when he made the decision to leave this dry, barren spot and cross the valley to the well-wooded foot of the Sangres. The road at the far left of the photo points toward the woods where he camped that evening. Photo by author.

sudden cold snap, perhaps the rapid approach of an arctic front, for Pike had not mentioned the chill the day before, and Grape Creek was still free of ice and flowing enough to soak the men's boots as they sloshed across the low point in the valley and began their ascent toward the woods. It was eight o'clock before they lit campfires. They had marched twenty-eight miles. The temperature had dipped to 10 degrees below zero, and the men were in trouble.[43]

FIGURE 5.9 Grape Creek, near where the party crossed, heading for the woods at the foot of the Sangres in the background. Photo by author.

Frostbite first grips the extremities of the circulatory system—fingers, noses, and toes—sometimes within as little as thirty minutes. After fording Grape Creek and hiking for several more miles, the men would have first felt stinging and burning. Then they would have begun to lose sensation in their extremities. By the time they reached camp, they probably were hobbling on feet they could no longer feel. A standard body of military medical knowledge equipped most officers of the day to set broken bones and tend to various injuries including cuts, gunshot wounds, and frostbite, but this knowledge was not well organized or systematically engrained in commanders, and Pike, who wrote far less frequently about his men's health than did Meriwether Lewis, may or may not have had the skills to cope with the unfolding emergency.

Probably Doctor Robinson took charge. If he knew what Lewis knew when treating frostbite at the Mandan village in January 1805, the doctor might have put the men's feet in cold water. This is a surprisingly modern treatment, however, not to mention counterintuitive. More likely, in Pike's camp, an ungainly dance ensued. After making campfires, fourteen men fumbled to unlace their boots and moccasins from numb feet with fingers they could barely feel. Once free of their icy shoes, the men thrust their toes before the flames. Firelight flickering over the bare skin would have illuminated a horrible pale coloring, and the feet would have felt cold to the touch and hard. Although warming by fireside responds to a powerful instinct to relieve the numbness, it is one of the worst things they could have done. In the Russian winter of 1812, Napoleon's panicky soldiers did the same thing. Their feet thawed rapidly, and then swelled and blistered so that by the time the boots dried and the men tried to put them back on, their engorged feet would not fit. At this point, there was no way to protect them from the cold. An aching pain set in and then gangrene. Better to leave the feet cold until they could be properly and permanently warmed rather than expose them to thawing and repeated freezing. Pike did not record how he and Robinson treated frostbite, but that evening the feet of nine of the men froze badly enough that they were unable to walk in the morning. Among them were Pike's personal attendant Thomas Daugherty and John Sparks, the party's best hunter.[44]

This calamity brought other problems. The men had not eaten in three days, during which they had exerted themselves to the limit. Their caloric intake had been dangerously low since the Christmas supper three weeks before, during which time they had alternated between gorging themselves and going several days at a time with little or no food. From these episodic feasts, their gastrointestinal systems would not have been able to absorb enough nutrients to restore the muscle and fat reserves the men had depleted during the fasts. With this latest foodless spell, the men would have been suffering the first effects of starvation: weight loss, weakness, apathy, irritability, violent anger, and impaired memory, concentration, and judgment. In the morning, the ones who were able to walk went out to hunt, but their bodies were not up to such vigorous activity. Pike and Robinson wounded a bison but could not give chase. It was enough to sap the fight even of a man like Pike. "We concluded," he later wrote, "it was useless to go home to add to the general gloom." They found some rocks to rest by and stayed awake all night, unable to sleep in the bitter cold. Now they could add exhaustion to the hunger and cold that afflicted them.[45]

And hypothermia, too. Unlike frostbite, which is a localized freezing of tissue, hypothermia occurs when the entire body's temperature drops below ninety-five degrees. At first the body copes by shivering, but this demands a surprisingly large amount of energy, more than the recent caloric intake of Pike's body probably could have sustained. So his temperature probably just kept falling, the chill sucking more heat out of him than his hungry body could produce. At this point, bodily functions slow down. The brain processes information sluggishly and makes poor decisions. Low morale, poor memory, lack of self-control, and even paranoia can further debilitate hypothermia victims. Confusion and apathy set in, and the mind is overcome by a sense that everything would be fine if the body could just lie down. The next morning, the hungry, exhausted, hypothermic bodies of Pike and Robinson crawled a mile in the snow to within shooting range of a small herd of bison. Eight times they shot, wounding a few, which immediately fled. "By this time," Pike wrote, "I had become extremely weak and faint." It was now four days without food, and the two men were despondent. One physician has even suggested suicidal. The supply of nutrients in their tissues had dropped to critical levels, slowing the body's chemical reactions that sustain the capacity to do work, and the time over which they could maintain brief maximum exertion had dropped by a factor approaching fifty percent. They gave up. It was better to "remain absent and die by ourselves rather than to return to our camp and behold the misery of our poor lads." Then some more bison appeared, and adrenaline surged through Pike's body. He fired, killing one beast with four shots.[46]

Luck had provided what the mind and body could no longer muster. Somehow Pike and Robinson managed to hack out some of the animal's flesh and haul it back to the hungry men. When Pike staggered into camp near midnight, he was cheered to behold on the faces of his cohort "not a frown, nor a desponding eye." They "hail[ed] their officer and companions," and Sergeant William Meek declared that "on the morrow the most robust had determined to set out in search of us; and not return unless they found us, or killed something to preserve the life of their starving companions."[47] The bonds among men of arms had endured. The party's recovery from "general gloom" to "not a frown, nor a desponding eye," might reflect the meal's transformation of the group's actual mood, or it may simply indicate the change in Pike's perceptions as his digestive system began to extract the protein from the meat and convert it into glucose to fuel his brain. Either way it was occasioned by calories, not culture, and depended primarily not on social bonds but on physiology.

The next morning, January 20, after three days of rest by campfire, five of the men were able to walk, and sticks picked up in the woods served as canes to enable two more to march, without packs. Sparks and Daugherty, however, were unable to proceed. Their toes probably had begun to blacken, a sign Pike recognized to mean that the men were going to lose them. Military practice at the time authorized a commander to do whatever necessary to protect the safety of his unit, even to the point of sacrificing individuals. Still, no officer could justify abandoning men except when the party's welfare required it, unless he provisioned them as well as possible, and unless he had a reasonable expectation of being able to rescue them. Under the circumstances, Pike could have turned the party around. The blockhouse on the Arkansas lay only four days distant over a route he knew was passable, and there they would find food and fuel, two healthy hunters, the beginnings of a crude shelter, and horses that might now be well enough to send back to save the soldiers nursing wounded feet. If Pike considered such an option, he did not mention it in his diary. Instead, on Wednesday, he hiked up to the foot of the mountains "to see what prospect there was of being able to cross." At the base, however, snow drifts four to five feet deep blocked his advance. The mountains appeared lower to his left, and he decided to take the party south, contouring the range in hopes of finding a pass free of snow. Something irresistible was drawing him across the Sangres. Pressing forward heedless of comfort and safety was without doubt part of Pike's character. It also fit with the impaired judgment of a man in his state. He may have had secret orders to get to Santa Fe, but they are not required to explain his decisions. At this point, Pike's stomach and circulatory system were probably doing much of his thinking.[48]

On January 22, the men who could carry burdens reallocated the weight in the bundles to relieve those who could not. The hikers carried only one meal, leaving the remains of the bison and as much ammunition as possible with Sparks and Daugherty, who were staying behind. Beyond that, Pike could offer the two frostbitten soldiers only Dodsley's now hollow advice. "Have fortitude," Pike told them, "to resist" your "fate." He promised to send a rescue party as soon as possible. They then parted with tears.[49] Nothing in the sentimental departure, however, obscured the fact that he was leaving two wounded men to possible death. The ties of camaraderie were fraying and soon would be as threadbare as the rags the men wore on their backs.

That afternoon the party stopped around three o'clock and went out to hunt. They killed nothing. For the next week they lumbered through the snow. Game eluded them, and hunger and cold dogged them. On Friday, January 23, it snowed so hard the men could see but ten yards in front of them. Pike found it "impossible to keep any course without the compass, continually in my hand," and he lost the rest of the crew. He found himself alone at nightfall, once more contemplating his own imminent mortality, "scarcely able to conceive a more dreadful idea than remaining on the wild, where inevitable death must have ensued." On top of hunger and hypothermia, he likely suffered fatigue, the condition in which full rest and recovery does not take place between bouts of exhausting exertion. Surges of adrenaline, such as the one that energized Pike to kill the bison near Grape Creek, may enable momentarily explosive activity, but without recuperation, fatigue accumulates and reduces mental and physical efficiency and saps a victim's initiative. This yields poor decision making and other mistakes, which in turn prolong or aggravate the fatiguing conditions. As one survival psychologist has observed, "the power of fatigue to undermine an individual's performance to the extent where it is at best ineffective and at worst counterproductive is one which has long been grossly underestimated." The next day Pike confided to his diary, "for the first time in the voyage found myself discouraged."[50]

By this time, Pike's purpose in crossing the mountains must have been unfathomable to the men. The expedition had already located the headwaters of the Arkansas. Tramping interminably through blizzards without sustenance was surely not necessary to find the Red. Laboring in the snow, apparently without purpose, the men likely lost sight of the connection between their suffering and the pursuit of national objects, which must have shaken their faith in their commander. If Pike's scant journal commentary about his men's health and the possibly inept handling of the frostbite disaster near Grape Creek indicate a low level of concern for his men's physical condition, then the medical emergencies that dogged the group might have further dampened their confidence in his leadership. They were also losing their connection to each other. First Pike had separated the group along the upper Arkansas, then in the Royal Gorge. Next he left Vazquez and Smith, then Sparks and Daugherty. Now the blizzard had separated the party further, and within a few days, he would leave Private Hugh Menaugh in the snow at the foot of a pass, the fifth man left behind in two weeks. When Pike finally did manage to rejoin his men on the twenty-fourth, he found them trudging along "silent and with downcast countenances." The frequent separations were becoming routine, and the party was disintegrating. The unit cohesion that had inspired cheers when Pike and Robinson brought in the bison near Grape Creek had frayed into an every-man-for-himself slow-motion scramble to get over the mountains. Each soldier must have wondered if he might be abandoned next.[51]

Perhaps this was on Private John Brown's mind—or his stomach, rather—on the afternoon of the twenty-fourth as the crew once again struggled up the Sangres in waist-deep snow. Hungry from three days without a meal, Brown grumbled that the physical burdens had become unbearable for humans, fit only for horses. Pike pretended not to hear. Was this a near brush with mutiny, the complete unraveling of the ties that bound soldiers? Pike feared so. Once more, though, he was rescued by full bellies. Late in the afternoon, the party killed another bison and devoured it by campfire. Not fully satisfied by this happy outcome, Pike took the opportunity to stifle any further disobedience that might arise. After the meal, he rebuked Brown in front of the other men, calling him "seditious and mutinous." Pike also excoriated him for complaining about burdens when all men in the group, including the commander, bore them "equally." He threatened to execute the private if such "ingratitude" ever escaped Brown's lips again. Concluding the tirade, Pike thanked the rest of the men for their "obedience and perseverance" and promised to secure them the future "rewards of our government and gratitude of your countrymen."[52]

Pike's outburst—though probably partly a product of the irritability that accompanies weeks of malnourishment—also reflected his commitment to the nation. Indeed, Pike devoted nearly the entire harangue to gratitude and equality, concepts heavily laden with nationalist implications. Equality among men came from nothing less than the Declaration of Independence itself. It was what had justified Pike's defiance of his wealthy father-in-law. All independent men were equal in their duty to sacrifice for the good of the nation. In return, the nation owed them gratitude, a sentiment that enabled Americans of different social statuses to claim and acknowledge cultural debts to one another and thereby negotiate their relationships to each other and to the nation. Gratitude was what the postrevolutionary generation owed to the revolutionaries. Gratitude was what gave Pike faith in army life as he contemplated his father's deterioration. Gratitude was what he expected would compensate Sparks and Daugherty for their toes. Pike said Brown had shirked his "duty as a soldier," but he had also blasphemed these two pillars of early American nationalism.[53]

For Pike, then, military fraternity and nationalism were complementary attachments, which worked in tandem. Fraternity had sustained the party through trials in Minnesota, at the Pawnee village, and into the Rockies. It wavered, though, as men lost faith in Pike, and as the repeated separations weakened their confidence that they could count on support from the unit or its leader. Pike's marriage, late night studying, river-running, and exploring, however, had given him one additional reservoir to draw from to boost morale. When western snows buried unit cohesion and froze the tissue of his men's feet, he appealed to national ideals like equality and gratitude. If Pike could no longer cajole them forward by binding them together, he would try to bind them to the nation.

More than ever, Pike was determined to cross the mountains. "Had the storm continued one day longer," he feared, "the animals would have continued in the mountains, and we should have became so weak as not to be able to hunt, and of course have perished." On the morning of the twenty-seventh, he left Menaugh with a cache of food and led the party uphill for one more assault on the Sangres. After a "bad days march" through snow three-feet deep, they crested the range and came upon westward flowing waters. They spent the night high in the mountains and the next day followed a creek down into an enormous valley, in the foreground of which rose hills of sand, whose "appearance," Pike wrote, "was exactly that of the sea in a storm." Making camp between the sand hills and the mountains, Pike climbed the highest dune with his spy glass and saw a broad river bisecting the valley. The Red? No, that was still in Texas, but Pike took it for the Red. The party was now in the San Luis Valley, an enormous basin, more than a hundred miles long and more than fifty miles wide, averaging 7,700 feet in elevation and surrounded by peaks as high as 14,000 feet. Today the dunes have been preserved as Great Sand Dunes National Park, a destination of recreation and relaxation.[54]

Over the next three days, Pike marched the men to the river, crossed it, and camped among some cottonwoods that lined one of its tributaries entering from the southwest. The site had plentiful water and wood to build boats for descending the river and to construct a temporary defensive structure.[55] February in the San Luis Valley can be bitterly cold, but Pike did not complain of it in the month he camped there. He went out hunting almost daily, and not once did he mention hunger. Although the men's well-being hardly rivaled the comforts of modern travelers in the valley, he had navigated what remained of his party out of immediate peril and begun to meet their daily bodily requirements. Next he returned his attention to the national objects.

His first task was to build some shelter. Pike said the task was for defense, but the party had seen no one for three months and had little reason to fear hostility from Indians or Spaniards. As much as for any other reason, he likely undertook the project in order to occupy soldiers who had little else to do and who were likely to be idle for a few weeks while rescue parties retrieved the men, horses, and baggage from the mountains. Whatever his motives, over the course of the next week, a stockade gradually took shape. It lay on the banks of a tributary, five miles up from its confluence with the larger river. The men felled cottonwood logs, as much as two-feet in diameter, and piled them atop one another until the structure stood twelve-feet high. It was thirty-six feet square and had bastions at the corners. A moat encircled it, and its occupants gained entrance by crossing the ditch on a plank and crawling under ground-level through a small hole below the base. Inside, they posted long poles, sharpened at one end, and pointed them over the walls to slow any intruders who might try to climb over the structure. "Thus fortified," he boasted, he could have fended off a hundred Spanish horsemen. For good measure, he raised an American flag.[56]

At this point, the story of the expedition took a startling turn. As the stockade neared completion, Robinson suddenly announced important business he had to attend to in Santa Fe. Ostensibly he aimed to collect a debt on behalf of one William Morrison, a Kaskaskia merchant and a man known to both Robinson and Pike. Sometime in the recent past, Morrison had entrusted a trader named Baptiste Lalande with some merchandise to take to sell in Santa Fe. Lalande never came back and was believed to have sold the goods, pocketed the proceeds, and remained in New Mexico.

FIGURE 5.10 Replica of Pike's stockade built on site, according to the specifications in his journal. In the background is Sierra del Ojito, a volcanic promontory Pike climbed to get the lay of the land. Photo by author.

There was a Baptiste Lalande living in the city at the time Pike camped in the San Luis Valley, and the claim was plausible enough that the Spanish governor would later promise to investigate it. But Pike also confessed in his journal that the story was something of a pretext. In fact, he called it "spurious." The party had reached the point in the expedition that Pike and Robinson "conceived...to be the most eligible" for reaching Santa Fe, Pike acknowledged, and "the idea suggested itself" of making Morrison's debt the excuse "to gain a knowledge of the country, the prospect of trade, force, &c." Moreover, Pike believed that American agreements with Spain guaranteed United States citizens "the right of seeking the recovery of all just debts." Pike had finally overstepped his orders. Unless he deluded himself into thinking that Robinson could get in and out of the provincial capital without detection or that the Spaniards, who had killed or detained all previous American visitors, would not mind Robinson's call, the junket clearly violated Wilkinson's order to avoid giving offense to the Spaniards when near their territory. Or, perhaps, getting a look at Santa Fe had been the real national object all along. The doctor's subsequent behavior in New Mexico hints at a third possibility, that the province was only Robinson's objective, and that he concocted the debt collection mission on his own and persuaded Pike of its appeal. In any case, on the morning of February 7, the doctor departed the little fortification, ostensibly to see if he could find Lalande, collect the money, and rejoin the party before it floated down the Red. Significantly, though not surprisingly, he set off upstream, to the southwest, in the right direction for Santa Fe according to the Santa Fe Trail map.[57]

That evening, Pike also dispatched a rescue party. Corporal Jeremiah Jackson and four men left to return to the scene of starvation and frostbite and bring out the "frozen lads," if they were alive and able to travel. While the four men who remained with Pike hobbled around putting the finishing touches on the stockade, he spent the next ten days hunting and reading (incredibly, he had deemed books among the essential items to carry over the mountains from the blockhouse on the Arkansas). On the seventeenth, some of the rescuers returned. Menaugh was on his way, they informed Pike, but Sparks and Daugherty were still unable to travel. The two soldiers had removed some of their frostbitten toes and sent them back with the rescuers. By this time, the digits would have blackened, and the skin and tissue would have shriveled. It is unlikely that enough time had passed for the toes to separate on their own—though that fate surely lay in their future. Instead, the men had probably self-amputated them, a gruesome procedure, though perhaps not as painful as it sounds because the toes had most likely lost all sensation. Along with their toes, Sparks and Daugherty gave the rescuers a message for Pike, begging him not to leave them stranded.[58]

Sparks and Daugherty selected the grisly medium of their toes in order to prevail on their commander's sensibility—his ability to perceive and respond to the suffering of others—in hopes it would incline him to rescue them. This was a reasonable thing to try, for after traveling with Pike for two seasons, they must have understood him well enough to know that he could be motivated by appeals to sentiment and compassion. Like many other men of the era, he took masculine pride in his sensitivity. He also, however, viewed the toes as a sacrifice for a "grateful country." The men owed their bodies to their nation. The nation owed them gratitude. This bargain, Pike believed, would "secure [the soldiers'] happiness." To him, suffering in the mountains was an act of nationalism. It was the same appeal he had used in diffusing Private Brown's disobedience.[59]

Before Pike was able to resolve these problems, he was saved by a new one. While hunting one day, he spotted a pair of men on horseback with lances. At first he avoided them—following his orders—but when he was unable to elude them, he invited them to the fort. The two riders were a Spanish soldier and a Hispanicized Indian. Robinson had been apprehended in Santa Fe, they informed Pike, and they had come to find any other Americans in the vicinity. They wanted to know why he was there and how many men he had. He told them he intended to descend the Red, but beyond that the conversation went nowhere. They spoke no English or French, and Pike commanded only halting Spanish and had no desire to satisfy their inquiries anyway. They departed for Santa Fe the next day, indicating the governor would send an emissary to whom Pike could explain himself. In the meantime, Pike dispatched Miller and Meek to cross the mountains and bring out all of the stranded men, including Smith and Vazquez from the Arkansas River. A Spanish emissary, Lieutenant Ignacio Saltelo, arrived on the morning of the February 26, backed by a hundred soldiers. Pike welcomed the commander into the stockade, and the Americans and Spaniards breakfasted together. Then Saltelo got down to business. He informed Pike, presumably in French, that the New Mexico governor, Joaquin del Real Alencaster, had invited Pike and his party to Santa Fe, from where the governor would provide an escort to the Red River. "What ...," Pike interrupted, "is not this the Red river?"[60]

"No sir!," Saltelo retorted, "the Rio del Norte." The Americans had camped on the Rio Conejos, a tributary of the Rio Grande, on Spanish soil. Immediately, Pike ordered his soldiers to lower the American flag. But Saltelo pressed for more: his mules and horses were nearby, he said, ready to take Pike and his men and their baggage to Santa Fe right then. Pike protested that his orders would not justify a detour to Santa Fe. Saltelo persisted. Pike was getting mad. He insisted he must wait for his men to come out of the mountains. Saltelo replied that, in that case, he would wait with Pike. Or Pike could come now and Saltelo would leave a detachment to escort the rescue party when it arrived. It did not matter to Saltelo. Pike decided to go. He was running out of arguments, and cooperating would be a gesture of goodwill. Sergeant Meek, the expedition's ranking member after Pike, was still in the mountains, but Pike left him orders for commanding the rump of the party, which would consist of Smith, Vazquez, Sparks, Daugherty, and Miller when they returned, and Jackson and Jacob Carter, whom Pike left at the stockade to wait for them. He invited Saltelo's soldiers to gather around the fort, and when they discovered there was not to be a fight, they cheerfully shared their provisions with Pike's men, "covering them with their blankets, &c." Meanwhile, Pike rode out twelve miles to spend the night with the Spanish officers. He would have some more labels to cross out on his maps that evening.[61]

Lost?

Pike's July 22 letter to Wilkinson had now come full circle. In that report, Pike had proposed that if he encountered Spaniards, he would pretend to have lost his way while looking for the Red River. When such a situation actually arose, he did just that. The coincidence has proven too much to swallow for those who suspect Pike had secret orders. A coherent story does follow from the starting assumption of secret orders. Pike went north from the Arkansas to follow what he took to be the Spanish trail to Santa Fe. When the trail petered out in the South Platte watershed, he crossed the Mosquito Range to the southwest, the direction of Santa Fe. Instead of wintering on the Arkansas or retreating from the Wet Mountain Valley, he foolishly pressed on, again to the southwest, willing to sacrifice anything to reach the New Mexican capital. In the San Luis Valley, the argument goes, he knew quite well he was on the Rio Grande and deliberately built a fort, raised a flag, and sent Robinson to Santa Fe on the flimsiest of excuses. He had executed an elaborate plot to follow his real orders to spy on Spanish territory, then feigned innocence of the plan when Saltelo showed up. His claim to being lost, as one of his most insistent doubters put it, was "so much applesauce."[62]

The secret-orders theory, however, depends on some assumptions that stretch the evidence. It requires a knowledgeable and rational Pike, who understood the geography not only well enough to navigate it himself but also simultaneously to concoct plausible counter-factual stories about it in the process. It also depends on a Pike who had time, energy, and foresight to falsify his journal and mislead his men, and who was cold-blooded enough to remain indifferent to their sufferings and his own in order to keep up his ruse. None of this fits well with the compassion he had exhibited throughout his life. Nor does it fit the apparent understanding of his character by his men, who faithfully executed orders through two brutal winter expeditions and who resolved to rescue him when he failed to return from the hunting trip near Grape Creek, even though some of them could barely walk. Nor does it square with the fallacies of Enlightenment geography that clouded Pike's understanding of the terrain, the sketchiness of the Santa Fe Trail map, or his physiological and cognitive impairment from Christmas Day until the arrival in the San Luis Valley. Moreover,

Pike published his July 22 letter in 1810 along with the rest of his maps and journals. Although he removed one critical line—about an unplanned trip to Santa Fe being a welcome serendipity—he evidently did not think the letter a damning document. Turning north from the Arkansas and twice crossing mountains to the southwest may to some observers seem to be evidence of secret orders or other disingenuousness. But they are not required to explain such behavior.

Pike's actions during those months were equally consistent with those of a man bumbling through the mountains looking for a river he does not know is three hundred miles away. In that case, the July 22 letter may be just what it appears to be—the hypothetical musings of a man embarking on a journey he knows will bring innumerable contingencies. Pike followed the human trail north from the Arkansas on December 10 because he had been unable to get the lay of the land by climbing the Grand Peak, and the geography as viewed from below did not match the picture he carried in his head or on his maps. He crossed southwest over the Mosquito Range from South Park on December 18 because that was the direction in which he believed the Red River lay. After Christmas, he descended the Arkansas, because that was exactly what a man who believed it to be the Red, which he had orders to follow home, would do. He crossed the Sangres the next month for the same reason he crossed the Mosquito Range—further emboldened perhaps by dose of irrational panic brought on by hunger, fatigue, and hypothermia that clouded his judgment of alternatives such as looking for the Red on the warmer, drier Plains or returning to the blockhouse and staging rescue operations from there.

In the San Luis Valley, the geography matched the Santa Fe Trail map Pike carried exactly. On that sketch, the Arkansas and Red both flowed south or southeast, roughly parallel. Between them, he had scrawled, "4 Days"—about what it took the party to get from the Arkansas to the San Luis Valley, after allowing for snow, frostbite, bad hunting, separation, and other setbacks. The map labeled the upper reaches of the Red "small branches" and showed three streams joining to form the main stem, two of which flowed from a chain of mountains from the west or southwest. Given all this, Pike might reasonably have concluded he was somewhere near the confluence of those branches, not far from the trail to Santa Fe. Finding themselves secure and with time on their hands Pike and Robinson cooked up the Santa Fe plan based on information one or both of them knew about Morrison back home. That Pike and Robinson believed they were on the Red is confirmed by the fact that Robinson departed upstream on the Conejos. Had they known that they were on the Rio Grande, the logical approach to Santa Fe would have been downstream. Although heading up the Conejos does—counterintuitively—in fact lead to a good route to Santa Fe, there was no way for Pike and Robinson to have that kind of nuanced knowledge of the local landscape, even if somehow they knew other things about the location of the rivers that Enlightenment geographers did not.

Pike's protest of innocence on the banks of the Rio Conejos, then, must be understood in the context of three months of puzzling behavior and bad decisions. He was utterly unprepared—physically or intellectually—for what befell the party in the mountains. Much of what he brought into the West—horses, clothing, maps, the ability to cajole and threaten people in the name of the United States of America—had given out. Having passed beyond the ability of the American state to support them, the men were reduced to relying on their bodies, the cultural knowledge they carried in their heads, and each other. It was not easy. At one point or another, but fortuitously never all at once, each of these resources failed them. Meanwhile, the Rocky Mountain winter pummeled the men's bodies and impaired their decision making. Although tantalizing, and perhaps plausible, the theory of secret orders ultimately rests on the speculative existence of such instructions. If everything can be explained by the available evidence, historians must be cautious in constructing explanations that require conjectural evidence. The counter story of Pike as an unenlightened geographer and physiologically and cognitively impaired organism, squares not only with the available evidence but also with his character and history of overreaching orders. Thus, his behavior is best explained as part of a larger set of mistakes and poor decisions occasioned by failure of his resources, including his body, to do for him what he had planned.

Pike's pursuit of national objects beyond his explicit orders also squares with his nationalist sensibilities. Western snows buried unit cohesion and froze the tissue of his men's toes. Shoes wore out and uniforms proved too flimsy for the season. He repeatedly had to revise what he had learned from Enlightenment geography, and the bodies and minds of horses and men broke down, and fortitude gave way to starvation, frostbite, hypothermia, and fatigue. When all his resources failed him, Pike drew from one additional reservoir: national attachment. Thus, he appealed to national ideas like equality and gratitude to sustain the party through Brown's grumbling and to justify the abandonment of Sparks and Daugherty. For the rest of their journey, Pike and his men traveled through

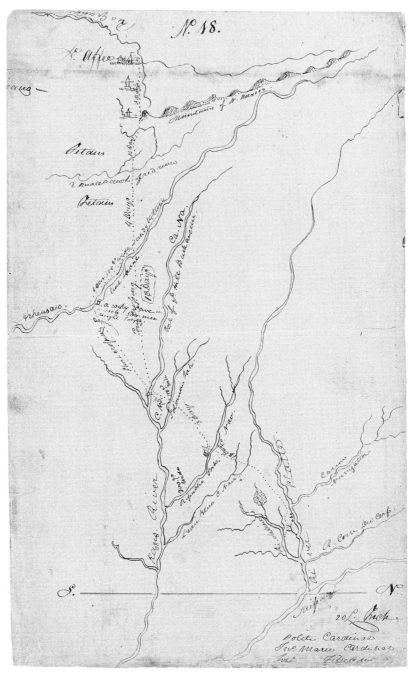

FIGURE 5.11 Santa Fe Trail map. National Archives and Records Administration.

equally unforgiving environments, but in navigating them, the Americans benefited from a new resource, Spanish hospitality, though it often grated against Pike's nationalism. Whether Pike went to Santa Fe by compulsion or design, the confused, trilingual encounter on the Rio Conejos was as much a rescue as an arrest.

6

A Comfortable Captivity

LEARNING NATIONALISM ABROAD IN NEW SPAIN,
FEBRUARY–JULY 1807

IT WAS NOT every day that seven scruffy American soldiers rode into Santa
Fe. When Pike's party presented just such a spectacle on March 3, 1807,
New Mexicans crowded into the narrow streets and followed the men and
their escorts to the center of the pueblo. Pike was dressed in blue trousers,
a blanket coat, a cap of scarlet cloth lined with fox skins, and moccasins.
His companions wore leggings, breech cloths, and leather coats. Not one
of them had a proper hat, and they had long since shed their uniforms. As
they dismounted in front of the government house, the plaza hummed as
townspeople puzzled over the ragged strangers. Do people dwell in houses
where you come from, someone asked, or in camps like Indians? Do you
wear hats in your country, inquired another? Pike tried to reassure himself
that back home his refinement was not in doubt. "Worth made the man,"
he recalled all the officers used to say in the Ohio Valley. In New Mexico,
however, he was not so sure. "The first impression made on the ignorant
is hard to eradicate," he feared. He was an American officer, and yet these
people were streaming out of their "miserable...houses" to gawk at his
tatters. It was all "extremely mortifying."[1]

The shabby arrival marked the beginning of a sojourn in northern New
Spain that was relieving to Pike's body but wrenching to his sensibilities.
Already confused by geographical boundaries, Pike soon found he had to
redraw the cultural borders he had expected as well. He carried in his head
a clear and uncomplicated division between American virtue and Spanish
degeneracy, but the townspeople's scorn had breached this mental
boundary. With their generosity, he donned a new shirt, tasted sweet
chocolate, and sipped fine wine. He also slept in beds, watched public
performances, and rode on horses, sometimes in coaches. In these months
in New Spain, he probably enjoyed more luxury than he ever had in his

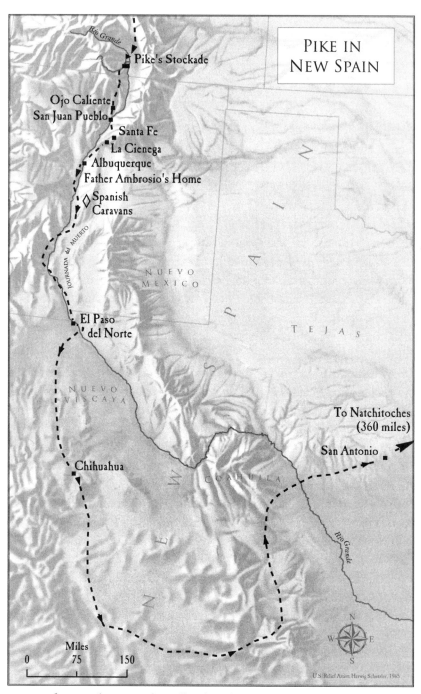

PIKE IN
NEW SPAIN

Río Grande

Pike's Stockade

Ojo Caliente
San Juan Pueblo

Santa Fe
La Cienega
Albuquerque
Father Ambrosio's Home

Spanish
Caravans

JOURNADA del MUERTO

NUEVO
MEXICO

N
E
W

S
P
A
I
N

TEJAS

El Paso
del Norte

NUEVO
VISCAYA

To Natchitoches
(360 miles)

San Antonio

Chihuahua

COAHUILA

Río Grande

Miles
0   75   150

N
W   E
S

U.S. Relief Artist. Herwig Schnitzler, 1965

FIGURE 6.1 Map by Steve Chignell and Sophia Linn.

life. Although he thoroughly indulged in these comforts, sometimes to excess, being restored to civilization by people who lived in mud houses jumbled the neat distinction he drew between American refinement and New Mexican coarseness. Moreover, at every turn, he met people of maddeningly perplexing nationality, who defied his mind's easy categorizations. There were Americans who had deserted their country, Mexican-born Spaniards ready to reject their sovereign's colonial domination, Catholic priests who craved Enlightenment learning, and Spanish gentlemen who matched Pike's own national loyalty and exhibited all the other virtues he most esteemed, except that they gave their allegiance to a regime he considered corrupt and backward. In New Spain, Pike encountered loyalty, refinement, self-discipline, love of knowledge, and pursuits of national and personal independence, discovering that he could neither exalt these as peculiarly American traits nor pin their opposites on Spaniards. Thus, as Pike shed his animal hides for Spanish linen, physical hardship gave way to a comfortable captivity that brought his understandings of American and Spanish national character into tension. Worse, although he did not know it while traveling in New Spain, by the time he edited his journals for publication, he learned that journeying to the West at Wilkinson's behest and the expedition's tenuous links to Aaron Burr had cast his own loyalty into doubt among his fellow Americans.

Nationalism provided the language for reconciling all this. In the descriptions of New Spain that he published after returning to the United States, Pike burnished his own nationalist credentials by comparing the Spanish colonial system unfavorably to American society. In particular, he played on American prejudices of Spanish and Catholic corruption, despotism, sensuousness, superstition, and excessive indulgence, a constellation of alleged vices that formed the early nineteenth-century version of the Black Legend, the long-term Anglo-American antipathy to Spanish colonialism, religion, and culture. In contrast, he characterized himself as a self-disciplined, rational, Protestant Yankee and highlighted how he had combatted wickedness in Spanish lands. Simultaneously, he extolled a few exceptional Spaniards who hungered for independence, exhibited admirable national loyalties, or appreciated education and Enlightenment ideas. In averring these individuals' desire for deliverance from various forms of tyranny, he rendered them fit for absorption into the American republic of one heart and mind and invited his readers vicariously to join him in their liberation. By praising virtuous individuals while denigrating the regime, he both reassured readers of his own national commitments

FIGURE 6.2 Pike's party arrives in Santa Fe, painting by Frederic Remington. "Great Explorers IX: Zebulon Pike," *Collier's Weekly*, June 16, 1906. Denver Public Library, Western History Collection.

and restored coherence to the moral distinctions he and his readers drew between themselves and Spaniards. His embrace of such stereotypes distorted his portrait of New Spain, but it highlights quite clearly and accurately his use of nationalism to collect the rewards he believed his sacrifice merited. Thus, confronting a foreign Other and recounting the meeting in a way that publically exhibited his loyalty crystallized the nationalist sensibilities that had been forming in his character since his childhood in a military family in the wake of the Revolution.

New Mexico

The comfortable captivity began on the third day of the march to Santa Fe, under the escort of Lieutenant Bartholomew Fernandez and a party of fifty men. They rode hard that day, making forty-five miles, and by the afternoon, Pike wrote, the "difference of climate was astonishing." Descending from the hills and snows, they came to a plain, where "vegetation was sprouting." There, they came to the village of Ojo Caliente. Adobe walls enclosed the town, which was filled with one-story houses with narrow doors and small windows. It was modest, but with five hundred residents and a mill nearby, it must have looked sumptuous to the ragged Americans. That night they were treated to a festive dance. As they passed more adobe towns the next day, townspeople streamed out, offering food and drink, dressings for sore feet, and the best bed in the house. Pike marveled at their conduct, which "brought to my recollection the hospitality of the ancient patriarchs, and caused me to sigh with regret at the corruption of that noble principle, by the polish of modern ages." For the next three weeks Pike and his men received similar treatment at every town they passed. They were traveling the busiest thoroughfare in New Mexico, the Camino Real, the royal road, which wended south generally following the Rio Grande through the most densely populated part of the province.[2]

In San Juan Pueblo on March 2, Pike got his first introduction to Spanish intellectual pursuits. San Juan, or St. John's as he called it, was another mud-walled village of flat-roofed houses, but even more substantial than any they had yet passed. It had double the population of Ojo Caliente and was home to the man Pike identified as the province's "president priest." As the strangers approached, people climbed onto the rooftops and crowded into the street. Fernandez dismounted and embraced the priest, and the villagers gathered to kiss the prelate's ring. Pike simply saluted the priest, who invited them in for coffee and chocolate. It was the "first good meal, wine, &c.," Pike had enjoyed in a long time, but he paid the price for his indulgence with acute gastrointestinal discomfort. In his journal, Pike apologized to his readers for succumbing to such immoderation and "determined to be more abstemious in the future."[3]

While Pike's stomach gurgled and cramped, the priest embarked on a two-hour dissertation about botany, literature, and other topics that Pike "enjoyed but little." The cleric droned on in Spanish and Latin. The house warmed. And Pike continued digesting his repast. But "by the exercise of a small degree of patience," he wrote, "I entirely acquired the esteem of this worthy father." The priest then turned to the subject of astronomy and invited Pike to take out his sextant and telescope, which enchanted everyone present. At first Pike was amazed that "a man who appeared to be perfect master of the antient languages, a botanist, mineralogist, and chemist, should be so ignorant of the powers of reflection and the first principles of mathematics." Pike claimed that Fernandez later informed him that the Spanish government prevented the pursuit of any science that "would have a tendency to extend the views of the subjects of the provinces to the geography of their country, or of any subject which would bring to view a comparison of their local advantages and situations with other countries."[4]

If the Spanish lieutenant said anything to this effect, Pike overstated its implications of inherent Spanish and Catholic ignorance. In the 1770s and 1780s, frontier officials under King Carlos III had enthusiastically encouraged science, exploration, and other Enlightenment pursuits in the Internal Provinces, bringing European thinking to the frontier in their private libraries and their personal relationships with Iberian intellectuals and disseminating it among the local intelligentsia. There was a thriving book trade, and censorship laws were loosened. Spanish promotion of the spread of knowledge, however, reversed with Carlos's death in 1788 and, more importantly, with the French Revolution's alarming demonstration of the practical implications of Enlightenment philosophy. Moreover, frontier officials feared that American attempts to undermine Spain's colonies would begin with a wave of seditious ideas. What Pike took in San Juan and elsewhere as the stunted intellect of Spaniards and the Church was actually a reflection of their calculated reaction to North American geopolitics. Fernandez and others who hungered for knowledge were not exceptions to Spanish backwardness so much as the still glowing remnants of an until recently vigorous Spanish Enlightenment that had diffused all the way to adobe towns in New Mexico. Spaniards marveled at instruments of science in this province not because they were ignorant but because they were enlightened.[5]

Another character Pike met in San Juan was none other than Baptiste Lalande, the ostensible object of Robinson's foray into New Mexico. As Pike walked to his men's quarters, Lalande accosted him in broken English. "My friend," he said, "I am very sorry to see you here: we are all prisoners in this country and can never return." Pike disputed the claim and then requested they switch to French, whereupon Lalande peppered him with questions. Where was Pike from? Why had he come to New Mexico? Lalande was not the first foreigner in New Mexico to take a particular interest in Pike. A few days before, an old Frenchmen in the escort party approached Pike and "expressed great regret" at Pike's capture and offered to hide Pike's papers. Suspicious, Pike gave the old man a few duplicate pages of his journal as a test and "charged him to guard [them] very carefully." Pike was sure that both men were spies, instructed by Spanish officials to lure the American into divulging more information than he otherwise intended. After Pike and Lalande entered the Americans' quarters, Pike ordered his men to fasten the door and grab Lalande. He accused Lalande of being a tool of the governor or someone else who had asked him to befriend and then betray the Americans. A creole from American Louisiana, French by culture, Lalande had absconded across national boundaries to avoid paying an American debt. Then, in New Mexico, as the trader Josiah Gregg would later say, opportunity overcame his "patriotism and probity," and he petitioned to become a Spanish subject. Now Lalande was betraying Americans to the Spaniards. Pike took out his sword, declaring that men who ratted on others "were scoundrels and never should escape punishment." A trembling Lalande confessed to the charge and begged Pike not to harm him. Pike then ordered the men to release him, calling him "too contemptible for further notice" and telling him to advise the governor, next time he wanted to pull such a trick, to choose a man "of more abilities and sense."[6]

The next day's journey brought more of the same. Lalande and his compromised nationality continued traveling with the party. They passed more villages, stopping to meet locals of importance. One priest, "understanding that I would not kiss his hand, would not present it to me." Another cleric strutted around with a knife in his boot, "whispering to one girl, chucking another under the chin, going out with a third, &c." The display, Pike grumbled, would have gotten the cleric "banished" from the priesthood "in our country." A third priest offered them coffee. It was only the third day since descending from the snows, but Pike was coming to disdain New Mexico.[7] It was filled with people of marginal nationality and priests who lived in obscene opulence, whose sexual transgressions, demand for idolatrous homage, and immoderate lifestyle turned Pike's stomach—both literally and figuratively. Even the comforts he enjoyed did not escape his disgust. Good food and drink tempted his self-discipline, and even the San Juan priest's pursuit of intellectual enlightenment became for Pike evidence of Spanish corruption. Thus he contrasted his rational, enlightened, self-disciplined, nationalist, Protestant American self to the idolatrous, backward, immoderate, nationally mongrel, Catholic world of New Mexico. Almost certainly, his Black-Legend biases distorted these descriptions of his first impressions of New Spain, though it is impossible to know how much. More certain is that it stung to have the population take him for a savage the night he arrived in Santa Fe, an error he took pains to set right for his reader.

Spanish officials, however, did not take him for a savage. To them, he constituted an ominous threat to a vast and valuable territory. Santa Fe was the capital of New Mexico, the northernmost outpost of Spanish settlement in the Interior Provinces. To the north and west lay millions of square miles that stretched to the Columbia River, a territory dimly known to the Spaniards but no less tantalizing for them than Louisiana was for Pike and Jefferson. The Missouri River, officials believed, provided an avenue to the commerce of the Pacific Rim. As Nemesio Salcedo, commandant general of the Interior Provinces, wrote to the Spanish foreign minister in 1805, the Americans took "as their objective no less than facilitating their commerce to Asia by making a port on the South Sea [the Pacific Ocean] between 40 and 45 latitude, at which parallels the Misuri has its sources." Salcedo and other officials also feared the Missouri's headwaters lay near the tributaries that fed the Rio Grande and the Colorado River and that enterprising Americans or Britons might find their way via the Missouri to the silver loads of Chihuahua and Sonora and "demand," as the Louisiana governor warned the crown in 1794, "the possession of the rich mines of the interior provinces of the very kingdom of Mexico."[8]

The waters of the Pacific Northwest, then, were the avenues by which empires might gather the furs and ores and other valuables of North America and distribute them throughout the Pacific Rim, a commerce Spain had long desired to control. The Nootka conflict of the 1790s, in which Britain had forced Spain to cede its exclusive sovereignty over the northern Pacific Coast, led the Spanish government to switch its efforts to protect its northwest interests by blocking encroachment by land from the east. The Nootka negotiations had also changed the rules of imperial territorial claims in North America. No longer was prior discovery sufficient to claim sovereignty. Increasingly, sovereignty depended on establishing mastery—through trade, forts, and the attachments of peoples. Whoever settled the land, tapped its resources, concentrated its energies, and allied with its natives could exert the most formidable claims to the borderlands between empires. Wilkinson had understood this when he sent Pike to map the land, follow the rivers, report on resources, and befriend Indians. So did the Spaniards, who placed on Salcedo's shoulders responsibility for blocking trespassers from entering this vast territory.[9]

Rumblings from the United States around the turn of the century indicated that the territory was also vulnerable. From the mines of Sonora to the mouth of the Columbia, Salcedo administered more territory than any other commandant in Spanish America, but his resources hardly matched the challenge. Since the 1780s, Spaniards had seen alliances with Indians as essential to the crown's hold on this northern frontier, and tenuous peace pacts had been concluded with the Navajos, Utes, and Comanches. By century's end, however, these exclusive agreements faced competition. Spaniards' efforts to establish themselves on the Great Plains in the 1790s repeatedly foundered on challenges from Indians hostile to the idea. In September 1804, Salcedo warned the Spanish viceroy that in addition to exploring the Missouri and searching for mines, the Americans were "ingratiating themselves to the Indian nations," and he ordered several expeditions to the Plains to win Indian loyalties. Amid such concerns came Wilkinson's 1804 letter warning that Lewis and Clark were starting across the continent in search of commercial routes and diplomatic ties with Indians. Soon after came news of the Freeman-Custis-Sparks expeditions on the Red and other potential incursions. In response to such trespasses, Spanish officials instructed Salcedo to arrest trespassers and confiscate their papers and instruments. They were to be treated humanely and returned to their homeland, but a complaint was to be registered with their government. Rumors of the Burr conspiracy intensified the alarm, as Spanish officials believed the former vice president's principal objective to be the invasion of Spanish territory, with the consent of the US government. Not trusting fellow officials to convey information reliably in such a delicate matter as the Burr threat raised, Salcedo even set personal envoys to the United States to set up a direct line of intelligence between Chihuahua and Philadelphia.[10]

All this, coupled with the tensions on the Sabine as well as Jefferson's bellicose speeches in early 1806, convinced Salcedo that war with the United States was imminent. Men from Louisiana had been trickling into New Mexico and Texas for years, but they had generally come as individuals. Pike, in contrast, led a military party with official orders from the United States of America. In this context, New Mexican governors acting under Salcedo's orders beginning in 1804 launched at least four military expeditions onto the Plains in hopes of capturing Lewis and Clark and intimidating the Indians of the grasslands into alliance with Spain. Three of these failed, crumbling in the face of natives' resistance and/or harsh conditions that led to mutiny and desertion. In the spring of 1806, just as Pike was preparing to depart St. Louis, Salcedo sent Spain's largest and most ambitious expedition onto the Plains, this time under the command of his most capable officer, Lieutenant Facundo Melgares. Pike's name did not appear in any of the Spanish documents that recorded these efforts, making it unlikely that officials knew of or aimed to capture him, as he mistakenly believed, but once he turned up in the San Luis Valley, Spanish officials had no difficulty fitting him into the larger American conspiracy that Lewis and Clark, the Burr scheme, American wooing of Indians, and the Sabine conflict had already conjured in their minds. The appearance of American soldiers in the vicinity of Santa Fe fulfilled Spanish officials' worst nightmares.[11]

Consequently, as soon as Robinson showed up, Governor Real Alencaster suspected that this stranger might be part of the larger American vanguard he and his superiors had feared. Robinson told the governor he was a Frenchman from St. Louis and that he had been visiting the Pawnees in order to collect a debt from some traders. Learning, while among the Pawnees, that his debtors were in New Mexico, he had joined a party of fifteen men who went hunting on the western Plains. After they turned back in the snows of the Rockies, he had come on alone, until finding some Utes who guided him to Santa Fe. Real Alencaster doubted this tale, assuming Robinson had been sent by Wilkinson. He turned the ersatz Frenchman over to a military escort bound for Chihuahua, the capital of the Internal Provinces, and dispatched a party to try to find the rest of Robinson's companions.[12] This was the detachment that first located Pike on the Conejos.

While Real Alencaster puzzled over the implications of Robinson's appearance, his emissaries came back and reported that the news was even worse. A party of American soldiers had camped on the Conejos, and they were flying an American flag. The governor sent a larger armed party, the one that brought Pike to Santa Fe. Capturing Pike turned out to be easier than keeping him. Real Alencaster had orders to detain Americans but not for what to do with them. Plenty of foreigners had managed to get to Santa Fe, but few had managed to get out. Pike, however, presented a more delicate case. Diplomatic relations with the United States were momentarily quiescent. Real Alencaster did not want to upset the apple cart by harming or offending an American military officer. For his part, Pike had heard from the old Frenchman who had offered to hide his papers that the Spanish expedition to the Pawnees the previous summer had been sent to capture Pike, something Fernandez had confirmed but which turned out to be not quite accurate.[13] As Pike arrived in Santa Fe, then, neither he nor Real Alencaster understood each other very well. They began a dance in which each tried to make sense of the other without giving the other much information to go on.

After dismounting in the plaza in Santa Fe and enduring the taunts about houses and hats, Pike was led into the palace of the governors. He passed through several rooms with animal-skin rugs and took a seat to wait for Real Alencaster. All rose when the governor entered, and he addressed Pike in French. "You come to reconnoiter our country, do you?" "I marched to reconnoiter our own," Pike replied. The governor continued the examination, twice asking if Robinson was with Pike, which Pike twice denied. Real Alencaster then inquired about when Pike had left St. Louis, which Pike indicated was in July. "I think you marched in June," the governor retorted. "No sir!" Pike shot back.[14] Real Alencaster was getting nowhere. He dismissed Pike and told him to return later in the evening with his trunk of papers. If confrontation wouldn't work, Real Alencaster would try a tack with a little more guile.

So would Pike. As he left the government house, Pike happened upon the man to whom he had given his journals. Believing the man had come to make a report to the governor, Pike sarcastically asked whether he had yet done so. The Frenchman replied in a "humble tone" and slunk away. No matter, Pike had not trusted him in the first place. Instead, he had ordered his men to stash his more sensitive papers on their persons and in their clothing.

When he returned to the governor's palace, the second meeting was different. The governor called in an American prisoner named Zalmon Cooley to translate the conversation. Cooley had joined an 1801 expedition to Texas under General Wilkinson's long-time aide, Philip Nolan. Ostensibly, Nolan came to trade horses, but he had no passport and had already made Spaniards suspicious of his previously shadowy sojourns in their territory. They attacked the party, believing it to be a filibustering mission. Nolan was killed, and the surviving members of his party, who claimed to know nothing about filibustering, were taken captive. Pike met two of them during his tour of Mexico, and he gathered news about eleven more. Although Nolan's actual objectives are unknown, Pike believed the men to be innocents, and Cooley later begged for his help. Cooley's presence in the conversation with Real Alencaster, however, turned out to be unnecessary, as Pike insisted on holding it in French, without an interpreter. After Pike read the expedition's instructions aloud in French, the governor rose and shook Pike's hand. He declared his pleasure to meet Pike "as a man of honor and gentleman" and invited Pike to retire and take his trunk with him. Pike believed the interrogation to be over.[15]

In the meantime, Pike's men had been enjoying their comfortable captivity. All along the Camino Real, as Pike had hobnobbed with priests and other dignitaries, his men found more raucous amusements. If wilderness had enforced some degree of equality within the party, the class distinctions that divided an American officer from his recruits resurfaced upon return to settled territory. Usually, Pike's men were quartered separately from him and consorted with a different stratum of Spanish society. They had considerable freedom to explore the towns and partake of available pleasures. They drank and danced with locals and had a wilder time than the polite conversation Pike's hosts offered him. After the interview with the governor, Pike learned the locals were "treating the men with liquor." Intoxicated men might reveal the papers they stowed. Or perhaps a hearty hug from a drinking buddy or the wandering hand of a female companion might inadvertently discover them. In light of Real Alencaster's new friendliness, Pike decided to reclaim the documents and return them to his trunk. But the governor outfoxed him.[16]

He recalled Pike and his trunk again the next day. After examining the container's contents, including the materials Pike had restored to it, Real Alencaster ordered Pike to prepare himself and his men to march to Chihuahua to appear before Salcedo, a plan the governor had actually intended before Pike had even arrived in Santa Fe. Pike demanded to know if he was a prisoner. Real Alencaster said no. Pike disagreed. His papers had been seized. He had been deprived of his arms. He was being marched nearly five hundred miles off course from his orders. "I cannot consent," he insisted, "without its being by force of arms." Real Alencaster assured him his consent was not voluntary. Both men then retired to commit their dispute to paper, with Pike receiving a certificate acknowledging that he and his men could keep their weapons but that they nevertheless went at the command of Spanish officials. At stake in this charade was more than the semantic duel over whether or not Pike was a prisoner. By insisting that Pike was not a prisoner, Spanish officials preserved their claim against the US government for the cost of escorting the party around the northern frontier while still maintaining the diplomatic pretense that they had not arrested an American officer. The arrangement also resolved a more immediate dilemma for Real Alencaster, who could neither allow Pike to go on exploring Spanish territory nor keep him, an American army officer, indefinitely in Santa Fe, as he had Cooley, Lalande, and others. In effect, he punted his problem to Salcedo.[17]

Before he sent Pike on his way, however, Alencaster made one last attempt to obtain information from him. Neither guile nor intimidation had yielded anything that the governor took to be the truth. Next he would try hospitality. In the morning, he had sent Pike a new shirt and a neck cloth, made by his sister in Spain, and invited the American to dine with him. This time, however, Pike got the best of him, or so he reported in his journal. "The dinner at the governor's was rather splendid," he wrote. They drank fine wine and ate delectable Spanish dishes. Cheered by the wine, Real Alencaster loosened his lips and revealed sensitive matters such as disputes among Spanish officials over foreign policy with the Americans. At the end of the meal, he ordered up his coach. Pulled by six mules, it lurched out of Santa Fe carrying the governor, Fernandez, Pike, and his new escort, Captain Anthony D'Almansa. Three miles out of town, the governor dropped them off, crying "Remember Alencaster, in peace or war."[18] Pike departed Santa Fe against his will, but he left much more presentable than he had arrived, well-dressed and riding in style.

Even as he played cat and mouse with Real Alencaster, Pike found much to admire among the Spaniards he met, especially their hospitality and interest in discussing science, geography, politics, international affairs, religion, and commerce. Despite the national barriers, shared intellectual interests made them kindred spirits, and both the American and his Spanish hosts exchanged information, hungry to learn about each other. As the party traveled south from Santa Fe, Pike delighted in conversing with Spaniards who were eager to hear about his country and forthcoming in describing theirs. One morning when they were delayed by snow, Pike visited an old invalid soldier "who received us in the most hospitable manner, giving us chocolate &c." He inquired about American politics and religion, and favorably compared American customs to Spanish. Pike eagerly held forth on rotation in office, freedom of conscience, and other topics, which, Pike noted approvingly, the old soldier found extraordinary and marvelous.[19] In encounters like this one, the descriptions of which must be taken as being aimed as much at his American readers as at the soldier he described, Pike discovered that military honor, love of knowledge, nationalist commitments, personal virtue, and other Enlightenment imprints that stamped his own sensibilities were abundant among the elite of northern New Spain.

Assigned to escort Pike was Captain Anthony D'Almansa. Lieutenant Fernandez, who had conducted Pike to Santa Fe and who Pike often referred to in his journals as "my friend," tagged along the first day as well. After taking leave of the governor, they climbed a hill on horseback and galloped through a snowstorm until they came after nightfall to a village, likely the town of Cienega. There, Pike and the two officers lodged at the home of a priest who was absent. Drink opened D'Almansa up as it had the governor earlier in the day, and he recounted his woes while the temperate Pike listened eagerly. D'Almansa was an old man. He was a *criollo*—the word for someone who could claim Spanish racial and cultural status but who had been born in the New World. *Peninsulares*, in contrast, were Spaniards born on the Iberian Peninsula, and they considered themselves a notch above their locally born compatriots. D'Almansa had served faithfully in his majesty's army for forty years. For that service, however, he had attained only the rank of first lieutenant and captain by brevet. Meanwhile, he had watched younger *peninsulares* regularly promoted over his head.[20] Perhaps Pike saw a bit of his own father in the aging, infirm, and underappreciated D'Almansa.

After drink put the old man to sleep, Pike and Fernandez talked late into the snowy evening. Fernandez elaborated on the *criollos'* dilemma. New World-born Spaniards like D'Almansa and probably Fernandez, too, were suspended in a frustrating status within the Spanish empire. Many ranked at the top of New Spain's social hierarchy, owning land, controlling labor of Indians and *mestizos*, and enjoying the honorable titles of *don* and *doña*. In a society that had a different set of laws for people of different social statuses, the *criollos* suffered no legal barriers to their position or advancement. They held government posts and military commissions. They dominated the priesthood. They could amass great wealth. Yet they chafed under the perceived haughtiness of Iberians, who generally held the best positions in colonial society. *Criollos* could, for example, be officers, but rarely did they achieve high rank. They were priests, but not bishops. In short, their status enabled them to aspire but not to achieve. They wanted, Fernandez informed Pike, a "change of affairs," including open trade with the United States.

To Pike such birth preferences were anathema. To prevent men from rising according to their abilities, as Pike believed he was doing, was an outrageous violation of independence, and he reported Fernandez's commentary in his journals as evidence of the Spanish empire's wickedness. Liquor had opened up Real Alencaster and D'Almansa, but it was sympathy that loosened Pike's lips. Taking a piece of chalk, he sketched on the ground the geography of Louisiana and New Mexico. He also provided his friend a letter addressed to US citizens attesting to Fernandez's friendliness and influence. The lieutenant was convinced that the United States would soon invade New Spain, and he believed such a certificate would benefit him. Lest the invaders take him for one of the haughty backward Iberians, he, too, wanted to be remembered by Pike in war and peace. The next morning, after finding common ground on a snowy night a few miles south of Santa Fe, the American and the Spaniard embraced and bid a tearful farewell.[21]

Continuing south with D'Almansa, Pike made many more friends. The day after Fernandez departed, they came to the house of a priest, Father Rubí, who received them with the standard hospitality. At dinner Pike sampled fine wines and enjoyed a musical performance of drums, horns, violins, and cymbals. It was the conversation, however, that most impressed Pike, and before he left "we seemed to have been friends for years past." Once again, the plight of the *criollos* was the topic of "candid conversation," and in expressing his opinion, Father Rubí "neither spared the government nor its administrators." He also "displayed a liberality of opinion and a fund of knowledge" about government and religion. What most interested Pike, however, were the cleric's statistical tables. For each town in New Mexico, the priest had compiled information on latitude, longitude, population, and a multitude of social, political, and economic data that Pike considered "a complete geographical, statistical, and historical sketch of the Province." Pike wanted a copy but sensed that D'Almansa looked askance at Father Rubí's forthcomingness. He decided not to press his luck.[22]

At Father Rubí's Pike also met an old Indian. The man inquired whether Pike and his men were Spanish, to which a Spanish gentleman replied in the affirmative. But, the Indian objected, "they do not speak Castilian." True enough, he was told, but just as the Keres and Ute nations are both Indians but speak different languages, the strange visitors were Spaniards who spoke a different language. "This reasoning," Pike recorded, "seemed to satisfy the poor savage, and I could not but smile at the ingenuity displayed to make him believe there was no other nation of whites but the Spaniards."[23] While the Spanish gentleman sought to prevent the spread of knowledge and preserve power by maintaining ignorance, disgruntled *criollos* and enlightened Spanish priests with gridded data were Pike's collaborators in prying that information from Spanish grips and disseminating it to American readers, whom Pike correctly believed eager for stories of Spanish degeneracy.

Next Pike met Father Ambrosio Guerra in Albuquerque. Like Rubí, Guerra had plenty of food and drink and some interesting data, but he offered something more as well. Father Guerra housed several young women whom he had liberated from captivity. Their role in the priest's household was unclear—Pike called them Guerra's "adopted children"—but the cleric ordered them to greet Pike affectionately. Two of them, whom Pike took to be English, were of light complexion, and when Pike paid them some attention, the priest directed them to sit on the sofa beside Pike and embrace him. What he was offering Pike is not clear, and Pike did not explain, observing only that they were beautiful and not loath in making the required advances. After dinner, Father Guerra made a clearer invitation. He led Pike into a room darkened by black silk curtains, apparently his private religious chambers. Pike called it his "sanctum sanctorum." There, Father Guerra showed Pike "majestic images of various saints" and "the crucified Jesus, crowned with thorns, with rich rays of golden glory." Donning a black gown and miter, Guerra knelt before a cross and took Pike's hand, attempting to tug the American to his knees as well. Pike refused. The priest then began to pray. After a few minutes Guerra rose, placed his hands on Pike's shoulder, blessed him, and cried, "You will not be a Christian; Oh! what a pity! oh! what a Pity!" At the end of the evening, a shaken Pike acknowledged to his journal that the episode had made a "serious...impression" on him.[24] The American soldier and Spanish priest parted with "great marks of friendship," but once again the self-disciplined Yankee seems to have resisted what he took (or quite possibly mistook) as Catholic sexual and religious deviance and made sure not to miss the opportunity to tell his readers about it.

In the next town below Albuquerque, Pike reunited with Robinson. Since leaving the stockade, the doctor had, like Pike, enjoyed the luxuries New Spain could offer, and his body showed it. This man, Pike wrote, was "not that Robinson who left my camp, on the head waters of the Rio del Norte, pale, emaciated, with uncombed locks and beard of eight months growth." This one glowed with "fire, unsubdued enterprise and fortitude." At first Pike pretended not to know Robinson, true to what both men had told the governor. But they could not long contain their elation at the reunion. As they exchanged a warm greeting, D'Almansa smiled as if to say, "I knew this." After going out to where the men were camped and leaving D'Almansa's earshot, Robinson recounted his adventures. He had been guided by Indians to Santa Fe, where Real Alencaster received him coolly at first, saying Lalande had no money or property and vaguely promising to secure Robinson's claims at some point in the future. Then Real Alencaster warmed up to Robinson, as he had to Pike, inviting Robinson to dinner before dispatching him with an escort to Chihuahua to appear before Salcedo. Once Pike turned up in Santa Fe, Robinson's escort was halted in the village of San Fernandez, south of Albuquerque. Since then

Robinson had been practicing medicine in the countryside, using the role to gather information about "the manners, customs, &c. of the people, and to endeavor to ascertain the political and religious feelings and to gain every other species of information which would be necessary to our country and ourselves."[25]

There was, however, probably more to Robinson's story than he told Pike. According to Real Alencaster's letter to Salcedo, Robinson told the governor that the United States planned to extend its borders to New Mexico, establish ports on Louisiana's rivers, populate the banks of the Missouri, explore the western rivers, and capture distant Indian commerce.[26] Why Robinson told the governor this is not clear, though certainly it was nothing that Real Alencaster and Salcedo did not already know or suspect. Nor does the information appear to have been specific enough to have been strategically useful. Whatever the reason, the motives of the always shadowy Robinson would later grow even murkier.

Pike gave no hint that he knew any of this. Instead, the reunion was a "joyful meeting" for Pike and his men, for "the whole party was enthusiastically fond of [Robinson]." As they celebrated their reunion, Robinson shared one additional bit of good news. The man who was to escort them to Chihuahua was Don Facundo Melgares, whom Robinson described as a gallant gentleman soldier. Melgares was an Iberian-born officer, younger than D'Almansa, but destined to be yet another *peninsular* who passed the old man in rank. Already he had commanded the expedition that had narrowly missed catching Pike in the Pawnee village, and he would later become the last Spanish governor of New Mexico. For now, he and Robinson had been looking forward to Pike's arrival, "anticipating the pleasure we three will enjoy, in our journey to Chihuahua." Pike had made friends easily since leaving Santa Fe, but he was doubtful. "I suspected [Melgares] would watch us close."[27]

Melgares, however, lived up to Robinson's billing, and then some. "He received me," Pike wrote, "with the most manly frankness and the politeness of a man of the world." Within two hours, "we were as well acquainted as some people would be in the same number of months." According to Pike, Melgares had "none of the haughty Castillian pride," but rather "the urbanity of a Frenchman." He was well-mannered, gallant, generous, warm, and loyal. To demonstrate his goodwill, he handed the trunk of papers over to Pike, and he also withdrew Robinson's guard, entrusting the doctor to Pike's supervision, two gestures that Pike appreciated as marks of "politeness and friendship." Pike also recognized in the Spanish lieutenant a man who shared Pike's sense of military and national loyalty. "He was one of the few officers or citizens whom I found," Pike wrote, "who was loyal to their king," though, to be sure, he was "indignant at the degraded state of the Spanish monarchy." He opposed the possibility of a war for independence "unless"—and this was important—"France should usurp the government of Spain." It was men like Melgares, Pike wrote, "who possess the heads to plan, the hearts to feel and the hands to carry this great and important work [independence] into execution." His description of Melgares reads as Pike must have wanted his own biography to be written. Perhaps because Melgares exhibited so many of the characteristics Pike most endeavored to cultivate in himself, he excused the Spanish officer for his loyalty to such a backward repressive country. Pike called him "my brother soldier," and the two became great friends.[28]

Before the party continued on to Chihuahua, Melgares gave a ball. He sent out a message to the *alcaldes* of all the villages in the area. "Send this evening six or eight of your handsomest young girls" to San Fernandez, where "I propose giving a fandango, for the entertainment of the American officers." Pike thought the gala a "handsome display of beauty," though he was appalled that such an order would be obeyed, and he took it as more evidence of "the degraded state of the common people." Similarly, he frowned on Melgares's "mode of living." In contrast to the austere American military crews Pike had captained, Melgares traveled in style, with eight mules loaded with camp equipment, wines, candies, and other delights. He played cards, hosted parties, and doled out handfuls of dollars to humble New Mexicans. "If a subaltern indulged himself with such a quantity of baggage," Pike wrote indignantly, "what would be the cavalcade attending an army?" Degraded villagers kowtowing to the whims of a passing army, junior officers traveling in the style of generals—it all "evince[d] the corruption of the Spanish discipline," Pike wrote, yet again titillating his readers and their anti-Spanish prejudices.[29]

Saying goodbye to D'Almansa on March 9, the party led by a wine-sipping, candy-eating Spanish lieutenant marched southward, a journey Pike used to apprise his readers both of New Spain's exploitable potential and its inhabitants' current dissatisfaction. Except for the difficult waterless stretch known as the *Jornada del Muerto*, Pike marveled at New Mexico's fertility. He and his troops had enjoyed plenty of "wood, water, provisions, &c." at Santo Domingo and found the town and surrounding scenery to provide "one of the handsomest views." At Albuquerque, he saw townspeople beginning to open the canals and cultivate the fields. "Men, women, and children of all ages and sexes" engaged in "joyful labor" that brought forth "rich abundance." "Every thing appeared to give life and gaiety to the surrounding scenery." The plantation of Don Francisco Garcia, with its twenty thousand sheep and thousand cows, made El Paso del Norte (modern Ciudad Juarez) "the most flourishing place we had been in." On March 12, they passed the encampment of a caravan of some three hundred men driving fifteen thousand sheep. Later in the day they met another outfit, this one with fifty men and two hundred horses. Caravans like these traveled between New Mexico and other northern provinces twice yearly, once in the spring and once in the autumn. They brought livestock and other New Mexican products out and brought merchandise in. The lushness that impressed Pike at El Paso and Albuquerque and the luxury that he enjoyed in the company of governors and officers depended on these kinds of connections. Such connections also brought into Pike's hand from Mexico City the January 17, 1807, edition of the *Gazetas de Mexico*, with ominous news about Burr's conspiracies back in the Mississippi Valley.[30]

But the connections between Madrid, Mexico City, and New Mexico were tenuous. Pike wrote that the caravans went out only in the spring and fall. In between, almost no one traveled the Camino Real.[31] It was a hard overland route from Chihuahua, which in turn was supplied by the Valley of Mexico and other points to the south. The light traffic could not possibly keep New Mexico supplied with all it needed. The commerce with Indians was even more tenuous, depending as it did on the vagaries of diplomatic relations and the feeble ability of the impoverished Spanish empire to keep New Mexico supplied with goods the Indians wanted. Spaniards had tamed the land enough to enrich a few people some of the time, but few profits stayed locally and access to wealth was not widely dispersed through the population. The frontier's prosperity was stunted by its thin ties to the outside world. To thwart Americans from establishing commercial connections, Spaniards had executed Nolan, imprisoned his partners, sent dragoons to capture Lewis and Clark, tried to woo Indians into the Spanish orbit, and deceived villagers into believing that Spaniards were the only white people.

The Spanish were right about American intentions. Pike sought to forge precisely those connections during his travel through New Spain. He was only in the first stage, of course—that of gathering information—but it was an essential step. To serve his nation in New Mexico, Pike struggled to keep his journals and maps, which contained his records and information, and was pleased when Melgares gave them back to him. He also eagerly read Father Rubí's data and Father Guerra's maps. He listened intently as Real Alencaster revealed feuds among his superiors and when D'Almansa and Fernandez complained about injustices to *criollos*. He admired Melgares's loyalty to the crown, but also took note of its limits. And he observed the degraded conditions under which he believed the majority of New Mexicans suffered, circumstances that might dispose them favorably to closer ties with the United States. All this and more Pike absorbed and, whenever he could, wrote down. For his American readers, eager to have their expectations of Spanish degeneracy confirmed, he formed a picture of a county desperate for liberation and ripe for exploitation by its northern neighbor. Pike cast himself, somewhat paradoxically, as the agent of both.

Chihuahua

Colonial Chihuahua has been called the "heartland" of the Spanish frontier. San Felipe el Real de Chihuahua, today's Ciudad Chihuahua, was founded in the early eighteenth century and had emerged as the largest among several communities in the region. In the bureaucratic nomenclature Spain imposed on its municipalities, it was a *villa*, bigger than a town (*pueblo*), smaller than a city (*ciudad*). As Pike approached on April 2, he would have seen smoke billowing from the silver refineries on the settlement's outskirts, their emissions testifying that this was still an important mining center. Over the course of the eighteenth century, mines in the vicinity yielded approximately $100 million of silver, or one-eighth of the total silver output of all of New Spain during that time. Its population had peaked perhaps at around twenty thousand in the middle of the century, and by the time Pike arrived, its inhabitants still numbered as many as eleven thousand. Although decades past its mining prime, Chihuahua continued to attract newcomers as the center of commerce between Mexico City and the settlements in Sonora and New Mexico. It processed ore mined throughout northern Mexico and served as a regional supply center. It also was the northern frontier's main military garrison, agricultural hearth, and the seat of government for the Internal Provinces.[32]

After the party made its way through dusty streets lined with the mud-walled single-story homes that had been ubiquitous on Pike's tour, the Americans would have found in the center of town a large plaza and elegant buildings reminiscent of much more substantial Spanish colonial

FIGURE 6.3 Chihuahua, circa 1850. Courtesy of Palace of the Governors Photo Archives (NMHM/DCA), Negative No. 171105.

cities. A variety of goods found their way into Chihuahua's shops—French laces and taffetas, English woolens, Chinese silk, Mexican cloth, Sonoran shrimp from the Gulf of California, and chocolate, sugar, and spices from around the world. It was home to a small number of *peninsulares*, almost all male, who made up less than one percent of the population, and who ruled the city despite being a numerical minority. Below them were *criollos*, locally called *españoles*, who made up about a third of the population, and the rest a variety of Indians and people of mixed race (*de color quebrado*). By the time Pike arrived, Apache attacks had waned in the regions to the south but still plagued the northern cities of Nueva Vizcaya around Chihuahua. Although pushed south, out of the range of the bison herds of the southern Plains during the eighteenth century by the Comanches, Apaches revised their ecology, raiding the Spanish settlements of northern Nueva Vizcaya to obtain livestock and other goods they consumed or later traded to substitute for the bison that had once met their needs.[33]

Salcedo received them graciously. Pike described him as a "middle sized man," about fifty-five, with a stern visage. A *peninsular* and the son of a noble military family, he had served the crown for nearly half a century before coming to Chihuahua in 1802. Although capable, he had not risen as quickly through the ranks as his knighted relatives.

Nevertheless, he had studied mathematics at the University of Barcelona and embraced Enlightenment ideas. As a sergeant major in the 1780s, he had trained volunteers for duty in the Spanish participation in the American Revolution.[34]

Salcedo beckoned his visitors to sit. "You have given us and yourself a great deal of trouble," he began. Next he ordered Pike's trunk to be brought in and directed Pike to explain the contents to an interpreter named Juan Pedro Walker. Born to an English father and French mother in New Orleans, Walker was a second lieutenant at a garrison near Chihuahua. He was also a skilled cartographer, who drew some of the best maps of the Internal Provinces. One by one, Walker and Pike went through the papers, explaining each to the general and piling personal papers in one stack and official documents in another. At one point, Pike protested that he wished to keep several letters from Clara, to which Salcedo assented, and Pike stashed them into his pocket. Next the commandant requested Pike to write a statement of his voyage and informed him he would be staying in Walker's quarters to afford Pike the company of someone who spoke English. Pike, who had encountered the by-now standard French greeter while waiting in the hall for Salcedo, took this latest gesture to be more a matter of espionage than hospitality. Finally, Salcedo ordered Robinson in and demanded to know who he was. Melgares explained he was a doctor accompanying Pike's party. Salcedo dismissed Robinson. He would deal with him later.[35]

Pike described the meeting as cordial, but he and Salcedo differed considerably on the seriousness of his crime. Reflecting the republican impulse to grid land into well-defined parcels, Pike defended his breach of Spanish territory. Sending a large military party all the way to the Pawnees, he insisted, was a much greater trespass than it was for Pike to get lost accidentally on the wrong side of the Rio Grande. Spanish correspondence, however, barely mentioned the territorial violation. What most alarmed Salcedo and other officials was the larger project of repeated American exploration of the rivers, collection of data, and, especially, the "subtle means" that Salcedo said the United States was employing "to separate the Indian Nations from dependence on us."[36] This made Pike's instructions from Wilkinson, which he thought legitimated his voyage, far more alarming to the Spaniards than Pike perhaps understood. As Salcedo protested a few days later to James Wilkinson, the documents contained "unequivocal proofs, that an offence of magnitude has been committed against his majesty." Salcedo's letters also indicated that he decided early on to free Pike but to keep the papers, so as to minimize the information the American carried home. But he did not inform Pike of this decision for several weeks. In the meantime, Pike proved to be as much trouble to keep around as to release.

His three-and-a-half weeks in Chihuahua afforded Pike his most extended and up-close chance to observe daily life on the Spanish frontier. During that time, he lived in Walker's quarters, though he had considerable freedom of movement throughout the city. The day after his arrival in Chihuahua, Melgares began introducing Pike to his friends. They included Don Alberto Mayner, Melgares's father-in-law, and Don Bernardo Villamil and Don Manuel Zuloaga, both secretaries to the commandant general. These men and other distinguished citizens Pike met, along with their spouses and Robinson, formed a lively social coterie over the next few weeks. In their company, Pike enjoyed dinner parties, outings, and walks on the public promenade, where the elite of Chihuahua society went to see and be seen. In the ample time between negotiating with Salcedo the question of what would happen to Pike's papers and who would pay his travel expenses, Pike took full advantage of this company to gather information about New Spain and its peoples. He believed he detected snippets of the kind of discontent that his *criollo* military escorts and Father Rubí had betrayed and which Pike took to be the tip of the iceberg that had wrecked the hull of the ship of the Spanish empire and would, Pike thought, ultimately sink it.[37]

On Saturday, April 4, Pike visited the hospital. There he met two officers, "fine looking young men," whom he was informed had once been "the gayest young men of the province." An unnamed disease, however, had changed their fortunes, and now they "were mouldering away" in the hospital, and "there was not a physician in his majesty's hospitals who was able to cure them." Pike tried to arrange for Robinson to help them, but the "jealousy" of Spanish doctors "made it impracticable"—evidence for Pike of the "deplorable state of the medical science in the provinces," and undoubtedly of Spanish incompetence and venality in general.[38]

Pike found estimable traits of citizenship as lacking in women as in men. Accompanying Melgares and his wife to the public walk one Sunday, Pike met some of Chihuahua's leading women. He noted their eyes, figures, and clothing, but especially that they had lost "every sentiment of virtue or ambition" to acquire the intellectual refinement that "would make them amiable companions, instructive mothers, or respectable members of society." This he blamed on their husbands. Spanish men, he said, treated women like horses—objects of conversation and entertainment and markers of status—but never as equals. "Finding that the men only regard them as objects of gratification to the sensual passions," Pike later wrote that the women "have lost every idea of that feast of reason and flow of soul, which arise from the intercourse of two refined and virtuous minds." Pike did meet two women who embodied the kind of republican womanhood that he valued in Clara and that had led him on the upper Mississippi to pine for the "cultivated and feeling mind of a civilized fair." Señora Maria Con. Caberairi and Señora Marguerite Vallois had generous husbands and "spirit sufficient" to "think themselves rational beings, to be treated on an equality." Their homes served as the "rendezvous" for Chihuahua's men of "science, art or arms," including Pike. The two women, however, were the exception that proved the rule, as their audacity made them "the subject of scandal." Along with suffering soldiers, then, Pike used female gender roles to construct his broad-minded American thinking as a contrast to Spanish backwardness.[39]

He reinforced this virtuous American persona with displays of masculine compassion and critiques of Spanish cruelty. One evening Pike met an American named David Fero. Fero had served as a first lieutenant under Pike's father and later joined Philip Nolan's mysterious incursion into Texas. Like Cooley, he was now a captive in Mexico. This night, Fero had slipped away from the place he was being held and wished to speak with Pike. Conferring with an alleged filibusterer could have jeopardized Pike's fragile relations with the already suspicious Salcedo, but national and military ties to "a countryman, an acquaintance, and formerly a brother soldier" persuaded Pike to risk the meeting. Pike found the tearful encounter "affecting," and he "promised to do all I could for him consistent with my character and honor, and their having entered the country without the authority of the United States." He gave Fero a little money—"what my *purse* afforded, not what my *heart* dictated"—and wrote a letter to Salcedo pleading for the release of the Nolan party survivors and for permission to carry letters to their friends and family, who had heard nothing of the captives since their disappearance.[40] Salcedo refused both requests, saying that in releasing them from the dungeon where they were being held upon his arrival in Chihuahua and striking the metal shackles in which they were clamped, he had already shown as much clemency as his position authorized him. He could do no more without instructions from the king.

Between dining with leading men, interceding for sick officers and captive Americans, and attending the salons hosted by scandalous women, Pike was becoming something of a local celebrity. Wherever he went conversation moved freely from science to religion to geography to politics. Even Walker, apparently assigned to keep an eye on Pike, "candidly confessed his disgust" with Spanish manners, morals, and politics and shared his personal frustration with being denied the opportunity to make the most of his skills and rise in station in Spanish society. On April 20, Pike learned about a rumored commercial treaty between Great Britain and the United States, which his Spanish friends were convinced portended a military alliance against Spain. Conversation that day also touched on news of an unexplained visit to Mexico City by an American official. Although Chihuahuans had not yet heard of Burr's treason trial, which opened three days before Pike arrived in the provincial capital, the mysterious official was Walter Burling, a Wilkinson aide who carried to the viceroy the general's request for a reward for thwarting the conspiracy. On other occasions, Pike and his friends discussed forbidden books. One officer, whom Pike discreetly did not name, regularly visited Pike to read Alexander Pope's *Essays on Man*. Pike offered to let the man borrow it, but the Church leaders, he wrote, "examine and condemn to the flames all books of a modern sentiment…and excommunicate any one in whose hands they may be found." The man decided he risked less visiting Pike than being caught with the impermissible literature in his own possession.[41]

But "the walls had ears." There was almost nothing that happened in Chihuahua that Salcedo did not learn about within a few hours. At sundown on April 24, one of the commandant's aides called on Pike. Salcedo was displeased to learn that Pike and Robinson had "held forth political maxims and principles" that "called into question" the "allegiance due…the [Spanish royal] court" and that might foment a "revolt" within the kingdom. Several Spaniards were implicated in these conversations, and their identities had been "noted" and they "would be taken care of." As for Pike, Salcedo's messenger warned him to refrain from discussing religion or politics. Pike refused, asserting his right "when called on" to "always give my opinions freely," but his Spanish friends were alarmed and perhaps embarrassed. They agreed to be more cautious. This was Pike's Chihuahua, where good officers lay dying for want of medical attention while professional envy blocked their cure, where women's intellect atrophied and men exercised theirs only in secret, where foreign innocents languished, and where a despot sought to control private conversation and block the light of the world's knowledge from shining on his subjects.[42]

Salcedo's Chihuahua, however, looked substantially different. Although ardent in his opposition to the perceived American threat, the general was no tyrant. Other sources portray him as a steady, honest, and hardworking bureaucrat who evinced a genuine concern for the well-being of his subjects. At the end of his long reign from 1802 to 1813, Salcedo could count many achievements. He held the border with the United States without triggering violence, minimized the Indian depredations that had long plagued the Spanish frontier, and prevented the Mexican War for Independence from engulfing his jurisdiction. He had encouraged smallpox vaccination, which one historian credits with fostering the province's early nineteenth-century population rise. Among his most signal achievements was his promotion of education in the Internal Provinces. From his first arrival in New Spain, he began ordering the creation of new schools at military posts and the improvement of existing ones. Each officer or soldier with a child in school was to pay a tax to support the school and schoolmaster. Attendance was mandatory for children under twelve. Costs of attendance for the poor would be paid for from a public charitable fund. Taking personal oversight of the initiative, Salcedo received semi-annual reports on every school and a sample of each child's work. In 1808 he donated more than 1,900 pesos of his own money to support education in Chihuahua and called for other wealthy citizens to follow suit. The resulting funds established the town's first school for girls. Although no precise evidence of literacy rates is available, one historian's examination of documents that recorded whether individuals could write their name indicates that literacy in the Internal Provinces was higher than might be expected of an early nineteenth-century frontier, certainly high enough to challenge Pike's dim view of the subjects' education. In fact, the formal education of an officer's child in Salcedo's Chihuahua undoubtedly exceeded that of a youngster at an Ohio Valley post at the same time.[43]

Pike, however, missed or ignored much of this. Judging from a small sample that he colored with preconceived anti-Spanish biases, Pike portrayed Chihuahua and the northern frontier in general as a landscape of discontent, in which tyranny repressed an otherwise enterprising and virtuous people. They were ripe for rebellion, he reported to Congress upon returning to the United States. The citizens of northern New Spain, he said, were like an "acorn," dormant under the shade of a parent tree, but ready to rise up when touched by "the light of heaven." The American and French examples had awakened their ambitions, and Spanish subjects now "turned their eyes towards the United States, as brethren of the same soil." If Napoleon were to seize the Spanish throne, an American army would have only "to march from province to province in triumph, and be hailed by the united voices of grateful millions as their deliverers and saviours, whilst our national character would be resounded to the most distant nations of the earth." The United States would become "their factors, agents, guardians, and...tutelar genius," and at the same time secure "to herself the almost exclusive trade of the richest country in the world."[44] Pike envisioned his nation as both Mexico's benefactor and exploiter. Unbeknownst to Pike, Robinson was already endeavoring to put such sentiments into action.

If Robinson was General Wilkinson's spy on behalf of the Burr conspiracy, he made a curious request to Nemesio Salcedo. On April 8, less than a week after arriving in Chihuahua, the doctor wrote to the general explaining his motives for coming to Mexico. Once again he denied any official connection to Pike, though he affirmed their friendship and mutual esteem. Rather, his intention was to come along on the voyage until they neared Mexico and then to depart for the northern towns to settle some "pecuniary matters" and to investigate whether Mexico might be a better place than the United States for doctoring. Whatever he found must have impressed him because he closed the letter by requesting permission to remain in New Spain and to become a "subject of His Catholic Majesty." He also hinted at a proposal he would soon offer Salcedo. That proposal was the subject of his second letter two weeks later. In that one, he reiterated his intent to become a Spanish subject and suggested a way by which he could "do the greatest services to my Country and...become a useful member of [its] society." That service lay in exploration. Robinson claimed great familiarity with the North American West and with British and American intentions for the region. He promised to lead a Spanish expedition to gather geographical and other information to aid Spain's claims to the territory against its imperial rivals. He closed by asking Salcedo not to inform "my friend Lieutenant Pike" of this plan, partly to keep the plan a secret from Spain's imperial rivals and partly to avoid confiscation of Robinson's possessions in the United States. Instead, he asked Salcedo to declare that Robinson was to be detained in Mexico for some time.[45]

Robinson was probably not candid. He was concerned about his reputation and assets in the United States, not to mention the new bride he had left behind in St. Louis. Moreover, his nationalist sentiments seemingly matched Pike's; a letter he wrote on July 5 after his return to the United States compared "the Glorious Anniversary of our Freedom & Independence" to New Spain's "Ignorance, Superstition, & Tyranny." Hence, Robinson's proposal likely reflects not a genuine desire to immigrate but rather a bid for adventure on the Spaniards' dime. The doctor's subsequent career was that of an inveterate nationalist and adventurer. He returned to Mexico several times, once as a special envoy of James Madison during the War of 1812, later as the organizer of filibustering expeditions, and finally as a fighter for Mexican independence. In an 1813 report to Secretary of State James Monroe, he echoed Pike's earlier assessment almost verbatim, urging US intervention in the great cause of Mexican independence, which would also "secure to ourselves an unrivaled commerce with one of the richest countries in the World." His final public act was the production of a map of the North American imperial boundaries based on his extensive travels and inquiries, and not a little conjecture. The generous territory Robinson claimed for the United States beyond the still unratified Adams-Onís Treaty boundaries has prompted the historian David Narrett to call the map "a map of imperial assertion" and "a bid for empire." Like Pike, then, Robinson championed both American expansion and Mexican independence, and it seems likely that some of this was already on the doctor's mind as he penned his proposal to Salcedo.[46]

Salcedo bought none of it. The two Americans were becoming a pack of trouble. Pike was spreading seditious ideas. Robinson was plotting something insincere. Sometime around April 21, Salcedo received a letter from Real Alencaster, who believed he had learned something more about Pike. The rest of Pike's soldiers had emerged from the mountains and been escorted to Santa Fe. One of them told the governor a much more incriminating tale than Pike or Robinson had offered. The informant, whom Real Alencaster described as having a "foot ailment" and whom subsequent Spanish correspondence identifies as Sparks, indicated that the American soldiers believed, while in the Wet Mountain Valley, that they were in Spanish territory and that they had demanded an explanation from Pike of why the expedition was going on. His response was that they were seeking the Red River, where they would meet another large party of American soldiers. This seems unlikely, as there is no record of any other American party with instructions to rendezvous with Pike. It is possible, however, that Sparks was referring to the abortive commercial expeditions Wilkinson dispatched around the time of Pike's journey. Garbling some of the details, Sparks also described the encounter with the Pawnees, claiming that Pike sought to sever the tribe's relations from the Spaniards, that Pike had asked them for directions to Spanish territory, and that Pike had instructions to arrest any Spaniards he met in American territory.[47] All in all, the report formed a more alarming account of American intentions than Pike or Robinson had provided the governor and confirmed Salcedo's fears that Pike was the vanguard of the American westward push to the Interior Provinces. Salcedo received Real Alencaster's letter by April 21. Two days later, Robinson proposed to go adventuring for the king. The next day, Salcedo cracked down on Pike's garrulousness. He had had enough of these Americans. Soon he ordered Pike to prepare himself and his party to leave, even though the men rescued from the mountains had not yet caught up. And Pike was to take Robinson with him. Pike departed Chihuahua on April 28, again under Melgares's escort, and now at last headed homeward to be delivered to American soil in Natchitoches.

Murder

Six days after Pike left Chihuahua, Theodore Miller was murdered. On the Mississippi voyage, Pike had found the private "obliging" and "agreeable," the only man on either voyage, other than Robinson, about whose personality Pike ever commented. On both expeditions, he often took Miller hunting and on other forays away from the main party. It was Miller who slogged with Pike along the snowy last leg of the march to Leech Lake to bang on the gates of McGillis's post. Pike also took Miller on the abortive attempt to climb the Grand Peak in November 1806 and to find the headwaters of the river he had assumed in December to be the Red. On February 19, when Pike sent a second rescue party back into the mountains for Sparks and Daugherty, Miller was one of the two who volunteered to go, for which Pike commended their "habit, discipline, and example," and service "in the interest of a nation." When Saltelo escorted Pike away from the stockade a week later, Miller was still in the mountains. Pike would never see him again.[48]

Volunteering for the rescue attempt along with Miller had been Sergeant William Meek. Meek had started the expedition as a corporal but was promoted to sergeant after Lieutenant Wilkinson took the party's other sergeant, Joseph Ballenger, down the Arkansas River. Both Meek and Miller were in their twenties and apparently were good friends. Together they had performed a heroic feat. Carrying only ten pounds of venison, they crossed back over the snowy Sangre de Cristos through the country in which the party had nearly frozen and starved the month before. They managed to get all the way back to the camp near the mouth of Royal Gorge and collected Vazquez and Smith and the party's remaining gear and horses. On the return, they picked up Sparks and Daugherty, who were now able to travel, probably on horseback. When they arrived at the stockade, about March 18, as Pike was trekking with Melgares's troops along the road between San Fernandez and El Paso, they found Lieutenat Saltelo waiting for them.[49] There was a note from Pike giving orders to obey the Spaniards and placing Meek in charge of the rump party, which now included Corporal Jeremiah Jackson, Private Hugh Menaugh, and the six men who had just come out of the mountains.

Departing the stockade, Meek and his men arrived by April 7 in Santa Fe, where they tarried long enough to be interrogated by Real Alencaster and to get into a bit of trouble. On the fifteenth, the governor complained in a letter to Salcedo that the inhabitants of Santa Fe were paying fond attention to the Americans, despite "their hardness of temperament and the many requirements and charges which they impose upon the citizenry." Somewhere in their engagements with the locals, the two friends bickered after Miller insulted Meek. Meek would later testify that Miller had apologized and that the incident was over. But their companions were not so sure. Smith later said that Meek hated Miller from that day on. In the meantime, Real Alencaster sent them along to Salcedo, and they traveled the same route Pike had, perhaps nursing resentment along the way.[50]

On May 4, Meek and his men arrived at Carrizal, a military garrison between El Paso del Norte and Chihuahua, and trouble started within hours. Perhaps because of the row in Santa Fe or perhaps for some other reason, Meek and Miller quarreled late in the afternoon as the sun was setting. Transcripts generated by Spanish investigations of the dispute detail what transpired. Officials at the presidio initially questioned witnesses, whose responses are summarized, though not quoted, in the transcripts. Over the next seven months, as the case worked its way up the Spanish chain of command, witnesses were recalled for additional testimony, and Meek changed his story about the events, claiming that Vazquez, who served as his interpreter, had so botched the job that Meek wished to revise his statement. Out of this morass of fragmentary and shifting testimony emerges a fairly clear picture as to what happened, but a lot of questions about why.

The fray began with Meek accusing Miller of stealing some of his vermillion. Miller hotly denied it and upped the ante by accusing Meek of having taken it himself from Pike. Juan Olguin, a Spanish sergeant nearby, intervened and managed to get Meek to give up his saber, but Meek quickly returned to the quarrel, accompanied by Jackson and Smith. As Miller and Meek came to blows, their countrymen separated them, and believed they had succeeded. Miller slumped down on a stone bench against the wall, while Meek went off. Within minutes, however, he was wrestling with Olguin for the sword, which hung in its sheath from the Spaniard's saddle horn. The horse shied. Olguin grabbed the saber with two hands, but could not hold on. Meek had extracted it too far. As Olguin let go and turned to settle his horse, Meek rushed at Miller, declaring, "This is the way that American Sgts. Punish Soldiers." The tip of the saber pierced Miller just above his left nipple and penetrated horizontally toward his back. "I'm killed," Smith heard the victim gasp three times. Witnesses arriving quickly on the scene pronounced him dead.

Meek confessed to having killed Miller, but claimed self-defense and military privilege. He testified that shortly before the incident, a drunken Miller had insulted and struck him when Meek had ordered him to retire to the barracks. Subsequent witnesses, however, denied seeing any such altercation themselves. Meek also said that he had not intended to kill Miller but rather had only wished to strike him with the flat of the saber to subdue him. Miller, he said, had impaled himself by charging at him. In Meek's defense, he argued that the death was unintentional and that under American military law he had a right to discipline a disobedient subordinate, even with death. Meek languished in prison for nearly eight months while his case continued. Testimony was taken again and again. Some witnesses were difficult to locate. In late December 1807, the Spanish prosecutor recommended that Meek had already served sufficient time for whatever crime he may have committed and advocated his release. But higher Spanish authorities continued the investigation, and the transcript ends in May 1808 with the case still unresolved. The six men never caught up with the rest of the party and did not arrive in the United States until 1809. Meek would not be allowed to return to the United States until 1821.[51]

Coahuila and Texas

The day after Meek's confession, Pike and Melgares parted ways, an occasion that prompted Pike to think about the relationship between independence and loyalty. On one hand, a deep friendship had transcended the two officers' national differences, and Pike admired Megalres's national loyalty. On the other, Melgares directed his fealty to a despot, whose regime deprived so many, including, Pike believed, Melgares himself, of personal independence.[52] After leaving his Spanish friend, Pike traveled under escort across the Spanish provinces of Coahuila and Texas, meeting numerous Americans and Spaniards whose independent-minded ways compromised their nationalism. As a man who had always found independence and nationalism compatible, Pike must have wondered if anyone in New Spain exhibited both.

Among the several Americans he encountered on the homeward leg of his journey, Pike saw none of Melgares's admirable loyalty, but he did find plenty of willfulness. On May 19, an American army deserter begged Pike to take him back to his company, but Pike would not "give any encouragement to the scoundrel." Later Pike met an American named Griffith, who had not only deserted but did not regret it. Indeed, he maintained the Spaniards had treated him far better than the American army, and he indicated he would never return to the United States. Pike rebuked the "impertinence" of addressing an American officer in such a manner, to which Griffith "muttered something about being in a country where he was protected." Pike then threatened the man into silence and ordered his soldiers to shun him. At dinnertime, Pike sent a message to his host saying that he did not presume to tell him whom to welcome at the table, but that if Griffith were present, Pike and his men would not eat. The host assured Pike that Griffith would not reappear and apologized for the "accident" that had brought them together in the morning. Finally, on June 1, at a presidio on the Rio Grande, Spanish authorities asked Pike to examine an American prisoner who had told a tall tale. Originally from Virginia, the man had gone adventuring in Texas. He was abandoned by comrades, nearly killed by Indians, and, by guile and luck, lived to reach the Rio Grande, where he discovered mines of gold and silver. Pike at first pegged the man for agent of Aaron Burr and was contemplating denouncing him, but one of the men recognized the Virginian as the murderer of an American army officer. Pike informed the Spanish authorities, who sentenced the man to perpetual confinement. "Thus vengeance," Pike wrote, overtook "the ingrate and murderer when he least expected it."[53]

Locals, too, seemingly valued independence over nationalism. For instance, his new *criollo* escort, Captain Varela, feared he had already achieved his ultimate rank. There were also Apaches in irons and a young priest "who was extremely anxious for a change of government." After seeing the "mass of people" at Mapimí, who were "naked and starved wretches," Pike laughed to think Salcedo had tried to prevent him from learning too much about the country, for "there were disaffected persons sufficient to serve as guides should an army ever come into the country." Independence and nationalism were compatible in Ohio, where the federal government had remade the landscape of Pike's youth with land sales, military supply contracts, army appointments, and Indian wars, but seemed incompatible in the Internal Provinces. A few Americans had gotten there by exercising liberty and disloyalty. As for locals, national allegiance like Melgares's required accepting a backward regime that squelched their independence. To crave independence, as the creole officers and priests did, verged on disloyalty. Nobody here, it seemed, was both independent and loyal. When he got to San Antonio, however, he met two remarkable men, whose virtues enabled Pike to find the language to reconcile loyalty and independence.[54]

When he arrived in June 1807, San Antonio was a town of approximately 1,500 people, one of the more substantial settlements on the northern frontier. It was also the provincial capital. Pike and Robinson were housed at the quarters of Colonel Antonio Cordero, governor of the province of Texas. They also met Lieutenant Colonel Simón de Herrera, commander of the troops who had confronted Americans on the Sabine River the previous fall. The two men impressed Pike as much as anyone he met in New Spain. On June 9, Cordero hosted a lavish dinner party, offering the first toast to "the President of the United States." Pike returned the compliment by toasting "His Catholic Majesty." Thereafter, General Wilkinson was toasted, as were Pike and his companions. Finally, the guests toasted "the continuation of the good understanding which exists between the two countries." The congeniality continued through several days of parties and conversation, during which the two gentlemen displayed "astonishing knowledge" of American politics. Pike described them as learned, gallant, and extremely popular among their people. They also "agree perfectly" in "their hatred to tyranny," and affirmed their determination never to see it take root in the New World, except under their king, "whom they think their honor and loyalty bound to defend with their lives and fortunes." Pike added that if Napoleon Bonaparte should "seize on European Spain, I risque nothing in asserting, those two gentleman would be the first to throw off the yoke, draw their swords, and assert the independence of the country." Although not entirely accurate (Herrera remained a royalist during Miguel Hidalgo's anti-colonial revolt and was murdered by insurgents in 1813), this declaration deftly enabled Pike to laud his friends' independence without impugning their loyalty.[55]

Individuals' virtue, however, did not mitigate Pike's contempt for the Spanish empire, as he wrote to his friend and fellow officer Jacob Kingsbury soon after his July 1807 arrival in Louisiana, one of his first written assessments of his travels. "I have found," he told Kingsbury, the Spaniards "as individuals" to be "the most hospitable generous and friendly People I never [sic] knew." As for the government, however, it was "Tyronical; Hypocritical; an[d] Superstitious." How could Pike so admire the Spaniards "as individuals" while so disdaining the regime they had made? Some of it can be chalked up to condescending sympathy, but that does not fully explain it. Pike's commitment to the friends he made in New Spain seems as deep and genuine as his belief in the Black Legend. The individuals who won his admiration were hardly the exceptions. Rather they encompassed virtually everyone he met. The cast included the refined and loyal officers Melgares, Cordero, and Herrera. It also included *criollos* who thirsted for independence, and the priests, officers, and women hungry for intellectual enlightenment. How could Spain be so barbaric if it was filled with delightful people who reflected the very qualities he fancied himself to possess?[56]

The question contains the answer: he was writing partly about himself. After his shabby arrival in Santa Fe, the challenge of exploration was no longer physical but rather social and cultural. It was an encounter with a difficult national other that wrenched his nationalist sensibilities. His sense of membership in his own national community would not let him accept a nation of contrary principles uncritically. His sense of individual honor would not let him criticize friends who had treated him well and displayed the traits he valued; after all, as he had reassured himself in Santa Fe, "worth made the man." He reconciled these poles of American nationalism—individualism and membership in a national community, independence and loyalty—by peopling his account with honorable individuals who suffered under a corrupt regime.

The problem of personal honor took on added urgency for him soon after he set foot back on American soil. Although there were no snickers about his apparel upon his return, he found that his virtue and nationalism were suddenly and unexpectedly called into question. In publishing his account of his travels, then, he found himself writing for an audience he wished to persuade of his merits. Criticizing a corrupt Spanish regime while applauding individual Spaniards who looked a lot like him was one way to do so.

7

"Citizen Soldier"

PIKE AND THE NATION, 1807–1813

"LANGUAGE CANNOT EXPRESS the gaiety of my heart," Pike wrote of his homecoming "when I once more beheld the standard of my country waved aloft!—'All hail' cried I, the ever sacred name of country, in which is embraced that of kindred[,] friends, and every other tie which is dear to the soul of man!" The nation of kindred and friends, however, did not embrace Pike at first. Alleging ties to the Burr conspiracy, newspaper editors called him "the beast of Santa Fé" and "a parasite of Wilkinson." One anonymous letter to the New Orleans *Gazette* even tried to connect Pike to Miller's murder, charging that its purpose was to cover up the expedition's ties to Wilkinson's "treachery." Over the next six years, Pike wielded both pen and sword to combat such accusations and restore his reputation. He would score a great triumph, but only at a terrible cost.[1]

Burr, Wilkinson, and Pike

On February 22, 1808, when the House of Representatives met to deliberate "what compensation ought to be made to Captain Pike and his companions for their services," Congressman John Rowan of Kentucky rose to object. He had received a letter from New Orleans indicating that one of Pike's sergeants, Joseph Ballenger, was a friend of Burr's and during the expedition had wooed Indians to the former vice president's cause. Rowan had spoken also with Ballenger's brother, who affirmed that Wilkinson had sent the sergeant on the expedition for that purpose. "If this is the case," Rowan insisted to his colleagues, "and Mr. Pike is privy to this confederacy, he ought not to receive compensation." In March the House committee investigating the matter recommended a reward similar to what Lewis and Clark and their men had recently won, but Congress

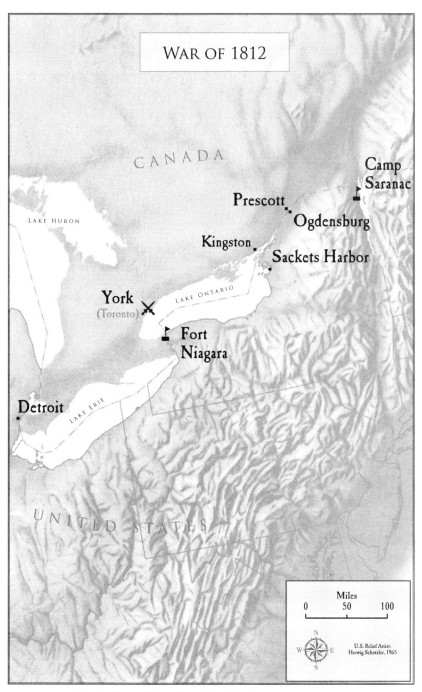

FIGURE 7.1 Map by Steve Chignell and Sophia Linn.

adjourned without voting. The matter resurfaced in December, but again the lawmakers declined to take action one way or another.[2]

Rowan had a point. Only one damning degree separated Pike from Burr, and that was James Wilkinson. On February 19, 1807, a few days before Real Alencaster's dragoons detained Pike in the San Luis Valley, a US army officer apprehended Burr in Alabama Territory and arranged to have him escorted to Virginia to stand trial for treason. On May 20, Wilkinson sailed from New Orleans for Richmond, where a grand jury was about to convene its investigation into the allegations against Burr. Armed with his doctored version of the cipher letter in which Burr appeared to plot treason, the general was to be the prosecution's star witness. Before he left New Orleans, however, Wilkinson wrote to Pike, who was long expected but had not yet returned. Reports of Pike's death had recently reached the Mississippi Valley, and Wilkinson had believed Pike a goner. A few days before departing, however, the general received a letter from Salcedo indicating that Pike was alive and would soon return. "You will hear of the scenes in which I have been engaged," Wilkinson then wrote Pike. "The traitors whose infamous designs against the constitution and government of our country I have detected, exposed, and destroyed, are vainly attempting to explain their own conduct by inculpating me." Therefore, be careful what you say, he added, because "they have asserted that your's and lieutenant Wilkinson's enterprise was a premeditated co-operation with Burr's." Pike's friendship for his general and Wilkinson's authorship of the expedition guaranteed that whatever brushes tarred Wilkinson would color Pike's reputation as well.[3]

Pike returned to the United States a week after the grand jury indicted Burr. Like the former vice president, whose trial was not set to begin until August 3, Pike spent the summer in limbo. Although Wilkinson had authorized him to return to his family in St. Louis, Pike chose to send for them instead and wait for his frozen lads and the rump of the party at Natchitoches. When they failed to arrive, he wrote to Salcedo inquiring about them. Clara and four-year-old Clarissa joined him by the end of the summer. Meanwhile, Pike wrote to Wilkinson and Dearborn that despite the seizure of his papers, he had managed to smuggle out a good portion of his documents. To pass the sweaty hours of the Natchitoches summer, he began the tedious task of transcribing the jumble of papers into some semblance of order. He also wrote a public letter to the Natchez *Herald* to publish what he had learned about the plights of David Fero and the rest of Nolan's party, whose fates had remained unknown to their family and friends. In August, in further testimony to his impotence, a party of Comanches—the very people whom he had been unable to locate on the western Plains—showed up at Natchitoches and visited him and other officials. Although he heard nothing from Salcedo, it gradually became evident his men were not going to return soon, and he must have wondered if they would suffer the same fate as Nolan's men.[4]

Meanwhile, Pike wanted to get to Washington—to advocate a promotion for his father, to secure a West Point appointment for his younger brother George, and to brief Wilkinson and maybe even the president on his travels. He also aimed to boost his own standing, perhaps recalling Wilkinson's warning of rumors linking the expedition to Burr. The night before sailing for Washington, Pike penned an anxious letter to his father. He was indignant about the old soldier's failed promotion and apprehensive about his own. "Many others have similar causes of Complaint," he lamented. "Should my Country attempt to do us such injustice," I will not extend "my right arm…to save her from ruin." In that case, he would "retire to the haunts of the untutored savage," where he would admittedly miss civilized life but at least be free of the "craft, and diplomatic deception of refined societies." But, he went on, if the nation would "do us *justice* which my pride, and hopes seems yet to dictate, and there should be War with G.B. I am determined to push my fortune in the sphere of military life—and nothing shall by me be omitted which honor will license." Rejecting the biblical injunction, "humble thyself and thou shall be exalted," he instead adopted a more self-reliant motto: "Respect thyself if you wish the World to respect you." As his sentences oscillated between thin-skinned indignation that the nation did not show him more appreciation and flourishes of sentimental nationalism, Pike reflected early-republic patriotism—a sentiment more frequently thin and volatile than hard and fixed. In a world in which the outcome of the American national experiment was still uncertain and in which people switched allegiances freely, patriotism was a useful discourse for men like Pike to assert their claims to the nation's rewards, but rarely an unswerving dedication that would abide the perceived insult of ingratitude. After two years of hardship abroad and a summer in an ungrateful nation at home, Pike's allegiances hung in the balance.[5]

On his arrival in the East, he began to reestablish his nationalist credentials, telling stories, distributing gifts, and cultivating the friendship of powerful people. No one anticipated Pike's arrival more eagerly than

Wilkinson, who wrote to Jefferson on September 13 that Pike "is on his Route to the City of Washington" and will "no doubt be able to communicate much Interesting Information." On landing in New York, Pike sent the president of the Military Philosophical Society a Spanish carbine and cartridge box. He also carried a letter of introduction to a senator from Captain Amos Stoddard, who called Pike "one of the first officers of his rank in our service" and a man whose travels "cannot fail to be interesting to individuals, and to the Government." Soon after arriving in Washington, Pike visited the naturalist and editor Samuel L. Mitchill, who had published Pike's *Medical Repository* article on Louisiana in 1804. According to Mitchill, now a New York congressman, Pike regaled him with "a forbidding and almost terrifying account of those Western Regions." To Secretary of War Henry Dearborn, Pike appealed for a commission "for the command of one of the Corps" in the event of war with Great Britain. "Twelve years service and military experience," he felt, amply justified such a request. To the Attorney General Caesar A. Rodney, Pike wrote that if he lacked the "genious" of some national leaders, "I will claim and [sic] equality on the scale of patriotism with the Great Worthies of our Country.... My Sword is always ready to defend her rights and my life to be sacrificed to the Great principals which have animated our forefathers."[6]

Pike made his biggest splash, however, with a pair of grizzly bear cubs he bestowed upon President Jefferson. Pike had purchased them from an Indian who had captured them in the mountains of New Mexico. At first his men rode with the cubs on their laps. Later Pike had a cage made for them and strapped it to the back of a mule. At night he let them out, and they roamed "like dogs through our camps," following the men, who fed them like pets. The pair completed their journey aboard ship from New Orleans to Washington. Jefferson, who had heard of but never encountered a grizzly, was delighted to see a live specimen of what he called "the most formidable animal of our continent," one "so little known in the U.S." Fashionable Washingtonians like Congressman Mitchill thought it "quite the style" to come down to the White House and "visit the Bears," which, according to Jefferson seemed "perfectly gentle" and "quite good humored." After a few weeks, Jefferson sent the cubs to Charles Willson Peale in Philadelphia to advance the cause of public science by having them "exhibited in your Museum to it's numerous visitors." In a brief thank-you note, the president "salute[d]" Pike "with esteem and respect."[7]

Bear cubs and professions of patriotism, however, could not shield Pike from the fallout of the Burr trial. The drama's curtain had lifted on

T.R.Peale delin

MISSOURI BEAR.
Ursus horribilis: Ord.

FIGURE 7.2 Grizzly bears Pike gave to Jefferson. Painting is by Titian Ramsay Peale. American Philosophical Society.

August 3, and the cast included many of the nation's leading men. Among the jury, attorneys, witnesses, and instigators were Thomas Jefferson, John Randolph, Andrew Jackson, Henry Clay, and James Wilkinson. Chief Justice John Marshall presided from the bench. The question before the court was whether a former vice president had conspired to commit treason. Although he did not testify, Pike's name came up several times, usually in connection with a prominent Missourian named Timothy Kibby. A few days after Pike had arrived in Natchitoches, Kibby gave a deposition to the grand jury claiming that Wilkinson had repeatedly approached him about joining the Burr conspiracy. Kibby also said that a few days before Pike's boats had launched from Bellefontaine in July 1806, Wilkinson had confided to Kibby a secret the general had acknowledged to only one other person. Pike's expedition was not a government project but rather "of a private nature." Its object was Santa Fe. If Pike succeeded, Wilkinson allegedly continued, the general would be able to put himself "beyond the reach of his enemies." Wilkinson also told Kibby that "Lt. Pike himself was as yet ignorant of the nature of his journey."[8]

FIGURE 7.3 "The trial of Aaron Burr." From the painting by C. W. Jefferys, published in Johnson and Corwin's *The Age of Jefferson and Marshall*, The Chronicles of America Series, Vol. 9, 1921. Print Collection, Miriam and Ira D. Wallach Division of Art, Prints and Photographs, the New York Public Library, Astor, Lenox and Tilden Foundations.

To support Kibby's statement, the defense called Major James Bruff to the witness stand the following October. In addition to recounting the alleged "grand scheme" that Wilkinson had hinted about to Bruff shortly after the general's June 1805 conference with Burr at Fort Massac, the major testified that Kibby was a "man of honor, whose word and oath would be taken where, perhaps, General Wilkinson's would be shaken." Wilkinson refuted Kibby's statement as "replete with falsehood" and accused Bruff of seeking to "take revenge...for past injuries." Although Wilkinson had ample incentive for lying to discredit his accusers, neither Kibby nor Bruff were completely credible witnesses either. Bruff had criticized Wilkinson publicly and to his superiors in Washington, and Wilkinson said the major had harbored a "long...[and] implacable hatred...towards me." Kibby's deposition rang hollow in failing to explain why the always-calculating general would loosen his lips before a man he barely knew and whose behavior, even by Kibby's testimony, kept him off balance.[9]

Despite Wilkinson's denials of Kibby's testimony, the trial damaged Pike's patron as much as Burr. Treason is a difficult charge to prove because conviction requires an overt act. Burr never raised a finger against the union. No gunboats came down the Mississippi. New Orleans and Veracruz never fell. No westerners moved to secede. The jury acquitted him of both treason and the misdemeanor of filibustering, the latter of which he probably had committed.[10] Late the following spring, Burr sailed for Europe and voluntary exile. Although he later returned to the United States and resumed his law practice, never again did he play a major role in national politics. Wilkinson, meanwhile, had made many enemies. For years he had imperiously blocked the ambitions of Bruff and other rival officers while his loyal supporters easily gained his favor. The arbitrary arrests and overruling of civilian law in his attempt to clamp down on Burr's friends in New Orleans in 1806 and 1807 had alienated others. Still more cringed at the pompous testimony of a general in full military regalia who had little to add to the proceedings beyond the cipher letter. And that document, even with Wilkinson's doctoring, hardly painted an innocent picture of him. By the time Burr's trial ended, many believed Wilkinson the greater villain.

In December, Congressman John Randolph of Virginia called for a presidential inquiry into Wilkinson's connections to the Spanish government and his involvement with the Burr conspiracy. The representatives' discussion of the matter foundered on the question of whether

Congress had a right to request such an investigation. Moreover, Congressman Rowan hinted that a presidential commission would not do its job anyway. Indeed, Jefferson had depended on Wilkinson to discredit Burr and could not have been eager to uncover evidence that would damn the man whom Jefferson and his party had stood behind. Before Congress acted, Jefferson appointed his own investigation panel composed of Wilkinson's military subordinates, including his staunch supporter Thomas Cushing, the aide to whom the general allegedly first confided the cipher letter. Not surprisingly, when the investigators reported in June 1808, they absolved the general of ever receiving payment from the Spanish government and of any connection to Burr's exploits. Absolution by his underlings, however, hardly ended Wilkinson's troubles. For the next three years he was beset by almost constant congressional and other inquiries into his conduct, ending in 1811 when a court-martial once again acquitted him of any wrongdoing, while the incriminating documents slept quietly deep in Spanish archives.[11]

Throughout all this, Pike's loyalty to Wilkinson never wavered. In November 1807, just after the Burr trial closed, Pike accompanied Wilkinson to Baltimore and gleefully reported to Attorney General Rodney that soldiers and civilians were hailing the general and that mobs were burning effigies of Aaron Burr. A year later, with Wilkinson expecting another congressional investigation, the general solicited a deposition from Pike. Under oath, Pike twice denied involvement with Burr and averred that Wilkinson had never proposed to him anything injurious to the United States or in violation of its constitution. On the contrary, he said, "I do most sincerely believe that General Wilkinson has, to the best of his judgment, and utmost zeal, pursued the interest, honor and safety of his country." In 1811, Pike testified at Wilkinson's court-martial at the general's request. Pike applauded the acquittal and later declared that Wilkinson was one of only two men fit for the soon-to-be-open position of secretary of war. Throughout his career, Pike confessed, "I have never Omitted anything in my power to serve him or ceased to assert his innocence and Honor."[12]

While Wilkinson was on trial, Pike was, too. In February 1806, a few days after the Spanish dragoons had rescued his party in the San Luis Valley, the House of Representatives had approved extra compensation for Lewis and Clark and their men. To the co-captains went land warrants for 1,600 acres each, to the men 320. Everyone got double pay. Pike sought something similar. Congress appointed a committee chaired by Representative John Montgomery to consider the question on February 22, 1808, but as had been the case with Lewis and Clark, the measure was hotly debated. Not even the appointment of the committee went uncontested. One representative objected to the phrasing of the committee's charge "to inquire what compensation ought to be made" instead of if any ought to be made at all. Then Rowan, who had already championed congressional investigation of Wilkinson, raised the matter of Pike's alleged ties to Ballenger and Burr. Learning of Rowan's insinuations within hours, Pike was incensed. He considered it a "duty to myself; my family; and my profession" to "shut the mouth of Calumny and strike dumb the voice of slander." In an open letter to the *National Intelligencer* he denied that Ballenger had ever informed him of any special instructions from Wilkinson or that the sergeant had any opportunity to "make use of any intrigue, or in fact hold any conference with the Indians." Simultaneously, he moved behind the scenes to secure the administration's support, writing that same day to Henry Dearborn to request exoneration. Rowan's accusations and Pike's denial forced Montgomery's committee to confront the question of whether Pike had leagued with Burr.[13]

The committee exonerated Pike. It did not fully explain its rationale, but an analysis of the extant evidence demonstrates Pike's innocence. There are only two ways that Pike might have served Burr. First, an expedition such as Pike's might have assessed Spanish resources and fortifications, the degree of attachment of local peoples to the crown, and routes by which filibusterers might have invaded. Second, Pike might have triggered an international incident, say by building a fort and raising an American flag on Spanish soil. Either Spanish retaliation for such a transgression or US reprisals for any imprisonment or other mistreatment of an American army officer might lead to armed hostilities, which would provide cover for a gang of filibusterers from the Mississippi Valley to overrun Spanish territory.

Although Pike's more suspicious chroniclers have accused him of both reconnoitering and provocateuring for Burr, the two are nearly mutually incompatible.[14] Successful reconnaissance would have required Pike to get in and out of Santa Fe and home in time to brief Wilkinson and Burr, all without raising a stir. Without a stir, however, he could not trigger an international incident. At the same time, provocateuring required getting captured, which would render him unable to bring back any timely intelligence. A man cannot spy and raise a ruckus at the same time.

Moreover, the timing was all wrong. The author of the cipher letter, whichever conspirator wrote it, aptly deemed "concert and harmony of movement" among the parts of the scheme "essential."[15] Yet Burr was planning for his western trip by the spring of 1806, weeks before Pike left, and the former vice president was already setting those plans in motion while Pike was fiddle-faddling among the Osages and Pawnees. Wilkinson and Burr cannot possibly have expected Pike to get to Santa Fe and back in time to provide them usable information. The timing was equally bad for triggering an international crisis, which required more precision than a clumsy expedition of unknown duration and into unknown space far distant from where Burr's strike would have to begin. Moreover, the very week that Wilkinson penned Pike's June 1806 instructions, he received orders from Jefferson to descend the Mississippi to confront the Spaniards at the Sabine. He no longer needed Pike to provoke a war; the general could stop or start one himself. Finally, Pike's detours to the Pawnee village and the Grand Peak and his lack of urgency exiting Chihuahua bespeak a man trying to get a look at people and geography—exactly what his instructions said—not a belligerent trying to incite hostilities.

Most importantly, however, conspiracy with Burr does not square with Pike's nationalist sensibilities. As "sufficient justification" for his innocence of Rowan's insinuations, Pike offered to Dearborn his own track record—his "early choice of Military life, the many arduous and confidential duties I have performed" and the "perfect knowledge which the Government must have of my military and political Character."[16] Such a man who had devoted his public and private actions and words so consistently to serving the nation at great physical sacrifice to himself is unlikely to have found much appeal in whatever Burr could promise. Even Kibby and Ballenger, the two who most closely linked Pike to Burr—if they are to be credited at all—refrained from impugning his patriotism and maintained his innocence of knowingly participating in the conspiracy.

Believing that Pike deliberately worked for Burr requires accepting that an ardent nationalist forsook a lifetime of words and actions for the ill-defined promises of a disgraced former vice president. It also requires accepting that after buying into Burr's scheme, Pike meandered across the Plains and when offered the chance to start shooting in the San Luis Valley, badger Salcedo in Chihuahua, or otherwise pick a fight, he passed up the opportunities. Even casting him as an unwitting collaborator rests on the premise that Wilkinson believed a clueless lieutenant leading an ill-timed and uncertain expedition could provide some timely critical data or a usable war, the latter of which the general could have launched without Pike. Finally, although Kibby's deposition gave them an opening, Burr's prosecutors barely took notice of Pike's possible involvement—even though soliciting reconnaissance or attempting to launch a war on behalf of the conspiracy would have constituted evidence of the overt treasonable act that the prosecution lacked. That the people with the greatest incentive for establishing a link between Pike and Burr disregarded it suggests the flimsiness of the charge. Hence, the incomplete, contradictory, and circumstantial evidence available points overwhelmingly to Pike's innocence. As with the possibility of secret orders from Wilkinson, the most consistent explanation is simply that Pike was telling the truth most of the time, that he zealously embraced a mission he believed entailed diplomatic and exploratory service to a nation he loved and sacrificed for, and that sometimes in his zeal, he overstepped his orders.

Meanwhile, Pike's attempt to court the administration's support initially bore fruit. Two days after Rowan's February 1808 accusations, Dearborn obliged Pike with a letter that affirmed that even though Jefferson had not directly ordered the expeditions, he approved of them and held Pike's services "in high estimation." The public, Dearborn said, is "much indebted to you for the interprising persevering and judicious manner in which you have performed." Ballenger himself wrote a letter denying the statements Rowan attributed to him, and Pike sent the letter, along with Dearborn's, to the newspapers and forwarded them to Congress as well. Meanwhile, Montgomery's committee interviewed Ballenger's brother, examined other evidence, and concluded that Pike was not involved with Burr. After Congress adjourned that spring without acting on the matter of Pike's reward, Dearborn sent another letter to the House when it reconvened the following fall. Pike's expeditions were "approved by the president," the secretary repeated, and indicated that Pike and his companions might justifiably expect "a liberal reward from the government." There "can be no reasonable doubt of the zeal, perseverance, and intelligence of the commander," or of the "faithful conduct and arduous exertions" of the men. "I trust," he urged, that there will be no objections "to a reasonable compensation for such meritorious services." A week later, Pike's congressional supporters introduced a bill to compensate him and his men with land warrants and double pay. Congress failed to vote on the bill, however, and although it took up the question several more times in subsequent years, it never acted. Decades later, a destitute Clara would still be petitioning for the reward.[17]

Although the *Journals* of the House do not record the debates, many possible explanations might account for Congress's dithering. Almost forty years later, a Senate committee on military affairs reviewed the incomplete documentary record and speculated that Pike's death had precluded any further action on the matter—though that does not explain why Pike's case dragged on for years before his death, whereas Lewis and Clark's had moved through in a matter of months. Later, the historian Donald Jackson proposed that Congress feared setting an expensive precedent that exploration merited greater compensation than other military duties. It is also important to remember that 1808 was a national election year, in which even Pike's supporters might have hedged at associating themselves too closely with anything that smacked of Aaron Burr. In addition, while all this was unfolding, threats to the young nation's independence menaced from many directions and may simply have distracted lawmakers from Pike's sideshow. There were critical matters of national security to attend to.[18]

Independence, Personal and National

In the years between Pike's return and the War of 1812, both he and his country worried about independence. The self-taught Pike had long hoped his siblings would obtain more formal education than he had. Shortly after returning from his western sojourn, he began arranging a West Point appointment for his youngest brother, George Washington Pike. In February 1808, the same week he was rebuffing Rowan's insinuations, he was also thinking about his little brother's improvement. "Secure your Independence by an early attention to economy without niggardness," he told George, and "let your Arms be the best, your Cloths appropriate to your rank and your Demeanor such as is becoming to the son of an Old Patriot and soldier—and the Brother of a man not unknown to the army— Pay great attention to your Grammar and orthography." In invoking both self-improvement and self-discipline as keys to independence, Pike's brotherly concerns mirrored America's.[19]

Neither the Revolution nor the Constitution had resolved the tension between liberty and order. Unbounded individualism had troubling implications for the sovereignty of an infant republic and hence continued to spark national debate. To many, it appeared that individual liberty and the accompanying entrepreneurialism yielded national economic prosperity. For instance, Pike's friend Representative Samuel Mitchill told Congress that "a spirit of business" animated Americans, who would never "surrender their birthright, the privilege of ploughing the ocean for a market." The Scottish merchant John Melish drew similar conclusions after a tour of the United States in 1806. He attributed America's impressive economic vitality to a "spirit of independence" that cut across class divides and defined the American character. In the minds of men like Mitchill and Melish, the spirit of business and the spirit of independence entwined inextricably. As independent people profited, so did the independent nation.[20]

But independence also made Americans ornery. While Mitchill and Melish praised the economic acquisitiveness that fueled Americans' pursuit of happiness, others feared that unbounded liberty yielded selfishness, resistance to authority, and unwillingness to serve the common good. The editor Hezekiah Niles wrote that the "calculating spirit of trade…sinks an individual to the level of a brute, and…the charities of his heart are concentrated on himself." Similarly, a writer for the Philadelphia *Aurora* worried that some individuals sought to "form an interest separate from and adverse to the general interest"—not unlike Aaron Burr. Even Mitchill, who was himself optimistic about his constituents' virtues, confessed that "our citizens are believed to be averse to [the] taxation" necessary to shoulder the burden of the national defense. It boiled down to this: were personal and national independence compatible? The revolutionary generation, including Zebulon Pike, Sr., had believed they were; their children were not quite so sure.[21]

As they had for generations, the Pikes embodied the conundrum. George entered West Point on January 20, 1808, but hardly lived up to his brother's hopes. He refused to study and clamored to quit the service to return home to live with his parents. "Have you lost your senses?" Pike asked him in one letter after George had gone over his commander's head to appeal directly to the secretary of war for a pay advance. You have benefited from "every possible advantage and favour," censured Pike, and nevertheless have failed to improve your mind "by science" or your body "by martial exercises," or even to display "manly fortitude in a profession which has given a name to your family." Pike further fumed that George "refused to support himself when an honorable position was afforded," while their tubercular middle brother James had "determined never to become an incumbrance on the bounty of his parents." "Is this the youth for whose good conduct—I have pledged myself?" Pike asked. "Is this my Brother!! No it cannot be: some fatal delusion has spread itself over him."

Within a year, however, even the severe older brother felt "disposed to quit" the army. "The Idea of always being poor is what I detest," he wrote to his father. Here were two brothers—sons of a man whose personal independence had intersected with the nation's thirty years before, but now the younger was unwilling to take authority's direction, and the older—who took it willingly—was unable to obtain its rewards. Could their country count on a generation so concerned with individual pursuits to unite, sacrifice, and obey enough to repel external threats to national independence?[22]

Indeed, such threats abounded, as Pike acknowledged in another letter to George. "I have much to complain of again to you," he wrote, "but in those times when we are threatened by the two greatest nations in the world—I will cease to upbraid—and again hail you brother." One of those nations was Great Britain. Since the end of the Revolution, the United States and its erstwhile parent had fundamentally disagreed on the practical meaning of personal independence. To Americans, independence included the right to declare one's own nationality through immigration and naturalization in a new homeland, a privilege many Britons had exercised by coming to the United States in the previous three decades. Britain, however, did not recognize its former subjects as naturalized American citizens—once a subject of the king, always a subject of the king. With Great Britain embroiled in the Napoleonic Wars and in need of all the subjects it could get, the British navy vigorously enforced British law, impressing into military service all men it considered subjects, including seamen on American ships. To most Americans this was a violation of American sovereignty, but the Jefferson administration was not willing to go to war over it.[23]

But neither could Jefferson indefinitely turn a blind eye to such violations. On June 22, 1807, the H.M.S. Leonard fired upon the U.S.S. Chesapeake off the coast of Virginia, disabling the American vessel and killing three of its crew. Boarding the Chesapeake, the British took into custody four men whom they deemed deserters. This attack on an American naval vessel infuriated Americans and worsened diplomatic tensions. Nevertheless, in October, Great Britain reiterated its right to impress natural-born British subjects regardless of their citizenship and in November required Europe-bound commercial vessels of neutral nations to stop first in British ports and pay duties. In response, two weeks after Pike set aside his complaints against George in the name of unity during national crisis, Congress acted on the administration's behest and embargoed American exports to Britain. Jefferson intended the measure to compel Britain to acknowledge American neutrality rights. Instead, the measure ruined the many American merchants and farmers who depended on the Atlantic trade and precipitated smuggling and disobedience in response. Although the unpopular prohibition ended in March 1809, the problems that provoked it did not. In January 1812, with both foreign rivals and American citizens flaunting national sovereignty, Representative Mitchill warned Congress of the horrors that might soon follow if the nation failed to respond to such abuses. Its naval stores would slip into enemy hands; its shipwrights and seamen would flee to foreign service; and its port towns might confederate into independent city states, "forming a new Hanseatic league in the Western hemisphere"—a coastal Atlantic version of the worst western nightmares the Burr conspiracy had conjured. On top of all this, the British were once again allegedly inciting Indians in territory the United States considered its own.[24]

Threats to national independence also emanated from France. In the spring of 1808, Napoleon forced the Spanish Bourbon King Carlos IV and his son Fernando to abdicate. On June 6, he installed his brother Joseph Bonaparte on the throne and cast the meaning of loyalty of men like Facundo Melgares in Spanish America into confusion.[25] Did loyalty to Spain mean allegiance to the usurper who now sat on the throne? Or did it mean faithfulness to the Bourbons and, hence, rebellion against Spanish colonial authority? Melgares had told Pike that his loyalty to the crown would endure unless there was a Napoleonic takeover. Now there was one, and plenty of colonials, whatever their pre-coup predilections toward rebellion, decided the only honorable path was revolt against the illegitimate Spanish crown. Others, perhaps including the disgruntled *criollos* Pike had met, had long resented New-World domination by *peninsulares* anyway and decided to chuck European rule for independence. Turmoil in Spain provided them the cover to revolt while appearing to remain loyal to the deposed Bourbons. From Argentina to Texas, the rumblings Pike had detected during his travels erupted in wars for independence that would last for nearly two decades.

The coup in Spain and revolution in the Americas eroded what little neutral ground the United States could claim. To support the colonial rebels directly invited Napoleon's wrath, but to stand pat while the Americas exploded in revolutions that adopted the rhetoric of the United States' own was tacitly to accept Napoleon's usurpation. Moreover, the appearance of siding with the French would aggravate already strained relations with Great Britain and might backfire catastrophically if the British prevailed in the war and gained influence or imperial control over Spain's New World colonies. Fifteen years before the Monroe Doctrine, revolution in Spanish America cast doubt on whether the United States was in fact an independent geopolitical actor in its own hemisphere. To Pike, however, the appropriate course of action was clear. "We cannot remain uninterested spectators of what is acting in our vicinage," he observed to his father. War with France was imminent, and it would "unite us—and cause us to rally round our Government." Like Mitchill and others, he believed that the prospect of hostilities would bring independent men together to defend an independent nation, just as it had reconciled him with his footloose younger brother.[26]

Thus, war seemed a solution to America's problems of both personal and national independence. George Washington's biographer Mason Locke Weems, for example, supported war as a way to strengthen among Americans the kind of self-control Pike had urged upon his brother. Pike's friend William Henry Harrison agreed, urging men of George's generation to join the military and to submit to the "minute observances" of its discipline. Meanwhile, Mitchell maintained war would invigorate both nation and men and call forth from individual citizens a "public spirit" to defend the country from the "pressure of commercial embarrassment, and the menace of the most serious evils." On the Fourth of July 1812, Richard Rush, a Treasury Department official and son of the signer of the Declaration of Independence Benjamin Rush, addressed Congress to justify war with Britain. "Man," Rush advised Congress, "in his individual nature, becomes virtuous by constant struggles" and "self-denials." So, too, for nations. By no other means can they secure "their prosperity, their rights, their liberties." "An ignoble peace," he added, produced "an inordinate love of money—rage of party spirit—and a willingness to endure even slavery itself." In contrast, "war in a just cause produces patriotism." War would also unshackle American cultural ties to Britain, a "contaminating...intimacy" that he maintained still rendered the United States "dependent upon her loom, dependent upon her fashions, dependent upon her judicature, dependent upon her drama—reading none but her books." In sum, war with Britain would have the effect of "making our liberty thrive more securely, and ourselves more independent—privately and politically." As it had for the revolutionary generation, personal and national independence entwined, and once again a Pike leapt into the thick of things. "I feel anxious," Pike wrote of his expectation of an imminent

British or French invasion, "to evince to them that the sons are able to maintain the Independence handed down to us by our Fathers."[27]

Like Pike, in calling Americans to make personal independence virtuous and sustainable through heroic defense of national independence, Rush and Mitchill invoked the stories of the revolutionary generation. "Revered be the memories of the statesmen and orators whose wisdom led to the act of Independence," Rush said, "and of the gallant soldiers who sealed it with their blood!" He called his countrymen to make themselves "worthy to have your names recounted with the illustrious fathers of our revolution." As for the present generation, "revered be the dust of those who fall, sweet their memories." When Mitchill enumerated Britain's recent maritime abuses, he concluded that "our predecessors in 1774 and 1775" had gone to war for "outrages infinitely less than these." Mitchill also urged his listeners to "examine the pages of history," most notably the recent American defeat of belligerent pirates in the Mediterranean. "May we at no time forget to pronounce eulogies and utter songs, upon the benefactors of our country." Doing so not only honored the benefactors but improved subsequent generations as well. While the orators in Congress debated these points, Pike turned to recounting his own performances.[28]

Widespread anxiety about personal and national independence opened the door for Pike to reestablish his claim to national gratitude by telling the story of his travels. Writing up his exploits had preoccupied him since his return from New Mexico in 1807. A few days after arriving at Natchitoches, he wrote to Wilkinson on the subject of his papers. Although Salcedo had seized many of them at Chihuahua, "I yet possess immense matter," he assured the general, enough to "enable me to exhibit a correct chart of the route." He also wrote to Dearborn, reiterating that while Salcedo had taken "what he conceived [to be] all my papers," Pike still retained "the whole of my Journals; courses; and distances." Officially forbidden to carry pen and paper by the Spaniards, he had furtively brought a small pencil with him and scrawled observations and journal entries on scraps of paper. He rolled pages from his notebooks and wadded them into his men's guns. Other documents he stashed on the men's bodies and in their clothing. In their "breasts," Pike reported to Wilkinson with relief, "lay the whole secret of my papers," and not one man betrayed the scheme. By journey's end, however, the papers were in a "mutilated and deranged state." Consequently, Pike spent much of his time at Natchitoches and en route to Washington putting the material into shape, starting with the laborious task of filing down the gun barrels to extract their documentary contents. Despite being so exhausted upon arrival at Natchitoches that he found it "almost impossible for me to continue for one hour with the pen in my hand," and despite his time-consuming official duties serving Wilkinson for most of November and December, he synthesized the fragments into a draft report of his discoveries and submitted it to Dearborn on January 26, 1808. This raises the question of just what was in that pile of scraps.[29]

Most importantly, it contained his journal. Real Alencaster had tricked him in Santa Fe by returning Pike's trunk, only to recall it the next day. But the trunk did not contain all of Pike's papers. As he approached the New Mexican capital, Pike had spirited away his key papers, leaving just enough of them in the trunk so as not to arouse suspicion that there might be more documents. By returning the trunk, Real Alencaster partly foiled this scheme, as Pike then conceived it safer to store the rest of the papers in the trunk than on the bodies of his drinking and carousing men. By chance, however, as he retrieved the papers and returned them to the trunk, the man with the journal on his person was nowhere to be found, and thus the most valuable and complete record of the expedition survived the governor's inspection the next day. Thereafter, Pike managed to continue his observations and diary keeping, though neither his letters nor journals explain how, exactly. Although formally prohibited from taking notes, Pike frequently wrote official statements and letters in Chihuahua with Salcedo's blessing, and it is not hard to imagine Pike taking such opportunities to scribble notes for himself and stashing them away unnoticed.

Sometimes his chaperones simply looked the other way. Apparently accustomed to writing unmolested, for example, Pike noticed one day "a new species of discipline" and the aroused "suspicions of my friend Melgares." The heightened scrutiny prompted Pike to rise late at night and begin stuffing papers into the rifles. On another occasion, Melgares reprimanded him as Pike sat down to write in his journal. Pike at first took offense, but instead of objecting interpreted Melgares's added comment, "you have a good memory," as a winking signal that the Spaniard assumed Pike would not actually obey the injunction. Pike merely smiled assent and at the next opportunity disappeared into the bushes, established one of his men as a lookout, and sat down to write in peace. Such examples suggest Pike did have access to writing materials and did not always feel the need to hide his activities from Melgares. Even when he did, however, he found few stumbling blocks to even the most transparent deception. With a little luck, some deceit, and plenty of Spanish forbearance, Pike

seems to have been able to smuggle out many of his most important documents and to continue making new ones, raw material that he massaged
over the next year into a manuscript account of his travels. Little of that
raw material, however, has survived. Most of what remains is the printed
version of the manuscript he polished out of the scraps he retrieved from
his men's rifles and clothing. Crafted primarily in 1807 and 1808, as the
Burr trial threatened to mar his reputation and as Congress denied him
compensation and investigated his mentor, Pike's story must be thought
of not only as an account of what happened on the expedition, but also as
a reconstructed portrait of it as he wanted it to be seen.[30]

One of that portrait's main audiences was Congress. Shortly after sub-
mitting the materials to Dearborn, he laid before Montgomery's committee
a packet of documents and maps relating to his two journeys, including
his diary from the second. He also furnished to the committee his letters
to Dearborn regarding his findings about the Internal Provinces of New
Spain. The journals especially, his cover letter said, conveyed a sense of
"the hardships undergone and the difficulties encountered." He added
that some members of the party had become invalids for life and that
others were still prisoners in New Spain. Later, Congress received additional papers, including Pike's official instructions and Dearborn's letter
applauding Pike's conduct. Thus, Congress—at the time considering his
party's compensation claims—became the first audience for his tale of
sacrifice made on behalf of the nation.

Sometime in May 1808, with Congress adjourned and the compensation
bill tabled, Pike left Washington. By this time, he had completed most or
all of his manuscript and had assembled many of the related papers for
publication. Although he was still working on the maps, he had also written an extensive "Dissertation... on the Internal Parts of Louisiana," which
he had laboriously extracted from nightly entries he had made based on
observations that occurred to him during the day. He paid his bill for the
boarding of a draftsman he had employed for thirteen weeks to work on
his map and departed for St. Louis in a long-delayed return to that city. On
his way west, he stopped in Philadelphia, where he contracted with
Conrad, Lucas and Company to publish the collection, and he filed for a
copyright. On June 8, the firm issued a prospectus for the publication of
his journals from the Mississippi and western expeditions. In addition to
a daily narrative of his travels, the volume's four-hundred pages would
contain reports on Indian tribes, British traders, and Spanish colonies
and remarks on geography, climate, rivers, and more. It also promised

complete maps of the country Pike traversed and beyond. All this would cost subscribers three dollars, payable on delivery. Before leaving Philadelphia, Pike wrote to Dearborn urging him to purchase some copies for the War Department, and a month later from Pittsburgh, he asked Secretary of State James Madison to buy the volume and to help publicize it. He needed their patronage badly; he had agreed to finance part of the publication costs himself and expected "but an extreame small profit" from the venture. Financial remuneration, however, was not his main quarry. His aims, he told Dearborn, were "more generally directed to fame."[31]

The volume, which finally appeared in print in 1810, detailed the expedition through a daily account. He divided this diary into three parts: his Mississippi River expedition, his western journey up to his capture on the Rio Conejos, and his travels through New Spain. To these, he appended letters and other documents related to the expeditions, including his instructions, correspondence with Wilkinson, and speeches to Indians. He also tabulated information into charts that catalogued population, customs, and political arrangements of Indians and other local peoples. Most

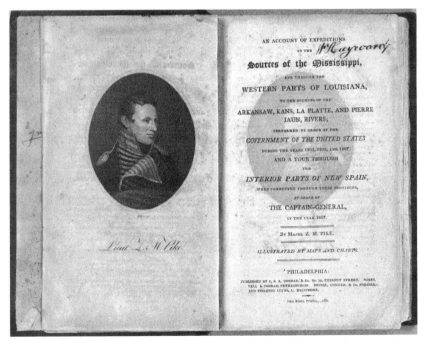

FIGURE 7.4 Title page of Pike's journal, published in 1810. David Rumsey Map Collection, www.davidrumsey.com.

importantly, he wrote three lengthy essays summarizing his observations on people and geography of the three segments of his travels and their potential benefits to the United States. Missouri's prairies, he said "will admit of a numerous, extensive and compact population." Beyond that, however, lay a "vast tract of untimbered country" whose soil was "generally dry and sandy," "barren," "parched," and "dried up for eight months of the year." It resembled the "sandy desarts of Africa" and would only allow "limited population." This wasteland, he indicated, nevertheless offered a useful buffer to prevent the US population from expanding beyond the nation's ability to attach it to the Union. The Indians who lived there were primitive but powerful and mostly under the influence of the Spanish. The United States must remedy this by supplying and withholding necessary trade goods to make them dependent and by guaranteeing peace among tribes. The provinces of New Spain, meanwhile, harbored potentially unlimited wealth. If Mexico were opened to free trade, Pike contended, "the country would immediately become rich and powerful." American ships "would fill every port," enabling "us to carry off at least nine-tenths of her commerce." Moreover, this potential abundance was only loosely tied to the Spanish crown. Abuses and backwardness in politics, religion, and economy, he believed, had produced a population longing for enlightened liberation. The United States could "at any time" easily "create and effect the revolution." In these passages and throughout the volume, Pike described North America's land and people as ripe for both exploitation and liberation, to the great benefit of the United States.[32]

The volume also constructed a patriotic persona for its author. Pike opened the preface by equating his expedition to Lewis and Clark's. He also confronted his Burr problem. "There has not been wanting," he wrote, "persons of various ranks, who have endeavored to infuse the idea into the minds of the public, that the last voyage was undertaken through some sinister designs of general Wilkinson." Pike condemned such insinuations as "groundless calumny," which had arisen from "the envenomed breasts" of Wilkinson's enemies and which the exonerating letters from Dearborn had "amply refuted." To leave no doubt of his innocence, Pike published the letters in one of the appendices. Also in the preface, he maintained that he had surpassed his instructions out of a "sense of duty" and that "as a man of humanity and feeling" he had put an end to warfare among Indians. In the journals, he trumpeted his compassion in narrating the trials of his "frozen lads" who feared abandonment. And he told how pity for a "brother soldier" moved him to risk his own welfare to visit

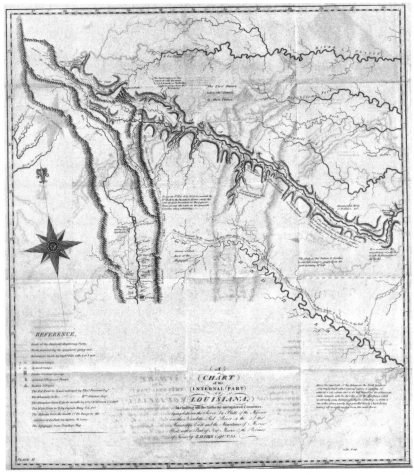

FIGURE 7.5 The map Pike drew of his travels in the Rocky Mountains. David Rumsey Map Collection, www.davidrumsey.com.

David Fero in Chihuahua, even as his unflagging patriotism forbade him from promising to the stranded *filibustero* anything that might compromise the nation's interests. "Could I deny him the interview from any motives of delicacy?" he asked his readers rhetorically; "No; forbid it humanity! Forbid it every sentiment of my soul!" To his April 4, 1807, declaration to Salcedo, he added a few lines (written in Washington after the fact). Here, he acknowledged that the spare sketch itself had omitted the details of the journey's hardships and then corrected that by reminding readers that he had often endured "thirst or famine," marched through "snows three or four feet deep," suffered exposure to "inclemency," and carried burdens of "60 or 70 pounds"—details "calculated to excite humanity." With these and many other flourishes, Pike simultaneously exhibited to readers his unfailing sacrificial patriotism and assured them of his humane sensibilities, constructing himself as a man of fortitude, honor, and feeling—the epitome of both Dodsley's advice and the era's idealized masculine sensitivity. Such a man, he hoped it was clear, could not possibly have leagued with Burr.[33]

The volume appeared in 1810, four years before Lewis and Clark's account, but hardly without hitch. Under the best of circumstances, Pike had taken down his observations by firelight after exhausting days, slapping at mosquitoes or with shivering hands clutching his cloak or animal skins to shield himself against the cold. Other times, he scribbled down whatever he could sneak between the prying glances of Spaniards, filling any handy scrap of paper available. Then, upon returning, while continuing his full military duties, he somehow arranged this disarray into a publishable narrative. Moreover, Pike never had been very skilled with the pen. His syntax and spelling were tortured, and the organization was confusing. The Prussian baron Alexander von Humboldt, from whom Pike borrowed liberally, charged him with plagiarizing the maps. Soon after the volume appeared, the publisher went bankrupt. In an editorial note in the opening pages of the book, one of the publishers doubted "whether any book ever went to press under so many disadvantages." Jefferson later asked Humboldt to excuse Pike's "oversight" in failing to acknowledge the rightful origins of the map's information. In any case, he told the baron, Pike did not even make "filthy shillings and pence" from the publication.[34]

The endeavor, however, yielded somewhat more fame than profit. Even before publication, Pike's version of his adventures was diffusing widely, as attested by letters by Joseph Ballenger and State Department official John Graham, both of whom judged Pike's statements about the expedition "correct." Ballenger added, "I think his party suffered as much as Clark and Lewis's, and deserves as well of their country." In addition, Pike's account induced Dearborn to acknowledge that Pike and his comrades had "performed...laborious and dangerous expeditions," a phrase that Montgomery's committee quoted in its recommendation for compensation. A few months after the American publication of the volume, the British publisher Thomas Rees obtained a copy of the manuscript, reworked the organization, corrected some spelling (though not enough, he lamented), and republished an 1811 version in London. Rees considered Pike's "discoveries" of "great importance to geographical science." Rees also expected that the reader would be gratified to know that "the persons whose adventures have excited his solicitude, whose tale of dangers and sufferings has awakened his sympathy, and drawn from him the sigh and the tear of commiseration, have not passed unrewarded by their grateful and applauding county." This was exactly the reputation Pike wanted.[35]

The only extant review of the volume, however, was less complimentary. In 1814, in the middle of the War of 1812, an anonymous British writer reviewed the London version for *Analectic Magazine*, a Philadelphia publication. Pike would have been pleased to read at the outset of the piece that the reviewer, like Rees, accepted the mission as being "altogether of a public nature" and having the "approbation" of the president. After this promising opening, however, the reviewer soured on the volume and its author. Some of Pike's discoveries, the reviewer complained, were not particularly new, and others were already out of date, given how the War of 1812 and the Spanish American revolutions had changed the territories through which Pike had traveled. If the volume offered little to science, the tedious and ungrammatical writing style caused it to fail also as a work of adventure. Although the review praised Pike's zeal and perseverance, it also highlighted the poor planning and many other foolhardy shortcomings of the expeditions. As Pike had hoped, the reviewer recognized Pike's "warm feelings" in connection with the frozen lads and other episodes, but added that Pike seemed "at the same time not a little ambitious of showing them." The reviewer even gloated about the strong fortifications of British traders on the upper Mississippi and their continued influence over the Indians and also predicted that the barren plains Pike found at mid-continent would buffer American expansion. "As a topographical survey," the article concluded, the book "is highly useful on the double ground of accuracy and perspicuity; but it can scarcely be accounted an amusing production."[36] Although the journals earned him recognition and some praise, it would take later writers to appreciate fully his exploits and complete the heroic picture that the journals had begun to sketch.

More immediately—and of great importance to Pike's pursuit of personal independence—the publication of the journals coincided with a series of rapid promotions. Upon return from the western expedition, he had discovered that he had been promoted to captain the previous August. In April 1808, as he was putting the finishing touches on his manuscript, he found himself at a crossroads. He angled for an appointment from Dearborn to head the army's new recruiting office in Kentucky (and asked that Robinson be posted there, too). A few days later, he rejected Dearborn's suggestion of a transfer to a rifle corps whose commander Pike thought incompetent. Instead, he begged to head a New Jersey regiment, an assignment the state's officers approved and that he considered "highly Honorable." On May 3, just before he departed for Philadelphia to finalize the agreement with his publisher, he was promoted to major in the sixth infantry. He spent 1808 and 1809 as Wilkinson's right-hand man, accompanying the general on several trips before departing with him to New Orleans, where they arrived in spring 1809. Over the next year, Pike played a key role in provisioning and ultimately relocating troops whom Wilkinson had ill-advisedly situated in a swampy, mosquito-ridden environment, resulting in the death of nearly half of the more than two thousand men stationed there. On December 31, 1809, the eve of the publication of his papers, his efforts earned him promotion to lieutenant colonel. At the age of thirty, he has passed his father in rank.[37]

In the waning days of November 1811, shortly before leaving his command in Baton Rouge for Washington, Pike wrote a letter to his friend Caesar A. Rodney, the nation's attorney general. In it, Pike declared himself "a Citizen Soldier."[38] As citizen, he had inherited the Revolution's promises of independence; as a soldier, he had elected to pursue them through the military. By that date, he had spent the past four-and-a-half years trying to get the nation of kindred and friends to embrace him. First by telling his story and giving gifts to friends in high places, then by disseminating the documents from his voyages, and finally by disclosing his actions for the public to judge, he had put to rest the Aaron Burr accusations. He had also persuaded a congressional committee to report a bill that would compensate the party, published his account on two continents, and scaled the military hierarchy. Of course, Congress had not passed the compensation bill, and his book had not made him any money. From time to time he himself had doubted whether the nation would reward his sacrifice at all.

Still, the nation's diplomatic troubles offered him some new prospects. The possibility of war, he told Rodney, meant "an Augmentation of the Army" and thus the chance to gain through military promotion and glory what his western adventures had won him only partially. In that event, he hoped Rodney would support a promotion for Pike. Pike, who as spurned explorer might have turned to private life and exemplified the selfishness that excessive liberty spawned, instead, as citizen soldier, declared to Rodney that his sword was always "ready to support" the nation's "political Truths" at "the risque of my blood and life." Meanwhile Republicans in

Congress were edging toward the conclusion that, as one representative soon proclaimed, "a resort to force will occasionally be indispensable" for "a nation...determined to be free." Pike and America both needed a good war.[39]

War of 1812

They would get a bad one. Pike left his post at Baton Rouge in the spring of 1812 and returned to Washington, where sabers were rattling in Congress. With the prospect of an enlarged army, he quickly resumed lobbying his high-ranking friends for a promotion, which he obtained shortly after President James Madison signed the act declaring war on Great Britain on June 18. Along with the new rank of colonel came orders to proceed to the northern front of a war that opened with an American attack on Canada. Expecting Canadians to welcome their invading neighbors as liberators, the Madison administration hoped that a decisive preemptive strike would induce Canadians to join the American side. Once Britain recognized the hopelessness of holding its disgruntled colony, the two governments could settle their many disagreements on terms to the administration's liking. En route to the front, Pike recruited and outfitted men in New Jersey for the fifteenth regiment, which Pike would command under his father's boyhood friend Brigadier General Joseph Bloomfield. Expecting "to be the advance Guard which enters Canada," Pike joined the regiment at Staten Island and then marched it first to Albany and then to Plattsburgh, on Lake Champlain at the mouth of the Saranac River, where the troops arrived in early fall. Clara accompanied him, but before they left he enrolled nine-year-old Clarissa in a "very celibrated school" in Philadelphia and secured a residence in the city for Clara to return to, presumably when weather or fighting grew intolerable for an officer's wife. On July 24, the day before he left to join his regiment, he wrote to Wilkinson, "If we go into Canada You will hear of my Fame or my death."[40]

The first year of war went badly for the United States. The quick victory did not materialize. Botched campaigns at Detroit and Niagara failed to secure strategic territorial gains (Detroit's actually lost ground) and soured Canadians to the American pretense of liberation. Instead, it was the Americans who refused to unite in support of the cause. Underfunded, under-provisioned, and often incompetently led, the army could not lure enough recruits or satisfactorily pay the ones it did manage to attract.

Federalists sniped at the Madison administration's follies, and Republicans retorted by calling them traitors. Residents along the border, who had not asked for war, continued the transborder commerce that had underwritten their livelihoods before the hostilities, and whenever restrictive laws or military orders cramped their activities, they simply disobeyed. Some even abetted the enemy, selling supplies and harboring spies. In November, Pike commanded a party of sixty men who advanced eight miles into Quebec, burning the barracks and blockhouses of a retreating force of Canadians and Indians, and prepared in high spirits to march toward the Canadian stronghold at Montreal. Dearborn, however, perhaps leery of a repetition of Detroit and Niagara, called the Americans back. As winter set in and made further campaigning impossible, top officers scrambled back to Washington to trumpet their exploits—coloring the facts as needed to win promotion—while the enlisted men hunkered down on the front.[41]

Pike stayed. From Camp Saranac, where he spent the winter drilling the troops and combating desertions and rumored mutinies, he witnessed the difficulties that had foiled the first year's campaign. For the first month, until lodges could be constructed, the camp's six thousand men slept on frozen ground and brushed the snow from their weary bodies when they awoke. Under such conditions, he found men hard to recruit and harder to keep. The ones who remained got sick. Ninety men died of illness in December, and he expected another seventy would succumb in January. Equally difficult to handle were the officers, who constantly jockeyed for stature and turned infantile at the slighted insult. Colonel Joseph Constant, for example, took umbrage that Pike and other officers were promoted over him and resigned his command of the third regiment. Pike, too, occasionally stooped to bickering over rank, such as when he gossiped to Rodney that William Eustis, the recently deposed secretary of war, was not "calculated to be at the Head of the War Department." He added that even the talents of the incoming secretary, John Armstrong, whom Pike esteemed greatly, were insufficient "to organize and bring into the field an Army to act with effect…out of such a heterogenious mass as the American forces." The military was a mess.[42]

Pike found even more fault with civilians. Some northern New Yorkers were "so void of all sense of honor" and "love of country," he complained, as to "hold correspondence with, and give intelligence to our enemies." In January 1813 he published excerpts of the *Articles of War*, the nation's code of military conduct, in the local newspapers: whoever aids or spies for the enemy shall be sentenced to death. And he warned that "henceforward, they shall be enforced with the greatest severity." Such open and persistent transgressions rankled Pike, who believed, as he wrote to a local landowner, Albon Mann, in February, "the present juncture demands the sacrifice from your fellow Citizens for which they will receive the thanks of their gratefull Country." With troop shortages, poor leadership, and a divided citizenry hamstringing operations during the war's first year, Pike despaired that only a handful of naval victories had "saved the Honor of the Nation and kept up the spirits of the people."[43]

In February 1813, Henry Dearborn, the major general in charge of operations on the Great Lakes, ordered Pike and his men to Lake Ontario. Dearborn wanted to concentrate his forces at the lake's primary American naval base, Sackets Harbor, in preparation for an attack on Kingston as soon as the spring ice thawed. At Kingston, the British housed most of their Great Lakes naval force, and its destruction would choke the Royal Navy's ability to supply and defend all points upstream. It was bitterly cold as Pike and four hundred men set out by snowshoe and sleigh in early March, with four hundred more trailing a few days behind. On March 6, one man froze to death and twenty more got frostbitten feet, which Pike predicted they would lose. He attributed the tragedy to the men's intoxication and noted two days later that he had not seen a drunken man in the outfit since. There remained, however, a few deserters and plenty of traitors with which to contend. In Ogdensburg, on the Saint Lawrence River in northern New York, local business leaders and officials who openly opposed the war had thwarted customs officer Alexander Richards's efforts to clamp down on cross-border traffic. A frustrated Richards prevailed upon Pike to skirt civilian authorities and hold some of the smugglers under military arrest. Pike called them "miscreants who possess so little patriotism as to wish success to an enemy," and after arriving at Sackets Harbor sent a detachment under Lieutenant Loring Austin to apprehend them. Richards, however, failed to provide a deposition attesting to the alleged violations, and Pike was forced to release the smugglers, who promptly filed counter charges protesting their unlawful military imprisonment. A local judge threw Austin in prison instead. In the end, the affair yielded Pike only embarrassment, a lot of ink spilled in letters explaining the episode to his superiors, and a reminder that not all American citizens embraced the sacrifice and reward he recommended to Albon Mann.[44]

By the time Pike reached Sackets Harbor in late March 1813, the United States desperately needed to win a battle—for public relations reasons as much as military ones. Opening the season with a victory would rally the troops and attract new ones. It would lure Indians, Canadians, and disgruntled Americans to the United States' side, and it would silence Federalists. Lose, however, and the disease, desertion, and dissent might continue. The unpopular war might handicap pro-war Republican candidates in upcoming New York state elections. And Ogdensburg's residents' disloyalty might metastasize along the entire border. Accordingly, Armstrong advised Dearborn to attack with his "whole strength" to ensure the first campaign would "be a successful one." If it failed, "the disgrace of our arms will be complete. The public will lose all confidence in us, and we shall even cease to have any in ourselves." The "good effects" of a win, however, would "be felt throughout the campaign."[45]

Spring brought Pike some good effects, too. Congress had established six new brigadier general appointments, and he learned on April 5 that he had received one. Now he could turn his attention from chasing smugglers to planning the spring campaign. To halt their losing streak, Pike's superiors switched their objective from the well-defended Kingston to the more vulnerable town of York on the northwestern shore of Lake Ontario. The United States already enjoyed a slight naval advantage on the lake and more warships were under construction at the Americans' primary Great Lakes naval base at Sackets Harbor, including a frigate called the *General Pike.* The British harbored several vessels of their own at York but had left the city poorly guarded. Capturing or destroying those vessels, Dearborn wrote to Armstrong, would give the United States "complete command of the lake" and provide a base from which to attack Niagara and other British posts around Ontario's shores. Dearborn's plan was for the navy to ferry Pike and at least a thousand troops (the number would turn out to exceed 1,700) across the lake from Sackets Harbor and to attack York by land, while the navy provided cover for the troops by bombarding the city from the water.[46]

As Pike contemplated the opening of the campaign, the most important service he had yet embarked upon in his career, his thoughts turned to honor and death. "I embark to-morrow," he wrote to his father, "in the fleet at Sackett's harbor at the head of a column of 1500 choice troops." He hoped to be "the happy mortal destined to turn the scale of war." If so, "honor and glory await my name." But if he were to perish, he yearned for a death "like Wolfe's—to sleep in the arms of victory." The ice broke on April 20, and the squadron of fifteen vessels assembled with 1,700 men, the naval forces under the command of Admiral Isaac Chauncey and the army under Major General Henry Dearborn. They launched on April 22 and 23, but a gale quickly chased them back to port. On April 25, they embarked once again for the two-day voyage across Lake Ontario. In the morning Pike announced the orders for the land attack, detailing who was to land first, when to shoot and when not to, who was to cover the left flank and the right, and which platoons would stay in reserve. After all the logistics, he reminded officers and soldiers alike to be "mindful of the honor of the American arms." "Courage and bravery in the field," he said, "do not more distinguish the soldier than humanity after victory." Treat "the unoffending citizens of Canada" with kindness, and respect their property. The orders were to be read in front of every corps, and every field officer was to carry a copy of his own. On board ship, the evening before the attack, he gave a letter to an aide with instructions to deliver it if Pike fell in battle. "My dear Clara,—We are now standing on and off the harbor of York, which we shall attack at daylight," he began. "I shall dedicate these last moments to you, my love, and to-morrow throw all other ideas but my country to the winds." Words eluded him in the weight of the moment. "I have no new injunction, no new charge to give you; nor no new ideas to communicate; yet we love to commune with those we love, more especially when we conceive it may be the last time." In closing, he passed on a "father's love" to young Clarissa and implored his wife, "Should I fall, defend my memory." He signed it, "with the warmest sentiments of love and friendship, Montgomery."[47]

The ships reached York on the afternoon of April 26. The capital of Upper Canada, York counted six hundred inhabitants and was built on a small inlet in Lake Ontario, just northeast of the ruins of an old French fort called Tarantah, which bequeathed its name and location to the modern city Toronto. Between York and the remains of the French post lay the main British fortress. A narrow spit of land and archipelago of small islands curved into the lake, culminating in Gibraltar Point and protecting the town and fortifications from storms and enemies that might attack from the water. Still, British General Sir Roger Sheaffe had few options. He commanded only seven hundred regulars, three hundred militiamen and local workers, and a few dozen Indians. Not all of his guns were fully operational, and a western battery between the fortress and Tarantah was not yet finished.[48]

As the sun rose on April 27, Chauncey's fleet was anchored about a mile from the beach. By eight o'clock, riflemen under Major Benjamin Forsyth were clambering into boats for the landing. They rowed for shore

FIGURE 7.6 *York Barracks, Lake Ontario, Upper Canada, May 13, 1804*, Library and Archives Canada, Acc. No. 1990-336-3.

near Tarantah, about a mile southwest of the fortress, but an east wind blew them off course toward some woods. Well-shielded by the thickets, several hundred British troops and Indians fired on the boats. Within feet of the shore, Forsyth ordered his men to begin shooting back. Some of the Americans splashed into the waves, eager to gain land, while oarsman, their backs to the musket balls whizzing by, pulled for the shore. Watching from one of the ships, an impatient Pike allegedly cried "I can't stay here any longer" and ordered his staff and several companies of infantry into boats to steer for the beach. Still under heavy fire, Forsyth's crew disembarked and charged into the teeth of the British bayonets, while Pike landed seven or eight hundred men, with more coming behind. As musicians bugled "Yankee Doodle," hundreds of American infantrymen scrambled up the steep bank "in high spirits," Pike's aide reported, and the badly outnumbered British and Indians quickly "shewed us their backs." With the troops landed, the schooners maneuvered around Gibraltar Point and drew within six hundred yards of the British stronghold and began firing the cannons. Meanwhile, Pike organized the infantry regiments and pursued the fleeing redcoats and Indians through the woods, capturing the western battery and some smaller works that the British had hastily assembled to forestall the landing. By early afternoon, Pike halted his troops in a clearing to bring up the heavy artillery for the final assault. The advancing American columns, greatly aided by the naval barrage from off shore, had nearly captured the main fortress.[49]

While he awaited the reinforcements, Pike sat down on a stump to interrogate a prisoner. His enemy was clearly retreating, but the Union Jack still flew over the fort, Sheaffe's last-ditch effort to confuse the Americans into delay while his soldiers carried off whatever of value they could and burned whatever they could not, including the nearly constructed *Sir Isaac Brock*. Pike wanted to know from the captive how many troops remained at the fort and whether they were prepared to defend it. He probably did not manage to extract this intelligence before a tremendous explosion rocked the battlefield. Before abandoning the fort, Sheaffe had ordered a powder magazine to be set ablaze, and the resulting detonation rocketed stones larger than a man's fist in every direction, killing at least forty Britons and a similar number of Americans, including one of Pike's assistants. Another aide sustained severe bruises but escaped with his life, protected beneath the portly corpse of the British prisoner. One of the projectiles struck Pike's forehead. Others pulverized his back and ribs. Within five minutes, however, his officers had formed the troops and resumed marching them toward the town, while the colonel who took over Pike's command sent a message ahead demanding immediate surrender. Around two o'clock, medics carried Pike from the battlefield. According to the surviving aide, Pike asked what was happening when a great "Huzza!" rang out from distant troops. "The British union jack is coming down, general," an attending sergeant said. "The stars are going up." According to another version, Pike gasped, "Push on, my brave fellows, and avenge your general." He was rowed out to the *U.S.S. Madison*, where the British flag that had decoyed him was brought and placed beneath his head as a pillow. Within hours he expired. Just thirty-four years old, he died the glorious death he had frequently contemplated.[50]

"We are in full possession of this place," Dearborn wrote in a terse note to Armstrong at eight o'clock that night. "We shall be prepared to sail for the next object" with the "first favorable wind. I have to lament the loss of the brave and active brigadier-general Pike." For two days, the American surgeons amputated limbs and sewed the mangled bodies of the more than three hundred men wounded by the explosion. They also found time to embalm Pike's body and encase it in a preservative of rum for the return voyage. Back in Sackets Harbor, it was hoisted out of a ship and placed in a fresh casket. Before he was interred, a few thirsty soldiers guzzled the rum that had preserved his corpse, a gruesome end to the body of a teetotaler who had once chased his soldiers through the bushes in the Ohio Valley to keep them from quenching their great thirst.[51]

DEATH OF GEN. PIKE,
At York, (U. C.) on the 27th of April, 1813.

FIGURE 7.7 *Death of Gen. Pike, At York, (U.C.) on the 27th April, 1813*, Library and Archives Canada, Acc. No. 1990-553-734.

In death Pike reaped the honor and gratitude that had escaped him in life. The first significant victory after nearly a year of false starts, the victory at York temporarily restored American confidence and helped keep US naval power on the Great Lakes on par with Britain's for the rest of the war. The news spread quickly, first across Lake Ontario to the Niagara district, and from there diffused throughout New York and to the nation at large. By May 11, Philadelphia's *Weekly Aurora* published an article confirming the rumors of military triumph and the demise of Pike. As word spread, the papers trumpeted the victory and lamented its hero. Eulogies and toasts were published everywhere. Between acts in a stage performance, a Baltimore theater company unveiled an obelisk with an inscription acclaiming Pike's glorious death, while the band played somberly and an actress dressed as Columbia mournfully pointed her spear to his name. Two lengthy poems commemorated his heroism. Hezekiah Niles dedicated the fourth volume of his *Weekly Register* to Pike and fellow martyr, the naval captain James Lawrence. And Congress appointed a committee to consider publicly honoring Pike and Lawrence and providing for the "support and comfort" of their families. Even the critics of the war celebrated him. A Federalist paper, for example, declared the war unnecessary and insisted that not even taking York could compensate for losing a man like Pike. Although the nation had forfeited a great military man, it had gained something potentially even more valuable: a martyr.[52]

Militarily, the rest of the war went much like its first year, with occasional dramatic victories sandwiched in between episodes of division, defeat, and tragicomic incompetence. By the end of 1814, the war effort was on the brink of financial collapse, and a few New England Federalists were contemplating secession. Despite the bleak prospects, British alarm about the possibility of renewed warfare in Europe enabled American diplomats to negotiate more favorable peace terms at Ghent than they had won on the battlefields of North America. At war's end the military had not conquered any new territory nor secured the nation's shipping. Nevertheless, the embattled Madison administration claimed victory by redefining the war it had launched to win a military basis for American sovereignty as being instead a defense of national honor. Calling the Treaty of Ghent "highly honorable to the nation," Madison claimed that it "terminates, with peculiar felicity, a campaign signalized by the most brilliant successes." James Monroe, the secretary of both the war and state departments, said that "our Union has gained strength, our troops honor, and the nation character, by the contest."[53] The administration brushed aside the absence of strategic territorial gains and took heart that the nation had responded with fortitude and sacrifice to the most powerful military in the world and had not lost. The memory of Pike and others who died honorably lent credibility to the intellectual sleight of hand that reinvented the war's rationale.

His earliest biographies appeared in this context. Initially, extended eulogies chronicled his life in magazines and newspapers alongside the published toasts and heroic accounts of the Battle of York. The first was a simple four-sentence statement in the *Weekly Aurora* on May 11 in the middle of an account of the fighting at York. Pike was born in New Jersey, it said. He had a talent for inspiring other men. His travels through Louisiana were a "monument of his intrepid character." He left a widow and a daughter. Another tribute, in the *Weekly Register* on June 5, hailed that he had risen, without the benefit of "adventitious circumstances" and "forced his way into the public affection by the power of his virtues and strength of his talents alone." The article also called for "some person competent to the performance" to take up the "sweet, yet melancholy duty of giving to the world a full and faithful portraiture."[54]

Someone did. An unsigned fourteen-page article titled "Biographical Memoir of the Late Brigadier-General Zebulon Montgomery Pike" appeared in the July issue of a magazine called the *Monthly Recorder*, barely two months after his death. The article opened by acknowledging that no two historical figures claim a tighter hold on the public's "imagination and sympathies" than "the hardy explorer" and the "defender of his country's rights." Pike was both. The article then briefly recounted his New Jersey birth to a military family, his modest, self-disciplined boyhood and youth, and the domestic commitments of husband and father from which he tore himself whenever his country called. The piece also mentioned his appreciation for Dodsley's *Economy of Human Life* and the comments Pike scrawled in its margins. For eight pages the memoir chronicled Pike's two expeditions, quoting liberally from his journals to illustrate the hardships he encountered and the fortitude and patriotism with which he met them. The final five pages were about the Battle of York and the last week of Pike's life. It quoted Pike's final letter to his father, his orders to his men, and the aide's account of the battle, which newspapers had repeatedly published by this time. "Thus fell, in the prime of an active and useful life, Brigadier-General Zebulon Montgomery Pike," the article concluded. "The deep and universal sorrow manifested for his loss, is the best eulogium upon his virtues."[55]

With no citations and an anonymous author, the piece obscured its own origins, but Pike had plenty of supporters with access to the information it contained and a desire to publicize it. One was the aide who published the account of York, which the last third of the memoir rendered nearly verbatim. The source also could have been one of the adoring officers of his fifteenth regiment, who formed a military honor society in his name out of "respect for our deceased commander" and a wish to perpetuate "his fame," and who resolved to solemnize future anniversaries of his death by dressing for mourning and foregoing all unnecessary duties for the day.[56] But what about the document's details of the family's multigenerational military history or the quotes of Pike's commentary in the margins of his copy of Dodsley? Such intimacies likely originated from someone closer to Pike than a comrade in arms.

Clara certainly knew such details and had an incentive to share them; promoting Pike's memory was her best chance for support in what promised to be a long and difficult widowhood. For all its glorification of her fallen husband, the always penny-pinching government outdid itself and failed to pay Pike's salary for the month in which he had died. Repeatedly, Clara attempted to claim her husband's unpaid wages and finally wrote directly to the secretary of war to inquire about the holdup. Her letter evoked a woman who matched her descendants' subsequent descriptions of her as a commanding and educated person. In flowing penmanship and with flawless grammar and spelling, she opened with ladylike apologies for intruding on the secretary's time and closed with unrelenting logic that demolished the lame excuses and endless runaround his underlings had given her. No pushover widow, Clara manipulated both the era's required feminine deference and a masculine style of argumentation to further her claim. The secretary apparently found her persuasive and scrawled on the back on her note, "answer this letter and give Mrs. Pike the information she requests." This episode and subsequent correspondence, in which she pleaded for the payment John Montgomery's committee had endorsed but which Congress never voted on, marked her as possessing both the motive and the skill to author or collaborate on the eulogizing biography of her late husband. If so, the memoir—and perhaps, too, the final letter Pike wrote her, which somehow found its way into print—suggest that with vigor and success she took up his final request to defend his memory.[57]

Whatever its origins, the biography boosted Pike's fame. Between 1813 and 1856, at least nine different authors reproduced the piece or portions of it nearly verbatim, changing a few details and sometimes the sequence of topics. Six of the nine appeared before 1820, and several of the writers issued multiple printings of their versions. One of them, Henry Whiting, conducted new research and expanded it to nearly a hundred pages in 1845. In national stature, Pike's name surpassed that of Meriwether Lewis, whose as-yet-unpublished expedition journals and embarrassed financial and political circumstances mired him in depression and in 1809 led to his suicide. By contrast, eulogists of War of 1812 martyrs frequently compared their heroes to Pike, making him a measuring stick for virtuous national sacrifice. Indeed, Pike's achievements seem to rival those of his namesake, Richard Montgomery. "Another Montgomery in fate," the "Biographical Memoir" called him on its final page, and similar comparisons to the fallen Revolutionary War general filled the pages of the newspapers. Collectively, the body of hagiography that emerged after his death traced his life from humble beginnings to a zealous and distinguished career serving the nation. Thus the memorialists completed the persona Pike had cultivated throughout his life and that he had begun to publicize through his journals.[58]

Curiously, the expeditions were not what these early biographers found most important. Rather, they most esteemed his sacrifice. Although they occupied ample space in the texts, his western travels mattered to the narratives primarily to foreshadow the virtues that peaked in his martyrdom. The intelligence he collected in the West, the maps he made, the treaties he negotiated, and even the US victory at York all mattered less than his self-discipline and sacrifice, virtues that Madison administration officials and other anxious early-republic nationalists sought to inculcate in young men as the antidote to excessive liberty. His martyrdom showed that American sons, absorbed as they were in profitable pursuits, could nevertheless sacrifice for the nation as their fathers had. On June 26, 1813, just before toasting, "Zebulon Montgomery Pike," who "fell in the arms of victory, and expired on the conquered flag of his enemy," diners aboard the *Chesapeake* also drank to "*the United States*—'76 made them independent at home; 1812 shall make them all independent abroad." The constructed memory of a self-disciplined and self-sacrificing Pike modeled what the second independent generation should be, while the toasts, poems, biographies, and congressional resolutions affirmed that the republic could show the kind of gratitude that Pike had faith it would.[59]

The reinvention of the memory of the war and its warriors between 1815 and 1820 also remade the relationship between the military and American nationalism and admitted soldiers to a privileged place among American patriots. In the 1780s, Americans had cast the Revolution as a citizens' victory and considered the army a necessary evil to be reduced or eliminated as soon as possible. Abhorring standing armies and privileged designations of classes of citizens alike, Congress refused to grant life pensions to the men of arms who had helped wrest national independence from an imperial parent. Pike, however, was alleged to have often said that "there are men in the army, who have courage enough to act without any other interest than that of a love of country," and the stories about him and others who fell in the War of 1812 bore this out. After the war, Americans increasingly embraced figures like Zebulon Pike, the elder, growing infirm in his dotage, and Zebulon Montgomery Pike, the son who gave his life at York, as suffering soldiers, an archetype that exemplified national courage and willingness to sacrifice for noble causes. The archetype's influence became visible with the Pension Act of 1818. Originating in the work of a congressionally appointed committee that the Pikes' friend General Joseph Bloomfield chaired, the act belatedly recognized the heroism of Revolutionary soldiers by awarding lifetime pensions to needy veterans of the first war for independence. Among the applications that inundated the War Department was one from near Cincinnati under the name of the destitute Zebulon Pike. Thus, Zebulon Montgomery Pike's memory, along with those of other War of 1812 dead and wounded, helped to cement the bond in the national imagination between soldiers' sacrifice and American patriotism, a link that did not exist at the time of the Revolution but that holds tight down to the present day.[60]

Suffering soldiers—and for a few years, Zebulon Montgomery Pike was the leading one—tempered the liberty-order conundrum. They made national and personal independence compatible. Self-disciplined, self-sacrificing individuals pursuing happiness posed no threat to the nation. The War of 1812, as ambiguous a victory as it was geopolitically, had accomplished many of its early proponents' cultural objectives. It brought independent men together to sacrifice for a national community. It also left a legacy of military martyrdom by which order could occasionally trump liberty in the future. The liberty-order conundrum would never go away completely, however. Tensions between national security and individual freedom resurfaced when courts heard cases on the constitutionality of the Union's suspension of habeas corpus during the Civil War, in 1918 when labor organizer Eugene Debs lectured a jury that had just convicted him of delivering an antiwar speech on the venerable tradition of American patriotic political dissent, when twenty-first century courts struggled to balance the Bill of Rights with the Patriot Act, and plenty of times in between. The dilemma has endured throughout American history, but Pike's generation, a generation in which many feared the liberty-order problem might splinter the country, resolved it sufficiently so that future generations of Americans would be able to debate it.

Pike, who had often written that he hoped for a glorious death, surely would have approved the memory that others made for him in the decade after his martyrdom. In pondering what might have been, it is tantalizing to consider the career paths of a pair of Pike's contemporaries, Andrew Jackson and William Henry Harrison, who also believed in physical sacrifice for national rewards and who did live to exploit the legends of their heroics. But Pike won the gratitude and distinction he coveted only in death—too late to enjoy the personal independence that he had believed would result from service to his nation. Zebulon Montgomery Pike and America grew up together and won their independence during his lifetime. In the end, he obtained what he had promised his "frozen lads": death delivered him into the "bosom of a grateful country."[61]

Epilogue

THE UNITED STATES might not have defeated Great Britain in the War of 1812, but it had clearly beaten the Indians. Native power in North America had always rested on playing empires against one another, securing favorable relationships with one by maintaining the possibility of giving their friendship and commerce to another. This was the basis of the middleman position that empowered the Mdewakantons and Osages, and it was Sharitarish's gambit for coping with successive visits by Spaniards and Americans in 1806 as well. The one thing that all these peoples refused Pike was a promise to live under only one flag. In 1815, however, the British arranged peace with the United States and promised to withdraw military and commercial presence from south of the now more firmly drawn border. Wabasha, who had given his peace pipe to Pike in 1806, and Le Petit Corbeau, who had been among those who sold him the land that became the Twin Cities, headed a delegation of western Indians who journeyed to protest to the British at Lake Huron's Drummond Island in 1816. Without the friendship and trade of the British, Wabasha said, "we cannot live long." In abandoning Indian allies to make their own accommodations with the Americans, the British deprived the natives of their greatest asset—the middle ground—and greatly facilitated the United States' westward expansion.[1]

As British traders and soldiers withdrew from the western and southern Great Lakes, the United States began to dictate the terms of its relations with Indians, as it had in Ohio after Fallen Timbers. As Le Petit Corbeau bitterly complained, "The Big Knives [the Americans] spoke to us with a Sword in their Left Hand, and a switch in their right, signifying that they would deprive us of our English Traders and build Forts on our land, with or without our permission."² That year, the United States constructed Fort Crawford at Prairie du Chien to bring that jumble of ethnicities, where Pike had toured potential fort sites with the boundary-crossing Fraser, firmly under American control. In 1819, the army established Fort Snelling (briefly called Fort St. Anthony) on the acreage Pike had purchased from Le Petit Corbeau and the Mdewakantons at the confluence of the Minnesota and Mississippi rivers. These and other frontier posts formed a chain that stretched from the Great Lakes to the Missouri River and empowered Americans to enforce a new federal law (and the old federal ambition) to prohibit commerce with foreign traders within the boundaries of the United States. The next year the government sent Major Stephen H. Long, who had selected the site for Fort Snelling, to explore the Rocky Mountains and to negotiate friendships with the Pawnees and other Indians, whose territory Spain had recently ceded to the United States through the Adams-Onís Treaty. As a representative of the sole remaining imperial power on the Great Plains, Long had to give far less ground in these talks than Pike had.

To the southwest, in the land of the Osages and French traders, Missouri Territory applied for admission to the republic in 1819 as a slave state, the second to be carved out of the Louisiana Purchase. A slave state's request for admission raised the question of whether the independence of some included the right to curtail the independence of others. Although the Missouri Compromise, which allowed slavery south of a latitude line drawn across the continent at 36°–30', temporarily corked the volatile question, this new nineteenth-century conundrum of independence pre-occupied the nation during the lives of Pike's children and grandchildren. By suffering for his nation in the West and sacrificing for it in war, Pike had contributed to the expansion that raised the question of whether slavery would swell along with the nation. His life and death helped resolve one kind of independence conundrum and unleash another. The creation and resolution of that second conundrum led to further improvement of the West and eventually redefined the relationship between western land-scapes and American nationalism.

Even before the War of 1812 ended, many followed Pike's southwestern footsteps, often carrying his memory in their hearts and a copy of his journal in their hands. First to come was Captain Daniel Hughes, who traveled to Chihuahua in 1809 to retrieve the remainder of Pike's damned rascals. With Dearborn's and Jefferson's approval, Wilkinson also instructed Hughes to obtain intelligence about Spanish designs on

FIGURE 8.1 Fort Snelling, 1844, with Pike's Island in the foreground. *Fort Snelling* by Joseph Casper Wild. Minnesota Historical Society.

American frontiers and to discern Mexican reaction to Napoleon's coup and other European affairs. Hughes returned in October with all the men, except the prisoner Meek.[3] Inspired by Pike's report of cheap local goods and the high prices fetched by imports, St. Louis traders also soon began trickling across the Plains. They found no El Dorado in New Mexico, however, instead enduring physical hardship to get there and frequently getting captured once they arrived. With Pike's journal in hand, James Baird and Robert McKnight reached Santa Fe in 1812 and remained as captives for eight years. In 1817, New Mexican officials arrested a son of the Chouteau family and his partner and confiscated their $30,000 worth of trade goods. The peddlers spent forty-eight days in a Santa Fe jail. Stephen Long's 1820 military exploration party, which encountered no trouble with Spaniards, nevertheless endured shortages of food, fuel, and water and made a dispiriting error, mistaking the Canadian River for the Red. At the foot of the Rockies one night, they boiled gritty flood water for their soup, first skimming off the buffalo dung that floated on the surface. Echoing Pike's assessment and undoubtedly recalling his own hardships, Long famously labeled the prairies between the Missouri River and the Rockies the "Great American Desert."[4]

In 1821, American travelers' fortunes began to improve when William Becknell, also guided by Pike's journal, reached Santa Fe with comparative

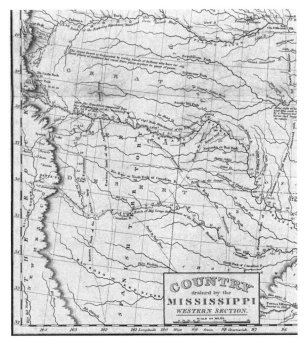

FIGURE 8.2 Excerpt of Stephen Long's 1823 map of the 1820 expedition. "Great American Desert" is printed across the Plains, and the Red River's headwaters are still depicted in the Rockies. David Rumsey Map Collection, www.davidrumsey.com.

ease. When he arrived, he met Facundo Melgares, by then governor of New Mexico, who welcomed the American instead of arresting him. Mexico had just won independence from Spain, and New Mexican officials immediately reversed Spanish prohibitions on trade with Americans. Becknell returned to Missouri with a wagonload of silver and stories that launched two decades of lucrative commerce along the Santa Fe Trail. The following year he outfitted another expedition to cross the Plains from Missouri and blazed a shorter route friendlier to wheeled vehicles. Becknell's trailblazing put in place one of the first pieces of national improvement, the network of canals, roads, wires, and rails that would soon knit the United States into a continental nation and transform Americans themselves. As traffic increased and the trail became better known, Pike's journal's importance as a manual faded but continued to provide inspiration. Josiah Gregg, whose 1844 *Commerce of the Prairies* replaced Pike's work as the trail's most commonly carried guide, opened his book by crediting Pike's "exciting descriptions of the new El Dorado" for spreading "like wildfire throughout the western country" and sparking the stampede to Santa Fe. Within two decades, New Mexicans became so reliant on American trade that in September 1846, in the midst of the Mexican-American War, one town hailed the arrival of the conquering American army by treating its members to a feast of wine and cakes. One of the army's officers, lieutenant colonel William Hemsley Emory, contrasted the welcome with the "hardships, trials, and perseverance of the gallant Pike." Transformed from a place where Americans tried to avoid capture—if they didn't starve first—into a feast of sweets, Emory's New Mexico was a haven where Americans secured their needs and rendered locals dependent.[5]

No one illustrated this better than Susan Shelby Magoffin. In the summer of 1846 Magoffin journeyed from St. Louis to Santa Fe, covering some of the territory that Pike had four decades earlier. The young bride of eight months, who celebrated her nineteenth birthday on the Plains, rode in a carriage alongside her maid servant as part of a large trading caravan of fourteen wagons, twenty men, dozens of mules, and some two hundred oxen hauling goods for sale and trade. Each night, she slept on a bed with sheets in a tent with a dressing bureau, combs, pillows, and a carpet manufactured in Philadelphia. She did not get lost. She was rarely wet, cold, or hungry and often enjoyed wine and dessert with her meals. So great was her comfort that when bored she would leave her carriage to rough it a bit, walking alongside the procession, picking flowers until she tired. To be sure, her trip after sighting Pikes Peak was not easy. She suffered a miscarriage, illness, and depression before her travels were over, but most of the time, her comfort and safety far exceeded Pike's, largely because she benefited from the system of connections that he had helped launch and that by the 1840s brought Philadelphia rugs to the grasslands and carried Mexican silver to Saint Louis. In fact, her greatest fear came from the incipient Mexican-American War. While she was dallying on the Plains, her merchant brother-in-law James, who had married a Mexican woman, was brokering a compromise by which a few people in Santa Fe who favored American rule would transfer the city to United States control, at last fulfilling Pike's prediction that New Mexico was so weakly attached to its rulers that an American army could take it without a fight.[6] When women with Philadelphia rugs found it necessary to ease the monotony of Plains travel by gathering wildflowers, the days of men proving themselves and their nationalism and claiming independence by suffering in the West were clearly numbered.

In the folds of Magoffin's tents lurked a new threat to nationalism, however. Even as the Santa Fe Trail tied New Mexico to Missouri, those connections threatened to sever the Union. The lands in New Mexico and California that brother-in-law James had helped wrest from Mexico had to be attached to the Union, much as McGillis's upper Mississippi country had had to be incorporated after the Louisiana Purchase. Still fearing Montesquieu's prophecy that distance would erode connections and foster distinctive regional interests in the now enlarged Union, Americans of all stripes—southerners and northerners, Democrats and Whigs—hatched plans for a transcontinental railroad to link New Mexico and California to the nation. But disputes over the location of the route entangled the project in sectional conflict, as southerners and northerners vied to direct the railroad along paths advantageous to their own region. After Congress failed to hammer out a Pacific railroad bill in 1853, Illinois Senator Stephen A. Douglas launched a daring plan. He proposed organizing the Kansas and Nebraska territories to open the way for settlement, survey, and federal land grants, all necessary for the building of a northern transcontinental route. To assuage southern opposition, the Kansas-Nebraska Act repealed the Missouri Compromise's ban on slavery north of the 36°-30' line, by allowing the territories' citizens to choose freedom or slavery. The measure, he believed, promised to resolve both the slavery and railroad impasses. Instead, the railroad question bedeviled Congress for the rest of the decade, while the pro-slavery implications of the Kansas-Nebraska Act arrayed much of northern society against it and sparked a bloody contest for Kansas.[7] Thus, the terms of the Missouri Compromise proved insufficient to incorporate the lands that Pike had explored and Becknell and James Magoffin had further tied to the nation. In the 1850s, North and South divided over the meaning of independence. Northerners argued that the nation would be made independent only by independent men pursuing their self-interest in public spirited, virtuous ways, as had Zebulon Montgomery Pike. To them, allowing one man to deprive another of independence threatened this. Southerners, in contrast, held that dark-skinned people were made to labor for white owners; to grant them independence would upset the natural social hierarchy and unleash chaos. Once again, order and liberty clashed.

And once again, a Pike stepped into the fray. Born in 1811, James Shepherd Pike descended from the branch of the family that had remained in Massachusetts in the 1660s, when their more radical Presbyterian cousins defected to New Jersey. James Shepherd's ancestors, however, were no less headstrong than the Woodbridge Pikes, from whom Zebulon Montgomery hailed.[8] A staunch Whig, James campaigned in 1840 for

William Henry Harrison, whose son had married Zebulon Montgomery's daughter Clarissa, and ran unsuccessfully for Congress from Maine in 1850. Having previously traded a successful business career for journalism, James joined Horace Greeley's *New York Tribune* as Washington correspondent and later as associate editor. Through the 1850s, his writing fired northern anti-slavery sentiment and brought him national prominence. In 1861, Lincoln named him ambassador to the Netherlands.

Among the several books he authored was *The New Puritan*, a biography of his ancestor Robert Pike, son of the John Pike who emigrated from England in 1635 and brother of the one who founded Woodbridge. Robert, James said, was constantly "engaged in improving his fortunes," which brought him considerable wealth, and also endured personal hardship and Indian depredations as a military officer on the New England frontier in order to build a new Israel in New England. Most importantly, as the *New Puritan*'s subtitle proclaimed, Robert "defended the Quakers, resisted clerical domination, and opposed the [Salem] witch trials," actions that reflected his "advanced views on 'civil and ecclesiastical liberty,'" ideas which "finally became dominant" in America. Remembering his ancestor almost two hundred years later, James wrote of Robert as the embodiment of the nation. Despite living, as James said, in an era of "civil" and "ecclesiastical tyranny" without "liberty of speech…criticism, and opposition"— conditions "doubly intensified at the period of witchcraft prosecutions"— Robert steadfastly opposed the "malignant fanaticism" of his time, maintaining an "intrepidity of spirit" that "represented no party, but… individual independence." Still, Robert was no "radical," but rather an "eminently orthodox and conservative man," who "held his advanced views in opposition to a society with which he sympathized, and whose general objects he earnestly aimed to promote.… He did not wish to change its purposes or modify its principles." His opposition stemmed instead from his passion to "save it from the effects of its own errors." And he was "anxious" to promote its "development"—not unlike the upstart Republican Party, which James joined in the aftermath of the Kansas-Nebraska Act's assault on freedom.[9]

Although, like most of his contemporaries, James was no racial egalitarian, he had inherited a family and national tradition committed to pursuit of personal independence, and when he confronted the second independence conundrum, he sided with liberty. The party he joined held that slavery competed with free white labor, squelched personal improvement, and prevented individuals—black and white—from enjoying the fruits of their sacrifice. Worse still, its political entanglements prevented the government from fostering such pursuits of personal independence through construction of railroads and other national improvements. As Israel Washburn wrote to James Pike in 1855, "had we passed Richardson's [transcontinental railroad] bill in 1853, we'd not have repealed the Missouri Compromise [through the Kansas-Nebraska Act] in 1854." Thus, slavery jeopardized the personal and national independence that Robert, Zebulon, Zebulon Montgomery, and James Shepherd all stood for and the improvements that made both possible. "A great democratic republic," James concluded, "cannot forever submit to the anomaly of negro Slavery in its bosom." Forty-eight years after the Battle of York, James Shepherd Pike and his fellow Americans once again fought a war in which personal independence entwined with the survival of a nation.[10]

This second war accelerated national improvements. With southern delegates vacating their congressional seats during the Civil War, lawmakers easily passed the Pacific Railway Act of 1862. Lincoln signed the measure in August, inaugurating a half century of railroad construction that overcame the distance and hardship that separated the West from the Union he had preserved. In 1874, the Denver and Rio Grande Railroad began laying track through Colorado's Royal Gorge, reaching Leadville, near the headwaters of the Arkansas River in 1880. By this time, the area around Pike's furthest foray into the mountains had become a booming silver mining district. In 1877, the D&RG climbed La Veta Pass over the Sangres and soon pushed into the San Luis Valley, passing a few miles from the disintegrated remains of Pike's stockade. Further making use of the absence of southern opposition during the Civil War, Congress passed the Homestead Act in 1862 to plant thousands of independent Jeffersonian yeomen on the Plains that Pike had labeled "incapable of cultivation" and recommended leaving to the "wandering and uncivilized aborigines."[11] That year, Congress also passed the Morrill Land Grant Act, to found agricultural colleges and ensure it all would be farmed scientifically.

As the century neared its close, Americans could cross the continent much more quickly and with greater comfort and safety than the slogging Pike and Lewis and Clark expeditions had managed at its opening or even than the mid-century excursion of the flower-picking Magoffin. Some people even bought train tickets to vacation in places where Pike and others had nearly perished. The continent's difficult middle part, which lacked the fabled mountains of salt and the height of land, nevertheless did abound in mineral and vegetable riches to be dug and harvested from the earth. The federally subsidized railroads brought it all to markets that converted the produce of the land into capital. Pike had predicted the useless Plains would restrict the American population geographically and guarantee "thereby a continuation of the union."[12] Instead, the war that resolved the second independence conundrum and restored the South to the Union also enabled the expansion that finally established Americans in the West. Improvement had accomplished what the American Sahara had failed to assure: the knitting together of the nation and the final refutation of Montesquieu.

Because of such improvement, in 1893 Katharine Lee Bates did something Zebulon Montgomery Pike had failed to do. She summited the Grand Peak. Her journey began in June, as her sleeper car carried the thirty-three-year-old chair of the Wellesley College English department from Boston to Niagara Falls, where decades of uncurbed pursuits of happiness had yielded chaos and turned one of the continent's most awesome spectacles into a mélange of bill boards, amusement parks, cheap hotels, tourist traps, hire-wire acts suspended over the chasm, and con men everywhere, a pageant of both the natural sublime and the excesses of unrestrained improvement. Both were also on display at her next stop, Chicago's World's Columbian Exposition, the so-called White City. Dynamos, electric lights, moving pictures, long-distance telephone calls, and the world's first Ferris wheel wowed visitors like Bates by harnessing nature's power and denying gravity and space to serve and delight humans, but so, too, did the wild animals, Idaho's rustic log cabin, and other symbols of a fading frontier. Another visitor to Chicago that summer, the historian Frederick Jackson Turner, made the uncomfortable juxtaposition explicit in an essay that lamented the closing of the frontier phase of American history while also touting the taming of wilderness as the engine of American democracy and freedom. Not very far below the surface of his celebratory remarks lurked a vexing question. If the frontier was the source of American character and the frontier was now gone, what next? If Magoffin's generation had beaten a path to the West and James Shepherd Pike's had laid the steel rails over which Bates rode so comfortably, where would future Americans learn about the fortitude, sacrifice, and other virtues that had kept their forebears independent? Bates, who wrote of her "quickened and deepened sense of America" as she sped past Kansas wheat fields aboard a train to Colorado on the Fourth of July, was on her way to find out.

The sense of loss that accompanied the decline of frontier and that prompted Bates to write patriotically of the contrast between the western

FIGURE 8.3 Katharine Lee Bates. 1890s. Wellesley College Archives.

open space and the hubbub of the White City also renewed Americans'
interest in the heroes they credited with opening the West by braving
hardship. Most famously, Buffalo Bill, whose Wild West show played
across the street from the World's Fair (Bates would take it in on her return
journey), sought to preserve a piece of America's lost past by staging reen-
actments of the battles through which the army and frontiersmen had
wrested the western landscape from American Indians. After the turn of
the century, Santa Fe, whose adobe buildings' "mean appearance" had
piqued Pike's scorn, began to draw vacationers by rail, the town's pueblo
revival architecture promising them a taste of the romanticized remnants
of a quaint Spanish past uncluttered by the financial panics, labor con-
flicts, and overcrowding of modern American cities. Less famously,
scholars began to recover the stories of some of the West's first explorers.
Mostly forgotten by the century they had helped launch, Lewis and Clark
found new fame in the hands of Elliott Coues, who edited, annotated, and
indexed their journals, the first major reissuing of the work since 1814.
Coues went on to produce edited versions of the journals of Zebulon
Montgomery Pike, a subsequent southwestern traveler named Jacob
Fowler, and others. The city of Colorado Springs, Bates's destination, also
took renewed interest in Pike, seeking, unsuccessfully, to disinter his body
from Sackets Harbor for reburial atop Pikes Peak in order to com-
memorate the upcoming centennial of his expedition. City leaders also
commissioned research expeditions to Spanish and Mexican archives that

eventually recovered much of the material that Salcedo had seized. Unlike Pike's first burst of fame right after his death, this time Americans remembered not his military martyrdom so much as his western exploration, unredeemed by Congress in his lifetime but now of vital interest to a nation struggling to cope with the implications of a disappearing frontier. Like Buffalo Bill's extravaganzas, preserving the memory of explorers who had suffered to make Bates's generation comfortable helped Americans hold on to a bit of their vital frontier past, even as they hailed the whirring dynamos, chugging railroad engines, and electrons pulsing through copper wires that rendered that past obsolete.[13]

Bates enjoyed a glorious summer in the West. She taught English at Colorado College in Colorado Springs, the tourist mecca that had mushroomed up in the shadow of Pikes Peak. The highlight of her vacation was a day outing to the summit with some colleagues. By this time a cog railway carried passengers to the top of the 14,115-foot peak, but on the day they had selected for their tour, it wasn't operating, so Bates and her fellow professors hired a horse-drawn wagon to haul them up the winding road. Halfway up, they switched to mules and continued their exhausting journey. But for Bates it was worth it. With "one ecstatic gaze," she took in the view. In front of her, the Plains stretched to the east, seemingly all the way to Chicago. Turning around, she beheld the endless crown of mountains to the west. It was the "most glorious scenery I ever beheld." Filled with the nationalist elation of a summer that had taken her from the White City to the mountaintop, the next day she drafted the lines that would soon become a famous song.[14]

> Oh beautiful for halcyon skies,
> For amber waves of grain,
> For purple mountain majesties
> Above the enameled plain!
> America! America!

Words tweaked and set to Samuel Ward's melody, it became "America the Beautiful," a beloved hymn that celebrated the aesthetics of American landscape as the pinnacle expression of Americans' rugged overrunning of a continent and making it beautiful by spreading freedom. Besides the glories of mountains and plains, "beautiful" were the "pilgrims" who beat "a thoroughfare of freedom...across the wilderness," while in their wake the nation's "alabaster cities gleam[ed] undimmed by human tears." To

FIGURE 8.4 View of spacious skies and fruited plains from the purple mountain majesty. Photo by author.

Bates, who rebuffed critics' scorn of her use of the sentimental word, "beautiful," America inspired its citizens' attachments because of both its magnificent landscape and the brave deeds of the people who improved it—and improved themselves in the process. As a friend wrote at Bates's death, "America the Beautiful" conveyed "the deepest, richest sense of the splendor of the material possession that has been given to us," and it "impress[ed] upon every American citizen...to be worthy of that posses-sion...by developing the great qualities that can alone make any nation beautiful."[15] Once a place for men to prove their nationalist mettle through physical sacrifice, the West had now become a place about which women wrote lyrical poetry patriotically proclaiming America's beauty.

Contemporaries in the 1890s lamented that the improvement of Bates's West had destroyed the ruggedness of Pike's. More accurate, how-ever, is just the opposite. Pike's West created Bates's. In his lifetime, Pike's two great passions were self- and national improvement. Although intel-lectuals of his day worried the two might be incompatible, he found a way to reconcile them through a rugged military life. From the Ohio Valley through Louisiana and back to York, Pike endured physical hardship with fortitude in difficult environments in order to establish the nation in the West and defend its independence from rival peoples. What he launched as mere establishment quickly begot improvement, as Americans first drove the pickets of fortress stockades into the ground he had selected and later blazed commercial trails, hung telegraph wires, and laid steel rails. Establishment eventually made the West comfortable for people such as Susan Magoffin, Frederick Jackson Turner, and Katharine Lee Bates. Americans less and less frequently suffered on the nation's behalf in the West, and by the end of the nineteenth century, the West was a place of weekend excursions and breathless scenery. Great Sand Dunes National Park, the modern boundaries of which Pike entered on the day he left poor Menaugh, who gave out in the snow, joined the National Park System in 1932 as a destination where people sought relaxation, enjoyment, and renewal. National parks like Great Sand Dunes were called "America's best idea," something that made the nation both distinctive and good, much like previous generations had seen the fortitude of men like Pike as something that made the country distinctive and good. Difficult western landscapes, then, remained central to American nationalism through the twentieth century and beyond, but their significance arose as places of recreation instead of as places of sacrifice. By suffering in them himself, Pike set in motion changes that would render such places comfortable, turning forbidding and unclimbable grand peaks into purple mountain majesties and the great American desert into amber waves of grain. The republican principle of independence, which Jefferson had said would make a nation of one heart and mind, proved strong enough and adaptable enough for people like Pike to deploy in meeting the material challenges of a continent of daunting hardship and stunning beauty.

Notes

INTRODUCTION

1. Zebulon Pike, "Diary of an Expedition Made Under the Orders of the War Department, by Captain Z. M. Pike, in the Years 1806 and 1807, to Explore the Internal Parts of Louisiana," in *The Journals of Zebulon Montgomery Pike with Letters and Related Documents* (hereinafter cited as ZPJ), ed. Donald Jackson (Norman: University of Oklahoma Press, 1966), 1: 370.

2. Pike, "Diary of an Expedition," ZPJ, 1: 381.

3. Charles de Secondat, Baron de Montesquieu, *The Spirit of the Laws* in Great Books of the Western World, ed. Robert Maynard Hutchins (1748; repr., Chicago: Encyclopedia Britannica, 1952), 58; *The Federalist Papers* (New York: 1787–1788), LC, http://thomas.loc.gov/home/histdox/fedpapers.html, accessed September 7, 2011.

4. Richard L.Bushman, *The Refinement of America: Persons, Houses, Cities* (New York: Alfred A. Knopf, 1992), xix.

5. Terry Bouton, *Taming Democracy: "The People," the Founders, and the Troubled Ending of the American Revolution* (New York: Oxford University Press, 2007).

6. Vaclav Smil, *Energy in Nature and Society: General Energetics of Complex Systems* (Cambridge: MIT Press, 2008), 10, 344; italics are in the original; Edmund Burke, III, "The Big Story: Human History, Energy Regimes, and the Environment," in *The Environment and World History*, ed. Edmund Burke, III, and Kenneth Pomeranz (Berkeley: University of California Press, 2009), 33–53.

7. Peter S. Onuf, *Jefferson's Empire: The Language of American Nationhood* (Charlottesville: University of Virginia Press, 2000), 8.

8. W. Eugene Hollon, *The Lost Pathfinder: Zebulon Montgomery Pike* (Norman: University of Oklahoma Press, 1949); Donald Jackson, ed., *The Journals of Zebulon Montgomery Pike*, 2 vols. (Norman: University of Oklahoma Press, 1966); John Upton Terrell, *Zebulon Pike: The Life and Times of an Adventurer* (New York: Weybright and Talley, 1968). Even the shorter, more recent writings on Pike tend

to eschew these methodologies in favor of political, diplomatic, and intellectual histories. See, for example, essays in Matthew L. Harris and Jay H. Buckley, *Zebulon Pike, Thomas Jefferson, and the Opening of the American West* (Norman: University of Oklahoma Press, 2012); Stephen G. Hyslop, *Bound for Santa Fe: The Road to New Mexico and the American Conquest, 1806–1848* (Norman: University of Oklahoma Press, 2002).

CHAPTER I

1. James Savage, *Genealogical Dictionary of the First Settlers of New England, Showing Three Generations of Those Who Came Before May, 1692, on the Basis of Farmer's Register* (1860–1862; repr., Baltimore: Genealogical Publishing Co., Inc., 1986), 4:435; Allen Raymond Pike, *The Family of John Pike of Newbury, Massachusetts, 1635–1695* (n.p.: Penobscot Press, 1995); Joshua D. Coffin, *A Sketch of the History of Newbury, Newburyport, and West Newbury from 1635 to 1845* (Boston: Samuel G. Drake, 1845), 314; James S. Pike, *The New Puritan: New England Two Hundred Years Ago, Some Account of the Life of Robert Pike, the Puritan Who Defended the Quakers, Resisted Clerical Domination, and Opposed the Witchcraft Prosecution* (New York: Harper & Brothers, Publishers, 1879), 15, 17, 25, 28; "Proclamation to Restraine the Kings [sic] Subjects from Departing out of the Realme without Licence [sic]," July 21, 1635, in *Stuart Royal Proclamations: Royal Proclamations of King Charles I 1625–1646*, ed. James F. Larkin (Oxford, England: Clarendon Press, 1983), 2:463; John E. Pomfret and Floyd M. Shumway, *Founding the American Colonies, 1853–1660* (Harper & Row, Publishers, 1970), 166–170. Pike cites James Savage, *Genealogical Dictionary of the First Settlers of New England . . .*, v. 4.

2. Coffin, *Sketch of the History of Newbury*, 291–292, 311; Orra Eugene Monnette, *First Settlers of Ye Plantations of Piscataway and Woodbridge Olde East New Jersey, 1664–1714* (Los Angeles: Leroy Carman Press, 1930), 753; Pike, *New Puritan*, 26; Pike, *Family of John Pike*, 1–7; Monnette, 753; [Charlotte Cowdey Brown], *The New Jersey Browns* (Milwaukee: 1931), 10.

3. Pike, *Family of John Pike*, 9–12, 28, 41, 42; Monnette, *First Settlers*, 752–755; Joseph W. Dally, *Woodbridge and Vicinity: The Story of a New Jersey Township* (New Brunswick, N.J.: A. E. Gordon, 1873), 160–161, 167–173, 234.

4. [Charlotte Cowdey Brown], *The New Jersey Browns* (Milwaukee: 1931).

5. *New Jersey Browns*, 3–9; Dally, *Woodbridge and Vicinity*, 168–172; "Deed Book '1,'" *Middlesex County Deed Abstracts*, 1, no. 1 (March 1996), 1–2; Brown's will can be found at the New Jersey State Archives; see "Will of George Brown of Middlesex Co., NJ," *Wills and Inventories*, vol. 21, New Jersey Department of State, Secretary of State's Office, pp. 17–20.

6. Terry Bouton, *Taming Democracy: "The People," the Founders, and the Troubled Ending of the American Revolution* (New York: Oxford University Press, 2007), 16; Monnette, *First Settlers*, 376. Allen Pike gives slightly different dates; A. Van Doren

Honeyman, ed., *Calendar of New Jersey Wills, Administrations, Etc., Volume 6, 1761–1770*, Documents Relating to the Colonial History of the State of New Jersey, 1st ser., 33 (Somerville, N.J.: The Unionist-Gazette Association, 1928), 30–31; "James Pike Will," (Middlesex County), 1761, 3731–3736L, "Zebulon Pike Will," (Middlesex County), 1762, 3859–3864L, and "Jennet Pike Will," (Middlesex County), 1770, 4633–4636L all available in *Wills and Inventories*, New Jersey State Archives, Trenton.

7. Douglas R. King, "A Soldier Named Zeb," 52–53; Bouton, *Taming Democracy*, 16–21.

8. In his pension application, Pike testified that he had been a saddler before joining the army; Zebulon Pike, Pension Declaration, June 23, 1823, Lawrenceburg, Indiana, Veteran's Administration, Pension Records, Microcopy Publication M804, roll 1936, frames 1378–1385, NARADC; King, "Soldier Named Zeb," 54.

9. King, "Soldier Named Zeb," 2, 51–52; W. Eugene Hollon, *The Lost Pathfinder: Zebulon Montgomery Pike* (Norman: University of Oklahoma Press, 1949), 8, 26, 230; "Will of George Brown of Middlesex Co., NJ"; "Will of John Brown of Boone County, KY," *Will Book B*, 1800–1829, County Clerk's Office, Boone County, KY. Hollon does not appear to have consulted these records; Nadine A. Hunt, "Pike-Brown Narrative of Research," 2009, in author's possession, 21–22.

10. Isabella's hand in the family Bible recorded the date as April 17, though New York State registered the license date as July 11. One possible explanation is that when she gave birth to a daughter, Mary, on November 19 of that year Isabella perhaps thought it prudent to back-date the family Bible entry to cover up the child's out-of-wedlock conception. It was not uncommon, however, for eighteenth-century children to be so conceived, and no particular legal or social stigma attended such origins. Given that the July date means that Mary was born after only four months' gestation yet lived for nine days, a springtime conception and April marriage date seems more plausible. Z. M. Pike Geneological Material, n.d., American Philosophical Association, Philadelphia, Pennsylvania; Gideon J. Tucker, *Names of Persons for Whom Marriage Licenses Were Issued by the Secretary of the Province of New York, Previous to 1784* (Albany: Weed, Parsons and Company, 1860), 301.

11. Virginia Bergen Troeger and Robert J. McEwen, *Woodbridge: New Jersey's Oldest Township* (Charleston, S.C.: Virginia Bergen Troeger and Robert J. McEwen, 2002), 41; Mark E. Lender and James Kirby, eds., *Citizen Soldier: The Revolutionary War Journal of Joseph Bloomfield* (Newark, N.J.: New Jersey Historical Society, 1982), 1–5; Bouton, *Taming Democracy*, 21–30.

12. Francis B. Heitman, *Historical Register of Officers of the Continental Army During the War of the Revolution, April, 1775, to December 1783* (Baltimore: Genealogical Publishing Co., Inc., 1973), 125; Ruth Wolk, *The History of Woodbridge, New Jersey* (Woodbridge, N.J.: 1970), 33–34. Jennet's name has also sometimes been

spelled Jenet and Janet. The will of her grandmother, for whom she was named, offers various spellings, too. I have chosen to follow the spelling used by her nephew in an 1812 letter, the only surviving source written by a relative who knew her; Troeger and McEwen, *Woodbridge*, 53.

13. Bloomfield, "Journal," [February] 19, 1776, 38.

14. Heitman, *Historical Register*, 442; King, "Soldier Named Zeb," 5; Zebulon Pike, Pension Declaration, NARADC.

15. King, "Soldier Named Zeb," 7; Troeger and McEwen, *Woodbridge*, 43; Bouton, *Taming Democracy*, 53–54.

16. Burt Garfield Loescher, *Washington's Eyes: The Continental Light Dragoons* (Fort Collins, Colo.: The Old Army Press, 1977), 101; Troeger and McEwen, 43, 45–46.

17. *Oaths of Allegiance: Allegiance Book # I Bucks County, Pennsylvania 1777* (Danboro, Pa.: Richard T. and Mildred C. Williams, 1973), BHC.

18. Loescher, *Washington's Eyes*, 1, 102; Zebulon Pike, Pension Declaration, NARADC.

19. Loescher, *Washington's Eyes*, 101; King, "A Soldier Named Zeb," 9, 13.

20. Loescher, *Washington's Eyes*, 102, 109.

21. Loescher, *Washington's Eyes*, 98.

22. Loescher, *Washington's Eyes*, 110, 111; Zebulon Pike, Pension Declaration, NARADC.

23. "General Zebulon M. Pike, A Native of Somerset," *Somerset County Historical Quarterly* 5, no. 4 (October 1916): 309–311; [A. Van Doren Honeyman], "The General Pike Article," *Somerset County Historical Quarterly* 8 (October 1919): 319–320. The birthplace was long in doubt, but has been decisively settled. The detective work leading to the puzzle's resolution is in Backes, "General Zebulon M. Pike, Somerset-Born," 16, 242–251. King, "A Soldier Named Zeb," 15.

24. Loescher, *Washington's Eyes*, 116–118, 120; George Washington, Morris Town, to Stephen Moylan, February 3, 1780, in *The Writings of George Washington from the Original Manuscript Sources, 1745–1799*, vol. 17, ed. John C. Fitzpatrick (Washington, D.C.: US GPO, 1931–1944), 482–483; King, "A Soldier Named Zeb," 18.

25. Dally, *Woodbridge and Vicinity*, 285; Wolk, *The History of Woodbridge*, 32–33; Troeger and McEwen, *Woodbridge*, 53–55.

26. Bouton, *Taming Democracy*, 31–32; Thomas Paine, *Common Sense* (1776; repr., New York: Penguin, 1986), 65, 118.

27. Richard H. Kohn, *Eagle and Sword: The Federalists and the Creation of the Military Establishment in America, 1783–1802* (New York: The Free Press, 1975), 17–39; Charles Royster, *A Revolutionary People at War: The Continental Army and American Character, 1775–1783* (Chapel Hill: University of North Carolina Press, 1979), 333–338.

28. Northumberland County, *Pennsylvania Deed Book*, vol. C, LDS US/CAN microfilm, pp. 199–200, #961193; Hollon, *Lost Pathfinder*, 9, interpreted the acquisition as

evidence of a westward move, but Northumberland Historical Society records show no evidence of the Pikes ever living there. On the contrary, they appear in various Bucks County records continuously from 1784 to 1787. "Bucks County Tax Records, Solebury Township, 1785–1787," photocopies of the original tax records, provided by Mercer Museum, Bucks County, Pennsylvania. I draw this conclusion by comparing his acreage and total property value to listings for other Bucks County residents in the tax records. Pike is far from the wealthiest, but neither is he at the bottom.

29. Thomas Perkins Abernethy, introduction to *Notes on the State of Virginia*, by Thomas Jefferson (Gloucester, Mass.: Peter Smith, 1976), vii–x; Donald Jackson, *Thomas Jefferson and the Stony Mountains: Exploring the West from Monticello* (Urbana: University of Illinois Press, 1981), 25–26; Thomas Jefferson, *Notes on the State of Virginia* (Gloucester, Mass.: Peter Smith, 1976), 157.

30. David Nye, *Consuming Power: A Social History of American Energies* (Cambridge: MIT Press, 1998), 8; Jefferson, *Notes*, 157–158; The Madison quote comes from the *National Gazette*, 1792, quoted in Richard Lyman Bushman, "A Poet, A Planter, and a Nation of Farmers," *Journal of the Early Republic* 19 (Spring 1999): 2.

31. Untitled manuscript documents relating to the case *Commissioners of Bucks County v. Zebulon Pike*, 1786, in General Zebulon Pike Papers (1751–1834), MSC 163, folder 1, Bucks County Historical Society, Doylestown, Pennsylvania (hereafter cited as BCHS); Northumberland County, *Pennsylvania Deed Book*, vol. D, LDS US/CAN microfilm, p. 511, #961193.

32. "Bucks County Tax Records, Solebury Township, 1785–1787," Mercer Museum; Eastburn Reeder, *Early Settlers of Solebury Township, Bucks County, Pa., Compiled from Deeds, Wills, and the Records of Friends' Meetings*, ed. Terry McNealy (1900; repr., Doylestown, Penn.: BCHS, 1971), 70–71; Warren C. Ely, Doylestown, PA, to H.D. Phillips, Trenton, N.J., August 26, 1916, in General Zebulon Pike Papers (1751–1834), BCHS.

33. Bouton, *Taming Democracy*, 70–87; Robert Morris to the President of Congress (John Hanson), July 29, 1782, in *The Papers of Robert Morris*, 1781–1784, vol. 6, ed. John Catanzariti and E. James Ferguson (Pittsburgh: University of Pittsburgh Press, 1984), 58, 61, 63, 65–69.

34. Terry Bouton, "A Road Closed: Rural Insurgency in Post-Independence Pennsylvania," *Journal of American History* 87 (December 2000): 859; Bouton, *Taming Democracy*, 102.

35. Bouton, *Taming Democracy*, 99–100.

36. Bouton, *Taming Democracy*, 220–221.

37. Kohn, *Eagle and Sword*, 109–111; R. Douglas Hurt, *The Ohio Frontier: Crucible of the Old Northwest, 1720–1830* (Bloomington: Indiana University Press, 1996), 111.

38. Bouton, *Taming Democracy*, 145–167, 197–225.

39. Bouton, *Taming Democracy*, 216–243.

40. "Bucks County Tax Records, Solebury Township, 1785–1787," Mercer Museum.

41. James C. Scott, *Seeing Like a State: How Certain Schemes to Improve the Human Condition Have Failed* (New Haven: Yale University Press, 1998); Akhil Reed Amar, *America's Constitution: A Biography* (New York: Random House, 2005).

42. John C. Weaver, *The Great Land Rush and the Making of the Modern World, 1650–1900* (Montreal: McGill-Queen's University Press, 2003), 229; Catharine Van Cortlandt Mathews, *Andrew Ellicott: His Life and Letters* (New York: The Grafton Press, 1908), chap. 3; Hurt, *Ohio Frontier*, 121, 138; Daniel Drake, "Dr. Daniel Drake's Memoir of the Miami Country, 1779–1794," *Quarterly Publication of the Historical and Philosophical Society of Ohio* 18 (April–September 1923): 90; John F. Carmichael, "Diary of Dr. Carmichael," 1795, HEH, 32–33.

43. Hollon, *Lost Pathfinder*, 13, 15; Hurt, *Ohio Frontier*, 111–112, 114–118; Kohn, *Eagle and Sword*, 114.

44. Thomas Taylor Underwood, *Journal of Thomas Taylor Underwood, March 26, 1792, to March 18, 1800: An Old Soldier in Wayne's Army* (Cincinnati: Society of Colonial Wars in the State of Ohio, 1945), BHC, iii–v, 2; see also Kohn, *Eagle and Sword*, 123–124; Edward Miller, *With Captain Edward Miller in the Wayne Campaign of 1794*, ed. Dwight L. Smith (Ann Arbor: William Clements Library, 1965), BHC, 7.

45. Hurt, *Ohio Frontier*, 122; Underwood, *Journal of Thomas Taylor Underwood*, 4–5, 11.

46. Hurt, *Ohio Frontier*, 119, 131; Miller, *With Captain Edward Miller*, introduction; Wayne, Hobson's Choice, to Henry Knox, August 8, 1793, in *Anthony Wayne: A Name in Arms: Soldier, Diplomat, Defender of Expansion Westward of a Nation: The Wayne-Knox-Pickering-McHenry Correspondence*, ed. Richard C. Knopf (Pittsburgh: University of Pittsburgh Press, 1960), 264.

47. Underwood, *Journal of Thomas Taylor Underwood*, 12; Miller, *With Captain Edward Miller*, introduction; Hurt, *Ohio Frontier*, 131; On the marching orders, see Underwood, *Journal of Thomas Taylor Underwood*, 15–16; Miller, *With Captain Edward Miller*, 1–7; Frazer E. Wilson, *Fort Jefferson: The Frontier Post of the Upper Miami Valley* (n.p.: Frazer Ells Wilson, 1950), 8–9.

48. Miller, *With Captain Edward Miller*, 3–4; Hurt, *Ohio Frontier*, 131–132; Underwood, *Journal of Thomas Taylor Underwood*, 16–17.

49. Hurt, *Ohio Frontier*, 132–134; Underwood, *Journal of Thomas Taylor Underwood*, 16; Miller, *With Captain Edward Miller*, 3, 7.

50. Miller, *With Captain Edward Miller*, 7–8; Underwood, *Journal of Thomas Taylor Underwood*, 17–18; Hurt, *Ohio Frontier*, 134–135.

51. Hurt, *Ohio Frontier*, 135–136; Miller, *With Captain Edward Miller*, 8–9; Underwood, *Journal of Thomas Taylor Underwood*, 19.

52. Underwood, *Journal of Thomas Taylor Underwood*, 20–21; Hurt, *Ohio Frontier*, 137; Carmichael "Diary of Dr. Carmichael," 1–13 (quotes are from 11–13). "Occation" is in the original.

53. Smil, *Energy in Nature and Society*, 351; Fiege, *Republic of Nature*; Nye, *Consuming Power*, 18–22, 39–40.

54. Underwood, *Journal of Thomas Taylor Underwood*, 20–21.

55. Richard C. Wade, *The Urban Frontier: The Rise of Western Cities, 1790–1830* (Harvard University Press, 1967), 66; Andrew R. L. Cayton, "'Separate Interests' and the Nation-State: The Washington Administration and the Origins of Regionalism in the Trans-Appalachian West," *Journal of American History* 79 (June 1992): 39–67.

CHAPTER 2

1. Thaddeus Mason Harris, "Journal of a Tour Northwest of the Alleghany Mountains," in *Early Western Travels, 1748–1846*, ed. Reuben Gold Thwaites (Cleveland: The Arthur H. Clark Company, 1904), 340–341, in Early Encounters in North America (hereinafter cited as EENA), http://lib.colostate.edu/databases/permlink.php?id=388 (accessed July 22, 2013). R. Carlyle Buley, *The Old Northwest Pioneer Period, 1815–1840*, vol. 1 (Indianapolis: Indiana Historical Society, 1950), 1–2, uses some of the same imagery as Harris.

2. Andrew Ellicott, "Journal," October 29, 1796, in *The Journal of Andrew Ellicott* (Chicago: Quadrangle Books, 1962) (hereinafter cited as JAE), 8, 26–28; For more on the geology of the falls, see Richard C. Wade, *The Urban Frontier: The Rise of Western Cities, 1790–1830* (Harvard University Press, 1967), 13–14.

3. John Cooke, *Diary of John Cooke*, 1794 (Fort Wayne, Ind.: Governing Boards of the Public Library of Fort Wayne and Allen County, 1953), BHC, 4–5, 10; Edward Miller, *With Captain Edward Miller in the Wayne Campaign of 1794*, ed. Dwight L. Smith (Ann Arbor: William Clements Library, 1965), BHC, 12–13; Thomas Taylor Underwood, *Journal of Thomas Taylor Underwood, March 26, 1792, to March 18, 1800: An Old Soldier in Wayne's Army* (Cincinnati: Society of Colonial Wars in the State of Ohio, 1945), BHC, 19; Miller, *With Captain Edward Miller*, 12, 16, 19; Rom 13:1–3 and 8:31 (King James Version).

4. Underwood, *Journal of Thomas Taylor Underwood*, 21.

5. Underwood, *Journal of Thomas Taylor Underwood*, 21; Orsi visit to 1802 replica of the fort, 2009.

6. Zebulon Pike, Fort Massac, to Anthony Wayne, February 24, 1796, and James Wilkinson, Greenville, to Zebulon Pike, May 6, 1796, NT, M0367; Underwood, *Journal of Thomas Taylor Underwood*, 24.

7. [Anthony Wayne], Detroit, to [Zebulon Montgomery] Pike, September 2, 1795, Zebulon Montgomery Pike Collection, Chicago Historical Society, Chicago, IL (hereafter cited as ZMPCHS); Underwood, *Journal of Thomas Taylor Underwood*, 22–23; Zebulon Pike, Fort Massac, to Underwood, April 1796, Zebulon Pike Papers, Library of Congress.

8. For descriptions of the crossing, see, Harris, "Journal of a Tour;" and Francois André Michaux, "Travels to the West of the Alleghany Mountains," in *Early Western Travels, 1748–1846,* ed. Reuben Gold Thwaites (Cleveland: The Arthur H. Clark Company, 1904), 111–306, Early Encounters in North America (hereafter cited as EENA), http://lib.colostate.edu/databases/permlink.php?id=388 (accessed July 22, 2013).

9. Michaux, "Travels to the West," 145; Harris, "Journal of a Tour," 334; Receipt for Zeb[ulon] Montgomery Pike, July 23, 1798, ZMPCHS.

10. Erik F. Haites, James Mak, and Gary M. Walton, *Western River Transportation: The Era of Early Internal Development, 1810–1860* (Baltimore: John Hopkins University Press, 1975), 15; Wade, *Urban Frontier,* 39–40.

11. Zebulon Montgomery Pike, Vincennes, to Zebulon Pike [senior], Cincinnati, February 28, 1802, MS2150, Zebulon Montgomery Pike Letters, Western Reserve Historical Society, Cleveland, Ohio (hereinafter cited as ZMPL); W. Eugene Hollon, *The Lost Pathfinder: Zebulon Montgomery Pike* (Norman: University of Oklahoma Press, 1949), 36.

12. Ellicott, "Journal," February 24–June 22, 1797, in JAE, 41–118; André Michaux, "Travels into Kentucky, 1793–96," December 14–16, 1795, in *Early Western Travels, 1748–1846,* ed. Reuben Gold Thwaites (Cleveland: The Arthur H. Clark Company, 1904), 80–81, EENA, http://lib.colostate.edu/databases/permlink. php?id=388 (accessed July 22, 2013).

13. James Ripley Jacobs, *Tarnished Warrior: Major General James Wilkinson* (New York: The MacMillan Company, 1938), 74–82; Eliga H. Gould, "Entangled Histories, Entangled Worlds: The English-Speaking Atlantic as a Spanish Periphery," *American Historical Review* 112 (June 2007): 782.

14. Wayne to James McHenry, July 8 and 28, September 30, and October 28, 1796, in *Anthony Wayne: A Name in Arms: Soldier, Diplomat, Defender of Expansion Westward of a Nation: The Wayne-Knox-Pickering-McHenry Correspondence,* ed. Richard C. Knopf (Pittsburgh: University of Pittsburgh Press, 1960), 495–497, 506–507, 530–531, 536–537; correspondence between Zebulon Pike, Anthony Wayne, and James Wilkinson, February 24–October 29, 1796, M0367, Northwest Territory Collection, Indiana Historical Society, Indianapolis, Indiana (hereafter cited as NT); Underwood, *Journal of Thomas Taylor Underwood,* 24, 29–30.

15. Zeb[ulo]n Pike, [Fort] Massac, to Andrew Ellicott, confluence of Ohio with Mississippi, December 31, 1796, Zebulon Pike Collection, Chicago Historical Society, Chicago, Illinois (hereafter cited as ZPCHS); Ellicott, "Journal," December 20, 1796–January 1, 1797, in JAE, 26–28.

16. Underwood, *Journal of Thomas Taylor Underwood,* 25; Henry Whiting, "Life of Zebulon Montgomery Pike," in *The Library of American Biography,* vol. 5, 2nd ser., ed. Jared Sparks (Boston: Charles C. Little and James Brown, 1845), 221; Francis B. Heitman, *Historical Register and Dictionary of the United States Army, from Its Organization, September 29, 1789, to March 2, 1903* (Washington, D.C.:

Government Printing Office, 1903) 1:792; Pike's own testimony, Z[ebulon] M[ontgomery] Pike, Camp Terre au Bouf, to the Assistant Adjutant General, Washington, June 4, 1809, ZMPCHS, says 1800, but John R. Williams, Detroit, to Amos Holton, May 20, 1845, in *The Expeditions of Zebulon Montgomery Pike, To Headwaters of the Mississippi River, Through Louisiana Territory, and in New Spain, During the Years* 1805-6-7, ed. Elliott Coues (New York: Frances P. Harper, 1895), (hereafter cited as ZPC), 1: xxv–xxvi, recalls it as January 1801. This date is confirmed by Mark J. Wagner, a Southern Illinois University (Carbondale) archeologist who has worked on the site; Mark J. Wagner, "Searching for Cantonment Wilkinsonville," May 2004; Hollon, *Lost Pathfinder*, 30–31, 34, 37–40; Receipt for Zeb[ulon] Montgomery Pike, July 23, 1798, ZMPCHS.

17. U.S. War Department, Adjutant General's Office, "Zebulon Pike," Compiled Service Records of Volunteer Soldiers Who Served from 1784 to 1811 (hereafter cited as CRSV), U.S. Levies, Second Regiment, Microcopy Publication M905, roll 6, NARADC; John Dwight Kilbourne, Virtutis Praemium: *The Men Who Founded the State Society of the Cincinnati of Pennsylvania*, vol. 2 (Rockport, Maine: Picton Press, 1998), Library of the Society of the Cincinnati, 797; U.S. War Department, Adjutant General's Office, "Zebulon Pike: Statement of Information Found Concerning His Military Service," 1927, CRSV, NARAD; Adjutant General, Fred[eric]k Town, Md., to Zebulon Pike, Detroit, March 13, 1804, Adjutant General's Office Records, RG 94, Letters Sent (hereafter cited as AGOS), 1800–1890, Main Series, Microcopy Publication M565, frame 41, NARADC; James Dill to John C. Calhoun, April 1824, Veteran's Administration, RG 15, Pension Records, Microcopy Publication M804, roll 1936, frames 1405–1407, NARADC; Winfield Scott to Mrs. W. A. Livingston, Fort Dodge, IA, April 18, 1927, M804, roll 1936, frames 1332–1333, NARADC; Zebulon Pike, Pension Declaration, June 23, 1823, Lawrenceburg, Indiana, M804, roll 1936, frames 1378–1385, NARADC.

18. Zebulon Pike Sr.'s pension application records, M804, reel 1936, NARADC; untitled manuscript documents relating to the case *Commissioners of Bucks County* v. *Zebulon Pike*, 1786, in General Zebulon Pike Papers (1751–1834), Bucks County Historical Society, Doylestown, Pennsylvania (hereafter cited as BCHS); Whiting, "Life of Zebulon Montgomery Pike," 220; Terry Bouton, *Taming Democracy: "The People," the Founders, and the Troubled Ending of the American Revolution* (New York: Oxford University Press, 2007); Jay Fliegelman, *Prodigals and Pilgrims: The American Revolution against Patriarchal Authority, 1750–1800* (Cambridge: Cambridge University Press, 1982).

19. Samuel Richardson, *Clarissa or The History of a Young Lady*, http://www.gutenberg.org/etext/9296; Fliegelman, *Prodigals and Pilgrims*, 9–35, 86–89; John Locke, *An Essay Concerning Human Understanding*, sect. 67 (1690), Oregon State University, http://oregonstate.edu/instruct/phl302/texts/locke/locke1/Essay_contents.html (accessed November 8, 2006); John Locke, *Some Thoughts*

Concerning Education, in *English Philosophers of the Seventeenth and Eighteenth Centuries* (37 vols., New York, 1910), http://www.fordham.edu/halsall/mod/1692locke-education.html (accessed November 8, 2006).

20. Fliegelman, *Prodigals and Pilgrims*, 35; Steven Watts, *The Republic Reborn: War and the Making of Liberal America, 1790–1820* (Baltimore: The Johns Hopkins University Press, 1987); Richard L. Bushman, *The Refinement of America: Persons, Houses, Cities* (New York: Alfred A. Knopf, 1992), 61–99; Eve Kornfeld, *Creating an American Culture, 1775–1800: A Brief History with Documents* (Boston: Bedford/St. Martin's, 2001); Sarah J. Purcell, *Sealed with Blood: War Sacrifice, and Memory in Revolutionary America* (Philadelphia: University of Pennsylvania Press: 2002), 11–48; Caroline Cox, *A Proper Sense of Honor: Service and Sacrifice in George Washington's Army* (Chapel Hill: University of North Carolina Press, 2004), 238; Mason L. Weems, *The Life of Washington*, ed. Marcus Cunliffe (Cambridge, Mass.: Harvard University Press, 1962); Jean Jacques Rousseau, *Émile, or On Education* (Paris, 1762), trans. Barbara Foxley (London and New York, 1911), bk. 2, p. 387.

21. Whiting, "Life of Zebulon Montgomery Pike," 220, 313; Williams to Holton, May 20, 1845, ZPC, 1: xxiv; William Shenstone, *Essays on Men and Manners* (1764; repr., Philadelphia: William W. Morse, 1804), 40; Weems, *Life of Washington*, 2–5.

22. Zebulon Montgomery Pike, Vincennes, to Zebulon Pike [senior], Cincinnati, February 28, 1802, ZMPL; Zebulon Montgomery Pike, Kaskaskias, to Maria H[eriot] Pike, Cincinnati, February 6, November 22, 1803, ZMPL; Z[ebulon] M[ontgomery] Pike, Washington City, to George W. Pike, Lawrence Burgh, Indiana Territory, February 25, 1808, ZMPL.

23. Zebulon Montgomery Pike to Maria Pike, February 6, November 22, 1803, ZMPL; Williams to Holton, May 20, 1845, ZPC, 1: xxiv; John M. Niles, *The Life of Oliver Hazard Perry* (Hartford: William S. Marsh, 1820), 317–318; Pike to Zebulon Pike, Sr., February 28, 1802, ZMPL.

24. Kornfeld, *Creating an American Culture*.

25. Robert Dodsley, *The Economy of Human Life: Translated from an Indian Manuscript, Written by an Ancient Bramin in a Letter From an English Gentleman Residing in China* (1750; repr., Philadelphia: Joseph Crukshank, 1795), in Early American Imprints First Series (hereinafter cited as EAI-1) #28582, University of Wyoming, Laramie, http://www-lib.uwyo.edu/find/subject.cfm?alpha=E, (accessed August 18, 2006), ii–xii.

26. Whiting, "Life of Zebulon Montgomery Pike," 314; Niles, *Life of Oliver Hazard Perry*, 319–320; Elliott Coues, ed., *The Expeditions of Zebulon Montgomery Pike, To Headwaters of the Mississippi River, Through Louisiana Territory, and in New Spain, During the Years 1805-6-7* (New York: Francis P. Harper, 1895), 1: xxxiii–xxxiv; Dodsley, *Economy of Human Life*, 9; Kenneth Lockridge, *On the Sources of Patriarchal Rage: The Commonplace Books of William Byrd and Thomas Jefferson and the Gendering of Power in the Eighteenth Century* (New York: New York

University Press, 1992), 3–5; Z[ebulon] M[ontgomery] Pike, New Orleans, to George W. Pike, West Point, August 17, 1809, ZMPL.

27. For a fuller discussion of Pike's relationship with Wilkinson, see Jared Orsi, "Reading with Pike: The Mystery of His Affection for James Wilkinson," *Wagon Tracks* 21 (May 2007), 17–20; Zebulon Montgomery Pike, "Interrogatories," November 17, 1808, *The Journals of Zebulon Montgomery Pike* (hereafter cited as ZPJ), ed. Donald Jackson (Norman: University of Oklahoma Press, 1966), 1:332–333; Hollon, *Lost Pathfinder*, 18.

28. Pike, Camp Independence, to James Wilkinson, August 28, 1806, ZPJ, 2:144. On another occasion, Pike closed a letter to Wilkinson, "You see my dear general, I write to you like a person addressing a father: at the same time I hope you will consider me not only in a professional, but a personal view, one who holds you in the highest respect and esteem;" Pike, Prairie du Chien, September 5, 1805, ZPJ 1:236–237; Dodsley, *Economy of Human Life*, 11, 33, 47, and 48.

29. Bettie Harrison Eaton, El Paso, to Elliott Coues, July 2, 1894, in ZPC, 1: xxxiii; Clara H. Pike, Boon County, Kentucky, to Amos Holton, April 25, 1845, in *The Case of Mrs. Clara H. Pike*, comp. by Amos Holton (Washington, [D.C.], T. Barnard, Printer, 1846), 5–9; Dodsley, *Economy of Human Life*, 26; Whiting, "Life of Zebulon Montgomery Pike," 313.

30. "John Brown's Will," *Will Book B*, Boone County, Kentucky, 156–161. Brown's will does not delineate an exact number of slaves, but several passages in the will that refer to slaves and the large amount of land owned by Brown, allow this estimate; Jefferson quoted in Clay S. Jenkinson, *Becoming Jefferson's People: Re-inventing the American Republic in the Twenty-first Century* (Reno: Marmarth Press, 2004), 47; Hollon, *Lost Pathfinder*, 8, 26. Hollon and other Pike biographers have said Clara's father was Pike's maternal uncle, making Clara his cousin. This seems unlikely. Although Pike's mother's maiden name was Brown, John Brown's father's will does not name an Isabella among his children. "Will of George Brown of Middlesex Co., NJ," *Wills and Inventories*, vol. 21, New Jersey Department of State, Secretary of State's Office, 17–20.

31. Hollon, *Lost Pathfinder*, 26, says the couple eloped to Cincinnati. This seems unlikely given that their marriage was recorded in the Boone County, Kentucky, records. They were married by Lewis Deweese, minister at the Bullitsburgh Baptist Church, and a neighbor of the Browns. The marriage record does not list any person giving consent to the nuptials, even though Clara was under twenty-one at the time and under Kentucky law would have needed permission from a father or guardian to get married; Jefferson, "Declaration of Independence," 1776; Thomas Paine, *Common Sense* (1776; repr., New York, 1986), 83; Fliegelman, *Prodigals and Pilgrims*, 4.

32. Pike to Zebulon Pike, Sr., October 12, 1801, ZMPL; John Demos, *Circles and Lines: The Shape of Life in Early America* (Cambridge, Mass.: Harvard University Press, 2004), 55.

33. Niles, *Life of Oliver Hazard Perry*, 319–320; Whiting, "Life of Zebulon Montgomery Pike," 314; Bushman, *The Refinement of America*, xvi.

34. Zebulon Montgomery Pike to Zebulon Pike, Sr., February 28, 1802, April 19, 1808, and July 10, 1810, ZMPL.

35. Williams to Holton, May 20, 1845, ZPC, 1: xxiv; Whiting, "Life of Zebulon Montgomery Pike," 220.

36. George Washington, "Rules of Civility and Decent Behavior in Company and Conversation," in the Papers of George Washington, http://gwpapers.virginia. edu/documents/civility/transcript.html; C. Dallet Hemphill, "Manners and Class in the Revolutionary Era: A Transatlantic Comparison," *William and Mary Quarterly*, 63 (April 2006): 351–352, 357–358; Dodsley, *Economy of Human Life*, 5; Shenstone, *Essays*, 111; Bushman, *The Refinement of America*; Joanne B. Freeman, *Affairs of Honor: National Politics in the New Republic* (New Haven: Yale University Press, 2001), 38–48; Locke, *Essay Concerning Human Understanding*, sect. 67.

37. Williams to Holton, May 20, 1845, ZPC, 1: xxvi; Zebulon Montgomery Pike to Zebulon Pike, Sr., February 28, 1802, July 10, 1810, ZMPL; Thomas Cushing to Henry Dearborn, April 10, 1806, AGOS; Hollon, *Lost Pathfinder*, 23.

38. Dodsley, *Economy of Human Life*, 12, 19, 92, 127, 129, and 130; Pike to George W. Pike, February 25, 1808, ZMPL.

39. Dodsley, *Economy of Human Life*, 119–120; Niles, *Life of Oliver Hazard Perry*, 319; Weems, *Life of Washington*; Stanley Elkins and Eric McKitrick, *The Age of Federalism* (New York: Oxford University Press, 1993), 43–44, 48–49; Simon P. Newman, *Parades and the Politics of the Streets: Festive Culture in the Early American Republic* (Philadelphia: University of Pennsylvania Press, 1997), 44–82; Purcell, *Sealed with Blood*, 96–98, 126–132; David Waldstreicher, *In the Midst of Perpetual Fetes: The Making of American Nationalism, 1776–1820* (Chapel Hill: University of North Carolina Press, 1997), 117–126; "Biographical Memoir of the Late Brigadier-General Zebulon Montgomery Pike," *Monthly Recorder* (New York State) 1 (July 1813), 222.

40. Pike to Zebulon Pike, Sr., April 19, 1808, ZMPL; Z[ebulon] M[ontgomery] Pike to George W. Pike, August 17, 1809, ZMPL.

41. Andrew Jackson to Rachel Jackson, December 29, 1813, in *The Papers of Andrew Jackson*, vol. 2, ed. Harold D. Moser and Sharon Macpherson (Knoxville: University of Tennessee Press, 1984), 515–516; Cox, *Proper Sense of Honor*, 73–117.

42. Williams to Holton, May 20, 1845, ZPC, 1: xxv.

43. Dodsley, *Economy of Human Life*, 15, 16, and 18; Williams to Holton, May 20, 1845, ZPC, 1: xxiv–xxv.

44. Hollon, *Lost Pathfinder*, 38, 40; Michaux, "Travels into Kentucky, 1793–96," 70–71.

45. Z[ebulon] M[ontgomery] Pike to Isabel[la] Pike, September 8, November 22, 1803, ZMPL; Zebulon Montgomery Pike to Maria Pike, February 6, 1803, ZMPL.

46. Nicole Eustace, *Passion Is the Gale: Emotion, Power, and the Coming of the American Revolution* (Chapel Hill: University of North Carolina Press, 2008), 244–249, 261; Sarah Knott, *Sensibility and the American Revolution* (Chapel Hill: University of North Carolina Press, 2009), 235; Dodsley, *Economy of Human Life*, 5, 24, 37, and 40.

47. "Interrogatories Proposed to Major Z.M. Pike," in ZPJ, 2:334. This document merits some discussion. It is a deposition sworn before John Creigh. Although the exact purpose of the deposition is not clear, Donald Jackson speculates that it was likely taken as part of James Wilkinson's attempts to exonerate himself of wrongdoing in the Burr affair. If so, Pike, who was a dogged defender of the general and haunted himself by connections to Burr (though much less so than Wilkinson), may have had reason to cast his invitation to exploration as emanating from some source other than Wilkinson, and the national hero explorer Lewis would have been a good source for establishing the legitimacy of Pike's own journeys. Thus, it is possible that he distorted or even fabricated Lewis's invitation. This, however, is unlikely. As we shall see later, there is scant evidence to connect Pike to Burr's activities at all, so Pike probably had little reason to lie about the origins of his exploration. Moreover, there was in fact a national plan to explore different parts of Louisiana. See Dan Flores, "Jefferson's Grand Expedition and the Mystery of the Red River," and Elliott West, "Lewis and Clark: Kidnappers," both in *A Whole Country in Commotion: The Louisiana Purchase and the American Southwest*, ed. Patrick G. Williams, S. Charles Bolton, and Jeannie M. Whayne (Fayetteville: University of Arkansas Press, 2005), 3–20, 21–39. Jefferson sent out several such expeditions and Wilkinson several more on the heels of the Corps of Discovery. Also, in late 1803, Lewis was chomping at the bit, bursting with hopes and plans, including one scheme he briefly entertained to take a side-trip toward Santa Fe from St. Louis before launching his main expedition up the Missouri. See Meriwether Lewis, Cincinnati, to Thomas Jefferson, October 3, 1803, and Jefferson, Washington, to Lewis, November 16, 1803, in *Letters of the Lewis and Clark Expedition with Related Documents, 1783–1854*, ed. Donald Jackson (Urbana: University of Illinois Press, 1962), 131. The overeager Lewis, who was certainly in a position to know of Jefferson's larger exploration projects, might very well have written to Pike to suggest the possibility that Pike head one himself. Finally, Lewis was still alive at the time of Pike's deposition, and Pike would have known that Lewis could easily have denied such a plan if it were not true. For all of these reasons, it is highly implausible that Pike was lying under oath, and we should take him at his word here.

CHAPTER 3

1. Zebulon Pike, "Journal of a Voyage to the Source of the Mississippi in the Years 1805 and 1806," January 29 through February 10, 1806, in *The Journals of*

Zebulon Montgomery Pike with Letters and Related Documents (hereinafter cited as ZPJ), ed. Donald Jackson (Norman: University of Oklahoma Press, 1966), 1:85–91; Pike, "Observations on the North West Company," ZPJ, 1:185.

2. Pike, "Observations on the North West Company," ZPJ, 1:183.

3. Pike, "Information Concerning Louisiana," in ZPJ, 1:227; Richard J. Kahn, and Patricia G. Kahn, "The *Medical Repository*: The First U.S. Medical Journal (1797–1824)," *New England Journal of Medicine* 337 (December 25, 1997): 1926–1930.

4. Pike, "Information Concerning Louisiana," in ZPJ, 1:226–227.

5. Richard C. Wade, *The Urban Frontier: The Rise of Western Cities, 1790–1830* (Cambridge, Mass.: Harvard University Press, 1967), 63.

6. Peter S. Onuf, *Jefferson's Empire: The Language of American Nationhood* (Charlottesville: University of Virginia Press, 2000), 7–8, 10–11, 53; James P. Ronda, "Pike and Empire," in *Zebulon Pike, Thomas Jefferson, and the Opening of the American West*, ed. Matthew L. Harris and Jay H. Buckley (Norman: University of Oklahoma Press, 2012), 61–80.

7. Donald Jackson, *Thomas Jefferson and the Stony Mountains: Exploring the West from Monticello* (Urbana: University of Illinois Press, 1981), 244.

8. James Ripley Jacobs, *Tarnished Warrior: Major General James Wilkinson* (New York: The MacMillan Company, 1938), 205–207; Vicente Folch, "Reflections on Louisiana," 1804, in *Louisiana under the Rule of Spain, France, and the United States, 1785–1807*, ed. James Alexander Robertson (1910–1911; repr., New York: Books for Libraries Press, 1969), 2:339–343; William E. Foley, "James Wilkinson: Pike's Mentor and Jefferson's Capricious Point Man in the West," in *Zebulon Pike, Thomas Jefferson, and the Opening of the American West*, ed. Matthew L. Harris and Jay H. Buckley (Norman: University of Oklahoma Press, 2012), 191–192.

9. Isaac Joslin Cox, "Opening the Santa Fe Trail," *Missouri Historical Review* 25 (October 1930–July 1931): 49–50; Foley, "James Wilkinson," 198–199; "Interrogatories Proposed to Major Z.M. Pike," in ZPJ 2:334–335; Jackson, *Thomas Jefferson*, 244.

10. Nancy Isenberg, *Fallen Founder: The Life of Aaron Burr* (New York: Viking, 2007), 224–231.

11. *New York Evening Post*, November 8, 1804, in *Political Correspondence and Public Papers of Aaron Burr* (hereafter cited as PCPPAB), ed. Mary-Jo Kline (Princeton: Princeton University Press, 1983), 2:896.

12. Andrew R. L. Cayton, "'Separate Interests' and the Nation State: The Washington Administration and the Origins of Regionalism in the Trans-Appalachian West," *Journal of American History* 79 (June 1992): 39–67; Thomas Jefferson to Robert R. Livingston, April 18, 1802, in *The Louisiana Purchase: Emergence of an American Nation*, ed. Peter J. Kastor (Washington, D.C.: CQ Press, 2002), 161; James Madison to Robert R. Livingston and James Monroe, March 2, 1803, in *The Louisiana Purchase*, Kastor, 174.

13. Isenberg, *Fallen Founder*, 293–297.

14. Anthony Merry, Philadelphia, to Lord Harrowby, August 6, 1804, in PCPPAB, 2:891; Merry, Washington, to Harrowby, March 29, 1805, in PCPPAB, 2:928.

15. Mary-Jo Kline, ed. *Political Correspondence and Public Papers of Aaron Burr* (Princeton: Princeton University Press, 1983), 930; Jacobs, *Tarnished Warrior*, 226; Brigadier General James Wilkinson to the House of Representatives, April 25, 1808, *American State Papers*, 37, Miscellaneous 1:572; "Interrogatories Proposed to Major Z.M. Pike," in ZPJ 2:335.

16. William E. Foley and C. David Rice, *The First Chouteaus: River Barons of Early St. Louis* (Urbana: University of Illinois Press, 1983), 92, 108–110.

17. "By the Governor and Superintendent of Indian Affairs in and over the Territory of Louisiana, A Proclamation," [July 10, 1806], in ZPJ, 1:228.

18. Willard H. Rollins. *The Osage: An Ethnohistorical Study of Hegemony on the Prairie-Plains* (Columbia, Mo.: University of Missouri Press, 1992), 6–8; Nye, *Consuming Power*, 15.

19. Jefferson to Joseph Anderson, December 28, 1805, quoted in Jackson, *Thomas Jefferson*, 243.

20. Wilkinson, St. Louis, to Dearborn, July 27, 1805, in ZPJ, 1:229; italics in original; Jackson, *Thomas Jefferson*, 245; Foley, "James Wilkinson," 199–200, 205–206; Jay H. Buckley, "Jeffersonian Explorers in the Trans-Mississippi West," 119–120.

21. Wilkinson, St. Louis, to Pike, July 30, 1805, in ZPJ, 1:304; Wilkinson, St. Louis, to Dearborn, July 27, 1805, in ZPJ, 1:230.

22. Pike, "Observation on the Country and the Indians," in ZPJ, 1:190; Pike, "Journal of a Voyage," August 9–19, 1805, in ZPJ, 1:6–12.

23. Pike, "Observation on the Country and the Indians," in ZPJ, 1:190–191, 191; Pike, "Journal of a Voyage," August 16, 17, 18, 19, 21, 23, 24, 26, 27, 28, 29, 30, and 31, 1805, in ZPJ, 1:10–11, 13–19; Pike, Head of the Rapids de Moyen, August 20, 1805, in ZPJ, 1:230.

24. Pike, "Journal of a Voyage," September 1, 1805, in ZPJ, 1:19–20; Pike, "Queries to Julien Dubuque," [September 1, 1805], in ZPJ, 1:234; Pike, Prairie de Chien, to Wilkinson, September 5, 1805, in ZPJ, 1:236.

25. Pike, Prairie de Chien, to Wilkinson, September 5, 1805, in ZPJ, 1:236.

26. Pike, "Journal of a Voyage," September 1, 1805, in ZPJ, 1:20.

27. Pike, "Observations," in ZPJ, 1:193, 196–198.

28. Pike, "Observations," in ZPJ, 1:197–198; Pike, "Journal of a Voyage," September 6, 1805, in ZPJ, 1:23.

29. Pike, "Journal of a Voyage," September 7 and 8, 1805, in ZPJ, 1:24–25; See Jackson's footnote 39 in Pike, "Journal of a Voyage," September 4, 1805, in ZPJ, 1:22; correspondence between Bleakley and Auguste Chouteau, 1804–1807, in Papers of the Saint Louis Fur Trade, Missouri Historical Society, microfilm (hereafter cited as PStLFT), vol. 1, reels 4 and 5; Pike, Prairie du Chien, to

Wilkinson, September 5, 1805, in ZPJ, 1:235; Pike, "Observations," in ZPJ, 1:197–198.

30. Pike, Prairie du Chien, to Wilkinson, September 5, 1805, in ZPJ, 1:235–236; Pike, "Journal of a Voyage," September 5–6, 1805, in ZPJ, 1:23.

31. Pike, Prairie du Chien, to Wilkinson, September 5, 1805, in ZPJ, 1:235; see also Pike, "Journal of a Voyage," September 7, 1805, in ZPJ, 1:23–24, and Jackson's footnote 41 for that date.

32. Warren L. Cook, *Flood Tide of Empire: Spain and the Pacific Northwest, 1543–1819* (New Haven/London: Yale University Press, 1973), 80–90; Salcedo, Chihuahua, to Alencaster, September 9, 1805, in ZPJ, 2:104–108.

33. James Wilkinson, St. Louis, to Henry Dearborn, September 8, 1805, in ZPJ 2:100–102.

34. Kline, PCPPAB, 2:940. Milton Lomask, *Aaron Burr: The Conspiracy and Years of Exile,* 1805–1836 (New York: Farrar, Straus, and Giroux, 1982), 81, gives the date as September 12; Lomask, *Aaron Burr,* 82–83; "Statement of Timothy Kibbey," July 6, 1807, in ZPJ, 1:246–249.

35. Kline, in PCPPAB, 2:940–941; Lomask, *Aaron Burr,* 82–83.

36. Pike, "Journal of a Voyage," September 10, 1805, in ZPJ, 1:27–28.

37. Pike, "Journal of a Voyage," September 14, 1805, in ZPJ, 1:31.

38. Pike, "Council with the Sioux," September 23, 1805, in ZPJ, 1:242; Pike, "Journal of a Voyage," September 17, 1805, in ZPJ, 1:33.

39. Patricia C. Albers, "Santee," in *Handbook of North American Indians* (Washington, D.C., Smithsonian Institution, 2001), 761–764; Raymond J. DeMallie, "Sioux Until 1850," in *Handbook of North American Indians* (Washington, D.C., Smithsonian Institution, 2001), 727–730.

40. Pike, "Council with the Sioux," September 23, 1805, in ZPJ, 1:243–245.

41. Albers, "Santee," 761; DeMallie, "Sioux Until 1850," 729; Jonathan Carver, *Three Years Travels Throughout the Interior Parts of North-America* (Boston: John Russell for David West, 1797).

42. Pike, "Council with the Sioux," September 23, 1805, in ZPJ, 1:243.

43. Pike, "Journal of a Voyage," September 23, 1805, in ZPJ, 1:38; Pike, "Council with the Sioux," September 23, 1805, in ZPJ, 1:242–243; Pike, "Treaty with the Sioux," September 23, 1805, in ZPJ, 1:245.

44. Pike, St. Piere, to Wilkinson, September 23, 1805, in ZPJ, 1:238; DeMallie, "Sioux Until 1850," 730.

45. Pike, "Journal of a Voyage," September 27, 1805, in ZPJ, 1:41.

46. Pike, "Journal of a Voyage," September 29 and October 16, 1805, in ZPJ, 1:42, 48.

47. Jackson, ed., *Journals,* footnote 110, 1:67.

48. Pike, "Journal of a Voyage," October 28 and 29, 1805, in ZPJ, 1:52.

49. Pike, "Journal of a Voyage," November 2 and 3, 1805, in ZPJ, 1:53–55.

50. Pike, "Journal of a Voyage," November 14, 1805, in ZPJ, 1:59.

51. Pike, "Journal of a Voyage," November 9, 15, 16, 17, 18 and December 6, 1805, in ZPJ, 1:58–60, 65.

52. Pike, "Journal of a Voyage," October 31, 1805, in ZPJ, 1:52–53.

53. Pike to Kennerman, October 1, 1805, in ZPJ, 1:247–249. Jackson notes (page 249), and I agree, that this letter is misdated. On October 1, Pike was still two weeks away from reaching Little Falls and deciding to leave part of the party for the winter. More likely, the date is October 19, on which date Pike's journal records him to be writing letters in preparation for continuing upstream. At that point, he still appears to have believed he would be leaving shortly; Pike, "Journal of a Voyage," December 10, 1805, in ZPJ, 1:67.

54. Pike, "Journal of a Voyage," November 26, 1805, in ZPJ, 1:62; Wilkinson, St. Louis, to Dearborn, November 26, 1805, in ZPJ, 1:249–256.

55. Jackson, ed., *Journals*, footnotes 9 and 11, 1:255–256; Wilkinson, St. Louis, to Dearborn, November 26, 1805, in ZPJ, 1:252.

56. Pike, "Journal of a Voyage," December 10, 19, 23, 27, and January 4, 1805, in ZPJ, 1:67–68, 71–73, 77; Pike, "Observations," in ZPJ, 1:205.

57. Pike, "Journal of a Voyage," December 12 and January 6, 1805, in ZPJ, 1:68–69, 77; Pike, "Observations," in ZPJ, 1:205.

58. Pike, "Journal of a Voyage," January 7 and 8, 1806, in ZPJ, 1:78–79.

59. Pike, "Journal of a Voyage," January 9, 1806, in ZPJ, 1:79–80.

60. Pike, "Journal of a Voyage," December 12, 1805, in ZPJ, 1:69.

61. Pike, "Journal of a Voyage," January 27, 1806, in ZPJ, 1:84.

62. Pike, "Description of the N.W. Company's Fort at Leech Lake, in February, 1806," n.d., in ZPJ, 1:184–185; Pike, "Return of Men Employed in the N. W. Company's Department of Fond du Lac, for 1805...," n.d., in ZPJ, 1:188; Pike, "Journal of a Voyage," February 2–3, 1806, in ZPJ, 1:89.

63. Pike, "Journal of a Voyage," February 2–3 and 10, 1806, in ZPJ, 1:89, 91.

64. Pike, "Journal of a Voyage," February 9, 1806, in ZPJ, 1:90–91.

65. Pike, "Recapitulation of Furs and Peltries...1804–5...," n.d., in ZPJ, 1:186–188; Pike, "Observations on the North West Company," n.d., in ZPJ, 1:180–181, 183.

66. Pike, "The Price of Goods in Exchange with the Indians of this Quarter," n.d., in ZPJ, 1:188; Pike, "Observations on the North West Company," n.d., in ZPJ, 1:180.

67. Pike to McGillis, February [7], 1806, in ZPJ, 1:256–259. There is no date on this letter. Jackson supplies February 6 without explanation. I am using the seventh, since in his journal, Pike twice referred to writing the letter on the seventh; Pike, "Journal of a Voyage," February 7 and 15, 1806, in ZPJ, 1:90, 93.

68. Pike, "Journal of a Voyage," February 16, 1806, in ZPJ, 1:93–94; "Answers of Several Indian Chiefs Made to an Address from Lieutenant Pike, at Leech Lake...," February 16, 1806, in ZPJ, 1:265.

69. McGillis to Pike, February 15, 1806, in ZPJ, 1:259–262.

70. McGillis to Pike, February 15, 1806, in ZPJ, 1:259–262.

71. Quoted in Jackson, ed., *Journals*, 1:262.

72. Pike, "Journal of a Voyage," April 6, 1806, in ZPJ, 1:115.

73. Jackson presents it in narrative form; ZPJ, 1:218–223. For a clearer visual representation of the information that is closer to what Pike produced, see "Abstract of the Nations of Indians on the Mississippi and Its Confluent Streams, from St. Louis, Louisiana, to Its Source, Including Red Lake and Lower Red River," n.d., in *The Expeditions of Zebulon Montgomery Pike, To Headwaters of the Mississippi River, Through Louisiana Territory, and in New Spain, During the Years* 1805-6-7 (hereafter cited as ZPC), 3 vols., ed. Elliott Coues (New York: Francis P. Harper, 1895), 1:346–347.

74. Pike, Prairie De Chien, to Wilkinson, April 18, 1806, in ZPJ, 1:268.

CHAPTER 4

1. Pike, "Diary of an Expedition," October 7, 1806, ZPJ, 1:331.

2. Vaclav Smil, *Energy in Nature and Society: General Energetics of Complex Systems* (Cambridge: MIT Press, 2008), 6, 61; Mark Fiege, *The Republic of Nature: An Environmental History of the United States* (Seattle: University of Washington Press, 2012), 362–365; E. A. Wrigley, *Continuity, Chance, and Change: the Character of the Industrial Revolution in England* (Cambridge: Cambridge University Press, 1988), 50–51; Jenika Howe, "Power in the Pasture: Energy and the History of Ranching in Western South Dakota," (master's thesis, Colorado State University, 2012); I have adapted the phrase, "farming sunshine" from Smil's description of petroleum as "buried sunshine," page 204.

3. Nancy Isenberg, *Fallen Founder: The Life of Aaron Burr* (New York: Viking, 2007), 297–298; Mary-Jo Kline, ed. *Political Correspondence and Public Papers of Aaron Burr* (hereafter cited as PCPPAB) (Princeton: Princeton University Press, 1983), 2:941; Milton Lomask, *Aaron Burr: The Conspiracy and Years of Exile, 1805–1836* (New York: Farrar, Straus, and Giroux, 1982), 87.

4. *National Intelligencer and Washington Advertiser* (hereafter cited as *NIWA*), April and May 1806, Library of Congress (hereafter cited as LC).

5. Wilkinson, St. Louis, to Pike, June 24, 1806, ZPJ, 1:285–288, Jefferson to Harrison, January 16, 1806, ZPJ, 1:287n1.

6. James Wilkinson, St. Louis, to Zebulon Pike, June 24, 1806, ZPJ 1:285–287; Scott, *Seeing Like a State*, 49–51; Wilkinson, Cantonment, Missouri, to Pike, July 12, 1806, ZPJ, 1:288–289.

7. Isaac Joslin Cox, "Opening the Santa Fe Trail," *Missouri Historical Review* 25 (October 1930–July 1931), 43–44, 49–50.

8. Pike, Capitol Hill, to Dearborn, December 2, 1808, *The Journals of Zebulon Montgomery Pike with Letters and Related Documents* (hereinafter cited as ZPJ), ed. Donald Jackson (Norman: University of Oklahoma Press, 1966), 2:349–350; Pike, St. Louis, to Daniel Bissell, June 15, 1806, ZPJ, 2:114; Pike, "Diary of an

Expedition," July 19, 1806, ZPJ, 1:292; Pike, Charette, to Bissell, July 22, 1806, ZPJ, 2:126; Pike, Charette, to Wilkinson, July 22, 1806, ZPJ, 2:127; Pike, Camp Independence, near the Osage Towns, August 28, 1806, ZPJ, 2:144; Wilkinson, Cantonment, Missouri, to Pike, July 12, 1806, ZPJ, 1:289; Jackson, ed., ZPJ, 1:290n5.

9. Pike, "Diary of an Expedition," August 13 and 18, 1806, ZPJ, 1:303, 306.

10. Wilkinson, "Report," ZPJ, 2:4, 16; Pike "Dissertation," ZPJ, 2:32–33, 40–41; Pike, "Diary of an Expedition," August 15, 1806, ZPJ, 1:304–305.

11. Pike, "Diary of an Expedition," August 19, 1806, ZPJ, 1:307; Pike, "Pike's Speech to the Osages," [August 22, 1806], ZPJ, 2:139–141.

12. Pike, "Diary of an Expedition," August 22, 1806, 1:309.

13. On the Lamie affair, see "Diary of an Expedition," July 17 and August 19–21, 1806, ZPJ, 1:291–292, 307–308; "Deposition of Baptiste Duchouquette," [August 21, 1806], ZPJ, 2:138–139; and Pike to Wilkinson, August 28, 1806, ZPJ, 2:142–144; Pike, "Dissertation," ZPJ, 2:32; William E. Foley and C. David Rice, *The First Chouteaus: River Barons of Early St. Louis* (Urbana: University of Illinois Press, 1983), 61–62; Wilkinson to Dearborn, August 2, 1806, ZPJ, 2:128–129; Wilkinson to Pike, August 6, 1806, ZPJ, 2:134–135.

14. Pike, "Diary of an Expedition," August 20, 1806, ZPJ, 1:308; Pike to Wilkinson, August 28, 1806, ZPJ, 2:143.

15. Pike to Wilkinson, August 28 and 30, 1806, ZPJ, 2:142–143, 145; Wilkinson to Pike, July 12, August 28, 1806, ZPJ, 1:289–290n4, 2:143.

16. Smil, *Energy*, 198.

17. Jackson, ed., *Journals*, 1:321–325, 2:6. On the likely contents of the meal that Pike was served, see David J. Wishart, *An Unspeakable Sadness: The Dispossession of the Nebraska Indians* (Lincoln: University of Nebraska Press, 1994), 23.

18. Douglas R. Parks, "Pawnee," in *Handbook of North American Indians*, vol. 13, ed. William C. Sturtevant (Washington, D.C.: Smithsonian Institution, 2001), 527; Waldo R. Wedel, *Central Plains Prehistory: Holocene Environments and Culture Changes in the Republican River Basin* (Lincoln: University of Nebraska Press, 1986), 171. For more on calumet ceremony in general, see Parks, "Pawnee," 538; Wishart, *Unspeakable Sadness*, 32; Waldo R. Wedel and George C. Frison, "Environment and Subsistence," in *Handbook of North American Indians*, vol. 13, ed. William C. Sturtevant, 49.

19. Wedel and Frison, "Environment and Subsistence," 49.

20. Warren L. Cook, *Flood Tide of Empire: Spain and the Pacific Northwest, 1543–1819* (New Haven/London: Yale University Press, 1973), 477; Wilkinson, "Report," ZPJ, 2:7; Pike to Dearborn, October 1, 1806, ZPJ, 2:149; Jackson, ed., *Journals*, 2:151.

21. "Pike's Speech to the Pawnees," September 29, 1806, ZPJ, 2:147; Jackson, ed., *Journals*, 1:328; Pike to Wilkinson, October 2, 1806, ZPJ, 2:150–151; "Lieutenant Wilkinson's Report," ZPJ, 2:6–7.

22. Parks, "Pawnee," 525–526; Wishart, *Unspeakable Sadness*, 25.

23. Wishart, *Unspeakable Sadness*, 23; Pike, "Dissertation on Louisiana," ZPJ, 1:36.

24. Wishart, *Unspeakable Sadness*, 24–25; Richard White, *Roots of Dependency: Subsistence, Environment, and Social Change among the Choctaws, Pawnees, and Navajos* (Lincoln: University of Nebraska Press, 1983), 178–198.

25. Nye, *Consuming Power*, 18; Charles S. Maier, "Consigning the Twentieth Century to History: Alternative Narratives for the Modern Era," *American Historical Review* 105 (June 2000): 807–831.

26. "Pike's Speech to the Pawnees," September 29, 1806, ZPJ, 2:147; Jefferson to Harrison, January 16, 1806, ZPJ, 1:287 n1.

27. Pike, "Diary of an Expedition," September 29, 1806, ZPJ, 1:329; Pike to Dearborn, October 1, 1806, ZPJ, 1:149; Pike, "Dissertation...on Louisiana," Washington, D.C., January 1808, ZPJ, 2:37.

28. Pike, "Dissertation...on Louisiana," ZPJ, 2:37–38.

29. "Pike's Speech to the Pawnees," ZPJ, 2:147; Nancy Shoemaker, *A Strange Likeness: Becoming Red and White in Eighteenth-Century North America* (New York: Oxford University Press, 2004); Ann M. Little, *Abraham in Arms: War and Gender in Colonial New England* (Philadelphia: University of Pennsylvania Press, 2007). On Pawnee authority, see Wishart, *Unspeakable Sadness*, 18–21, 36–37, and earlier, too; Pike, "Diary of an Expedition," September 29, 1806, ZPJ, 1:329.

30. Pike, "Diary of an Expedition," September 29, 1806, ZPJ, 1:328; Joaquín del Real Alencaster, Santa Fe, to Nemesio Salcedo, April 7, 1807, ZPJ, 2:182; Wilkinson, "Report," ZPJ, 2:7.

31. Pike, "Diary of an Expedition," September 29, 1806, ZPJ, 1:329; Pike, "Dissertation...on Louisiana," ZPJ, 2:37.

32. Pike "Diary of an Expedition," October 1, 1806, ZPJ, 1:329–330. The italics are Pike's; Pike to Wilkinson, October 2, 1806, ZPJ, 2:151–152.

33. Wishart, *Unspeakable Sadness*, 35–37; Pike to Wilkinson, October 2, 1806, ZPJ, 2:152.

34. Parks, "Pawnee," 530–531; Pike, "Dissertation...on Louisiana," ZPJ, 2:35.

35. Wishart, *Unspeakable Sadness*, 4–5; Wilkinson, "Lieutenant Wilkinson's Report," New Orleans, April 6, 1807, ZPJ, 2:5; Pike, "Diary of a Journal," September 27, 1806, ZPJ, 1:327.

36. George C. Sibley, "Notes on an Official Excursion," [June 1811], ZPJ, 2:371; Wilkinson, "Lieutenant Wilkinson's Report," New Orleans, April 6, 1807, ZPJ, 2:12–13.

37. Pike, "Diary of an Expedition," October 2, 1806, ZPJ, 1:330.

38. Pike, "Diary of an Expedition," October 2, 1806, ZPJ, 1:330; Pike to Wilkinson, October 2, 1806, ZPJ, 2:153.

39. Pike, "Diary of an Expedition," October 2, 1806, ZPJ, 1:330; Pike to Wilkinson, October 2, 1806, ZPJ, 2:153; Pike, "Diary of an Expedition," October 3–6, 1806, ZPJ, 1:330–331; Wilkinson, "Lieutenant Wilkinson's Report," New Orleans, April 6, 1807, ZPJ, 2:7.

40. Pike, "Diary of an Expedition," October 7, 1806, ZPJ, 1:331.

41. Sibley, "Notes on an Official Excursion," [June 1811], ZPJ, 2:375.

42. Sibley, "Notes on an Official Excursion," [June 1811], ZPJ, 2:376. Donald Jackson believed that "allowing for some elaboration," given the hostility between the Pike party and the Pawnees during the Americans' stay, the account has a "credible ring." See Jackson, ed., *Journals*, 2:377n3. Moreover, Pike's journal has already whitewashed the first showdown with the Pawnees. The tension at the flag exchange was much sharper as described in the accounts of Wilkinson and one of Pike's men, likely Sparks, who gave a version to the New Mexico governor. See Wilkinson, "Lieutenant Wilkinson's Report," April 6, 1807, ZPJ, 2:7; Alencaster to Salcedo, April 7, 1807, ZPJ, 2:181; Pike, "Diary of an Expedition," September 25, 1806, ZPJ, 1:327n86.

43. Pike, "Diary of an Expedition," October 7, 1806, ZPJ, 1:331.

44. Wrigley, *Continuity, Chance, and Change*, 52; Nye, *Consuming Power*, 17.

45. Parks, "Pawnee," 519–520; Wishart, *Unspeakable Sadness*, 63–69; 80–81; Richard White, *Roots of Dependency*, 199–206.

46. Pike, "Diary of an Expedition," September 25, October 8, 12, 29 and November 7, 1806, ZPJ, 1:321, 332, 334, 341, and 344.

47. Pike to Wilkinson, October 24, 1806, in ZPJ, 2:157; James B. Wilkinson to James Wilkinson, October 28, 1806, ZPJ, 2:161; James B. Wilkinson to Pike, October 26, 1806, ZPJ, 2:158–160.

48. Pike, "Diary of an Expedition," October 31, November 4–6, 1806, ZPJ, 1:341, 343.

49. Pike, "Diary of an Expedition," October 29, 31, November 4–8, 10, 12–14, 1806, ZPJ, 1:341, 343–345, 347; James B. Wilkinson to Wilkinson, October 28, 1806, ZPJ, 2:161.

50. Pike, "Diary of an Expedition," November 22, 1806, ZPJ, 1:349.

CHAPTER 5

1. Zebulon Montgomery Pike, "Diary of an Expedition," November 15–17, 1806, *The Journals of Zebulon Montgomery Pike* (hereafter cited as ZPJ), ed. Donald Jackson (Norman: University of Oklahoma Press, 1966), 1:345–346; italics in original.

2. Pike, "Diary of an Expedition," October 17, November 4 and 11, 1806, ZPJ, 1:336, 343–344; Sarah J. Purcell, *Sealed with Blood: War, Sacrifice, and Memory in Revolutionary America* (Philadelphia: University of Pennsylvania Press, 2002); David Waldstreicher, *In the Midst of Perpetual Fetes: The Making of American Nationalism, 1776–1820* (Chapel Hill: University of North Carolina Press, 1997).

3. James Wilkinson, St. Louis, to Zebulon Pike, June 24, 1806, in ZPJ, 1:285–287.

4. Milton Lomask, *Aaron Burr: The Conspiracy and Years of Exile, 1805–1836* (New York: Farrar, Straus, and Giroux, 1982), 5, 109; Aaron Burr, Philadelphia, to

Albert Gallatin, July 31, 1806, in *Political Correspondence and Public Papers of Aaron Burr* (hereafter cited as PCPPAB), ed. Mary-Jo Kline (Princeton: Princeton University Press, 1983), 2:992; Aaron Burr, Lexington, to William Wilkins, October 21, 1806, PCPPAB, 2:994.

5. Nancy Isenberg, *Fallen Founder: The Life of Aaron Burr* (New York: Viking, 2007), 303–304; Harman Blennerhassett to Aaron Burr, December 21, 1805, PCPPAB, 2:949–953; Kline, ed., PCPPAB, 2:994–997; Lomask, *Aaron Burr*, 128–130.

6. James Wilkinson, St. Louis, to Samuel Smith, March 29, 1806, *The Territorial Papers of the United States*, vol. 13 (hereafter cited as TP), (Washington, D.C.: US GPO, 1948), 13:366; Samuel Smith, Baltimore, to Thomas Jefferson, April 28, 1806, TP, 13: 502–503; Henry Dearborn to James Wilkinson, May 6, 1806, TP, 13:505–507; James Wilkinson, St. Louis, to Henry Dearborn, June 17, 1806, TP, 13:520–521; James Wilkinson, St. Louis, to Samuel Smith, June 17, 1806, TP, 13: 521–522; Lomask, *Aaron Burr*, 154, 164; James Ripley Jacobs, *Tarnished Warrior: Major General James Wilkinson* (New York: The MacMillan Company, 1938), 226–229; Burr to Wilkinson, April 16, 1805, PCPPAB, 2:968.

7. [Burr] to James Wilkinson, [22–29] July 1806, PCPPAB, 2:986–988; Kline, Lomask, and Isenberg agree that Burr was not the author of the letter. Kline makes a compelling case that the author likely was the former Ohio Senator Jonathan Dayton in PCPPAB, 2:973–990; Lomask, 114–122, Isenberg, 312.

8. Kline, ed., PCPPAB, 2:976; Lomask, *Aaron Burr*, 168–169; Thomas Perkins Abernethy, *The Burr Conspiracy* (New York: Oxford University Press, 1954), 187–188.

9. Kline, ed., PCPPAB, 2:979–980, 1000; Abernethy, *Burr Conspiracy*, 185–188; James Wilkinson, New Orleans, to Vicente Folch, January 3, 1807, Achivo General de Indias, Seville, Spain, legajo Cuba 2375, documentos 98–99.

10. Kline, ed., PCPPAB, 2:999, 1007; Abernethy, *Burr Conspiracy*, 108–110.

11. Jefferson would later praise Wilkinson's "honor of a soldier and fidelity of a good citizen." Kline, ed., PCPPAB, 2:982; Abernethy, *Burr Conspiracy*, 159–161.

12. Wilkinson to Pike, July 19, 1806, ZPJ, 2:120–121; Pike, "Diary of an Expedition," July 21–22, 1806, 1:294; Zebulon Pike, Charrette, Missouri, to James Wilkinson, July 22, 1806, ZPJ, 2:124. "Passd" is Pike's spelling.

13. A few authors have maintained that Pike's expedition was part of some larger scheme related to Burr and/or Wilkinson. See Elliott Coues, ed., *The Expeditions of Zebulon Montgomery Pike, To Headwaters of the Mississippi River, Through Louisiana Territory, and in New Spain, During the Years 1805–6–7* (New York: Francis P. Harper, 1895), 2: 500n44, 504n46, 571–72n6; Jack Kyle Cooper, *Zebulon Montgomery Pike's Great Western Adventure, 1806–1807* (Colorado Springs: Clausen Books, 2007) 164–171; Kyle S. Crichton, "Zeb Pike," *Scribner's*

Magazine 82 (July–December 1927), 462–467; M. R. Montgomery, *Jefferson and the Gun-Men: How the West Was Almost Lost* (New York: Three Rivers Press, 2000), 202–203, 207–209, 263–264, 270, 273, 286–290, 321.

14. Doug Erickson, Jeremy Skinner, and Paul Merchant, eds., *Jefferson's Western Explorations: Discoveries Made in Exploring the Missouri, Red River and Washita by Captains Lewis and Clark, Doctor Sibley, and William Dunbar, and compiled by Thomas Jefferson, the Natchez Edition*, 1806 (Spokane: The Arthur H. Clark Company, 2004); Dan Flores, "Jefferson's Grand Expedition and the Mystery of the Red River," in *A Whole Country in Commotion: The Louisiana Purchase and the American Southwest*, ed. Patrick G. Williams, S. Charles Bolton, and Jeannie M. Whayne (Fayetteville: University of Arkansas Press, 2005), 21–39; Dan L. Flores, *Southern Counterpart to Lewis & Clark: The Freeman & Custis Expedition of 1806* (1984; repr., Norman: University of Oklahoma Press, 2002); Donald Jackson, *Thomas Jefferson and the Stony Mountains: Exploring the West from Monticello* (Urbana: University of Illinois Press, 1981), 223–236, 248; Elliot West, "Lewis and Clark: Kidnappers," in *A Whole Country in Commotion: The Louisiana Purchase and the American Southwest*, ed. Patrick G. Williams, S. Charles Bolton, and Jeannie M. Whayne. (Fayetteville: University of Arkansas Press, 2005), 3–20; Jay H. Buckley, "Jeffersonian Explorers in the Trans-Mississippi West," in *Zebulon Pike, Thomas Jefferson, and the Opening of the American West*, ed. Matthew L. Harris and Jay H. Buckley (Norman: University of Oklahoma Press, 2012), 101–138.

15. Pike to Wilkinson, July 22, 1806, ZPJ, 2:124.

16. Pike, "Diary of an Expedition," November 18–20, 1806, ZPJ, 1:346–347.

17. John Logan Allen, *Passage Through the Garden: Lewis and Clark and the Image of the American Northwest* (Urbana: University of Illinois Press, 1975), 18–23; Jackson, *Thomas Jefferson and the Rocky Mountains*, 129–133.

18. Lawrence J. Burpee, *The Search for the Western Sea: The Story of the Exploration of North-Western America* (London: Alston Rivers, 1908), 293–295. Burpee suggests Carver's narrative was not an eyewitness account as it claims to be; Pike, "Journal of a Voyage," September 12, 1805, ZPJ 1:29; Nicolas King, "An Account of a Voyage Up the Mississippi River, from St. Louis to Its Source, &c.," ZPJ, 1:202; Allen, *Passage Through the Garden*, 23–26; Jonathan Carver, *Three Years Travels Throughout the Interior Parts of North-America* (Boston: John Russell for David West, 1797), 8–9, 45–46; Jackson, *Thomas Jefferson and the Rocky Mountains*, 93; Pike, "Information Concerning Louisiana," 1803, ZPJ, 1:227.

19. Pike, "Diary of an Expedition," November 23 and 24, 1806, ZPJ, 1:349–350.

20. Pike, "Diary of an Expedition," November 23–24, 1806, ZPJ, 1:349–350; Pike, "Dissertation on Louisiana," ZPJ, 2:26–27.

21. Pike, "Diary of an Expedition," November 24, 26, and December 3, 1806, ZPJ, 1:350, 353. Pike again calculated the altitude on December 3, recording it to be more than 18,000 feet.

22. Pike, "Diary of an Expedition," November 26, 1806, ZPJ, 1:350. Pike drew no map of his course to the summit of the peak, and his route has eluded historians for two hundred years. Inspired by the coming bicentennial of his expedition, numerous Pike enthusiasts in Colorado began working on the problem in the early twenty-first century. The description of Pike's climb in this paragraph and the next is based on this excellent new work as well as my own hiking along Pike's path. Frank Sanders, "The Pike Expedition and the Strange Anglo-American Entrada to the Spanish Southwest," unpublished manuscript in author's possession, 2006, 125–150; Dave Philipps, "What Peak Did Pike Climb? Lawyer Tracks Final Destination of Wayward Trek to Mount Rosa," Colorado Springs *Gazette*, April 25, 2004.

23. Pike, "Diary of an Expedition," November 26, 1806, ZPJ, 1:350–351.

24. Pike, "Diary of an Expedition," November 26–29, 1806, ZPJ, 1:350–351.

25. The men's attire was inadequate for the season because upon departing St. Louis, Pike expected to cross the Plains and return before winter set in.

26. Pike, "Diary of an Expedition," November 30, December 1–3, 1806, ZPJ, 1:351–353.

27. John Keegan, *The Face of Battle* (New York: Viking, 1976), 71–73, 114, 183–192; S. L. A. Marshall, *Men Against Fire: The Problem of Battle Command* (Norman: University of Oklahoma Press, 2000), 105, 165; Charles Royster, *A Revolutionary People at War: The Continental Army and American Character, 1775–1783* (Chapel Hill: University of North Carolina Press, 1979), 351–353; Fred Anderson, *A People's Army: Massachusetts Soldiers and Society in the Seven Years' War* (New York: W. W. Norton & Company, 1985), 159–164; Sarah Knott, *Sensibility and the American Revolution* (Chapel Hill: University of North Carolina Press, 2009), 163; William E. Foley, *Wilderness Journey: A Life of William Clark* (Columbia: University of Missouri Press, 2004), 105; James M. McPherson, *For Cause and Comrades: Why Men Fought in the Civil War* (New York: Oxford University Press, 1997), 82–89.

28. Pike, "Diary of an Expedition," December 9, 11–14, 1806, ZPJ, 1:356–358.

29. Pike, "Diary of an Expedition," December 13, 15–16, 1806, ZPJ, 1:357–358.

30. Pike, "Diary of an Expedition," December 16 and 18, 1806, ZPJ, 1:358–359.

31. Pike, "Diary of an Expedition," December 19–20, 22–24, 1806, ZPJ, 1:359–361. A roadside plaque and picnic site marks an approximate location of Pike's campsite for travelers on US Highway 285, just north of Poncha Springs.

32. Pike, "Diary of an Expedition," December 25, 1806, ZPJ, 1:361–362.

33. Pike, "Diary of an Expedition," December 26–28, 1806, ZPJ, 1:362–363.

34. Pike, "Diary of an Expedition," December 29–31, January 3, 1807, ZPJ, 1:363–364.

35. Pike, "Diary of an Expedition," January 1–3, 1807, ZPJ, 1:363–364.

36. Pike, "Diary of an Expedition," January 4, 1807, ZPJ, 1:364.

37. Pike, "Diary of an Expedition," January 4–5, 1807, ZPJ, 1:364–366; T. S. Eliot, "Little Gidding," No. 4 in *Four Quartets*, 1943, http://www.columbia.edu/itc/history/winter/w3206/edit/tseliotlittlegidding.html (accessed July 22, 2013).

38. Antillon, Isidoro de, *"La America Septentrional desde su extremo Norte hasta 10 [degrees] de Latitud, segun Las ultimas observaciones y descrubrimientos, para el Curso de Geografía,"* 1802, reproduced in Warren L. Cook, *Flood Tide of Empire: Spain and the Pacific Northwest, 1543–1819* (New Haven: London: Yale University Press, 1973).

39. Pike, "Diary of an Expedition," December 14, 1806, and January 9, 1807, ZPJ, 1:358, 367.

40. Pike, "Diary of an Expedition," January 9, 1807, ZPJ, 1:367; T. S. Eliot, "Little Gidding."

41. Pike, "Diary of an Expedition," January 13–14, 1807, ZPJ, 1:368.

41. Pike, "Diary of an Expedition," January 17, 1807, ZPJ, 1:368–369.

43. Pike, "Diary of an Expedition," January 17, 1807, ZPJ, 1:369.

44. Pike, "Diary of an Expedition," January 17, 1807, ZPJ, 1:369; Heggers, et al., "Experimental and Clinical Observations," *Annals of Emergency Medicine* 16 (September 1987), 1056; Bruce C. Paton, "Zebulon Pike in Colorado: His Struggle to Survive," in *"To Spare No Pains": Zebulon Montgomery Pike and his 1806–1807 Southwest Expedition*, ed. Tim Blevins, et al. (Colorado Springs: Pikes Peak Library District and Colorado Springs Pioneers Museum, 2007), 108–109; Bruce C. Paton, *Lewis and Clark: Doctors in the Wilderness* (Golden, Colo.: Fulcrum Publishing, 2001), 100–106; David Dary, *Frontier Medicine: From the Atlantic to the Pacific, 1492–1941* (New York: Alfred A. Knopf, 2008), 44–48, 85, 93–94, and 139; Meriwether Lewis, William Clark, et al., September 4, 1806, entry in *The Journals of the Lewis and Clark Expedition*, ed. Gary Moulton (Lincoln, Neb.: University of Nebraska Press/University of Nebraska-Lincoln Libraries-Electronic Text Center, 2005), http://lewisandclarkjournals.unl.edu/read/?_xmlsrc=1805-01-10.xml&_xslsrc=LCstyles.xsl (accessed October 7, 2011).

45. Author's conversation with physician Dr. Douglas Krohn, Fort Collins, Colorado, November 30, 2011; Paton, "Zebulon Pike in Colorado," 106–107; John Leach, *Survival Psychology* (New York: New York University Press, 1994), 87–96. One of the first systematic studies of human starvation was conducted at the University of Minnesota in 1944–1945. Thirty-two men were placed on semi-starvation diets for twenty-four weeks, during which the physical and psychological effects they exhibited were monitored. The men, whose ages ranged from twenty to thirty-three years and averaged 25.5 years, very closely resembled the age of Pike's men. Their semi-starvation diets included twice-a-day feedings of suboptimal caloric intake, which is somewhat different from

Pike's party's experience between December 25, 1806, and January 27, 1807, during which several multi-day stretches with no food at all were punctuated by feasting for a day or two after a kill. The study also entailed daily or weekly exercise, including various chores, walking, cycling, and periodic bursts of maximum exertion; taken together these added up to an active lifestyle, comparable though not quite equal to the level of physical activity Pike's men endured. Along with the works of Paton and Leach, the Minnesota study's results regarding the effects of the early phases of semi-starvation diets forms the basis for much of my discussion of the impact of hunger on Pike and his comrades. See especially, Ancel Keys et al., *The Biology of Human Starvation* (Minneapolis: University of Minnesota Press, 1950), 1:66–74, 106 and 2:808–826, 835–837, 851–863; Pike, "Diary of an Expedition," January 18, 1807, ZPJ, 1:369.

46. Paton, "Zebulon Pike in Colorado," 103, 107–108; Leach, *Survival Psychology*, 61, 74–76; Keys et al., *Biology of Human Starvation*, 1:289, 714–715; Pike, "Diary of an Expedition," January 19, 1807, ZPJ, 1:369.

47. Pike, "Diary of an Expedition," January 19, 1807, ZPJ, 1:370.

48. Pike, "Diary of an Expedition," January 20–21, 1807, ZPJ, 1:370–371. Thanks to Fred Anderson for providing context on the military practice of the time; Paton, "Zebulon Pike in Colorado," 106–109.

49. Pike, "Diary of an Expedition," January 22, 1807, ZPJ, 1:370.

50. Pike, "Diary of an Expedition," January 23–24, 1807, ZPJ, 1:371; Leach, *Survival Psychology*, 60–66.

51. Dary, *Frontier Medicine*, 49, 85–94; Pike, "Diary of an Expedition," January 24, 1807, ZPJ, 1: 371–372.

52. Pike, "Diary of an Expedition," January 24, 1807, ZPJ, 1: 371–372.

53. Jack Drummond, foreword to *Biology of Human Starvation*, 1:xiii-xiv; Purcell, *Sealed with Blood*, 49–91; Royster, *A Revolutionary People*, 8, 360–368; John Resch, *Suffering Soldiers: Revolutionary War Veterans, Moral Sentiment, and Political Culture in the Early Republic* (Amherst: University of Massachusetts Press, 1999), 5.

54. Pike, "Diary of an Expedition," January 25, 27–28, 1807, ZPJ, 1:373–374.

55. Pike, "Diary of an Expedition," January 29–31, 1807, ZPJ, 1:374.

56. Pike, "Diary of an Expedition," January 31 and February 6, 1807, ZPJ, 1:374, 377; Carrol Joe Carter, *Pike in Colorado* (Fort Collins, Colo.: The Old Army Press, 1978), 41.

57. James Wilkinson, St. Louis, to Henry Dearborn, August 10, 1805, TP, 13:183; Charles Gratiot, St. Louis, to William Morrison, Kaskaskia, May 12, 1804, in *Letters of the Lewis and Clark Expedition with Related Documents, 1783–1854*, ed. Donald Jackson (Urbana: University of Illinois Press, 1962), 189; Pike, "Diary of an Expedition," February 6–7 and March 7, 1807, ZPJ, 1:376–379, 403; "Santa Fe Trail Map," ZPJ, 1:Plate 60.

58. Pike, "Diary of an Expedition," February 7–17, 1807, ZPJ, 1:378–381; Paton, *Lewis and Clark*, 104.

59. Pike, "Diary of an Expedition," February 17, 1807, ZPJ, 1:381; Nicole Eustace, *Passion Is the Gale: Emotion, Power, and the Coming of the American Revolution* (Chapel Hill: University of North Carolina Press, 2008), 244–249, 261; Knott, *Sensibility and the American Revolution*, 235.

60. Pike, "Diary of an Expedition," February 16, 19, and 26, 1807, ZPJ, 1:379–384.

61. Pike, "Diary of an Expedition," February 26, 1807, ZPJ, 1:384–385.

62. Crichton, "Zeb Pike," 465.

CHAPTER 6

1. Zebulon Montgomery Pike, "Diary of an Expedition," March 3–4, 1807, in *The Journals of Zebulon Montgomery Pike* (hereafter cited as ZPJ), ed. Donald Jackson (Norman: University of Oklahoma Press, 1966), 1:391–396.

2. Pike, "Diary of an Expedition," March 1–2, 1807, ZPJ, 1:387–388.

3. Pike, "Diary of an Expedition," March 2, 1807, ZPJ, 1:388–391.

4. Pike, "Diary of an Expedition," March 2, 1807, ZPJ, 1:390. "Antient" is Pike's spelling.

5. Rosalind Z. Rock, "Dying Quijote: Nemesio Salcedo and the Last Years of Spain in the Internal Provinces," PhD diss., University of New Mexico, 1981, 173–190.

6. Pike, "Diary of an Expedition," February 28 and March 2, 1807, ZPJ, 1:386, 388–389; Josiah Gregg, *Commerce of the Prairies: Or the Journal of a Santa Fé Trader, during Eight Expeditions Across The Great Western Prairies, and a Residence of Nearly Nine Years in Northern Mexico* (New York: Henry G. Langley, 1844), 2; Joaquín del Real Alencaster, Santa Fe, to Nemesio Salcedo, July 7, 1805, and Salcedo, Chihuahua, to Alencaster, September 9, 1805, SGM, legajo 1787–1807, 1–10.

7. Pike, "Diary of an Expedition," March 2, 1807, ZPJ, 1:391.

8. Salcedo, Chihuahua, to Pedro Cevallos, February 5, 1805, SpAGI (Aud. Guad. 398), AT, quoted in Warren L. Cook, *Flood Tide of Empire: Spain and the Pacific Northwest, 1543–1819* (New Haven/London: Yale University Press, 1973), 465; The Barón de Carondolet to Don Luis de las Casas, November 24, 1794, in *Louisiana under the Rule of Spain, France, and the United States, 1785–1807*, ed. James Alexander Robertson (1910–1911; repr., New York: Books for Libraries Press, 1969), 1:298; Cook, *Flood Tide of Empire*, 434.

9. Cook, *Flood Tide of Empire*, 249, 434, 475–476.

10. Cook, *Flood Tide of Empire*, 436–437, 475–476; Salcedo, Chihuahua, to José de Iturrigaray, August 14, 1804, Archivo General y Público, Mexico, Provincias Internas, Archivo General y Público, Mexico, Provincias Internas (hereafter cited as AGP), *tomo* 200, 324; Joaquín del Real Alencaster to José de Iturrigaray,

April 1, 1807, AGP, *tomo* 200, 87–88; Joaquín del Real Alencaster, Santa Fe, to Nemesio Salcedo, October 11, 1805, SGM, *legajo* 1787–1807, 14–16; Marqués de Casa Calvo, Nueva Orleans, June 27, 1804, to Nemesio Salcedo, AGP *tomo* 200, 318; Joaquín del Real Alencaster, Santa Fe, to Nemesio Salcedo; Joaqín de Zarauz, New York, to Aguirre, January 26, 1807, AGP *tomo* 200, 94; Joaquín de Zarauz, New York, to Ciriaco González Carvajal, January 27, 1807, AGP *tomo* 200, 95–96; Rock, "Dying Quijote," 162–163.

11. Cook, *Flood Tide of Empire*, 460–472, 476–483.

12. Alencaster to Salcedo, [February 16, 1807], ZPJ, 2:165–166.

13. Pike, "Diary of an Expedition," March 2, 1807, ZPJ, 1:386.

14. Pike, "Diary of an Expedition," March 3, 1807, ZPJ, 1:392.

15. Pike, "Diary of an Expedition," March 3, 1807, ZPJ, 1:393–394.

16. Pike, "Diary of an Expedition," February 26, March 2, 4, and 7, 1807, ZPJ, 1:385, 388, 394, and 405.

17. Pike, "Diary of an Expedition," March 4, 1807, ZPJ, 1:394; Pike to Real Alencaster, March 3, and Real Alencaster to Pike, March 3, 1807, ZPJ, 2:167–168.

18. Pike, "Diary of an Expedition," March 4, 1807, ZPJ, 1:395–396.

19. Pike, "Diary of an Expedition," March 5, 1807, ZPJ, 1:397.

20. Pike, "Diary of an Expedition," March 4, 1807, ZPJ, 1:396–397.

21. Pike, "Diary of an Expedition," March 4, 1807, ZPJ, 1:397–398.

22. Pike, "Diary of an Expedition," March 6, 1807, ZPJ, 1:399.

23. Pike, "Diary of an Expedition," March 6, 1807, ZPJ, 1:400.

24. Pike, "Diary of an Expedition," March 7, 1807, ZPJ, 1:400–401.

25. Pike, "Diary of an Expedition," March 7, 1807, ZPJ, 1:402–404.

26. Real Alencaster to Salcedo, [February 16, 1807], ZPJ, 2:165–166.

27. Pike, "Diary of an Expedition," March 7, 1807, ZPJ, 1:402–404.

28. Pike, "Diary of an Expedition," March 8, 1807, ZPJ, 1:405–406.

29. Pike, "Diary of an Expedition," March 8–9, 23, 1807, ZPJ, 1:405–407, 410.

30. Pike, "Diary of an Expedition," March 5, 7, 12, 21, 27, 1807, ZPJ, 1:398–399, 401, 407, 409, 411, 411n212.

31. Pike, "Diary of an Expedition," March 12, 1807, ZPJ, 1:407.

32. Oakah L. Jones, Jr., *Nueva Vizcaya: Heartland of the Spanish Frontier* (Albuquerque: University of New Mexico Press, 1988), 229, 249; Cheryl English Martin, *Governance and Society in Colonial Mexico: Chihuahua in the Eighteenth Century* (Stanford: Stanford University Press, 1996), 1; Susan M. Deeds, "Colonial Chihuahua: Peoples and Frontiers in Flux," in *New Views of Borderlands History*, ed. by Robert H. Jackson (Albuquerque: University of New Mexico Press, 1998), 33.

33. Martin, *Governance and Society*, 29–46; Deeds, "Colonial Chihuahua," 34.

34. Pike, "Diary of an Expedition," April 2, 1807, ZPJ, 1:412–413; Rock, "Dying Quijote," 31–32.

35. Juan Pedro Walker, "Map of the Route Through New Mexico," [*c*. 1805], 2049 Huntington Manuscripts (hereafter cited as HM), Huntington Library, San Marino, California; Juan Pedro Walker, "Mapa Geografico…de las Provincias de Texas, Coahuila, Nueva Biscaya y Nuevo Mexico…," 1805,2050 HM; "[Mapa de la] Expedicion de S. Anto. De Bejar a Santa Fe…" [March 30–May 19, 1808], 2051 HM; Pike, "Diary of an Expedition," April 2, 1807, ZPJ, 1:413.

36. Salcedo to Wilkinson, April 8, 1807, ZPJ, 2:185–186; Alencaster, Santa Fe, to Jose de Iturrigaray, April 1, 1807, Nemesio Salcedo to Jose de Iturrigaray, April 20, 1807, Nemsio Salcedo, Chihuahua, to William C. C. Claiborne, September 18, 1806, Nemesio Salcedo, Chihuahua, to Jose de Iturrigaray August 14, 1804, all in AGP, *tomo* 200, 87–90, 134–141, 324; Salcedo to Casa Yrujo, April 8, 1807, ZPJ, 2: 187–188.

37. Pike, "Diary of an Expedition," April 2–28, 1807, ZPJ, 1:412–422.

38. Pike, "Diary of an Expedition," April 4, 1807, ZPJ, 1:414–415.

39. Pike, "Diary of an Expedition," April 5, 1807, ZPJ, 1:415; Pike, "Geographical, Statistical, and General Observations," ZPJ 2:83–84.

40. Pike, "Diary of an Expedition," April 9, 1807, ZPJ, 1:416–417; Pike to Salcedo, April 4, 1807, ZPJ, 2:171–173. This letter was published in the 1810 edition of Pike's journals. There is some inconsistency about dates. Pike's journal records his meeting with Fero as taking place on April 9, but this letter describing the encounter is dated the fourth.

41. Pike, "Diary of an Expedition," April 20 and 27, 1807, ZPJ, 1:417–418, 422; Pike, "Geographical, Statistical, and General Observations," ZPJ 2:93.

42. Pike, "Diary of an Expedition," April 24, 1807, ZPJ, 1:419.

43. Rock, "Dying Quijote," 198–219; Jones, Jr., *Nueva Vizcaya*, 207–215.

44. Pike, "Geographical, Statistical, and General Observations," ZPJ 2:95–97.

45. Robinson to Salcedo, April 8 and 23, 1807, ZPJ, 2: 192–193, 204–206.

46. Robinson to Kingsbury, July 5, 1807, ZPJ, 2:245; Donald Jackson, ed., *The Journals of Zebulon Montgomery Pike* (Norman: University of Oklahoma Press, 1966), 2:206; David E. Narrett, "Liberation and Conquest: John Hamilton Robinson and U.S. Adventurism Toward Mexico, 1806–1819," *Western Historical Quarterly* 40 (Spring 2009): 33, 48–49; Article in *Lexington Reporter* reprinted in *Missouri Gazette*, St. Louis, May 24, 1817, folder 9, DM.

47. Real Alencaster to Salcedo, April 7, 1807, ZPJ, 2:181–184; Nemesio Salcedo, Chihuahua, to Joaquín del Real Alencaster, April 19, 1807, SGM, legajo 1787–1807, 27–29; William E. Foley, "James Wilkinson: Pike's Mentor and Jefferson's Capricious Point Man in the West," in *Zebulon Pike, Thomas Jefferson, and the Opening of the American West*, ed. Matthew L. Harris and Jay H. Buckley (Norman: University of Oklahoma Press, 2012), 206.

48. Pike, "Journal of a Voyage," November 2, 1805, ZPJ, 1:53; Pike, "Diary of an Expedition," February 19, 1807, ZPJ, 1:382; Jackson ed., *Journals*, 2:209n; Jack Kyle Cooper, *Zebulon Montgomery Pike's Great Western Adventure, 1806–1807* (Colorado Springs: Clausen Books, 2007).

49. Real Alencaster to Salcedo, April 7, 1807, ZPJ, 2:194.

50. Real Alencaster to Salcedo, April 15, 1807, ZPJ, 2:199; "The Murder of Theodore Miller," 1807, ZPJ, 2:215, 217, 219.

51. "The Murder of Theodore Miller," 1807, ZPJ, 2:209–224; "American Captives at Liberty," *St. Louis Enquirer*, March 31, 1821, DM folder 8.

52. Pike, "Diary of an Expedition," May 6, 1807, ZPJ, 1:425.

53. Pike, "Diary of an Expedition," May 19, 29, and June 1, 1807, ZPJ, 1:429, 431–435.

54. Pike, "Diary of an Expedition," May 2, 11, 14, and 17, 1807, ZPJ, 1:424, 426, 428–429.

55. Pike, "Diary of an Expedition," June 9, 13, 1807, ZPJ, 1:438, 441.

56. "Never" is in the original; Pike means "ever"; Pike to Kingsbury, July 20, 1807, ZPJ, 2:252.

CHAPTER 7

1. Pike, "Diary of an Expedition," July 1, 1807, *The Journals of Zebulon Montgomery Pike* (hereafter cited as ZPJ), ed. Donald Jackson (Norman: University of Oklahoma Press, 1966), 1:447–448; W. Eugene Hollon, *The Lost Pathfinder: Zebulon Montgomery Pike* (Norman: University of Oklahoma Press, 1949), 165–167.

2. U.S. Congress, *Annals of the Congress of the United States, 1789–1824*, 10th Cong., 1st sess., 1658–60, available at http://memory.loc.gov/ammem/amlaw/lwac.html (accessed July 22, 2013); *U.S. House Journal*, 10th Cong., 1st sess., February 22, 1808, 189, available at http://memory.loc.gov/ammem/amlaw/lwac.html (accessed July 22, 2013); U. S. Congress, House, Committee on Compensation to Capt. Zebulon Pike and His Companions, "Compensation to the Persons Engaged in the Several Exploring Expeditions under Captain Pike," March 10, 1808, *American State Papers* (hereafter cited as ASM), 37, Miscellaneous 1:719, available at http://infoweb.newsbank.com (accessed March 7, 2011); U. S. Congress, House, Committee on Compensation to Capt. Zebulon Pike and His Companions, "Compensation to the Persons Engaged in the Several Exploring Expeditions under Captain Pike," December 16, 1808, ASM 37, Miscellaneous 1:942–944; *Monitor* (Washington, D.C.), June 13, 1809, Early American Newspapers, Series II: (1758–1900), University of Colorado, Boulder (hereafter cited as EAN-2), 2; Donald Jackson, ed., *The Journals of Zebulon Montgomery Pike* (Norman: University of Oklahoma Press, 1966), 357–358.

3. Bates to Dearborn, May 17, 1807, ZPJ, 2:227; Wilkinson to Pike, May 20, 1807, ZPJ, 2:228.

4. Zebulon Pike, Natchitoches, to Nemesio Salcedo, August 20, 1807, ZPJ, 2:264–266; Pike, Natchitoches, to Zebulon Pike, August 12, 1807, ZPJ, 2:259–260; Pike, Natchitoches, to James Wilkinson, July 5, 1807, ZPJ, 2:238–244; Pike,

Natchitoches, to Henry Dearborn, July 15, 1807, ZPJ, 2:249–250; Zebulon Pike, Natchitoches, to the *Natchez Herald*, July 22, 1807, ZPJ, 2:255–258; "John Sibley's Council with the Comanches," [August 18, 1807], ZPJ, 2:260–262; Hollon, *Lost Pathfinder*, 173.

5. Pike to Zebulon Pike, August 12, 1807, ZPJ, 2:259–260; Pike to Wilkinson, July 5, 1807, ZPJ, 2:238–244; Pike, New Orleans, to Zebulon Pike, September 17, 1807, ZPJ, 2:271–272; italics in original.

6. James Wilkinson, Richmond, to Thomas Jefferson, September 13, 1807, ZPJ, 2:271; Pike, New York, to Jonathan Williams, October 19, 1807, ZPJ, 2:274–275; Amos Stoddard, Fort Adams, to Nicholas Gilman, September 4, 1807, ZPJ, 2:269–270; Samuel L. Mitchill, Washington, to Catherine Mitchill, November 7, 1807, Samuel L. Mitchill Papers, William L. Clements Library, University of Michigan, Ann Arbor, Michigan (hereafter cited as MP); Pike to Dearborn, Washington, December 17, 1807, ZPJ, 2:282–283; Pike, Baltimore, to Caesar A. Rodney, November 12, 180[7], Zebulon Montgomery Pike Collection, Chicago Historical Society, Chicago, Illinois (hereafter cited as ZMPCHS); "genious," "claim and equality," and "principals" in the original.

7. Pike, Washington, to Jefferson, February 3, 1808, ZPJ, 2:292–294; Jefferson, Washington, to Pike, November 5, 1807, ZPJ, 2:278; Samuel L. Mitchill, Washington, to Catherine Mitchill, November 9, 1807, MP; Jefferson, Washington, to Charles Willson Peale, November 6, 1807, ZPJ, 2:278–279. "It's" is Jefferson's error.

8. Buckner F. Melton, *Aaron Burr: Conspiracy to Treason* (New York: John Wiley & Sons, Inc., 2002), 1; Timothy Kibby, "Statement of Facts," July 6, 1807, ZPJ, 2:246–249.

9. *American State Papers* 37, Misc. 1: 548, 555, 571, 582; James Ripley Jacobs, *Tarnished Warrior: Major General James Wilkinson* (New York: The MacMillan Company, 1938), 218, applies this logic to Bruff, though it relates even better to Kibby, whom Wilkinson did not know at all and over whom he held no military authority.

10. Nancy Isenberg, *Fallen Founder: The Life of Aaron Burr* (New York: Viking, 2007), 272.

11. "General Wilkinson," *Annals of Congress*, 10th Cong., 1st sess., January 7, 1808, 1333–1357; Dearborn to Burbeck, January 2, 1808, ASM 37, Misc. 1:706; Details of the various Wilkinson investigations can be followed in the documents republished in Arthur M. Schlesinger, Jr., and Roger Bruns, ed. *Congress Investigates: a Documented History, 1872–1974* (1975: repr., New York: Chelsea House, 1983), 1:103–243, and in Jacobs, *Tarnished Warrior*, 240–275; examples of Wilkinson's dealings with Spaniards include (but are hardly limited to) James Wilkinson to Esteban Miro, 1787, 57, legajo Cuba 2373, Archivo General de Indias, Seville, Spain; Vicente Folch, "Reflections on Louisiana," 1804, in *Louisiana under the Rule of Spain, France, and the United States, 1785–1807*,

ed. James Alexander Robertson (1910–1911; repr., New York: Books for Libraries Press, 1969), 2:339–343.

12. Pike, Baltimore, to Caesar A. Rodney, n.d., ZMPCHS; "Interrogatories proposed to Major Z. M. Pike," [November 17, 1808], ZPJ, 2:331–336; *Weekly Register* (hereafter cited as *NWR*), October 12, 1811; Pike, Baton Rouge, to Caesar A. Rodney, November 29, 1811, ZMPCHS; Pike, Cantonment Saranac, to Caesar A. Rodney, January 24, 1813, ZMPCHS; Pike to Rodney, November 29, 1811, ZMPCHS.

13. "The Act Compensating Lewis and Clark," March 3, 1807, in *Letters of the Lewis and Clark Expedition*, 377; *Annals of Congress*, 10th Cong., 1st sess., 1658–1659; Pike to the *National Intelligencer*, February 22, 1808, ZPJ, 2:299; Pike to Dearborn, February 22, 1808, ZPJ, 2: 299–300.

14. M. R. Montgomery, *Jefferson and the Gun-Men: How the West Was Almost Lost* (New York: Three Rivers Press, 2000), 213–214, 255, 270–271, and 286; Frank Sanders, "The Pike Expedition and the Strange Anglo-American Entrada to the Spanish Southwest," unpublished manuscript in author's possession, 2006, 91–92, 172, 192; and Isaac Joslin Cox, *The Early Exploration of Louisiana* (Cincinnati: University of Cincinnati Press, 1906).

15. "Burr's Conspiracy—Arrests," January 26, 1807, ASM, 37, Misc.1:472.

16. Pike to Dearborn, February 22, 1808, ZPJ, 2:299–300.

17. Dearborn to Pike, February 24, 1808, ZPJ, 2:300–301; "Compensation to Persons Engaged in the Several Exploring Expeditions Under Captain Pike," March 10 and December 16, 1808, ASM, 37, Misc. 1: 719, 944; Pike to editor of *Baltimore American and Daily Advertiser*, May 15, and Ballenger to Wilkinson, April 3, 1808, in *Monitor* (Washington, D.C.), May 24, 1808, EAN-2, 4; Dearborn to Montgomery, December 7, 1808, ZPJ, 355.

18. U.S. Senate, Committee on Military Affairs, *Report to accompany bill S. No. 50*, January 15, 1846, in Amos Holton, *The Case of Mrs. Clara H. Pike Widow of Gen. Z. Montgomery Pike, Now Pending Before the U.S. Congress…* (Washington, [D.C.]: T. Barnard, Printer, 1846), (hereafter cited as CHP), 15; Jackson, ed., *Journals*, 2:358.

19. Pike to Zebulon Pike, September 17, 1807, ZPJ, 2:271–272; Pike, Washington City, to George W. Pike, Lawrence Burgh, Indiana Territory, February 25, 1808, MS2150, Zebulon Montgomery Pike Letters, Western Reserve Historical Society, Cleveland, Ohio (hereinafter cited as ZMPL).

20. Steven Watts, *The Republic Reborn: War and the Making of Liberal America, 1790–1820* (Baltimore: The Johns Hopkins University Press, 1987); *Annals of Congress*, 12th Cong., 1st sess., 870; Melish quoted in Watts, *Republic Reborn*, 5.

21. Niles quoted in Watts, *Republic Reborn*, 74; *Aurora* quoted in Watts, *Republic Reborn*, 220; *Annals of Congress*, 12th Cong., 1st sess., 874.

22. Francis B. Heitman, *Historical Register and Dictionary of the United States Army, from Its Organization, September 29, 1789, to March 2, 1903* (Washington, D.C.:

US GPO, 1903), 1:792; Pike, New Orleans, to George W. Pike, West Point, August 17, 1809, ZMPL; Pike, Canton, Washington, to Zebulon Pike [senior], Lawrence Burgh, Indiana Territory, July 10, 1810, ZMPL.

23. Pike, Baltimore, to George W. Pike, Poughkeepsie, N.Y., December 20, 1808, ZMPL; Alan Taylor, *The Civil War of 1812: American Citizens, British Subjects, Irish Rebels, and Indian Allies* (New York: Alfred A. Knopf, 2010), 101–123.

24. Taylor, *Civil War of 1812*, 101; *Annals of Congress*, 12th Cong., 1st sess., 873–874.

25. Gabriel H. Lovett, *Napoleon and the Birth of Modern Spain: The Challenge to the Old Order* (New York University Press, 1965), 1:98–124.

26. Pike, Canton, Washington, to Zebulon Pike [senior], Lawrence Burgh, Indiana Territory, July 10, 1810, ZMPL.

27. Watts, *Republic Reborn*, 150, 153, 162–163; *Annals of Congress*, 12th Cong., 1st sess., 874–875; Richard Rush, "An Oration, delivered by Richard Rush on the 4th of July, 1812, in the Hall of the House of Representatives, at the Capitol, Washington," Early American Imprints, 2nd Ser. (hereinafter cited as EAI-2), number 26671, http://infoweb.newsbank.com (accessed May 20, 2011), 4, 39, 46–47; Pike, Belle Fontaine, to Dearborn, August 18, 1808, Adjutant General's Office Records, RG 94, Letters Received (hereafter cited as AGOR), 1805–1821, Microcopy Publication M566, NARADC, roll 1, frames 197–201.

28. Rush, "Oration," 42–43, 47; *Annals of Congress*, 12th Cong., 1st sess., 872, 875.

29. Pike, Natchitoches, to Wilkinson, July 5, 1807, ZPJ, 2:240–242; Pike, "Diary of a Tour," May 1, 1807, ZPJ, 1:424; Pike to Dearborn, July 15, 1807, ZPJ, 2:249; Pike, Washington, to Dearborn, January 26, 1808, ZPJ, 2:286.

30. Pike, "Diary of a Tour," April 29 and May 1, 1807, ZPJ, 1:423–424; Thomas P. Slaughter, *Exploring Lewis and Clark: Reflections on Men and Wilderness* (New York: Alfred A. Knopf, 2003).

31. Pike, Philadelphia, to Dearborn, May 27, 1808, ZPJ, 2:321; Z. M. Pike, "A Dissertation on the Soil, Rivers, Productions, Animal and Vegetable, with General Notes on the Internal Parts of Louisiana, Compiled from Observations Made by Capt. Z.M. Pike, in a late tour from the Mouth of the Missouri, to the Head Waters of the Arkansaw and Rio Del Norte in the Years 1806 and 1807; Including Observations on the Aborigines of the Country," in *An Account of Expeditions to the Sources of the Mississippi and Through the Western Parts of Louisiana, to the Sources of the Arkansaw, Kans, La Platte, and Pierre Juan, Rivers; Performed by Order of the Government of the United States during the Years 1805, 1806, and 1807. And a Tour Through the Interior Parts of New Spain, When Conducted Through These Provinces, by Order of the Captain-General in the Year 1807* (hereafter cited as AOE), (Philadelphia: C. & A. Conrad, & Co., 1810), Appendix to Part II, 2, 18; Zebulon Montgomery Pike, *Exploratory Travels Through the Western Territories of North America: Comprising a Voyage from St. Louis, on the Mississippi, to the Source of That River, and a Journey Through the Interior of Louisiana and the North-Eastern Provinces of New Spain. Performed in*

the Years 1805, 1806, 1807, *by Order of the Government of the United States* (hereafter cited as ET), (London: Longman, Hurst, Rees, Orme, and Brown, 1811), vi; Jackson, ed., *Journals*, 2:321–322; "Prospectus of Pike's Expedition," June 8, 1808, ZPJ, 2:322–323. The prospectus was reprinted numerous times in many papers. See for example, "Prospectus of Pike Expedition," *Monitor* (Washington, D.C.), October 6, 8, November 24, and December 31, 1808, and January 3, 19, and February 4, 1809, Early American Newspapers, Series I: (1690–1876), University of Wyoming, Laramie (hereafter cited as EAN-1); Pike, Pittsburgh, to Madison, June 20, 1808, ZPJ, 2:324; Jackson, ed., *Journals*, 1:xxvi.

32. Z. M. Pike, AOE. Page numbers for the quotations below are given for the more readily accessible ZPJ. The 1810 version I consulted to construct this paragraph can be found at HEH; Pike, "Dissertation…on…Louisiana," ZPJ, 2:26–28, 37. "Desarts" is in the original; Pike, "Geographical, Statistical, and General Observations," ZPJ, 2:84, 96–97.

33. Pike, AOE, 3, 5; Pike, "Diary of an Expedition," February 17 and April 9, 1807, ZPJ, 1:381, 416; Pike, "Sketch of an Expedition," AOE, Appendix to Part III, 77; also in *The Expeditions of Zebulon Montgomery Pike, To Headwaters of the Mississippi River, Through Louisiana Territory, and in New Spain, During the Years 1805–6–7*, (hereafter cited as ZPC), ed. Elliott Coues (New York: Francis P. Harper, 1895), 2:852–853; Nicole Eustace, *Passion Is the Gale: Emotion, Power, and the Coming of the American Revolution* (Chapel Hill: University of North Carolina Press, 2008), 244–249, 261; Sarah Knott, *Sensibility and the American Revolution* (Chapel Hill: University of North Carolina Press, 2009), 235.

34. Jackson, ed., *Journals*, xxvi; John Conrad, editorial noted in "To the Public," AOE, 5; Jefferson to Alexander von Humboldt, December 6, 1813, ZPJ, 2:387–388.

35. Joseph Ballenger to James Wilkinson, April 3, 1808, in *Monitor* (Washington, D.C.), May 24, 1808, EAN-2. 4; John Graham to George Ewing, May 26, 1808, ZPJ, 2:319–320; Dearborn to Montgomery, December 7, 1808, ASM, 37, Misc. 1:942; "Communicated to the House of Representatives," December 16, 1808, ASM, 37, Misc.1:942; Rees, "Advertisement," January 28, 1811, ET, v, ix.

36. "Pike's Exploratory Travels," *The Analectic Magazine Containing Selections from Foreign Reviews and Magazines Together with Original Miscellaneous Compositions and a Naval Chronicle* 3 (February 1814): 89–104.

37. Heitman, *Historical Register*, 1:792; Pike, Washington, to Dearborn, March 11, April 4, and April 14, 1808, AGOR, 1:177–184, 186–188; Pike to Z[ebulon] Pike [senior], April 19, 1808, ZMPL; Joseph Bloomfield, Trenton, attestation of Pike's New Jersey Birth, March 23, 1808, AGOR, 1:184–185; James Wilkinson, *Memoirs of My Own Times* (Philadelphia: Abraham Small, 1816), 2:468–470; Jacobs, *Tarnished Warrior*, 260; documents in AGOR, 1:225–311.

38. Pike to Rodney, November 29, 1811, ZMPCHS.

39. Pike to Rodney, November 29, 1811, ZMPCHS; *Annals of Congress*, 12th Cong., 1st sess., 859.

40. Pike, Washington, to William Eustis, June 4, 1812, ZMPCHS; Pike, Washington, to Alex[ander] Macomb, July 4, 1812, ZMPCHS; Heitman, *Historical Register*, 1:792; Pike, Trenton, to [James] Wilkinson, July 24, 1812, ZMPCHS.

41. Taylor, *Civil War of 1812*; Hollon, "Zebulon Montgomery Pike," 264.

42. Hollon, "Zebulon Montgomery Pike," 265; Pike, Cantonment Saranac, to Caesar A. Rodney, January 24, 1813, ZMPCHS; Taylor, *Civil War of 1812*, 321–324; *NWR*, October 16, 1813, 116–117.

43. *"Military," NWR*, January 30, 1813, 344; Pike, Cantonment Saranac, to Albon Mann, February 28, 1813, *Bloomfield-Pike Letterbook*, William L. Clements Library, University of Michigan, Ann Arbor, Michigan (hereafter cited as BPL); Pike to Rodney, January 24, 1813, ZMPCHS.

44. Hitsman, *Incredible War of 1812*, 136; Pike, Chautauqua, N.Y., to Colonel Pierce, March 7, 1813, BPL; Pike, Hopkington, N.Y., to Dearborn, March 8, 1813, BPL; Pike, Sackets Harbor, to John Chandler, April 8, 1813, BPL; Pike, Sackets Harbor, to [Alexander] Richards, March 25, 1813, BPL; Taylor, *Civil War of 1812*, 269–279; Pike, Sackets Harbor, to Jacob Jennings Brown, March 22, 1813, BPL; Pike to Richards, March 25, 1813, BPL; Pike, Sackets Harbor, to [no recipient named], March 25, 1813, BPL; Pike, Sackets Harbor to Dearborn, March 26, 1813, BPL; Pike, Sackets Harbor, to [Loring] Austin, April 13, 1813, BPL; Pike, Sackets Harbor, to [Alexander] Richards, April 13, 1813, BPL; Pike, Sackets Harbor, to John Chandler, April 14, 1813, BPL; Pike, Sackets Harbor, to Amos Benedict, April 14, 1813, BPL; Pike, Sackets Harbor, to N. Williams, April 14, 1813, BPL; Pike, Sackets Harbor, to John Armstrong, April 14, 1813, BPL; Pike, Sackets Harbor, to Eli Collins, April 22, 1813, BPL; Harvey Strum, "Smuggling in the War of 1812," *History Today* 29 (1979), 537.

45. Taylor, *Civil War of 1812*, 201, 214; John Armstrong to Henry Dearborn, March 29, 1813, in *NWR*, March 5, 1814.

46. *NWR*, October 30, 1813, 147–148; Isaac Chauncey, U.S. Ship *Madison*, April 27, 1813, *NWR*, May 15, 1813, 179; Hollon, "Zebulon Montgomery Pike," 267; *NWR*, 6, Supplement to March 5, 1814, 20.

47. Pike, Brownsville, N.Y., to Zebulon Pike, Cincinnati, ca. April 21, 1813, *NWR*, July 10, 1813, 304; "General Order," April 25, 1813, *NWR*, June 5, 1813, 229–230; *Analectic Magazine* 6 (August 1815): 149–150.

48. Hitsman, *Incredible War of 1812*, 137–139; Hickey, *War of 1812*, 129; Latimer, 1812, 131.

49. Henry Dearborn, York, to John Armstrong, Washington, April 28, 1813 and Isaac Chauncey, York, to William Jones, April 28, 1813, both in *NWR*, May 15, 1813, 178–180; "Extract of a Letter from a Field Officer in the Force Which Landed at York, to the Department of War," *NWR*, May 22, 1813, 193–194; Unsigned letter published in *Weekly Aurora* (Philadelphia), May 11, 1813, EAN-2, 8; Letter from Major General Lewis, *Weekly Aurora* (Philadelphia), May 11, 1813, EAN-2, 8; "Capture of York, in Canada," *NWR*, June 5, 1813, 225–226 (this article

was originally published in the *Aurora*); Hitsman, *Incredible War of* 1812, 137–140; Cooper, *Ned Myers*, 46–47.

50. "Capture of York, in Canada," *NWR*, June 5, 1813, 225–226; "Gen. Z. M. Pike," *NWR*, June 5, 1813, 229; Hitsman, *Incredible War of* 1812, 140.

51. Henry Dearborn, York, to John Armstrong, Washington, April 27, 1813, Henry Dearborn, York, to John Armstrong, Washington, April 28, 1813, and Isaac Chauncey, York, to William Jones, April 28, 1813, all in *NWR*, May 15, 1813, 178–180; "Extract of a Letter from a Field Officer in the Force Which Landed at York, to the Department of War," *NWR*, May 22, 1813, 193–194; "Capture of York, in Canada," *NWR*, June 5, 1813, 225–226; "Gen. Z. M. Pike," *NWR*, June 5, 1813, 229; "Captain James Lawrence," *NWR*, July 10, 1813, 303; Jon Latimer, *1812 War with America* (Cambridge, Mass.: Harvard University Press, 2007), 132; Latimer, *1812*, 132; "Gen. Z. M. Pike," *NWR*, June 5, 1813, 229; Samuel Dung[an] to Elisa [Dungan], May 29, 1813, quoted in Robert M. Warner, "The Death of Zebulon M. Pike," *Annals of Iowa*, 3rd ser., 33 (July 1955–April 1957), 44–46; James Fenimore Cooper, *Ned Myers or A Life Before the Mast* (New York: G. P. Putnam's Sons, 1900), 51; Taylor, *Civil War of* 1812, 343. Myers described the corpse as "the body of an English officer, preserved in rum, which, they said, was General Brock's." Myers was almost certainly wrong. Brock had died the previous October at Queenston Heights, across Lake Ontario from York and was buried at Fort George on the Niagara River. Nor have I found any other record of the Americans capturing an officer's body at York and bringing it back to Sackets Harbor—something the papers or the military reports would surely have mentioned. The only officer's body recorded as being returned on ship from York to Sackets Harbor was Zebulon Montgomery Pike's.

52. *Weekly Aurora* (Philadelphia), May 11, 1813, 8; For a few examples of many, see "Gen. Z. M. Pike," *NWR*, June 5, 1813, 228–230; *NWR*, June 26, 1813, 270; *Chronicle* (Harrisburg), July 26, 1813, EAN-2, 4; "Gen. Z. M. Pike," *NWR*, June 5, 1813, 229; *Columbian*, May 26, 1813, EAN-2, 2; "Monody on the Death of Brigadier-General Zebulon Montgomery Pike, Who Fell at the Battle of York, Upper Canada, April 27, 1813," in *The Fall of Palmyra: And Other Poems* by N. H. Wright (1814; repr. Middlebury, Vt.: William Slade, 1817); *NWR*, vol. 4 March–September 1813, backside of title page; *Federal Republican and Commercial Gazette* (Georgetown), July 30, 1813, EAN-2, 2; *NWR*, July 31, 1813, 358; *Washingtonian*, May 24, 1813, EAN-2, 3; *NWR*, March 4, 1815, 417–418; *NWR*, March 18, 1815, 39.

53. Taylor, *Civil War of* 1812, 381–439; Madison and Monroe quotes are from page 420.

54. *Weekly Aurora* (Philadelphia), May 11, 1813, EAN-2, 8; "Gen. Z. M. Pike," *NWR*, June 5, 1813, 228–229.

55. "Biographical Memoir of the Late Brigadier-General Zebulon Montgomery Pike," *Monthly Recorder* (New York State) 1, no. 4 (July 1813): 220–234.

56. "Tribute of Respect to the Memory of General Z. M. Pike," *NWR*, Supplement to vol. 5, 1814, 59–60; "Brigadier-General Pike," *NWR*, May 14, 1814, 176.

57. Clara H. Pike, Boone County, Kentucky, to the Secretary of War, May 22, 1814, ZMPCHS; Clara H. Pike, Boon County, Ky., to Amos Holton, April 25, 1845, and January 12, 1846, CHP, 5–10.

58. *Biographical Memoir of the Late Brigadier-General Zebulon M. Pike, Who Was Killed in the Attack on York (Upper Canada), April 29, 1813, from the Monthly Recorder for July 1813 (Accompanied by an Elegant Likeness of the Deceased)* (New York: 1813); "Biographical Memoir of the Late Brigadier General Zebulon Montgomery Pike," *Analectic Magazine* November 4, 1814: 380–395; James McBride, *Naval Biography, Consisting of the Memoirs of the Most Distinguished Officers of the American Navy, to which Is Annexed the Life of General Pike* (Cincinnati: Morgan, Williams, & Co., 1815), 275–295; Thomas Wilson, *The Biography of the Principal American Military and Naval Heroes, Comprehending Details of Their Achievements During the Revolutionary and Late Wars* (New York: John Low, 1819), 5–24; John M. Niles, *The Life of Oliver Hazard Perry* (Hartford: William S. Marsh, 1820), 317–337; Henry Whiting, "Life of Zebulon Montgomery Pike," in *The Library of American Biography*, vol. 5, 2nd ser., ed. Jared Sparks (Boston: Charles C. Little and James Brown, 1845), 217–314; John S. Jenkins, *The Generals of the Last War With Great Britain* (Buffalo: G. H. Derby & Co., 1851), 323–337; *Life of Jacob Brown, to Which Are Added Memoirs of Generals Ripley and Pike* (1847; repr., New York: Sheldon, Blakeman, & Co., 1856); "Captain James Lawrence," *NWR*, July 10, 1813, 303; *NWR*, December 4, 1813, 231; *NWR*, February 5, 1814, 382.

59. Watts, *Republic Reborn*, 151–160; *NWR*, June 26, 1813, 270; *NWR*, April 16, 1814, 112–113.

60. Charles Royster, *A Revolutionary People at War: The Continental Army and American Character, 1775–1783* (Chapel Hill: University of North Carolina Press, 1979); *NWR*, Supplement to vol. 5, 1814, 60; John Resch, *Suffering Soldiers: Revolutionary War Veterans, Moral Sentiment, and Political Culture in the Early Republic* (Amherst: University of Massachusetts Press, 1999); John Dwight Kilbourne, Virtutis Praemium: *The Men Who Founded the State Society of the Cincinnati of Pennsylvania*, vol. 2 (Rockport, Maine: Picton Press, 1998), Library of the Society of the Cincinnati, 1796.

61. Pike, "Diary of an Expedition," ZPJ, 1:381.

EPILOGUE

1. Jeremy Adelman and Stephen Aron, "From Borderlands to Borders: Empires, Nation-States, and the Peoples in Between in North American History," *American Historical Review* 104 (June 1999), 814–841; Richard White, *The Middle Ground: Indians, Empires, and Republics in the Great Lakes Region, 1650–1815*

(Cambridge, U.K.: Cambridge University Press, 1991); "Indian Council," *Historical Collections of the Michigan Pioneer and Historical Society* 16 (1890), 481, University of Michigan Digital Library, http://quod.lib.umich.edu/cgi/t/ text/text-idx?c=genpub;idno=0534625.0016.001, (accessed August 26, 2011); Robert S. Allen, *His Majesty's Indian Allies: British Indian Policy in the Defence of Canada, 1774–1815* (Toronto: Dundurn Press, 1992); Colin G. Calloway, "The End of an Era: British-Indian Relations in the Great Lakes Region after the War of 1812," *Michigan Historical Review* 12 (Fall 1986), 1–20; Alan Taylor, *The Civil War of 1812: American Citizens, British Subjects, Irish Rebels, and Indian Allies* (New York: Alfred A. Knopf, 2010), 426–430.

2. "Indian Council," 482.

3. Dearborn to Wilkinson, [September 8, 1808], *The Journals of Zebulon Montgomery Pike* (hereafter cited as ZPJ), ed. Donald Jackson (Norman: University of Oklahoma Press, 1966), 2:324–326; Wilkinson to Salcedo, October 10, 1808, ZPJ, 2:326–327; Wilkinson, Carlisle, to Thomas Cushing, October 12, 1808, ZPJ, 2:327–328; Wilkinson, Carlisle, to Daniel Hughes, October 13, 1808, ZPJ, 2:328–330; "American Captives at Liberty," *St. Louis Enquirer*, March 31, 1821, folder 8, Dale Morgan Collection, Huntington Library (hereafter cited as DM).

4. Jules de Munn to William Clark, November 25, 1817, in *News of the Plains and Rockies, 1803–1865, Original Narratives of Overland Travel and Adventure*, ed. David A. White (Spokane: Arthur H. Clark Company, 1996), 2:43–48; Roger L. Nichols and Patrick L. Halley, *Stephen Long and American Frontier Exploration* (Newark: University of Delaware Press, 1980), 115–157.

5. John Lauritz Larson, *Internal Improvement: National Public Works and the Promise of Popular Government in the Early United States* (Chapel Hill: University of North Carolina Press, 2001); Daniel Walker Howe, *What Hath God Wrought: The Transformation of America, 1815–1848* (New York: Oxford University Press, 2007); Elliott West, *The Last Indian War: The Nez Perce Story* (New York: Oxford University Press, 2009); Pike, "Geographical, Statistical, and General Observations," ZPJ, 2:50–51, 97; Stephen G. Hyslop, *Bound for Santa Fe: The Road to New Mexico and the American Conquest, 1806–1849* (Norman: University of Oklahoma Press, 2002), 21, 37–42; *Missouri Gazette*, St. Louis, September 13, 1817, folder 9, DM; Josiah Gregg, *Commerce of the Prairies: Or the Journal of a Santa Fé Trader, during Eight Expeditions Across The Great Western Prairies, and a Residence of Nearly Nine Years in Northern Mexico* (New York: Henry G. Langley, 1844), 10; W. H. Emory, *Notes of a Military Reconnaissance from Ft. Leavenworth in Missouri to San Diego in California, Including Part of the Arkansas, Del Norte, and Gila Rivers* (Washington, D.C.: Wendell and Van Benthuysen, Printers, 1848), 38. Another who appears to have carried Pike's journal is Jacob Fowler, who explored the Arkansas River and Rio Grande while trapping beaver in 1821 and 1822; Jacob Fowler, *The Journal of Jacob Fowler, Narrating an Adventure from Arkansas through the Indian Territory, Oklahoma, Kansas, Colorado, and New*

Mexico, to the Sources of Rio Grande del Norte, 1821–22 (New York: Francis P. Harper, 1898).

6. Susan Shelby Magoffin, *Down the Santa Fe Trail and into Mexico: The Diary of Susan Shelby Magoffin, 1846–1847* (1926; repr., Lincoln: University of Nebraska Press, 1982), especially 4, 6–7, 37, and 67; Pike, "Geographical, Statistical, and General Observations," ZPJ, 2:97.

7. Larsen, *Internal Improvement*, 240–252; James M. McPherson, *Battle Cry of Freedom: The Civil War Era* (New York: Oxford University Press, 1988), 121–124.

8. On James S. Pike's biography, see Robert F. Durden, *James Shepherd Pike: Republicanism and the American Negro, 1850–1882* (Durham: Duke University Press, 1957); on his genealogy, see Allen Raymond Pike, *The Family of John Pike of New burry, Massachusetts, 1635–1695* (n.p.: Penobscot Press, 1995).

9. James S. Pike, *The New Puritan: New England Two Hundred Years Ago, Some Account of the Life of Robert Pike, the Puritan Who Defended the Quakers, Resisted Clerical Domination, and Opposed the Witchcraft Prosecution* (New York: Harper & Brothers, Publishers, 1879), 10, 11, 16, 22, 24, 131–146.

10. On James's less than charitable beliefs about blacks' capacities, see James S. Pike, *The Prostrate State: South Carolina under Negro Government* (1874; repr., New York: Harper and Row, 1968); Israel Washburn to James S. Pike, January 19, 1855, in James Shepherd Pike, *First Blows of the Civil War: The Ten Years of Preliminary Conflict in the United States, from 1850 to 1860, a Contemporaneous Exposition, Progress of the Struggle Shown by Public Records and Private Correspondence* (New York: American News Company, 1879), 263; James S. Pike, *New York Tribune*, March 12, 1860, quoted in Pike, *Prostrate State*, xi.

11. Pike, "Dissertation on Louisiana," ZPJ, 2:28.

12. Pike, "Dissertation on Louisiana," ZPJ, 2:28.

13. Lynn Sherr, *America the Beautiful: The Stirring True Story Behind Our Nation's Favorite Song* (New York: Public Affairs, 2001), 29; Richard White, "Frederick Jackson Turner and Buffalo Bill," in *The Frontier in American Culture: An Exhibition at the Newberry Library, August 26, 1994–January 7, 1995*, ed. James R. Grossman (Berkeley: University of California Press, 1994), 7–66; Louis S. Warren, *Buffalo Bill's America: William Cody and the Wild West Show* (New York: Alfred A. Knopf, 2005); Hal K. Rothman, *Devil's Bargains: Tourism in the Twentieth-Century American West* (Lawrence: University Press of Kansas, 1998), 81–112; Pike, "Observations on New Spain," April 12, 1808, ZPJ, 2:50; Paul Russell Cutright, *A History of the Lewis and Clark Journals* (Norman: University of Oklahoma Press, 1976), 102–103; Elliott Coues, ed., *The Expeditions of Zebulon Montgomery Pike, To Headwaters of the Mississippi River, Through Louisiana Territory, and in New Spain, During the Years 1805-6-7* (New York: Francis P. Harper, 1895), 1:xxiii–xxx; Herbert E. Bolton, "Papers of Zebulon M. Pike, 1806–1807," *American Historical Review* 13 (July 1908), 798–827; Jackson,

Journals, 2:191; Stephen Harding Hart and Archer Butler Hulbert, eds., *The Southwestern Journals of Zebulon Pike, 1806–1807* (1932; repr., Albuquerque: University of New Mexico Press, 2006), 22–27.

14. Quoted in Dorothy Burgess, *Dream and Deed: The Story of Katharine Lee Bates* (Norman: University of Oklahoma Press, 1952), 102; Katharine Lee Bates, "Diary," July 22, 1893, box 3, Katharine Lee Bates Collection, Wellesley College Archives, Wellesley, Massachusetts.

15. Burgess, *Dream and Deed*, 106.

Bibliography

PRIMARY SOURCE COLLECTIONS AND ABBREVIATIONS

AGI: Archivo General de las Indias, Seville, Spain, Library of Congress, Manuscripts Division, Washington, D.C.

AGP: Archivo General y Público, Mexico, Provincias Internas, Archivo General y Público, Mexico, Provincias Internas, Tomos 200–201, 239

AGOR: Adjutant General's Office Records—Letters Received, National Archives and Records Administration, Washington, D.C.

AGOS: Adjutant General's Office Records—Letters Sent, National Archives and Records Administration, Washington, D.C.

AHN: Archivo Histórico Nacional, Madrid, Spain, Library of Congress Manuscripts Division, Washington, D.C.

AOE: Pike, Z. M. *An Account of Expeditions to the Sources of the Mississippi and Through the Western Parts of Louisiana, to the Sources of the Arkansaw, Kans, La Platte, and Pierre Juan, Rivers; Performed by Order of the Government of the United States during the Years 1805, 1806, and 1807. And a Tour Through the Interior Parts of New Spain, When Conducted Through These Provinces, by Order of the Captain-General in the Year 1807.* Philadelphia: C. & A. Conrad, & Co., 1810

APS: Zebulon Montgomery Pike Papers, American Philosophical Society, Philadelphia, Pennsylvania

ASP: *American State Papers*

BCHS: Bucks County Historical Society, Doylestown, Pennsylvania

BPL: *Bloomfield-Pike Letterbook*, William L. Clements Library, University of Michigan, Ann Arbor, Michigan

BHC: Burton Historical Collection, Detroit Public Library

CHP: Amos Holton, *The Case of Mrs. Clara H. Pike, Widow of Gen. Z. Montgomery Pike, Now Pending Before the U.S. Congress, with Some Extracts from Her Letters, Pertaining Thereto, Ect [sic].; Her Petition, Praying Compensation for Extraordinary Services, Rendered by Her Late Husband, in Conducting the Two Exploring*

Expeditions, to the Sources of the Mississippi River, and Through the Interior and South-Western Extremity of the Territory of Louisiana, in the Years 1805, '6 and '7; and the Report Made Thereon, by Col. Benton, Chairman of the Committee on Military Affairs in the Senate, as Prepared for the "Union," Newspaper, (But Its Unexpected Length Induces Its Publication in the Form). Washington, [D.C.]: T. Barnard, Printer, 1846.

CHS: Chicago Historical Society, Chicago, Illinois

CSRV: Compiled Service Records of Volunteer Soldiers Who Served from 1784 to 1811, U.S. Levies, Second Regiment, Microcopy Publication M905, roll 6, NARADC

CRSR: Compiled Records of Soldiers Who Served in the American Army During the Revolutionary War, Continental Troops, Fourth Regiment Light Dragoons, Microcopy Publication M 881, roll 48, NARADC

DM: Dale Morgan Collection, Huntington Library

DPL: Denver Public Library, Denver, Colorado

EAI-1: *Early American Imprints, Series I: Evans (1639–1800)*, University of Wyoming, Laramie, Wyoming

EAI-2: *Early American Imprints, Series II: Shaw-Shoemaker (1801–1819)*, University of Wyoming, Laramie, Wyoming

EAN-1: *Early American Newspapers, Series I: (1690–1876)*, University of Wyoming, Laramie, Wyoming

EAN-2: *Early American Newspapers, Series II: (1758–1900)*, University of Colorado, Boulder, Colorado

EENA: *Early Encounters in North America.* Colorado State University, Fort Collins, Colorado

ET: Zebulon Montgomery Pike, *Exploratory Travels Through the Western Territories of North America: Comprising a Voyage from St. Louis, on the Mississippi, to the Source of That River, and a Journey Through the Interior of Louisiana and the North-Eastern Provinces of New Spain. Performed in the Years 1805, 1806, 1807, by Order of the Government of the United States.* London: Longman, Hurst, Rees, Orme, and Brown, 1811.

HEH: Henry E. Huntington Library, San Marino, California

JFC: *John F. Carmichael Diary*, Huntington Library

JWBHC: James Wilkinson Papers, Burton Historical Collection, Detroit Public Library

JWCHS: James Wilkinson Collection, Chicago Historical Society, Chicago, Illinois

HM: Huntington Manuscripts, Huntington Library

KLB: Katharine Lee Bates Collection, Wellesley College Archives, Wellesley, Massachusetts

LC: Library of Congress, Washington, D.C.

LCM: Library of Congress Manuscripts Division, Washington, D.C.

LCN: Library of Congress Newspapers and Current Periodicals Room, Washington, D.C.

MCDA: Middlesex County Deed Abstracts, Middlesex County, New Jersey

MHS: Massachusetts Historical Society Library, Boston Massachusetts

MP: Samuel L. Mitchill Papers, William L. Clements Library, University of Michigan, Ann Arbor, Michigan

NARARM: National Archives and Records Administration, Rocky Mountain Region, Denver, Colorado

NARADC: National Archives and Records Administration, Washington, D.C.

NCDB: *Deed Books*, Northumberland County, Pennsylvania

NIWA: *National Intelligencer and Washington Advertiser*, Library of Congress

NJSA: New Jersey State Archives, Trenton, New Jersey

NT: Northwest Territory Collection, Indiana Historical Society, Indianapolis, Indiana

NWR: *Niles' Weekly Register*

PAB: Papers of Aaron Burr

PCPPAB: Mary-Jo Kline, ed. *Political Correspondence and Public Papers of Aaron Burr.* Princeton: Princeton University Press, 1983.

PFAA: Pike Family Association of America

PStLFT: Papers of the Saint Louis Fur Trade, Missouri Historical Society, microfilm

SANM: Spanish Archives of New Mexico

WGR: William Gillet Rich Collection, Huntington Library, San Marino, California

SGM: Secretaria de Guerra y de Marina, Mexico. Seccion de Varios Asuntos. Legajo 1787–1807, Library of Congress Manuscripts Division, Washington, D.C.

TP: Clarence Edwin Carter, ed., *The Territorial Papers of the United States*

TPBHC: Thomas Pasteur Papers, Burton Historical Collection, Detroit Public Library

WBBC: *Will Book*, Boone County, Kentucky

WCCC: William Claiborne Letter Books

WRHC: Western Reserve Historical Society, Cleveland, Ohio

ZMPCHS: Zebulon Montgomery Pike Collection, Chicago Historical Society

ZMPL: Zebulon Pike Letters, Western Reserve Historical Society, Cleveland, Ohio

ZPC: Zebulon Pike journals—Coues edition

ZPCHS: Zebulon Pike Collection, Chicago Historical Society

ZPJ: Zebulon Pike journals—Jackson edition

RARE BOOKS AND PUBLISHED PRIMARY SOURCES

"Autograph Letters: Tract 39." In *Western Reserve Historical Society Tracts 37–72.* Cleveland: Western Reserve Historical Society, 1888. WRHS.

Biographical Memoir of the Late Brigadier-General Zebulon M. Pike, Who Was Killed in the Attack on York (Upper Canada), April 29, 1813, from the Monthly Recorder *for July 1813 (Accompanied by an Elegant Likeness of the Deceased).* New York: 1813.

"Biographical Memoir of the Late Brigadier-General Zebulon Montgomery Pike," *Monthly Recorder* (New York State) 1, no. 4 (July 1813), 220–234.

"Biographical Memoir of the Late Brigadier General Zebulon Montgomery Pike." *Analectic Magazine* 4 (November 1814): 380–395.

Bloomfield, Joseph. "Journal of Joseph Bloomfield." In *Citizen Soldier: The Revolutionary War Journal of Joseph Bloomfield*, edited by Mark E. Lender and James Kirby, 35–142. Newark, N.J.: New Jersey Historical Society, 1982.

Bolton, Herbert E. "Papers of Zebulon M. Pike, 1806–1807." *American Historical Review* 13 (July 1908): 798–827.

Bradley, Jared William, ed. *Interim Appointment: W. C. C. Claiborne Letter Book, 1805–1805.* Baton Rouge: Louisiana State University Press, 2002.

[Brown, Charlotte Cowdey]. *The New Jersey Browns.* Milwaukee: n.p., 1931.

Carter, Clarence Edwin, ed. *The Territorial Papers of the United States.* Vol. 13, "The Territory of Louisisana-Missouri, 1803–1806." Washington, D.C.: US GPO, 1948.

Carver, Jonathan. *Three Years Travels Throughout the Interior Parts of North-America.* Boston: John Russell for David West, 1797.

Catanzariti, John and E. James Ferguson, eds. *The Papers of Robert Morris, 1781–1784.* Vol. 6. Pittsburgh: University of Pittsburgh Press, 1984.

Coffin, Joshua D. *A Sketch of the History of Newbury, Newburyport, and West Newbury from 1635 to 1845.* Boston: Samuel G. Drake, 1845.

Cooke, John. *Diary of John Cooke, 1794.* Fort Wayne, Ind.: Governing Boards of the Public Library of Fort Wayne and Allen County, 1953. BHC.

Cooper, Jack Kyle. *Zebulon Montgomery Pike's Great Western Adventure, 1806–1807.* Colorado Springs: Clausen Books, 2007.

Cooper, James Fenimore. *Ned Myers or A Life Before the Mast.* New York: G. P. Putnam's Sons, 1900.

Dodsley, Robert. *The Economy of Human Life: Translated from an Indian Manuscript, Written by an Ancient Bramin in a Letter From an English Gentleman Residing in China.* Philadelphia: Joseph Crukshank, 1795. Early American Imprints First Series #28582. University of Wyoming, Laramie, Wyo. http://www-lib.uwyo.edu/find/subject.cfm?alpha=E. Accessed August 18, 2006.

Drake, Daniel. *Natural and Statistical View or Picture of Cincinnati and the Miami Country.* Cincinnati: Looker and Wallace, 1815. Early American Imprints Second Series #34595. University of Wyoming, Laramie, Wyo. http://www-lib.uwyo.edu/find/subject.cfm?alpha=E. Accessed September 13, 2006.

Drake, Daniel. "Dr. Daniel Drake's Memoir of the Miami Country, 1779–1794." *Quarterly Publication of the Historical and Philosophical Society of Ohio,* 18 (April–September 1923): 37–117.

Ellicott, Andrew. *The Journal of Andrew Ellicott.* Chicago: Quadrangle Books, 1962.

Emory, W. H. *Notes of a Military Reconnaissance from Ft. Leavenworth in Missouri to San Diego in California, Including Part of the Arkansas, Del Norte, and Gila Rivers.* Washington, D.C.: Wendell and Van Benthuysen, Printers, 1848.

Erickson, Doug, Jeremy Skinner, and Paul Merchant, eds. *Jefferson's Western Explorations: Discoveries Made in Exploring the Missouri, Red River and Washita by Captains Lewis* and Clark, Doctor Sibley, and William Dunbar, and compiled by Thomas Jefferson, the *Natchez Edition, 1806.* Spokane, The Arthur H. Clark Company, 2004.

The Federalist Papers. New York: 1787–1788. Library of Congress. http://thomas.loc. gov/home/histdox/fedpapers.html. Accessed frequently, 2006–.

Fitzpatrick, John C., ed. *The Writings of George Washington from the Original Manuscript Sources, 1745–1799.* Vol. 17. Washington, D.C.: US GPO, 1931–1944. Society of the Cincinnati Library, Washington, D.C.

Flores, Dan L. ed., *Southern Counterpart to Lewis & Clark: The Freeman & Custis Expedition of 1806.* 1984. Reprint, Norman: University of Oklahoma Press, 2002.

Folch, Vicente. "Reflections on Louisiana." In *Louisiana Under the Rule of Spain, France, and the United States, 1785–1807: Social, Economic, and Political Conditions of the Territory Represented in the Louisiana Purchase as Portrayed in Hitherto Unpublished Contemporary Accounts by Dr. Paul Alliot and Various Spanish, French, English, and American Officials,* edited by James Alexander Robertson. Vol. 2, 323–347. 1910–11. Reprint. Freeport, N.Y., Books for Libraries Press, 1969.

Fowler, Jacob. *The Journal of Jacob Fowler, Narrating an Adventure from Arkansas through the Indian Territory, Oklahoma, Kansas, Colorado, and New Mexico, to the Sources of Rio Grande del Norte, 1821–22.* New York: Francis P. Harper, 1898.

Glover, Richard, ed., *David Thompson's Narrative 1784–1812.* Toronto: The Champlain Society, 1962.

Gregg, Josiah. *Commerce of the Prairies: Or the Journal of a Santa Fé Trader, during Eight Expeditions Across The Great Western Prairies, and a Residence of Nearly Nine Years in Northern Mexico.* New York: Henry G. Langley, 1844.

Gregg, Josiah. *Commerce of the Prairies.* 1844. Reprint. Norman: University of Oklahoma Press, 1954.

Griswold, Bert J., ed. *Fort Wayne, Gateway of the West, 1802–1813: Garrison Orderly Books, Indian Agency Account Book.* Indianapolis: Historical Bureau of the Indiana Library and Historical Department, 1927.

Harbison, Massy, "Account of the Sufferings of Massy Herbeson and Her Family, Who Were Taken Prisoners by a Party of Indians. Given on Oath, before John Wilkins, Esq. One of the Justices of the Peace for the Commonwealth of Pennsylvania." In *A Selection of Some of the Most Interesting Narratives of Outrages Committed by the Indians in Their Wars, With the White People,* edited by Archibald Loudon, 69–74. Carlisle, Pa.: A. Loudon, 1808. Reprint, New York: Arno Press, 1971.

Harris, Thaddeus Mason. "Journal of a Tour Northwest of the Alleghany Mountains." In *Early Western Travels, 1748–1846,* edited by Reuben Gold Thwaites, 308–381. Cleveland: The Arthur H. Clark Company, 1904. Early Encounters in North America. Colorado State University, Fort Collins, Colo., http://vulture.library. colostate.edu/databases/. Accessed September 6, 2006.

Hart, Stephen Harding and Archer Butler Hulbert, eds. *The Southwestern Journals of Zebulon Pike, 1806–1807*. 1932. Reprint. Albuquerque: University of New Mexico Press, 2006.

Historical Collections of the Michigan Pioneer and Historical Society 16 (1890). University of Michigan Digital Library, http://quod.lib.umich.edu/cgi/t/text/text-idx?c=genpub;idno=0534625.0016.001. Accessed August 26, 2011.

History of the American War, of Eighteen Hundred and Twelve from the Commencement until the Final Termination Thereof, on the Memorable Eighth of January 1815, at New Orleans: Embellished with a Striking Likeness of General Pike, and Six Other Engravings. Philadelphia: W. M. M'Carty & Davis, 1816.

Holton, Amos. *The Case of Mrs. Clara H. Pike, Widow of Gen. Z. Montgomery Pike, Now Pending Before the U.S. Congress, with Some Extracts from Her Letters, Pertaining Thereto, Ect [sic].; Her Petition, Praying Compensation for Extraordinary Services, Rendered by Her Late Husband, in Conducting the Two Exploring Expeditions, to the Sources of the Mississippi River, and Through the Interior and South-Western Extremity of the Territory of Louisiana, in the Years 1805, '6 and '7; and the Report Made Thereon, by Col. Benton, Chairman of the Committee on Military Affairs in the Senate, as Prepared for the "Union," Newspaper, (But Its Unexpected Length Induces Its Publication in the Form), by Amos Holton*. Washington, [D.C.]: T. Barnard, Printer, 1846.

Iles, George, ed. *Little Masterpieces of Science: Explorers*. New York: Doubleday, Page & Company, 1902.

An Important Visit: Zebulon Montgomery Pike 1805. [St. Paul: 1925?] WRHS.

Irving, Jr., John Treat. *Indian Sketches Taken During an Expedition to the Pawnee Tribes (1833)*. Edited by John Francis McDermott. Norman: University of Oklahoma Press, 1955.

Jackson, Donald, ed. *Letters of the Lewis and Clark Expedition with Related Documents, 1783–1854*. Urbana: University of Illinois Press, 1962.

Jefferson, Thomas. *Notes on the State of Virginia*. Gloucester, Mass.: Peter Smith, 1976.

Jenkins, John S. *The Generals of the Last War With Great Britain*. Buffalo: G. H. Derby & Co., 1851.

Kauffman, C. H. *The Dictionary of Merchandise, and Nomenclature in All Languages; for the Use of Counting-Houses: Containing, the History, Places of Growth, Culture, Use, and Marks of Excellency, of Such Natural Productions as Form Articles of Commerce; with Their Names in All European Languages*. Philadelphia: James Humphreys, 1805.

Kilbourne, John Dwight. Virtutis Praemium: *The Men Who Founded the State Society of the Cincinnati of Pennsylvania*, volume 2. Rockport, Maine: Picton Press, 1998. Library of the Society of the Cincinnati, Washington, D.C.

King, Douglas R. "A Soldier Named Zeb," unpublished manuscript in author's possession. 2003.

Kline, Mary-Jo, ed. *Political Correspondence and Public Papers of Aaron Burr*. Princeton: Princeton University Press, 1983.

Knopf, Richard C., ed. *Anthony Wayne: A Name in Arms: Soldier, Diplomat, Defender of Expansion Westward of a Nation: The Wayne-Knox-Pickering-McHenry Correspondence*. Pittsburgh: University of Pittsburgh Press, 1960.

Knopf, Richard C. "Report on Surgeons of the Indian Wars." Columbus: Anthony Wayne Parkway Board, n.d. BHC.

Larkin, James F., ed. *Stuart Royal Proclamations: Royal Proclamations of King Charles I 1625–1646*. Vol. 2. Oxford: Clarendon Press, 1983.

Lea, Tom. Calendar of Twelve Travelers Through the Pass of the North. [El Paso: El Paso Electric Co.], 1946.

Life of Jacob Brown, to Which Are Added Memoirs of Generals Ripley and Pike. 1847. Reprint, New York: Sheldon, Blakeman, & Co., 1856.

Locke, John. *An Essay Concerning Human Understanding* (1690). Oregon State University, http://oregonstate.edu/instruct/phl302/texts/locke/locke1/Essay_contents.html. Accessed November 8, 2006.

Locke, John. *Some Thoughts Concerning Education* (1693). In *English Philosophers of the Seventeenth and Eighteenth Centuries* volume 37. New York: P. F. Collier & Son, 1910. Modern History Sourcebook, Fordham University. http://www.fordham.edu/halsall/mod/1692locke-education.html. Accessed November 8, 2006.

Magoffin, Susan Shelby. *Down the Santa Fe Trail and into Mexico: The Diary of Susan Shelby Magoffin, 1846–1847*. 1926. Reprint. Lincoln: University of Nebraska Press, 1982.

Mathews, Catharine Van Cortlandt. *Andrew Ellicott: His Life and Letters*. New York: The Grafton Press, 1908.

Mathews, Catharine Van Cortlandt. *Andrew Ellicott: His Life and Letters*. 1908. Reprint, Alexander, N.C.: WorldComm, 1997.

McBride, James. *Naval Biography, Consisting of the Memoirs of the Most Distinguished Officers of the American Navy, to which is Annexed the Life of General Pike*. Cincinnati: Morgan, Williams, & Co., 1815.

Melish, John. *Travels in the United States of America, in the Years 1806 & 1807, and 1809, 1810, & 1811: Including an Account of Passages Betwixt America and Britain and Travels Through Various Parts of Great Britain, Ireland, and Upper Canada*. 2 vols. Philadelphia: Thomas & George Palmer, 1812.

Michaux, André. "Travels into Kentucky, 1793–96." In *Early Western Travels, 1748–1846*, edited by Reuben Gold Thwaites, 11–104. Cleveland: The Arthur H. Clark Company, 1904. Early Encounters in North America. Colorado State University, Fort Collins, Colorado. http://lib.colostate.edu/databases/permlink.php?id=388. Accessed September 6, 2006.

Michaux, Francois André. "Travels to the West of the Alleghany Mountains." In *Early Western Travels, 1748–1846*, ed. Reuben Gold Thwaites, 111–306. Cleveland: The Arthur H. Clark Company, 1904. Early Encounters in North America. Colorado State University, Fort Collins, Colorado. http://lib.colostate.edu/databases/permlink.php?id=388. Accessed September 6, 2006.

Miller, Edward. *With Captain Edward Miller in the Wayne Campaign of 1794*. Edited by Dwight L. Smith. Ann Arbor: William Clements Library, 1965.

Miller, Francis W. *Cincinnati's Beginnings: Missing Chapters in the Early History of the City and the Miami Purchase, Chiefly From Hitherto Unpublished Documents*. Cincinnati: Peter G. Thomson, Publishers, 1880.

Montesquieu, Charles de Secondat, Baron de. *The Spirit of the Laws*. In Great Books of the Western World, ed. Robert Maynard Hutchins. 1748. Reprint. Chicago: Encyclopedia Britannica, 1952.

Moser, Harold D. and Sharon Macpherson, eds. *The Papers of Andrew Jackson*. Vol. 2. Knoxville: University of Tennessee Press, 1984.

Nasatir, A. P. *Before Lewis and Clark: Documents Illustrating the History of the Missouri, 1785–1804*. Norman: University of Oklahoma Press, 2002.

Niles, John M. *The Life of Oliver Hazard Perry*. Hartford: William S. Marsh, 1820.

Niles, John M. *The Life of Oliver Hazard Perry*. Hartford: Oliver D. Cooke, 1821.

Paine, Thomas. *Common Sense*. New York: Penguin, 1986.

Pike, Allen Raymond. *The Family of John Pike of New burry, Massachusetts, 1635–1695*. N.p.: Penobscot Press, 1995.

Pike, James S. *The New Puritan: New England Two Hundred Years Ago, Some Account of the Life of Robert Pike, the Puritan Who Defended the Quakers, Resisted Clerical Domination, and Opposed the Witchcraft Prosecution*. New York: Harper & Brothers, Publishers, 1879.

Pike, James S. *The Prostrate State: South Carolina under Negro Government*. 1879. Reprint, New York: Harper & Row, Publishers, 1968.

Pike, James Shepherd. *First Blows of the Civil War: The Ten Years of Preliminary Conflict in the United States, from 1850 to 1860, a Contemporaneous Exposition, Progress of the Struggle Shown by Public Records and Private Correspondence*. New York: American News Company, 1879.

Pike, Z. M. *An Account of Expeditions to the Sources of the Mississippi and Through the Western Parts of Louisiana, to the Sources of the Arkansaw, Kans, La Platte, and Pierre Juan, Rivers; Performed by Order of the Government of the United States during the Years 1805, 1806, and 1807. And a Tour Through the Interior Parts of New Spain, When Conducted Through These Provinces, by Order of the Captain-General in the Year 1807*. Philadelphia: C. & A. Conrad, & Co., 1810.

Pike, Zebulon Montgomery. *Exploratory Travels Through the Western Territories of North America: Comprising a Voyage from St. Louis, on the Mississippi, to the Source of That River, and a Journey Through the Interior of Louisiana and the North-Eastern Provinces of New Spain. Performed in the Years 1805, 1806, 1807, by Order of the Government of the United States*. London: Longman, Hurst, Rees, Orme, and Brown, 1811.

Robertson, David. *Reports of the Trials of Colonel Aaron Burr*. Philadelphia: Hopkins and Earle, Fry and Kammerer, 1808.

Robertson, James Alexander, ed. *Louisiana under the Rule of Spain, France, and the United States.* 2 Vols. 1910–1911. Reprint. New York: Books for Libraries Press, 1969.

Rush, Richard. "An Oration, delivered by Richard Rush on the 4th of July, 1812, in the Hall of the House of Representatives, at the Capitol, Washington." Early American Imprints Second Series, #26671. http://infoweb.newsbank.com. Accessed May 20, 2011.

Sanders, Frank. "The Pike Expedition and the Strange Anglo-American Entrada to the Spanish Southwest." Unpublished manuscript, 2006.

Savage, James. *Genealogical Dictionary of the First Settlers of New England, Showing Three Generations of Those Who Came Before May, 1692, on the Basis of Farmer's Register.* Vol. 3. 1860–1862. Reprint. Baltimore: Genealogical Publishing Co., Inc., 1986.

Schlesinger, Jr., Arthur M. and Roger Bruns, ed. *Congress Investigates: a Documented History, 1872–1974.* Vol. 1. New York: Chelsea House, 1983; originally printed 1975.

Scott, Charles. *Scott's Wabash Expedition, 1791.* Fort Wayne, Ind.: Governing Boards of the Public Library of Fort Wayne and Allen County, 1953. BHC.

Shenstone, William. *Essays on Men and Manners.* 1764. Reprint. Philadelphia: William W. Morse, 1804.

Smith, James, "Journey Through Kentucky and into the Northwest Territory, 1795." In "Tours into Kentucky and the Northwest: Three Journals by the Rev. James Smith of Powhatan County, Va., 1783–1795–1797," ed. Josiah Morrow, 364–386. *Ohio Archaeological and Historical Publications* XVI (1907).

Symmes, John Cleves. *To the Respectable Public.* Trenton: Isaac Collins, 1787. Early American Imprints First Series #20738. Colorado State University, Fort Collins, Colo., http://docs.newsbank.com/openurl?ctx_ver=z39.88-2004&rft_id=info:sid/iw.newsbank.com:EVAN&rft_val_format=info:ofi/fmt:kev:mtx:ctx&rft_dat=0F301AA4064B9280&svc_dat=Evans:eaidoc&req_dat=109302F5AFBA2724. Accessed September 5, 2006.

Tyler, Royall. *The Contrast, a Comedy; in Five Acts: Written by a Citizen of the United States.* Philadelphia: Prichard & Hall, 1790. Early American Imprints First Series #28582. Colorado State University, Fort Collins, Colo. http://docs.newsbank.com/openurl?ctx_ver=z39.88-2004&rft_id=info:sid/iw.newsbank.com:EVAN&rft_val_format=info:ofi/fmt:kev:mtx:ctx&rft_dat=0F301AA4064B9280&svc_dat=Evans:eaidoc&req_dat=109302F5AFBA2724. Accessed September 8, 2006.

Underwood, Thomas Taylor. *Journal of Thomas Taylor Underwood, March 26, 1792, to March 18, 1800: An Old Soldier in Wayne's Army.* Cincinnati: Society of Colonial Wars in the State of Ohio, 1945. BHC.

University of Nebraska Press/University of Nebraska-Lincoln Libraries-Electronic Text Center. *The Journals of the Lewis and Clark Expedition.* http://lewisandclark-journals.unl.edu. Accessed October 7, 2011.

Washington, George. "Rules of Civility and Decent Behavior in Company and Conversation." Papers of George Washington. http://gwpapers.virginia.edu/documents/civility/transcript.html.

White, David A. ed. *News of the Plains and Rockies, 1803–1865, Original Narratives of Overland Travel and Adventure.* Vol. 2. Spokane: Arthur H. Clark Company, 1996.

Whiting, Henry. "Life of Zebulon Montgomery Pike." In *The Library of American Biography*, Vol. 5, 2nd ser., edited by Jared Sparks, 217–314. Boston: Charles C. Little and James Brown, 1845.

Wilkinson, James. *Memoirs of My Own Times.* Philadelphia: Abraham Small, 1816.

Wilson, Thomas. *The Biography of the Principal American Military and Naval Heroes, Comprehending Details of Their Achievements During the Revolutionary and Late Wars.* New York: John Low, 1819.

Wright, N. H. *The Fall of Palmyra: And Other Poems.* Middlebury, Vt.: William Slade, 1817.

SECONDARY SOURCES

Abernethy, Thomas Perkins. *The Burr Conspiracy.* New York: Oxford University Press, 1954.

Adelman, Jeremy, and Stephen Aron. "From Borderlands to Borders: Empires, Nation-States, and the Peoples in Between in North American History." *American Historical Review* 104 (June 1999): 814–841.

Albers, Patricia C. "Santee." In *Handbook of North American Indians*, volume 13, part 2, edited by William C. Sturtevant. Washington, D.C., Smithsonian Institution, 2001.

Allen, John Logan. *Passage Through the Garden: Lewis and Clark and the Image of the American Northwest.* Urbana: University of Illinois Press, 1975.

Allen, Robert S. *His Majesty's Indian Allies: British Indian Policy in the Defence of Canada, 1774–1815.* Toronto: Dundurn Press, 1992.

Amar, Akhil Reed. *America's Constitution: A Biography.* New York: Random House, 2005.

Anderson, Benedict. *Imagined Communities: Reflections on the Origin and Spread of Nationalism.* London: Verso, 1991.

Anderson, Fred. *A People's Army: Massachusetts Soldiers and Society in the Seven Years' War.* New York: W. W. Norton & Company, 1985.

Anderson, Fred. *Crucible of War: The Seven Years' War and the Fate of Empire in British North America, 1754–1766.* New York: Vintage Books, 2000.

Anfinson, John O. *The River We Have Wrought: A History of the Upper Mississippi.* Minneapolis: University of Minnesota Press, 2003.

Appleby, Joyce. *Inheriting the Revolution: The First Generation of Americans.* Cambridge, Mass.: Harvard University Press, 2000.

Arnell, Barbara. *John Locke and America: The Defence of English Colonialism*. Oxford: Clarendon Press, 1996.

Aron, Stephen. *How the West Was Lost: The Transformation of Kentucky from Daniel Boone to Henry Clay*. Baltimore: Johns Hopkins University Press, 1996.

Aron, Stephen. *American Confluence: The Missouri Frontier from Borderland to Border State*. Bloomington: Indiana University Press, 2006.

Backes, William J. "General Zebulon M. Pike, Somerset-Born." *Somerset County Historical Quarterly* 8 (October 1919): 240–251.

Bailey, Garrick A. "Osage." In *Handbook of North American Indians*, volume 13, edited by William C. Sturtevant. Washington, D.C., Smithsonian Institution, 2001.

Barber, John W., and Henry Howe. *Historical Collections of the State of New Jersey*. New York: S. Tuttle, 1844.

Barr, Juliana. "From Captives to Slaves: Commodifying Indian Women in the Borderlands," *Journal of American History* 92:1 (June 2005), 19–46.

Barr, Juliana. *Peace Came in the Form of a Woman: Indians and Spaniards in the Texas Borderlands*. Chapel Hill: University of North Carolina Press, 2007.

Battle, J. H., ed. *History of Bucks County, Pennsylvania*. Philadelphia: A. Warner & Co., Publishers, 1887.

Belich, James. *Replenishing the Earth: The Settler Revolution and the Rise of the Anglo-World, 1783–1939*. Oxford: Oxford University Press, 2009.

Bennet, Robert Ames. *A Volunteer with Pike: The True Narrative of One Dr. John Robinson and of His Love for the Fair Señorita Vallois*. Chicago: A.C. McClurg & Co., 1909.

Bickham, Troy. *The Weight of Vengeance: The United States, the British Empire, and the War of 1812*. New York: Oxford University Press, 2012.

Blevins, Tim, et al., ed. *"To Spare No Pains": Zebulon Montgomery Pike and His 1806–1807 Southwest Expedition*. Colorado Springs: Pikes Peak Library District and Colorado Springs Pioneers Museum, 2007.

Bloch, Ruth. *Gender and Morality in Anglo-American Culture, 1650–1800*. Berkeley: University of California Press, 2003.

Bolton Valencius, Conevery. *The Health of the Country: How American Settlers Understood Themselves and Their Land*. New York: Basic Books, 2002.

Bond, Beverley W. *The Civilization of the Old Northwest: A Study of Political, Social, and Economic Development, 1788–1812*. New York: Ams Press, 1934.

Bouton, Terry. "A Road Closed: Rural Insurgency in Post-Independence Pennsylvania." *Journal of American History* 87 (December 2000): 855–887.

Bouton, Terry. *Taming Democracy: "The People," the Founders, and the Troubled Ending of the American Revolution*. New York: Oxford University Press, 2007.

Bradsby, H. C., ed. *History of Luzerne County, Pennsylvania, with Biographical Selections*. Chicago: S.B. Nelson & Co., Publishers, 1893.

Brown, Kate. "Gridded Lives: Why Kazakhstan and Montana Are Nearly the Same Place." *American Historical Review* 106 (February 2001): 17–48.

Brynn, Edward. "Patterns of Dissent: Vermont's Opposition to the War of 1812." *Vermont History* 40 (1972): 10–27.

Buckely, Jay H. "Jeffersonian Explorers in the Trans-Mississippi West." In *Zebulon Pike, Thomas Jefferson, and the Opening of the American West*, edited by Matthew L. Harris and Jay H. Buckley, 101–138. Norman: University of Oklahoma Press, 2012.

Buley, R. Carlyle. *The Old Northwest Pioneer Period, 1815–1840.* Vol. 1. Indianapolis: Indiana Historical Society, 1950.

Burgess, Dorothy. *Dream and Deed: The Story of Katharine Lee Bates.* Norman: University of Oklahoma Press, 1952.

Burke, III, Edmund. "The Big Story: Human History, Energy Regimes, and the Environment." In *The Environment and World History*, edited by Edmund Burke, III, and Kenneth Pomeranz, 33–53. Berkeley: University of California Press, 2009, 33–53.

Burke, III, Edmund, and Kenneth Pomeranz. *The Environment and World History.* Berkeley: University of California Press, 2009.

Burpee, Lawrence J. *The Search for the Western Sea: The Story of the Exploration of North-Western America.* London: Alston Rivrs, 1908.

Bushman, Richard L. *The Refinement of America: Persons, Houses, Cities.* New York: Alfred A. Knopf, 1992.

Bushman, Richard Lyman. "Markets and Composite Farms in Early America." *William and Mary Quarterly*, third series, 55 (July 1998): 351–374.

Bushman, Richard Lyman. "A Poet, A Planter, and a Nation of Farmers." *Journal of the Early Republic* 19 (Spring 1999): 1–14.

Butler, Judith. *Bodies that Matter: The Discursive Limits of Sex.* New York: Routledge, 1993.

Calloway, Colin G. "The End of an Era: British-Indian Relations in the Great Lakes Region after the War of 1812." *Michigan Historical Review* 12 (Fall 1986): 1–20.

Camp, Stephanie M. H. *Closer to Freedom: Enslaved Women and Everyday Resistance in the Plantation South.* Chapel Hill: University of North Carolina Press, 2004.

Cañizares Esguerra, Jorge. "New World, New Stars: Patriotic Astrology and the Invention of Indian and Creole Bodies in Colonial Spanish America, 1600–1650." *American Historical Review* 104 (February 1999): 33–68.

Carpenter, John C. "Pike: A Typical American Soldier." *Transactions of the Kansas State Historical Society* 7 (1901–1902): 284–287.

Carter, Carrol Joe. *Pike in Colorado.* Fort Collins, Colo.: The Old Army Press, 1978.

Carter II, Edward C., ed. *Surveying the Record: North American Scientific Exploration to 1930.* Philadelphia: American Philosophical Society, 1999.

Cayton, Andrew R. L. "'Separate Interests' and the Nation State: The Washington Administration and the Origins of Regionalism in the Trans-Appalachian West." *Journal of American History* 79 (June 1992): 39–67.

Chaplin, Joyce E. *Subject Matter: Technology, the Body, and Science on the Anglo-American Frontier, 1500–1676*. Cambridge, Mass.: Harvard University Press, 2001.

Chaplin, Joyce E. "Expansion and Exceptionalism in Early American History." *Journal of American History* 89 (March 2003): 1431–1455.

Christian, Shirley. *Before Lewis and Clark: The Story of the Chouteaus, the French Dynasty That Ruled America's Frontier*. New York: Farrar, Straus and Giroux, 2004.

Colley, Linda. *Captives*. New York: Pantheon, 2002.

Cook, Warren L. *Flood Tide of Empire: Spain and the Pacific Northwest, 1543–1819*. New Haven: Yale University Press, 1973.

Cox, Caroline. *A Proper Sense of Honor: Service and Sacrifice in George Washington's Army*. Chapel Hill: University of North Carolina Press, 2004.

Cox, Issac Joslin. *The Early Exploration of Louisiana*. Cincinnati: University of Cincinnati Press, 1906.

Cox, Isaac Joslin. "The Louisiana-Texas Frontier." *The Quarterly of the Texas State Historical Association* 10 (July 1906): 1–75.

Cox, Isaac Joslin. "The Pan-American Policy of Jefferson and Wilkinson." *Mississippi Valley Historical Review* 1 (September 1914): 212–239.

Cox, Isaac Joslin. "Opening the Santa Fe Trail." *Missouri Historical Review* 25 (October 1930–July 1931): 30–66.

Crackel, Theodore J. *Mr. Jefferson's Army: Political and Social Reform of the Military Establishment, 1801–1809*. New York: New York University Press, 1987.

Crichton, Kyle S. "Zeb Pike." *Scribner's Magazine* 82 (July–December 1927): 462–467.

Cutright, Paul Russell. *A History of the Lewis and Clark Journals*. Norman: University of Oklahoma Press, 1976.

Cutter, Donald C., ed. and trans. *The Defenses of Northern New Spain: Hugo O'Connor's Report to Teodoro de Croix, July 22, 1777*. Dallas: Southern Methodist University Press, 1994.

Dary, David. *Frontier Medicine: From the Atlantic to the Pacific, 1492–1941*. New York: Alfred A. Knopf, 2008.

Davis, W. W. H. *The History of Bucks County, Pennsylvania, from the Discovery of the Delaware to the Present Time*. Doylestown, Pa.: Democrat Book and Job Office, 1876.

Dean, Virgil W., ed. *The Pike Expedition: A Bicentennial Reflection*. Special issue, *Kansas History* 29, no. 1 (Spring 2006).

deBuys, William. *Enchantment and Exploitation: The Life and Hard Times of a New Mexico Mountain Range*. Albuquerque: University of New Mexico Press, 1985.

Deeds, Susan M. "Colonial Chihuahua: Peoples and Frontiers in Flux." In *New Views of Borderlands History*, edited by Robert H. Jackson. Albuquerque: University of New Mexico Press, 1998.

Deeds, Susan M. *Defiance and Deference in Mexico's Colonial North: Indians Under Spanish Rule in Nueva Vizcaya*. Austin: University of Texas Press, 2003.

DeMallie, Raymond J. "Sioux Until 1850." In *Handbook of North American Indians*, Vol. 13, pt. 2, edited by William C. Sturtevant. Washington, D.C., Smithsonian Institution, 2001.

Demos, John. *Circles and Lines: The Shape of Life in Early America*. Cambridge, Mass.: Harvard University Press, 2004.

Durden, Robert F. *James Shepherd Pike: Republicanism and the American Negro, 1850–1882*. Durham: Duke University Press, 1957.

Elias, Norbert. *The Civilizing Process*. Translated by Edmund Jephcott. New York: Urizen Books, 1978.

Eliot, T. S. "Little Gidding." No. 4 in *Four Quartets*. 1943. http://www.columbia.edu/itc/history/winter/w3206/edit/tseliotlittlegidding.html (accessed July 22, 2013).

Elkins, Stanley and Eric McKitrick. *The Age of Federalism*. New York: Oxford University Press, 1993.

Engeman, Thomas S., ed. *Thomas Jefferson and the Politics of Nature*. Notre Dame, Ind.: University of Notre Dame Press, 2000.

Eustace, Nicole. *Passion Is the Gale: Emotion, Power, and the Coming of the American Revolution*. Chapel Hill: University of North Carolina Press, 2008.

Evans, Peter B., Dietrich Rueschemeyer, and Theda Skocpol, eds. *Bringing the State Back In*. Cambridge and New York: Cambridge University Press, 1985.

Fausz, J. Frederick. *Founding St. Louis: First City of the New West*. Charleston: The History Press, 2011.

Fenn, Elizabeth. *Pox Americana: The Great Small Pox Epidemic of 1775–1782*. New York: Hill and Wang, 2001.

Fett, Sharla. *Working Cures: Healing, Health, and Power on Southern Slave Plantations*. Chapel Hill: University of North Carolina Press, 2002.

Fischer, Kirsten. *Suspect Relations: Sex, Race, and Resistance in Colonial North Carolina*. Ithaca, N.Y.: Cornell University Press, 2002.

Fitzgerald, William. "Boone County, Kentucky, Family Graveyards." *The Kentucky Genealogist* 2 (January–March 1960), 32–35.

Fliegelman, Jay. *Prodigals and Pilgrims: The American Revolution Against Patriarchal Authority, 1750–1800*. Cambridge: Cambridge University Press, 1982.

Flores, Dan. "Jefferson's Grand Expedition and the Mystery of the Red River." In *A Whole Country in Commotion: The Louisiana Purchase and the American Southwest*, edited by Patrick G. Williams, S. Charles Bolton, and Jeannie M. Whayne, 21–39. Fayetteville: University of Arkansas Press, 2005.

Foley, William E. "James Wilkinson: Pike's Mentor and Jefferson's Capricious Point Man in the West." In *Zebulon Pike, Thomas Jefferson, and the Opening of the American West*, edited by Matthew L. Harris and Jay H. Buckley, 185–225. Norman: University of Oklahoma Press, 2012.

Foley, William E. *Wilderness Journey: A Life of William Clark*. Columbia: University of Missouri Press, 2004.

Foley, William E., and C. David Rice. *The First Chouteaus: River Barons of Early St. Louis*. Urbana: University of Illinois Press, 1983.

Foner, Eric, ed. *The New American History*. Philadelphia: Temple University Press, 1990.

Freeman, Joanne B. *Affairs of Honor: National Politics in the New Republic*. New Haven: Yale University Press, 2001.

Fresonke, Kris. *West of Emerson: The Design of Manifest Destiny*. Berkeley: University of California Press, 2003.

Geary, Michael M. "Ramparts of Sand: An Environmental History of Great Sand Dunes National Monument and the San Luis Valley." Master's thesis, Colorado State University, 1997.

Giddens, Anthony. *The Constitution of Society: Outline of the Theory of Structuration*. Berkeley: University of California Press, 1984.

Giles, Janice Holt. *The Land Beyond the Mountains*. Lexington: University Press of Kentucky, 1995.

Glenn, Myra C. "Troubled Manhood in the Early Republic: The Life and Autobiography of Sailor Horace Lane." *Journal of the Early Republic* 26 (Spring 2006): 59–93.

Goetzmann, William H. *Army Exploration in the American West, 1803–1863*. New Haven: Yale University Press, 1959.

Goetzmann, William H. *New Lands, New Men: America and the Second Great Age of Discovery*. New York: Viking, 1986.

Gould, Eliga H. "Entangled Histories, Entangled Worlds: The English-Speaking Atlantic as a Spanish Periphery." *American Historical Review* 112 (June 2007): 764–786.

Greely, A. W. *Explorers and Travellers*. New York: Charles Scribner's Sons, 1904.

Greene, Jack P. "Colonial History and National History: Reflections on a Continuing Problem." *William and Mary Quarterly* 64 (April 2007), http://www.jstor.org/stable/4491615 (July 23, 2013).

Greenfeld, Liah. *Nationalism: Five Roads to Modernity*. Cambridge, Mass.: Harvard University Press, 1992.

Greenfeld, Liah. *The Spirit of Capitalism: Nationalism and Economic Growth*. Cambridge, Mass.: Harvard University Press, 2001.

Haggard, J. Villasana. "The Neutral Ground Between Louisiana and Texas, 1806–1821." *The Louisiana Historical Quarterly* 28 (October 1945): 1001–1128.

Haites, Erik F., James Mak, and Gary M. Walton. *Western River Transportation: The Era of Early Internal Development, 1810–1860*. Baltimore: Johns Hopkins University Press, 1975.

Hämäläinen, Pekka. "The Western Comanche Trade Center: Rethinking the Plains Indian Trade System." *Western Historical Quarterly* 29 (Winter 1998): 485–513.

Hämäläinen, Pekka. "The Rise and Fall of Plains Indian Horse Cultures." *Journal of American History* 90 (December 2003): 833–862.

Hampson, Norman. *The First European Revolution, 1776–1815.* New York: W.W. Norton and Company, 1969.

Harper, John Lamberton. *American Machiavelli: Alexander Hamilton and the Origins of U.S. Foreign Policy.* Cambridge: Cambridge University Press, 2004.

Harris, Matthew L., and Jay H. Buckley. *Zebulon Pike, Thomas Jefferson and the Opening of the American West.* Norman: University of Oklahoma, 2012.

Hart, Stephen Harding, and Archer Butler Hulbert, eds. *The Southern Journals of Zebulon Pike, 1806–1807.* Albuquerque: University of New Mexico Press, 2006.

Harvey, Charles M. "The Pike Exploration Centennial." *The American Monthly Review of Reviews* 34 (July–December 1906): 333–337.

Hay, Thomas Robson and M. R. Werner. *The Admirable Trumpeter: A Biography of General James Wilkinson.* Garden City, N.Y., Doubleday, Doran & Company, Inc., 1941.

Heggers, John P., et al. "Experimental and Clinical Observations on Frostbite." *Annals of Emergency Medicine* 16 (September 1987): 1056–1062.

Heidler, David S., and Jeanne T. Heidler, eds. *Encyclopedia of the War of 1812.* Santa Barbara, Calif.: ABC-Clio, 1989.

Heitman, Francis B. *Historical Register and Dictionary of the United States Army, from Its Organization, September 29, 1789, to March 2, 1903.* Vol. 1. Washington, D.C.: US GPO, 1903.

Hemphill, C. Dallett. "Manners and Class in the Revolutionary Era: A Transatlantic Comparison." *The William and Mary Quarterly* 63 (April 2006): 345–372.

Hickey, Donald R. *The War of 1812: A Forgotten Conflict.* Urbana: University of Illinois, 1989.

Hijiya, James. "Why the West Is Lost." *William and Mary Quarterly*, 3rd Series, 51 (April 1994): 276–292.

Hinderaker, Eric and Peter Mancall. *At the Edge of Empire: The Backcountry in British North America.* Baltimore: Johns Hopkins University Press, 2003.

Hitsman, J. Mackay. *The Incredible War of 1812: A Military History.* Toronto: University of Toronto Press, 1965. Reprinted with updates by Donald E. Graves. Toronto: Robin Brass Studio, 2005. Page references are to the 2005 edition.

Hobbs, Jr., Gregory J. "The Role of Climate in Shaping Western Water Institutions." *University of Denver Water Law Review* 7 (Fall 2003): 1–46.

Hoffer, Peter Charles. *Sensory Worlds in Early America.* Baltimore: Johns Hopkins University Press, 2003.

Hollon, W. E. "Zebulon Montgomery Pike and the York Campaign, 1813." *New York History* 30 (July 1949): 259–275.

Hollon, W. Eugene. *The Lost Pathfinder: Zebulon Montgomery Pike.* Norman: University of Oklahoma Press, 1949.

Holmberg, James J., ed., *Dear Brother: The Letters of William Clark to Jonathan J. Clark.* New Haven: Yale University Press, 2003.

Horsman, Reginald. *Expansion and American Indian Policy, 1783–1812.* Norman: University of Oklahoma Press, 1992.

Howe, Daniel Walker. *What Hath God Wrought: The Transformation of America, 1815–1848.* New York: Oxford University Press, 2007.

Howe, Jenika. "Power in the Pasture: Energy and the History of Ranching in Western South Dakota." Master's Thesis, Colorado State University, 2012.

Hunt, Lynn, ed. *Eroticism and the Body Politic.* Baltimore: Johns Hopkins University Press, 1991.

Hurst, James Willard. *Law and the Conditions of Freedom in the Nineteenth-Century United States.* Madison: University of Wisconsin Press, 1956.

Hurt, R. Douglas. *The Ohio Frontier: Crucible of the Old Northwest, 1720–1830.* Bloomington: Indiana University Press, 1996.

Hyde, Anne F. *Empires, Nations, and Families: A History of the North American West, 1800–1860.* Lincoln: University of Nebraska Press, 2011.

Hyde, George E. *The Pawnee Indians.* 2nd ed. Norman: University of Oklahoma Press, 1974.

Hylsop, Stephen G. "One Nation Among Many: The Origins and Objectives of Pike's Southwest Expedition." In "The Pike Expedition: A Bicentennial Reflection," ed. Virgil W. Dean. Special issue, *Kansas History* 29, no. 1 (Spring 2006): 2–13.

Hyslop, Stephen G. *Bound for Santa Fe: The Road to New Mexico and the American Conquest, 1806–1848.* Norman: University of Oklahoma Press, 2002.

Igler, David. "Diseased Goods: Global Exchanges in the Eastern Pacific Basin, 1770–1850." *American Historical Review* 109, no. 3 (June 2004): 693–719.

Isenberg, Andrew C. "The Market Revolution in the Borderlands: George Champlin Sibley in Missouri and New Mexico, 1808–1826." *Journal of the Early Republic* 21 (Fall 2001): 445–465.

Isenberg, Nancy. *Fallen Founder: The Life of Aaron Burr.* New York: Viking, 2007.

Jackson, Donald. *Thomas Jefferson and the Stony Mountains: Exploring the West from Monticello.* Urbana: University of Illinois Press, 1981.

Jackson, Donald. *Thomas Jefferson and the Rocky Mountains: Exploring the West from Monticello.* Reprint. Norman: University of Oklahoma Press, 2002.

Jacobs, James Ripley. *Tarnished Warrior: Major General James Wilkinson.* New York: The MacMillan Company, 1938.

Jenkinson, Clay S. *Becoming Jefferson's People: Re-inventing the American Republic in the Twenty-first Century.* Reno: Marmarth Press, 2004.

Johnson, Walter. *Soul by Soul, Life Inside the Antebellum Slave Market.* Cambridge, Mass.: Harvard University Press, 1999.

Jones, Jr., Oakah L. *Nueva Vizcaya: Heartland of the Spanish Frontier.* Albuquerque: University of New Mexico Press, 1988.

Joseph, Gilbert M. and Daniel Nugent, eds. *Everyday Forms of State Formation: Revolution and the Negotiation of Rule in Modern Mexico.* Durham: Duke University Press, 1994.

Kahn, Richard J., and Patricia G. Kahn. "The *Medical Repository*: The First U.S. Medical Journal (1797–1824)." *New England Journal of Medicine* 337 (December 25, 1997): 1926–1930.

Kastor, Peter J., ed. *The Louisiana Purchase: Emergence of an American Nation.* Washington, D.C.: CQ Press, 2002.

Kastor, Peter J. *William Clark's World: Describing America in an Age of Unknowns.* New Haven: Yale University Press, 2011.

Katznelson, Ira. "Flexible Capacity: The Military and Early American Statebuilding." In *Shaped by War and Trade: International Influences on American Political Development*, edited by Katznelson and Martin Shefter, 82–110. Princeton: Princeton University Press, 2002.

Katznelson, Ira. "Rewriting the Epic of America." In *Shaped by War and Trade: International Influences on American Political Development*, edited by Katznelson and Martin Shefter, 3–23. Princeton: Princeton University Press, 2002.

Katznelson, Ira, and Martin Shefter, eds. *Shaped by War and Trade: International Influences on American Political Development.* Princeton: Princeton University Press, 2002.

Keegan, John. *The Face of Battle.* New York: Viking, 1976.

Kerber, Linda. "Revolutionary Generation: Ideology, Politics, and Culture in the Early Republic." In *The New American History*, edited by Eric Foner. Philadelphia: Temple University Press, 1990.

Keys, Ancel, Josef Brŏzek, Austin Henschel, Olaf Mickelsen, and Henry Longstreet Taylor. *The Biology of Human Starvation.* 2 vols. Minneapolis: University of Minnesota Press, 1950.

Kilbourne, John Dwight. Virtutis Praemium: *The Men Who Founded the State Society of the Cincinnati of Pennsylvania.* Vol. 2. Rockport, Maine: Picton Press, 1998.

Klepp, Susan E. *Revolutionary Conceptions: Women, Fertility, and Family Limitation in America, 1760–1820.* Chapel Hill: University of North Carolina Press, 2009.

Knopf, Richard C., ed. "A Surgeon's Mate at Fort Defiance: The Journal of Joseph Gardner Andrews for the Year 1795." *Ohio History: The Scholarly Journal of the Ohio Historical Society* 66 (January 1957): 57–86.

Knott, Sarah. *Sensibility and the American Revolution.* Chapel Hill: University of North Carolina Press, 2009.

Kohn, Richard H. *Eagle and Sword: The Federalists and the Creation of the Military Establishment in America, 1783–1802.* New York: The Free Press, 1975.

Kornfeld, Eve. "Crisis in the Capital: The Cultural Significance of Philadelphia's Great Yellow Fever Epidemic." *Pennsylvania History* 51, no.3 (1989): 189–205.

Kornfeld, Eve. *Creating an American Culture, 1775–1800: A Brief History with Documents.* Boston: Bedford/St. Martin's, 2001.

Kukla, Jon. *A Wilderness So Immense: The Louisiana Purchase and the Destiny of America.* New York: Random House, 2003.

Lamar, Howard R. *The New Encyclopedia of the American West.* New Haven, Conn.: Yale University Press, 1998.

Langston, Nancy. "Gender Transformed: Endocrine Disruptors in the Environment." In *Seeing Nature Through Gender,* ed. Virginia Scharff, 129–166. Lawrence: University Press of Kansas, 2003.

Laqueur, Thomas. *Making Sex: Bodies and Gender from the Greeks to Freud.* Cambridge, Mass.: Harvard University Press, 1990.

Larson, John Lauritz. *Internal Improvement: National Public Works and the Promise of Popular Government in the Early United States.* Chapel Hill: University of North Carolina Press, 2001.

Latimer, Jon. *1812 War with America.* Cambridge, Mass.: Harvard University Press, 2007.

Lawson, Russell M. *The American Plutarch: Jeremy Belknap and the Historian's Dialogue with the Past.* Westport: Praeger, 1998.

Leach, John. *Survival Psychology.* New York: New York University Press, 1994.

Lee, Francis Bazley. *New Jersey: As a Colony and as a State.* New York: Publishing Society of New Jersey, 1902.

Lewis, Jr., James E. "The Burr Conspiracy and the Problem of Western Loyalty." In *The Louisiana Purchase: Emergence of an American Nation,* edited by Peter J. Kastor, 64–73. Washington, D.C.: CQ Press, 2002.

Licht, Daniel. *Ecology and Economics of the Great Plains.* Lincoln: University of Nebraska Press, 1997.

Lindman, Janet Moore, and Michelle Lise Tarter, eds. *A Centre of Wonders: The Body in Early America.* Ithaca, N.Y.: Cornell University Press, 2001.

Linklater, Andro. *An Artist in Treason: The Extraordinary Double Life of General James Wilkinson.* New York: Walker Publishing Company, 2009.

Little, Ann M. *Abraham in Arms: War and Gender in Colonial New England.* Philadelphia: University of Pennsylvania Press, 2007.

Lockridge, Kenneth. *On the Sources of Patriarchal Rage: The Commonplace Books of William Byrd and Thomas Jefferson and the Gendering of Power in the Eighteenth Century.* New York: New York University Press, 1992.

Loescher, Burt Garfield. *Washington's Eyes: The Continental Light Dragoons.* Fort Collins, Colo.: The Old Army Press, 1977.

Lomask, Milton. *Aaron Burr: The Conspiracy and Years of Exile, 1805–1836.* New York: Farrar, Straus, and Giroux, 1982.

Lovett, Gabriel H. *Napoleon and the Birth of Modern Spain: The Challenge to the Old Order.* Vol. 1. New York: New York University Press, 1965.

Lynn-Sherow, Bonnie. *Red Earth: Race and Agriculture in Oklahoma Territory.* Lawrence: University Press of Kansas, 2004.

Maier, Charles S. "Consigning the Twentieth Century to History: Alternative Narratives for the Modern Era." *American Historical Review* 105 (June 2000): 807–831.

Marietta, Jack D., and G. S. Rowe. *Troubled Experiment: Crime and Justice in Pennsylvania, 1682–1800.* Philadelphia: University of Pennsylvania Press, 2006.

Markowitz, Harvey, ed. *Ready Reference American Indians,* 3 vols. Pasadena, Calif.: Salem Press, Inc., 1995.

Marshall, S. L. A. *Men Against Fire: The Problem of Battle Command.* Norman: University of Oklahoma Press, 2000.

Martin, Cheryl English. *Governance and Society in Colonial Mexico: Chihuahua in the Eighteenth Century.* Stanford: Stanford University Press, 1996.

McCaleb, Walter Flavius. *The Aaron Burr Conspiracy.* New York: Wilson-Erickson, Inc., 1936.

McCaleb, Walter Flavius. *The Aaron Burr Conspiracy and A New Light on Aaron Burr.* New York: Argosy-Antiquarian, Ltd., 1966.

McCusker, John J. "The Demise of Distance: The Business Press and the Origins of the Information Revolution in the Early Modern Atlantic World." *American Historical Review* 110 (April 2005): 295–321.

McEvoy, Arthur F. "Working Environments: An Ecological Approach to Industrial Health and Safety." *Technology and Culture* 36 (April 1995): 145–172.

McPherson, James M. *Battle Cry of Freedom: The Civil War Era.* New York: Oxford University Press, 1988.

McPherson, James M. *For Cause and Comrades: Why Men Fought in the Civil War.* New York: Oxford University Press, 1997.

Melton, Buckner F. *Aaron Burr: Conspiracy to Treason.* New York: John Wiley & Sons, Inc., 2002.

Melton, James Van Horn. *The Rise of the Public in Enlightenment Europe.* Cambridge: Cambridge University Press, 2001.

Menand, Louis. *The Metaphysical Club.* New York: Farrar, Strauss, and Giroux, 2001.

Michel, Peter. "The St. Louis Fur Trade: Fur Company Ledgers and Account Books in the Archives of the Missouri Historical Society." *Gateway Heritage* 6 (Fall 1985): 10–17.

Miller, Charles A. *Jefferson and Nature: An Interpretation.* Baltimore: Johns Hopkins University Press, 1988.

Mitchell, Timothy. *Carbon Democracy: Political Power in the Age of Oil.* London: Verso, 2011.

Montgomery, M. R. *Jefferson and the Gun-Men: How the West Was Almost Lost.* New York: Three Rivers Press, 2000.

Morgan, Edmund S. *Inventing the People: The Rise of Popular Sovereignty in England and America.* New York: W. W. Norton & Company, 1988.

Morgan, Jennifer. *Laboring Women: Reproduction and Gender in New World Slavery.* Philadelphia: University of Pennsylvania Press, 2004.

Narrett, David E. "Liberation and Conquest: John Hamilton Robinson and U.S. Adventurism Toward Mexico, 1806–1819." *Western Historical Quarterly* 40 (Spring 2009): 23–50.

Narrett, David E. "Geopolitics and Intrigue: James Wilkinson, the Spanish Borderlands, and Mexican Independence." *William and Mary Quarterly* 69 (January 2012): 101–146.

Nash, Linda. "Finishing Nature: Harmonizing Bodies and Environments in Late-Nineteenth Century California." *Environmental History* 8 (January 2003): 25–52.

Nash, Linda. *Inescapable Ecologies: A History of Environment, Disease, and Knowledge.* Berkeley: University of California Press, 2004.

Newman, Simon P. *Parades and the Politics of the Streets: Festive Culture in the Early American Republic.* Philadelphia: University of Pennsylvania Press, 1997.

Newman, Simon P. *Embodied History: The Lives of the Poor in Early Philadelphia.* Philadelphia: University of Pennsylvania Press, 2003.

Newton, Cody. "The Protohistoric Period in Northcentral Colorado: Analysis of the Lykins Valley Site (5LR263)." Master's thesis, Colorado State University, 2007.

Nichols, Roger L. and Patrick L. Halley. *Stephen Long and American Frontier Exploration.* Newark: University of Delaware Press, 1980.

Nye, David E. *Consuming Power: A Social History of American Energies.* Cambridge, Mass.: MIT Press, 1998.

Oliva, Leo E. "Enemies and Friends: Zebulon Montgomery Pike and Facundo Melgares in the Competition for the Great Plains, 1806–1807." In "The Pike Expedition: A Bicentennial Reflection," ed. Virgil W. Dean. Special issue, *Kansas History* 29 (Spring 2006): 34–47.

Oliva, Leo E., ed. "'Sent Out by Our Great Father': Zebulon Montgomery Pike's Journal and Route across Kansas, 1806." In "The Pike Expedition: A Bicentennial Reflection," ed. Virgil W. Dean. Special issue, *Kansas History* 29 (Spring 2006): 14–33.

Olsen, Michael L. "Zebulon Pike and American Popular Culture, or, Has Pike Peaked?" In "The Pike Expedition: A Bicentennial Reflection," ed. Virgil W. Dean. Special issue, *Kansas History* 29 (Spring 2006): 48–59.

O'Neill, Robert V. "Is It Time to Bury the Ecosystem Concept? (With Full Military Honors, of Course)." *Ecology* 82:12 (2001): 3275–3284.

Onuf, Peter S. *Jefferson's Empire: The Language of American Nationhood.* Charlottesville: University of Virginia Press, 2000.

Opie, John. *The Law of the Land: Two Hundred Years of American Farmland Policy.* Lincoln: University of Nebraska Press, 1987.

Orsi, Jared. "Invisible Rivers: The Struggle of Early American Explorers to Map Colorado's Rivers." In *Citizens Guide to Colorado's Water Heritage*, edited by Karla A. Brown. Denver: Colorado Foundation for Water Education, 2004, 9–13.

Orsi, Jared. "Reading with Pike: The Mystery of His Affection for James Wilkinson." *Wagon Tracks* 21 (May 2007): 17–20.

Orsi, Jared. "State Making and Unmaking (and Making It Back at All): Following Zebulon Pike across the Plains in 1806." In *The Grasslands of the United States:*

An Environmental History, edited by James E. Sherow. Santa Barbara: ABC-Clio, 2007, 159–175.

Orsi, Jared. "Zebulon Pike and His 'Frozen Lads': Bodies, Nationalism, and the West in the Early Republic." *Western Historical Quarterly* 42 (Spring 2011): 55–75.

Owens, Robert M. *Mr. Jefferson's Hammer: William Henry Harrison and the Origins of American Indian Policy.* Norman: University of Oklahoma Press, 2007.

Parks, Douglas R. "Pawnee." In *Handbook of North American Indians*, Vol. 13, edited by William C. Sturtevant. Washington, D.C.: Smithsonian Institution, 2001.

Pasley, Jeffrey L. *"The Tyranny of Printers": Newspaper Politics in the Early American Republic.* Charlottesville: University of Virginia Press, 2001.

Pasley, Jeffrey L., Andrew W. Robertson, and David Waldstreicher. *Beyond the Founders: New Approaches to the Political History of the Early American Republic.* Chapel Hill: University of North Carolina Press, 2004.

Paton, Bruce C. *Lewis and Clark: Doctors in the Wilderness.* Golden, Colo.: Fulcrum Publishing, 2001.

Paton, Bruce C. "Zebulon Pike in Colorado: His Struggle to Survive." In *"To Spare No Pains": Zebulon Montgomery Pike and his 1806–1807 Southwest Expedition*, edited by Tim Blevins, et al. Colorado Springs: Pikes Peak Library District and Colorado Springs Pioneers Museum, 2007.

Philipps, Dave. "What Peak Did Pike Climb? Lawyer Tracks Final Destination of Wayward Trek to Mount Rosa." *Colorado Springs Gazette.* April 25, 2004, A1.

Pike, James S. *The Prostrate State: South Carolina under Negro Government.* 1874. Reprint. New York: Harper and Row, 1968.

Pomfret, John E. and Floyd M. Shumway. *Founding the American Colonies, 1853–1660.* New York: Harper & Row, Publishers, 1970.

Preston, Douglas and Jose Antonio Esquibel. *The Royal Road: El Camino Real From Mexico City to Santa Fe.* Albuquerque: University of New Mexico Press, 1998.

Purcell, Sarah J. *Sealed with Blood: War, Sacrifice, and Memory in Revolutionary America.* Philadelphia: University of Pennsylvania Press: 2002.

Resch, John. *Suffering Soldiers: Revolutionary War Veterans, Moral Sentiment, and Political Culture in the Early Republic.* Amherst: University of Massachusetts Press, 1999.

Richter, Daniel K. *The Ordeal of the Longhouse: The Peoples of the Iroquois League in the Era of European Colonization.* Chapel Hill: University of North Carolina, 1992.

Roberts, Clarence V. *Early Friends and Families of Upper Bucks, With Some Accounts of Their Descendants.* Philadelphia: The Compiler, 1925.

Rock, Rosalind Z. "Dying Quijote: Nemesio Salcedo and the Last Years of Spain in the Internal Provinces." PhD Dissertation, University of New Mexico, 1981.

Rohrbough, Malcolm J. *The Land Office Business: The Settlement and Administration of American Public Lands, 1789–1837.* New York: Oxford University Press, 1968.

Rohrbough, Malcolm J. *Trans-Appalachian Frontier: People, Societies, and Institutions, 1775–1850.* Third Edition. Bloomington: Indiana University Press, 2008.

Rollins, Willard H. *The Osage: An Ethnohistorical Study of Hegemony on the Prairie-Plains*. Columbia, Mo.: University of Missouri Press, 1992.

Ronda, James P. *Lewis and Clark among the Indians*. Lincoln: University of Nebraska Press, 1984.

Ronda, James P. "Pike and Empire." In *Zebulon Pike, Thomas Jefferson, and the Opening of the American West*, edited by Matthew L. Harris and Jay H. Buckley, 61–80. Norman: University of Oklahoma Press, 2012.

Rothman, Hal K. *Devil's Bargains: Tourism in the Twentieth-Century American West*. Lawrence: University Press of Kansas, 1998.

Royster, Charles. *A Revolutionary People at War: The Continental Army and American Character, 1775–1783*. Chapel Hill: University of North Carolina Press, 1979.

Saunt, Claudio. "Go West: Mapping Early American Historiography." *William and Mary Quarterly* 3rd ser. 65 (October 2008): 745–778.

Scarry, Elaine. *The Body in Pain: The Making and Unmaking of the World*. New York: Oxford University Press, 1985.

Scharff, Virginia J., ed. *Seeing Nature Through Gender*. Lawrence: University Press of Kansas, 2003.

Scott, James C. *Seeing Like a State: How Certain Schemes to Improve the Human Condition Have Failed*. New Haven: Yale University Press, 1998.

Sellers, Christopher C. *Hazards of the Job: From Industrial Disease to Environmental Health Science*. Chapel Hill: University of North Carolina Press, 1997.

Sellers, Christopher C. "Thoreau's Body: Towards an Embodied Environmental History." *Environmental History* 4 (1999): 486–514.

Sherow, James E. "Workings of the Geodialectic: High Plains Indians and Their Horses in the Region of the Arkansas River Valley, 1800–1870." *Environmental History Review* 16 (Summer 1992): 61–84.

Sherow, James E. "Water, Sun, and Cattle: The Chisholm Trail as an Ephemeral Ecosystem." In *Fluid Arguments: Five Centuries of Western Water Conflict*, ed. Char Miller, 141–155. Tucson: University of Arizona Press, 2001.

Sherow, James E. *The Grasslands of the United States: An Environmental History*. Santa Barbara: ABC Clio, 2007.

Sherr, Lynn. *America the Beautiful: The Stirring True Story Behind Our Nation's Favorite Song*. New York: Public Affairs, 2001.

Shoemaker, Nancy. *A Strange Likeness: Becoming Red and White in Eighteenth-Century North America*. New York: Oxford University Press, 2004.

Shriver, Phillip R. and Clarence E. Wunderlin, Jr., eds. *The Documentary Heritage of Ohio*. Athens: Ohio University Press, 2000.

Simmons, Marc. *Spanish Government in New Mexico*. Albuquerque: University of New Mexico Press, 1968.

Simmons, Marc. *Coronado's Land: Essays on Daily Life in Colonial New Mexico*. Albuquerque: University of New Mexico Press, 1991.

Skowronek, Stephen. *Building a New American State: The Expansion of New Administrative Capacities, 1877–1920.* Cambridge: Cambridge University Press, 1982.

Slaughter, Thomas P. *The Whiskey Rebellion: Frontier Epilogue to the American Revolution.* New York: Oxford, 1986.

Slaughter, Thomas P. *Exploring Lewis and Clark: Reflections on Men and Wilderness.* New York: Alfred A. Knopf, 2003.

Smil, Vaclav. *Energy in Nature and Society: General Energetics of Complex Systems.* Cambridge, Mass.: MIT Press, 2008.

Spary, Emma. "Political, Natural, and Bodily Economies." In *Cultures of Natural History,* ed. N. Jardine, J. A. Secord, and E. C. Spary, 178–196. Cambridge: Cambridge University Press, 1996.

Steinberg, Ted. "Down to Earth: Nature, Agency, and Power in History." *American Historical Review* 107 (June 2002): 798–820.

Stroud, Ellen. "Reflections from Six Feet Under the Field: Dead Bodies in the Classroom." *Environmental History* 8 (October 2003): 618–628.

Sturtevant, William C. *Handbook of North American Indians,* 20 vols. Washington, D.C.: Smithsonian Institution, 1978–2008.

Swagerty, William R. "History of the United States Plains Until 1850." In *Handbook of North American Indians.* Vol. 13, edited by William C. Sturtevant. Washington, D.C.: Smithsonian Institution, 2001.

Taylor, Alan. *The Civil War of 1812: American Citizens, British Subjects, Irish Rebels, and Indian Allies.* New York: Alfred A. Knopf, 2010.

Terrell, John Upton. *Zebulon Pike: The Life and Times of an Adventurer.* New York: Weybright and Talley, 1968.

Thelen, David. "The Nation and Beyond: Transnational Perspectives on United States History." *Journal of American History* 86 (December 1999): 965–975.

Thrapp, Dan L. *Encyclopedia of Frontier Biography,* 3 vols. Spokane: The Arthur Clark Company, 1990.

Twitchell, Ralph Emerson. *The Leading Facts of New Mexican History.* 4 vols. Cedar Rapids, Iowa: The Torch Press, 1912.

Twitchell, Ralph Emerson. *The Spanish Archives of New Mexico: Compiled and Chronologically Arranged with Historical, Genealogical, and Geographical, and Other Annotations, by Authority of the State Of New Mexico.* 2 vols. Cedar Rapids, Iowa: The Torch Press, 1914.

Vermeule, Cornelius C. "Revolutionary Days in Old Somerset." *Proceedings of the New Jersey Historical Society,* n.s. 8 (October 1923): 265–281.

Wade, Richard C. *The Urban Frontier: The Rise of Western Cities, 1790–1830.* Cambridge, Mass.: Harvard University Press, 1967.

Wagner, Mark J. "Searching for Cantonment Wilkinsonville." May 2004.

Waldstreicher, David. *In the Midst of Perpetual Fetes: The Making of American Nationalism, 1776–1820.* Chapel Hill: University of North Carolina Press, 1997.

Wall, Helena M. "Confessions of a British North Americanist: Borderlands Historiography and Early American History." *Reviews in American History* 25 (March 1997): 1–12.

Warren, Louis S. *Buffalo Bill's America: William Cody and the Wild West Show.* New York: Alfred A. Knopf, 2005.

Watts, Steven. *The Republic Reborn: War and the Making of Liberal America, 1790–1820.* Baltimore: Johns Hopkins University Press, 1987.

Weaver, John C. *The Great Land Rush and the Making of the Modern World, 1650–1900.* Montreal: McGill-Queen's University Press, 2003.

Weber, David. *The Spanish Frontier in North America.* New Haven: Yale University Press, 1992.

Weber, David. "The Spanish Borderlands of North America: A Historiography." *Magazine of History* 14 (Summer 2000): 5–11.

Weber, David. *The Taos Trappers: The Fur Trade in the Southwest, 1540–1846.* Norman: University of Oklahoma Press, 2005.

Wedel, Waldo R. *Central Plains Prehistory: Holocene Environments and Culture Changes in the Republican River Basin.* Lincoln: University of Nebraska Press, 1986.

Wedel, Waldo R., and George C. Frison. "Environment and Subsistence." In *Handbook of North American Indians.* Vol. 13, edited by William C. Sturtevant. Washington, D.C.: Smithsonian Institution, 2001.

Weems, Mason L. *The Life of Washington.* Cambridge, Mass.: Harvard University Press, 1962.

West, Elliott. *Contested Plains: Indians, Gold Seekers, and the Rush to Colorado.* Lawrence: University Press of Kansas, 1998.

West, Elliott. "Lewis and Clark: Kidnappers." In *A Whole Country in Commotion: The Louisiana Purchase and the American Southwest,* edited by Patrick G. Williams, S. Charles Bolton, and Jeannie M. Whayne, 3–20. Fayetteville: University of Arkansas Press, 2005.

West, Elliott. *The Last Indian War: The Nez Perce Story.* New York: Oxford University Press, 2009.

White, Richard, *Roots of Dependency: Subsistence, Environment, and Social Change among the Choctaws, Pawnees, and Navajos.* Lincoln: University of Nebraska Press, 1983.

White, Richard. *The Middle Ground: Indians, Empires, and Republics in the Great Lakes Region, 1650–1815.* Cambridge: Cambridge University Press, 1991.

White, Richard. "Frederick Jackson Turner and Buffalo Bill." In *The Frontier in American Culture: An Exhibition at the Newberry Library, August 26, 1994, to January 7, 1995.* Edited by James R. Grossman. Chicago: The Library, 1994.

White, Richard. "The Nationalization of Nature." *Journal of American History* 86 (December 1999): 976–986.

Wibberly, Leonard. *Zebulon Pike: Soldier and Explorer.* New York: Funk & Wagnalls Company, 1961.

Wickberg, Daniel. "What Is the History of Sensibilities?" *American Historical Review* 112 (June 2007): 661–684.

Williams, Patrick G., S. Charles Bolton, and Jeannie M. Whayne, eds. *A Whole Country in Commotion: The Louisiana Purchase and the American Southwest.* Fayetteville: University of Arkansas Press, 2005.

Wilson, Frazer E. *The Treaty of Greenville: Being an Official Account of the Same.* Piqua, Ohio: The Correspondent Press, 1894.

Wilson, Frazer E. *Around the Council Fire: Proceedings at Fort Greene Ville in 1795 Culminating in the Signing of the Treaty of Greene Ville by General Anthony Wayne and the Indian Chiefs of the Old Northwest.* Greenville, Ohio: Frazer E. Wilson, 1945.

Wilson, Frazer E. *Fort Jefferson: The Frontier Post of the Upper Miami Valley.* Greenville, Ohio: Frazer E. Wilson, 1950.

Wishart, David J. *An Unspeakable Sadness: The Dispossession of the Nebraska Indians.* Lincoln: University of Nebraska Press, 1994.

Wood, Gordon S. *The Radicalism of the American Revolution.* New York: Vintage Books, 1991.

Woodley, Richard. *Zebulon Pike: Pioneer Destiny.* Wayne, Pa.: Banbury Books, 1982.

Worster, Donald. *Nature's Economy: A History of Ecological Ideas.* Cambridge: Cambridge University Press, 1988.

Worster, Donald. *A River Running West: The Life of John Wesley Powell.* Oxford: Oxford University Press, 2001.

Wrigley, E. A. *Continuity, Chance and Change: The Character of the Industrial Revolution in England.* New York: Cambridge University Press, 1988.

Yokota, Kariann Akemi. *Unbecoming British: How Revolutionary America Became a Postcolonial Nation.* New York: Oxford University Press, 2011.

Young, Alfred F. *The Shoemaker and the Tea Party: Memory and the American Revolution.* Boston: Beacon Press, 1999.

"Zebulon M. Pike in Reading PA." *Historical Review of Berks County* 3 (April 1938): 93–94.

Index

Santa Fe, 12, 86, 103, 154, 238, 239
  Americans detained in, 214, 216, 281
  as capital of New Mexico, 212
  commerce with United States, 137,
    167, 282
  commerce with Mexico
  distance from St. Louis, 84
  on map, 2–3, 177, 206
  military access to, 149
  Pawnees and, 144, 148
  Pike arrives in, 205, 208, 211, 214,
    216, 238
  Pike escorted to, 198, 208, 214, 217
  Pike in, 205–217, 257
  Pike's instructions regarding,
    166–168, 170, 184–186, 191, 196,
    199–203, 244, 248–249
  Pike's men escorted to, 232, 234
  Red River headwaters near,
    176–177, 183
  Robinson visit to, 195–200, 214, 220
  romanticization of, 288
  Santa Fe Trail, 176, 281–283
  silver mines near, 85
  Susan Magoffin travels to, 283–284
  Wilkinson's plans for exploring, 95, 130
Santa Fe Trail map, 176, 179, 197,
  199–202
Santee Sioux, 105–107
Sauks, 92, 93, 97, 99–100, 104
Senate, 86, 88, 90, 251
Seven Years' War, 20, 21, 36, 91
Sharitarish, 279
  Pike's departure, 149, 152
  insult done to, 148–149, 151
  Pawnee politics and, 150–153
  Spaniards and, 142, 148, 149
  welcoming Pike, 140
Shays's Rebellion, 54
Shenstone, William, 64, 72, 118
Sibley, George C., 152–153
Smil, Vaclav, 9

Smith, Patrick, 184, 193, 198, 234–235
Solebury, PA, 3, 27–28, 33, 35, 36
Somerset County (N.J.), 6, 22, 25, 26,
  28–29
Sonora, 212, 224
South Park, 160, 178–179, 200
South Platte River, 160, 179, 199
Spain, 89, 217, 224. *See also* Spaniards
  borders dispute over Louisiana, 77,
    87, 90
  control of Mississippi, 11, 38, 58, 131
  coup by Napoleon, 222, 237, 254
  empire of, 58, 175, 218, 223, 227,
    238, 255
  Enlightenment and, 209–210
  fur trade and, 212
  king of, 86, 102, 164, 254 , 260
  Mexican independence of, 282
  North American territories of, 102,
    166, 173, 231
  opposition to westward expansion,
    58, 113
  Pawnee allegiance to, 157
  relations with Indians, 103, 213, 219
  relations with United States, 95, 101,
    113, 130–132, 149, 162–167, 196,
    229, 249, 280
  rivalry with Britain, 103, 212, 229
  rule in Louisiana, 98,
  western discontent and, 11, 38, 54,
    58–59, 131
  Wilkinson working for, 246–247
Spaniards, 11, 14, 94, 135, 195, 223,
  229, 234. *See also* Spain
  arrest of Pike, 7, 13, 198
  Burr courting, 89
  confused about the Red River
    location, 183
  fur trade and, 137
  geographical knowledge of, 212
  Humboldt and, 175
  Louisiana and, 86, 91–92